Paul, Theologian of God's Apocalypse

Paul, Theologian of God's Apocalypse

Essays on Paul and Apocalyptic

Martinus C. de Boer

CASCADE *Books* · Eugene, Oregon

PAUL, THEOLOGIAN OF GOD'S APOCALYPSE
Essays on Paul and Apocalyptic

Cascade Books
An Imprint of Wipf and Stock Publishers
199 W. 8th Ave., Suite 3
Eugene, OR 97401

www.wipfandstock.com

PAPERBACK ISBN: 978-1-5326-8680-1
HARDCOVER ISBN: 978-1-5326-8681-8
EBOOK ISBN: 978-1-5326-8682-5

Cataloguing-in-Publication data:

Names: de Boer, Martinus C., author.

Title: Paul, theologian of God's apocalypse: essays on Paul and apocalyptic / by Martinus C. de Boer.

Description: Eugene, OR: Cascade Books, 2020 | Includes bibliographical references and index.

Identifiers: ISBN 978-1-5326-8680-1 (paperback) | ISBN 978-1-5326-8681-8 (hardcover) | ISBN 978-1-5326-8682-5 (ebook)

Subjects: LCSH: Paul, the Apostle, Saint. | Bible. Epistles of Paul—Theology. | Bible. Epistles of Paul—Criticism, interpretation, etc. | Eschatology—Biblical teaching.

Classification: BS2650.2 D43 2020 (print) | BS2650.2 (ebook)

Manufactured in the U.S.A.   05/11/20

For Paula

Contents

Preface

WHEN J. LOUIS MARTYN published his magisterial commentary on the Letter to the Galatians in 1997, the interpretation of Paul as an apocalyptic theologian re-entered scholarly discussion and debate in a significant way. I was privileged to write my dissertation on Paul's apocalyptic eschatology under Martyn's supervision, defending it in 1983 and publishing a revised version in 1988. The revised version provided the basis for an essay published the following year in a festschrift for Martyn. That contribution to Martyn's festschrift is now included as the opening chapter of this collection of essays on Paul and apocalyptic. I have been both perplexed and pleased by the fact that this essay has played a significant role in the ongoing debate about Paul as an apocalyptic theologian, perhaps because Martyn's commentary made use of it. I have had occasion to return to the subject matter of Paul as an apocalyptic theologian over the years, particularly in connection with Paul's letters to the Romans and to the Galatians, culminating in a retrospective essay in 2016. The latter now concludes this collection.

It is a pleasure to be able to publish these essays in one volume. I am indebted in particular to Michael Thomson who despite my hesitations about this project unfailingly encouraged it over the years, first at Eerdmans and then at Cascade Books. I am also grateful to the editors and staff at Cascade for their invaluable assistance in bringing this book to fruition.

I dedicate this collection to my wife of more than forty years, Paula Pumplin, who was there when these essays came into being and thus knows what it took to get them published in the first place and now again in this collection.

Acknowledgments and Original Publications

THE TWELVE CHAPTERS OF this book consist of ten articles that have been published previously and two that have not. I gratefully acknowledge, where required, the permission to reprint the previously published articles in this volume. Full bibliographical information for these articles, including their original titles, is provided in the list below.

Chapter 1: "Paul and Jewish Apocalyptic Eschatology." In *Apocalyptic and the New Testament. Essays in Honor of J. Louis Martyn*, edited by Joel Marcus and Marion L. Soards, 169-90. JSNTSS 24. Sheffield: JSOT (subsequently Sheffield Academic Press), 1989. Used by permission of Bloomsbury Publishing Plc.

Chapter 2: "Paul, Theologian of God's Apocalypse." *Interpretation* 56 (2002) 21-33.

Chapter 3: "Paul's Mythologizing Program in Romans 5-8." In *Apocalyptic Paul: Cosmos and Anthropos in Romans 5-8*, edited by Beverly Roberts Gaventa, 1-20. Waco, TX: Baylor University Press, 2013. Used by permission of Baylor University Press.

Chapter 4: "Sin and Soteriology in Romans." Not previously published. Also forthcoming in *Sin and its Remedy in Paul*, edited by Nijay K. Gupta and John K. Goodrich, 15–32. Eugene, OR: Cascade, 2020.

Chapter 5: "Cross and Cosmos in Galatians." In *The Unrelenting God*, edited by David J. Downs and Matthew L. Skinner, 208–25. Grand Rapids: Eerdmans, 2013. Used by permission of Wm. B. Eerdmans Publishing Co. and the editors.

Chapter 6: "Paul's Use and Interpretation of a Justification Tradition in Galatians 2.15-21." *JSNT* 28.2 (2005) 189-216.

Chapter 7: "Justification in Paul: From Galatians to Romans." Not previously published.

Chapter 8: "Salvation History in Galatians? A Response to Bruce W. Longenecker and Jason Maston," *JSPL* 2.2 (2012) 105–114. Copyright © 2011 by Eisenbrauns, Inc. Used by permission of The Pennsylvania State University Press.

Chapter 9: "Observations on the Significance of the Old Testament in Galatians." In *The Scriptures of Israel in Jewish and Christian Tradition: Essays in Honour of Maarten J. J. Menken*, edited by Bart J. Koet, Steve Moyise, and Joseph Verheyden, 211-26. NovTSup 148. Leiden: Brill, 2013. Used by permission of Koninklijke Brill NV.

Chapter 10: "Paul's Quotation of Isaiah 54.1 in Galatians 4.27." *NTS* 50 (2004) 370–89. Used by permission of Cambridge University Press.

Chapter 11: "De Psalmen bij Paulus: LXX Psalm 142:2 in Galaten 2:16 en Romeinen 3:20," *Amsterdamse Cahiers voor Exegese van de Bijbel en zijn Tradities* 25 (2010) 83–94. Used by permission by P. J. van Midden (University of Tilburg, Netherlands) of 2VM Press.

Chapter 12: "Apocalyptic as God's Eschatological Activity in Paul's Theology." In *Paul and the Apocalyptic Imagination*, edited by Ben C. Blackwell et al., 45–63. Minneapolis: Fortress, 2016. Used by permission of Fortress Press.

Abbreviations

Aet.	Philo, *De aeternitate mundi* (*On the Eternity of the World*).
ANRW	*Aufstieg und Niedergang der römischen Welt: Geschichte und Kultur Roms im Spiegel der neueren Forschung.* Edited by H. Temporini and W. Haase. Berlin: De Gruyter, 1972–.
ABD	*Anchor Bible Dictionary.* 6 vols. Edited by David Noel Freedman. New York: Doubleday, 1992.
As. Mos.	*Assumption of Moses* (*Testament of Moses*)
BAG	Walter Bauer, W. F. Arndt, and F. W. Gingrich. *Greek-English Lexicon of the New Testament and Other Early-Christian Literature.* Chicago: University of Chicago Press, 1957
BAGD	Walter Bauer, W. F. Arndt, F. W. Gingrich, and Frederick W. Danker. *Greek-English Lexicon of the New Testament and Other Early-Christian Literature.* 3rd ed. Chicago: University of Chicago Press, 2000.
2 Bar.	*2 (Apocalypse) Baruch*
BCE	Before the common era
BDB	Francis Brown, S. R. Driver, and Charles A. Briggs, *A Hebrew and English Lexicon of the Old Testament.* Oxford: Clarendon, 1907.
BDF	Friedrich Blass and Albert Debrunner. *A Greek Grammar of the New Testament and Other Early Christian Literature.* Translated and revised by Robert W. Funk. Chicago: University of Chicago Press, 1961.
BDR	Friedrich Blass and Albert Debrunner, *Grammatik des neutestamentlichen Griechisch.* 17th ed. Revised by Friedrich Rehkopf. Göttingen: Vandenhoeck & Ruprecht, 1990.
BHT	Beiträge zur historischen Theologie

BJRL	*Bulletin of the John Rylands University Library of Manchester*
BZNW	Beihefte zur Zeitschrift für die neutestamentliche Wissenschaft
CBQ	*Catholic Biblical Quarterly*
CD	Damascus Document (Cairo Genizah copy of a document also found at Qumran)
CE	Common era
col., cols.	column(s)
Col	Colossians
Congr.	Philo, *De congressu quaerendae eruditionis gratia* (*On the Preliminary Studies*)
Contempl.	Philo, *De vita contemplativa* (*On the Contemplative Life*)
1 Cor	1 Corinthians
2 Cor	2 Corinthians
CTJ	*Calvin Theological Journal*
Dan	Daniel
Deut	Deuteronomy
Eccl	Ecclesiastes
Ezek	Ezekiel
1 En.	*1 Enoch (Ethiopic Apocalypse)*
Eph	Ephesians
EvQ	*Evangelical Quarterly*
EvT	*Evangelische Theologie*
FRLANT	Forschungen zur Religion und Literatur des Alten und Neuen Testaments
Gal	Galatians
Gen	Genesis
Hab	Habakkuk
Heb	Hebrews

IDB	*The Interpreter's Dictionary of the Bible.* 4 vols. Edited by George Arthur Buttrick. Nashville: Abingdon, 1962.
IDBSup	*The Interpreter's Dictionary of the Bible. Supplementary Volume.* Edited by Keith Crim. Nashville: Abingdon, 1976.
Isa	Isaiah
JBL	*Journal of Biblical Liteture*
Jer	Jeremiah
JSNT	*Journal for the Study of the New Testament*
JSNTSS	Journal for the Sudy of the New Testament, Supplement Series
JSPL	*Journal for the Study of Paul and His Letters*
Jub.	*Jubilees*
KJV	King James Version
LAB	*Liber antiquitatem biblicarum* (Pseudo-Philo)
Lev	Leviticus
LNTS	Library of New Testament Studies
LSJ	Henry George Liddell, Robert Scott, and Henry Stuart Jones. *A Greek-English Lexicon.* 9th ed. Oxford: Clarendon, 1996.
LXX	The Septuagint (the Greek OT)
m.'Abot	The tractate *'Abot* of the Mishnah
m.Ber.	The tractate *Berakot* of the Mishnah
m.Sanh.	The tractate *Sanhedrin* of the Mishah
1 Macc.	1 Maccabees
2 Macc.	2 Maccabees
Matt	Matthew
N.B.	Nota bene (take note)
Nestle-Aland[27]	27th edition of *Novum Testamentum Graece* (see bibliography)
Nestle-Aland[28]	28th edition of *Novum Testamentus Graece* (see bibliography)
NICNT	New International Commentary on the New Testament

NIV	New International Version
NJB	New Jerusalem Bible
NovTSup	Supplements to Novum Testamentum
NRSV	New Revised Standard Version
NT	New Testament
NTAbh	Neutestamentliche Abhandlungen
NTS	*New Testament Studies*
OT	Old Testament
OTS	Old Testament Studies
1 Pet	1 Peter
2 Pet	2 Peter
Phil	Philippians
Phlm	Philemon
Praem.	Philo, *De praemiis et poenis* (*On Rewards and Punishments*)
Ps, Pss	Psalm(s)
Pss. Sol.	*Psalms of Solomon*
1QH	*Hodayot* (*Thanksgiving Hymns*) from cave 1 at Qumran
1QM	*Milhamah* (War Scroll) from cave 1 at Qumran
1QS	*Serek Hayahad* (Rule of the Community) from cave 1 at Qumran
4QMMT	*Miqsat Maʿăśê ha–Torah* (*Collection of Works of the Law*) from cave 4 at Qumran
REB	Revised English Bible
Rev	Revelation
Rom	Romans
RSV	Revised Standard Version
1 Sam	1 Samuel
2 Sam	2 Samuel
SBL	Society of Biblical Literature

Sir	Sirach/Ecclesiasticus
SP	Sacra pagina
SJT	*Scottish Journal of Theology*
Str–B	Strack, H.L. and P. Billerbeck, *Kommentar zum Neuen Testament aus Talmud und Midrasch*. 6 Vols. Munich: Beck, 1922–1961.
T. Reub.	*Testament of Reuben*
T. Naph.	*Testament of Naphthali*
TDNT	*Theological Dictionary of the New Testament*. 10 vols. Edited by Gerhard Kittel and Gerhard Friedrich. Translated by Geoffrey W. Bromiley. Grand Rapids: Eerdmans, 1964-76.
TWNT	*Theologischer Wörterbuch zum Neuen Testament*. 10 vols. Edited by Gerhard Kittel and Gerhard Friedrich. Stuttgart: Kohlhammer, 1932-79.
1 Tim	1 Timothy
2 Tim	2 Timothy
vol., vols.	volume(s)
vs., vss.	verse(s)
WBC	Word Biblical Commentary
Wis	Wisdom of Solomon
WTJ	*Westminster Theological Journal*
WUNT	Wissenschaftliche Untersuchungen zum Alten und Neuen Testament
ZNW	*Zeitschrift für die neutestamentliche Wissenschaft und Kunde der älteren Kirche*

Introduction

Apocalyptic Paul

Paul's Apocalyptic Eschatology

To THE MINDS OF many readers, Paul's apocalyptic eschatology[1] is most readily, or even exclusively, discernible in those passages which present a scenario of events to occur at Christ's Parousia (from the Greek, *parousia*, presence, coming, advent), an event which Paul can refer to as "the revelation (*apokalypsis*, apocalypse) of our Lord Jesus Christ" (1 Cor 1:7; cf. 2 Thess 1:7).[2] First Thess 4:13–18 and 1 Cor 15:20–28, 50–56 are the classic examples from the undisputed letters. Both concern the future resurrection of the dead. In the first, Paul (pro)claims,

> we [believers] who are alive, who are left until the coming (*parousia*) of the Lord, will by no means precede those who have died. For the Lord himself, with a cry of command, with the archangel's call and the sound of God's trumpet, will descend from heaven and the dead in Christ will rise first. Then we who are alive, who are left, will be caught up in the clouds together with them to meet the Lord in the air; and so we will be with the Lord forever.[3]

In the second, Paul announces,

> all will be made alive in Christ. But each in his own order: Christ the first fruits, then at his coming (*parousia*) those who belong to Christ. Then is the end, when he hands over the kingdom to God the Father, after he has destroyed every ruler and every authority and power . . . The last enemy to be destroyed is Death . . . We will not all die, but we will all be changed, in a moment,

---

1. In this volume, I use the term "apocalyptic" nominally as shorthand for "apocalyptic eschatology."

2. The following has been adapted from de Boer, "Paul and Apocalyptic Eschatology," 345–57.

3. Translations follow NRSV, with occasional changes.

1

in the twinkling of an eye, at the last trumpet. For the trumpet will sound, and the dead will be raised imperishable, and we will be changed . . . (15:23–24, 26, 51–52).[4]

It is the case, however, that apocalyptic eschatology in the letters and thought of Paul cannot be confined to these scenarios of the Parousia, nor then to the expectation of such a Parousia.[5] Jesus' Parousia, along with the events which shall accompany it, is the culmination of a series of apocalyptic-eschatological events. For Paul, this series began with God raising Jesus from the dead, an event which has already taken place. As Paul writes in 1 Thessalonians, Christians eagerly await God's "Son from heaven, *whom he raised from the dead*, Jesus, who rescues us from the wrath to come" (1 Thess 1:10). Here two references to the Parousia (awaiting the Son from heaven, rescue from the wrath to come) sandwich a reference to Jesus' own resurrection. In 1 Corinthians 15, Paul claims that "Christ has been raised from the dead," who for this reason is "the first fruits of those who have died" (1 Cor 15:20), the first installment of the full harvest of resurrection to come. God's raising of Christ thus constitutes the first act in the apocalyptic-eschatological drama of which the Parousia is but one element:

each in his own order:

(1) Christ the first fruits,

(2) then at his coming (*parousia*) those who belong to Christ.

(3) Then is the End (*eschaton*) . . . (1 Cor 15:23–24).[6]

Paul's understanding of Christ and his saving work is permeated from beginning to end (from Christ's resurrection to his Parousia) by the categories and the perspectives of apocalyptic eschatology. Indeed, Paul goes further since he also applies these categories and perspectives not

4. A notable (and challenging) example from the disputed Pauline letters occurs in 2 Thess 2:1–12, which reads in part: "As to the coming (*parousia*) of our Lord Jesus Christ and our being gathered together to him, . . . let no one deceive you in any way; for that day will not come unless the rebellion comes first and the man of lawlessness is revealed, the son of destruction . . . whom the Lord Jesus will destroy with the breath of his mouth, annihilating him by the manifestation of his coming (*parousia*)."

5. Scholars such as Albert Schweitzer, Ernst Käsemann, and J. Christiaan Beker, who have made significant contributions to an understanding of Paul as an apocalyptic-eschatological thinker, have also tended to identify the expectation of an imminent Parousia as the central or defining element of Paul's apocalyptic eschatology. See Schweitzer, *Mysticism of Paul*, 52; Käsemann, "Primitive Christian Apocalyptic," 109n1; Beker, *Paul the Apostle*, 18.

6. See further on this passage, de Boer, "Paul and Apocalyptic Eschatology," 371–74, 377–78.

only to Jesus' resurrection but also to his death by crucifixion, and even, in some contexts, to God's sending of Jesus into the world (Gal 4:4–6; Rom 8:3; cf. Phil 2:6–8).[7] The coming of Christ into the world, which leads to his death and resurrection and makes them possible, has inaugurated a unified apocalyptic drama that reaches its conclusion at the Parousia, which marks the End (*eschaton*).

The understanding of Paul as an apocalyptic thinker probably owes most to Albert Schweitzer who wrote two studies on Paul and his eschatology early in the twentieth century[8]: Schweitzer claimed that Paul lived "in the conceptions of the dramatic world-view" of Jewish apocalyptic eschatology, which Schweitzer referred to, somewhat unfortunately, as "the late Jewish Eschatology."[9] Schweitzer thus interpreted Paul's eschatology with primary reference not to the eschatology of Jesus nor to that of other early Christians but to the eschatology to be found among Jews of Paul's time. The writings attesting the Jewish eschatological view were for Schweitzer "mainly the Book of Enoch [*1 Enoch*], the Psalms of Solomon, and the Apocalypses of Baruch [*2 Baruch*] and Ezra [*4 Ezra*]." As additional sources, Schweitzer listed the book of *Jubilees*, the *Testaments of the Twelve Patriarchs*, and the "Ascension" (*Assumption*) of Moses, with a passing nod also to "the earlier and later Prophets."[10] (Schweitzer did not of course know the Dead Sea Scrolls). Ever since Schweitzer, students of Paul have tended to label Paul's eschatology (and even his theology as a whole) as "apocalyptic" largely because, following Schweitzer's lead, they have discerned conceptual affinities between Paul's eschatological ideas and first-century Jewish eschatological expectations that are also understood to be "apocalyptic" in some sense (e.g., the resurrection of the dead). It is thus difficult if not impossible to discuss Paul's apocalyptic eschatology apart from Jewish apocalyptic eschatology, and what scholars have said about the latter since the time of Schweitzer.

Many scholars of Jewish apocalyptic, though not all, have found it appropriate and useful to distinguish between apocalypses (a literary type or genre), apocalyptic eschatology (a religious perspective not confined to apocalypses), and apocalypticism (a socioreligious movement or community which has recourse to apocalyptic eschatology as a way of dealing with social

---

7. See the work of Martyn, "Apocalyptic Antinomies" and *Galatians*.

8. Schweitzer, *Paul and His Interpreters*, published in 1911, and *Mysticism of Paul*, published in 1931. The former volume began an introduction to the latter which was actually given a first draft in 1906 (see *Mysticism of Paul*, vii) and was intended as a sequel to the former volume.

9. Schweitzer, *Mysticism of Paul*, 11.

10. Schweitzer, *Mysticism of Paul*, 54–55.

or political alienation).[11] Only the second of these (apocalyptic eschatology) can apply to Paul. He wrote no apocalypses and his apocalyptic-eschatological understanding of Christ did not emerge from social or political or any other kind of alienation. Indeed, according to his own testimony, exactly the *reverse* is true in his case as in that of the communities he founded: Social and political alienation (often leading to persecution) was a *consequence* of faith in Christ (the Christ whose Parousia was eagerly awaited), *not* its cause (cf., e.g., Phil 3:5–9; 1 Thess 2:14). According to Hanson, "Apocalyptic eschatology is neither a genre, not a socioreligious movement, nor a system of thought, but rather a religious perspective, a way of viewing divine plans in relation to mundane reality. . . . [I]t is a perspective which individuals or groups can embrace in varying degrees at different times,"[12] and be given a home in different genres of literature, including letters. This book of essays thus treats Paul's *apocalyptic eschatology* as it comes to expression in his (undisputed) letters,[13] Romans and Galatians in particular.

In an important and influential article, first published in German in 1964, Philipp Vielhauer maintains that "the essential characteristic" of the apocalyptic-eschatological perspective is what he called "the eschatological dualism" of two world ages, "this age" and "the age to come"[14] (see *1 En.* 71:15; *4 Ezra* 7:50, 112, 119; *2 Bar.* 44:8–15; 83:4–9; *m. 'Abot* 4:1; *m. Sanh.* 10:1; *b. Ber.* 9:5; cf. Mark 10:30; Matt 12:32; Luke 18:30; Eph 1:21; 2:7; Heb 6:5). This claim has been echoed by Hanson who writes that as "a religious perspective," the "essential characteristics" of Jewish apocalyptic eschatology are two ages separated by "a great judgment."[15] Similarly, D. S. Russell writes that the "dualistic view of the world, which is characteristic of apocalyptic eschatology, finds expression in a doctrine of two ages."[16]

The dualism of the two ages is "eschatological" (and thus also temporal) because it entails the final, definitive replacement of "this age," which is completely evil or bad, by "the age to come." The latter puts an end to the former.

---

11. See esp. the work of Hanson, "Apocalypse, Genre," "Apocalypticism," *Dawn of Apocalyptic*, "Apocalypses and Apocalypticism (Genre, Introductory Overview)." I return to the issue of genre at a number of points in the essays of this volume. See esp. chapters 1 and 12.

12. Hanson, "Apocalypse, Genre," 27.

13. These are Romans, 1 Corinthians, 2 Corinthians, Galatians, Philippians, 1 Thessalonians, and Philemon.

14. Vielhauer, "Introduction" 588–89 (Vielhauer and Strecker, "Introduction," 549–50); Vielhauer, "Einleitung," 413.

15. Hanson, *Dawn of Apocalyptic*, 432, 440.

16. Russell, *Method and Message*, 269.

There is and can be "no continuity" between the two ages,[17] since "this age" is the epoch and the realm (or sphere) of sin, evil, and death, whereas "the age to come" is the epoch and the realm (or sphere) of God and thus of righteousness, well-being, and life. As realms (or spheres) of activity, the categories "this age" and "the age to come" have spatial as well as temporal aspects. The locus of "this age" is the earth, whereas the locus of "the age to come" is heaven (God's realm), from which the benefits of the new age will descend at the end of time or history. The dualism of the two ages characteristic of apocalyptic eschatology is thus *at once temporal and spatial*.[18]

Furthermore, although Jewish apocalyptic eschatology naturally finds its focus in God's covenantal relationship with Israel, the scope of the two ages is cosmic: They both involve all people and all times. As Schweitzer pointed out, redemption in apocalyptic eschatology is "not a mere transaction" between an individual and God, but "a world-event in which someone has a share."[19]

That Paul was familiar with some form of this eschatological dualism is minimally suggested by his use of the expression "this age" (*ho aiōn houtos*; Rom 12:2; 1 Cor 1:20; 2:6, 8; 3:18; 2 Cor 4:4; cf. Eph 1:21). In Gal 1:4, he refers to "the present evil age" (*ho aiōn ho enestōs*). The phrase "this world" (*ho kosmos houtos*) is a synonym (1 Cor 3:19; 5:10; 7:31; cf. Eph 2:2; 4 *Ezra* 4:2; 8:1), as is shown by the parallelism in 1 Cor 3:18–19:

> If you think that you are wise in *this age*, you should become
> fools so that you may become wise. For the wisdom of *this world*
> is foolishness with God.

The corresponding expression "the age (or world) to come" occurs only in Ephesians among the Pauline letters (1:21; cf. 2:7), though there may be an allusion to it in the reference to "the ends of the ages" (i.e., the end of the old age and the beginning of the new) in 1 Cor 10:11. But the idea of a coming age is implied when the present world-age is characterized as *this* world-age.[20] Moreover, such expressions as "the kingdom of God" (Rom 14:17; 1 Cor 4:20; 6:9, 10; 15:24, 50; Gal 5:21; 1 Thess. 2:12),[21] "eternal life" (Rom 2:7; 5:21; 6:22,

---

17. Vielhauer and Strecker, "Introduction," 550.

18. This should occasion no surprise since time is simply a method for keeping track of changes that take place in space.

19. Schweitzer, *Mysticism of Paul*, 54 (translation slightly modified).

20. Keck, "Paul and Apocalyptic Theology," 234.

21. See also Eph 5:5; Col 4:11; 2 Thess 1:5; cf. *As. Mos.* 10:1.

23; Gal 6:8),[22] and "new creation" (2 Cor 5:17; Gal 6:15)[23] are surely other ways of speaking about the age or world to come. These are eschatological realities, i.e., the realities of the New Age of God.

While a two-ages dualism characteristic of Jewish apocalyptic eschatology underlies Paul's thought, he does not, of course, write about "apocalyptic eschatology." He does not use this technical phrase, nor do other ancient writers of his time. The phrase is an invention, and also a convention, of biblical scholars.[24] It provides a convenient, shorthand way of labeling and discussing a distinctive form of eschatology (teaching concerning "last things") which scholars have discerned not only in Paul's letters but also in other ancient Jewish and Christian literature. In the use of this phrase, it is normally assumed, as pointed out above, that Christian versions of apocalyptic eschatology, including that of Paul, are deeply indebted to, or are modifications of, Jewish apocalyptic eschatology since the latter already existed when Jesus and the church were born. Jewish apocalyptic eschatology, in short, was the matrix within which Christian apocalyptic eschatology, including that of Paul, arose and developed.[25]

Eschatology has traditionally (within the history of Christian thought) referred to the four theological doctrines of heaven, hell, judgment, and life after death, often treated separately and with an eye on the destiny of the individual believer. *Apocalyptic* eschatology, however, concerns visible, objective, and public events which are cosmic in scope and implication, e.g., the general resurrection of the dead and the Last Judgment.[26] Apocalyptic eschatology is fundamentally concerned with God's active and visible rectification (putting right) of the created world (the "cosmos") which has somehow gone astray and become alienated from God. This form of eschatology is in turn often differentiated from the eschatology of the OT prophets (e.g., Amos, Isaiah, Jeremiah), which has a more limited frame of reference. This "prophetic" eschatology is often seen as the precursor of the apocalyptic variety,[27] though this is a much debated question.[28] Prophetic

22. See also 1 Tim 1:16; 6:12; Titus 1:2; 3:7; cf. Dan 12:2.

23. Cf. *1 En.* 72:1; *4 Ezra* 7:75; *2 Bar.* 32:6

24. See Sturm, "Defining the Word 'Apocalyptic.'"

25. Collins, *Apocalyptic Imagination.*

26. These events signal and effect the end of the world as previously known and experienced by human beings (i.e., the world characterized by sin, evil, death, and forces of lawlessness and rebellion, as in the scenarios of the Parousia quoted above), as well as the transition to a new world marked by righteousness, peace, and life.

27. See Rowley, *Relevance of Apocalyptic,* 13–53; Russell, *Method and Message,* 73–103; Collins, "From Prophecy to Apocalypticism."

28. Collins, *Apocalyptic Imagination,* 19–28.

eschatology—the eschatology of the OT prophets—has in view a future divine intervention in the ongoing history of Israel. This divine intervention is a corrective measure in the continuing story of God's people. Furthermore, God's intervention is not publicly visible but hidden in the historical process of national disaster or restoration. Post-exilic or "late" prophecy (e.g., Ezekiel, Zechariah, Trito-Isaiah) tends to portray God's intervention in the affairs and history of Israel against a backdrop of cosmic upheaval and discontinuity, which gives this "late" prophecy a proto-apocalyptic flavor.[29] According to Collins, a "novelty" of apocalyptic eschatology (relative to prophetic eschatology) is a judgment of the dead as well as of the living (cf. already Isa. 25:8; 26:19, part of the so-called Isaiah Apocalypse; Dan 12:1–3).[30] A distinctive element of apocalyptic eschatology, at least in such works as *1 Enoch*, *2 Baruch*, and *4 Ezra*, is its cosmic scope and interest: All times and places and thus all human beings are involved and at stake in the eschatological drama about to unfold, so that God's eschatological action of rectifying the creation reaches back to the beginning of human history even as it brings it to an end.

But why call this form of eschatology "apocalyptic"? The adjective is derived from the noun "apocalypse," a near transliteration of the Greek *apokalypsis*, literally meaning "unveiling" (which is also the meaning of the Latin *revelatio*, from which the English term "revelation" comes). The use of this term to characterize "apocalyptic" eschatology was inspired primarily by the New Testament book of Revelation, also known as the Apocalypse of John. The opening verse, from which the traditional title derives, reads: "The revelation (*apokalypsis*, apocalypse) of Jesus Christ, which God gave him to show his servants what must soon take place" (Rev 1:1). Apocalyptic eschatology refers, then, to the kind of eschatology found in the book of Revelation, and this eschatology is a matter of divine revelation: Apocalyptic eschatology is *revealed* eschatology.[31] It needs also to be recognized,

29. Cf. Hanson, *Dawn of Apocalyptic*.

30. Collins, "Apocalypses and Apocalypticism," 283.

31. The genre designation "apocalypse" is also derived from Revelation, namely, its opening verse. For understandable reasons, apocalyptic eschatology has been closely associated with books which are seemingly of the same genre as the NT book of Revelation and thus sharing its distinctive generic features at least to some extent. Daniel, *1 Enoch*, *4 Ezra*, and *2 Baruch* are the commonly cited examples (though unlike these works Revelation is not pseudonymous). In recent years, in fact, some scholars have begun to insist that the term "apocalyptic" should be used exclusively in connection with works of this genre or with the themes attested in them. These scholars also maintain that the term "apocalyptic" cannot then be limited to eschatology (understood narrowly as expectations about future events) since eschatology is not always the sole or even the major concern or topic of an apocalypse. Christopher Rowland (*Open Heaven*) is

however, that the book of Revelation is in many ways distinctive and cannot be taken as the measure of all expressions of an apocalyptic-eschatological worldview. The sheer quantity and richness of Revelation's symbolism and imagery are really without parallel in contemporary sources, whether Jewish or Christian.[32] Apocalyptic eschatology can be given expression in much less vivid, certainly less lurid, imagery and language, and Jewish apocalyptic eschatology, of course, would not have the Christian elements found in Revelation. Nevertheless, what is called "apocalyptic eschatology," whether in Jewish or Christian sources, is normally assumed to bear at least a "family resemblance" to the eschatology found in the book of Revelation; the family resemblance is discernible in the dualism of the two world ages, which is a matter of divine revelation.

If, then, the essential characteristic of apocalyptic eschatology is the dualism of two ages, cosmically conceived, the notion of revelation in "apocalyptic" eschatology encompasses *both* ages, not just the one to come, since it is only through the disclosure of the coming age that the present can be perceived as "*this* (evil) age," as one which is destined to be brought to an end by God. Along similar lines, Martyn has written that apocalyptic involves "the conviction that God has now given to the elect true perception both of present developments (the real world) and of a wondrous transformation in the near future." A central concern of apocalyptic is "the birth of a new way knowing both present and future."[33] The knowledge granted of the future, of the Last Judgment and of the new age beyond the Judgment, thus bears a close and reciprocal relationship to the knowledge granted of "this age"—which is to say that the solution (the age to come) must address the problem (this age). In apocalyptic eschatology, then, the notion of revelation applies not only to the Last Judgment and the coming age but also to "this age," its true nature and its destiny.

The opening line of Revelation, with its claim that the revelation is "of Jesus Christ," points to a crucial modification of Jewish apocalyptic eschatology, one shared by Paul. In Revelation, the eschatological events of the imminent future take their point of departure from an eschatological event of the recent past, the resurrection (and thus ascension) of Jesus Christ to God's heavenly throne (cf. 1:9–20; 5:1–14). This event, in *Paul*

---

the major proponent of this view. Rowland's approach has been enormously influential in Great Britain (see e.g., Reynolds and Stuckenbruck, *Jewish Apocalyptic Tradition*). I evaluate Rowland's proposal in chapter 2 below. On the problems with identifying an apocalypse as a literary genre prior to the second century CE, see chapter 1, nn. 31, 37; chapter 12, nn. 9, 18, 20.

32. Cf. Bauckham, *Theology of Revelation*, 9–12.

33. Martyn, "Apocalyptic Antinomies," 424n28; cf. Martyn, "Epistemology."

as in Revelation, constitutes a crucial Christian modification of Jewish apocalyptic eschatology. For Paul (as for John of Revelation), the hour of the eschaton was not, as in Jewish apocalyptic eschatology, about to strike; it had already struck in God's raising of Jesus from the dead, an apocalyptic-eschatological event, as Schweitzer clearly perceived:

> While other believers held that the finger of the world-clock was touching on the beginning of the coming hour and were waiting for the stroke that would announce this, Paul told them that it had already passed beyond the point, and that they had failed to hear the striking of the hour, which in fact struck at the Resurrection of Jesus.[34]

Paul's apocalyptic eschatology, as that of Revelation, is thus as much a matter of a *past* eschatological event (the resurrection of Jesus, the Messiah) as of an event still to occur (the Parousia). Believers such as Paul and John of Revelation were convinced that God's Messiah had already made an appearance on the human scene and, just as important, that this appearance of the Messiah provided the essential and inescapable clue to a "right" understanding of this world and its events, of the human condition or plight, as well as of what was expected to happen in the near future. "For the person of insight who dares to see things as they really are," Schweitzer wrote, "faith ceases to be simply a faith of expectation. It takes up present certainties into itself"; someone "who has true knowledge [a believer in Christ] can be conscious of himself [or herself] as at one and the same time" living in both ages, in what Schweitzer here refers to as "the transient world and the eternal world."[35] It would be better, however, to say that believers live at what Martyn called "the juncture of the ages,"[36] i.e., where the two ages, or rather the realities that characterize the two ages, are in conflict, with those of the new age seeking to replace those of the old, whereby God finally and irrevocably establishes God's sovereignty over the world. Paul's apocalyptic eschatology thus has a christological focus and foundation, one that determines the life of the believer both now and in the future.

Overview of the Essays in this Volume

The essays included in this volume seek to investigate and to illuminate various aspects of Paul's christologically focused apocalyptic eschatology,

34. Schweitzer, *Mysticism of Paul,* 99.
35. Schweitzer, *Mysticism of Paul,* 99.
36. Martyn, "Epistemology."

as outlined above, including its relationship and indebtedness to Jewish antecedents. The essays focus on Romans and Galatians, supplementing my monograph on Romans 5 and 1 Corinthians 15.[37]

Chapter 1, "Paul and Jewish Apocalyptic Eschatology," outlines two distinct patterns, or "tracks," of Jewish apocalyptic eschatology, the one labeled "cosmological" and the other "forensic." I argue here that Paul's letters show familiarity with both tracks but that he favors the former as the framework for explaining the theological significance of the Christ event.[38] This opening chapter also contains an addendum with a response to some representative criticisms of my proposal in recent publications by N. T. Wright (2015) and Jörg Frey (2016).[39]

Chapter 2, "Paul, Theologian of God's Apocalypse,"[40] argues that to speak of apocalyptic with respect to Paul is to concentrate not on the theme of direct communication of heavenly mysteries to a human being, as in the influential work of Christopher Rowland, but on the theme of God's own visible eschatological activity, activity that will constitute the actual revelation, i.e., the Apocalypse of God.[41] The chapter analyzes Paul's apocalyptic language (his use of the Greek term *apokalypsis* and its cognate verb) to support this claim.

37. De Boer, *Defeat of Death.* Full bibliographic information, along with the original titles, may be found above, in the section entitled "Acknowledgements and Original Publications." All the articles have been slightly edited and adapted for inclusion in this volume.

38. This essay was originally published in the festschrift for J. Louis Martyn (Marcus and Soards, *Apocalyptic and the New Testament,* 169–90.). It was written and completed in the fall of 1986 while I was also revising my dissertation (which I defended in 1983) for publication. The latter appeared as *The Defeat of Death* in 1988, a year before the article. Material from the article and book were incorporated into a subsequent encyclopedia article, "Paul and Apocalyptic Eschatology," published in 1998. See also "Excursus 2: Galatians and Apocalyptic Eschatology," in de Boer, *Galatians,* 31–35, which contains a concise summary.

39. Frey, "Demythologizing Apocalyptic?," 508-10; Wright, *Paul and His Recent Interpreters,* 155-67.

40. The original article was based on my inaugural address, "De apocalypticus Paulus," given to the Faculty of Theology of Vrije Universiteit Amsterdam on November 5, 1998, and on material found in de Boer, 'Paul and Apocalyptic Eschatology,' also published in 1998.

41. In the approach championed by Rowland and his followers, 2 Cor 12:1–4 is the most apocalyptic text to be found in Paul's letters (see discussion in chapter 2 below). It is difficult to see how this understanding of Paul's apocalyptic, with its spatial, experiential, and individualistic emphases, is to be distinguished from mysticism as such. Cf., e.g., Rowland, "Paul as an Apocalyptist [= Mystic]"; Collins et al., *Apocalypticism and Mysticism.*

The title of Chapter 3, "Paul's Mythologizing Program in Romans," contains an obvious allusion to Rudolf Bultmann's claim that Paul began a process of demythologizing apocalyptic eschatology, one that Bultmann himself believed he could bring to completion for the modern world. With an assist from the work of Ernst Käsemann, the chapter counters Bultmann's approach with the argument that Paul is actually *mythologizing* certain traditions derived from one strand of Jewish apocalyptic eschatology (the "forensic" variety)[42] with traditions from another strand (the "cosmological" variety). The characterization of Sin and Death as cosmological (and cosmic) powers is a key part of Paul's mythologizing program. One of the main reasons Paul programmatically mythologizes Sin and Death in Romans 5–8 is to explain why the Law is not, or no longer, a viable option for those who have come to believe in Christ.

Chapter 4, "Sin and Soteriology in Romans" (previously unpublished), explores Paul's mythologization of Sin (and its partner, Death) and its implications for soteriology further.[43] It argues that while human beings are indeed the victims of Sin for Paul, they also cannot entirely escape responsibility for the wrong that they do, i.e., for their complicity with (or consent to) Sin's hegemony. By the same token, if they become believers who put their trust in Christ, they cannot claim full credit for the good that they may subsequently do, for they cannot achieve or do what is right without assistance and guidance from the Spirit of Christ.

Chapter 5, "Cross and Cosmos in Galatians," focuses on Paul's twofold use of the term *kosmos* in Galatians. Paul uses this term in 4:3 to refer to the physical universe which is comprised of certain elements (*ta stoicheia tou kosmou*); in 6:14, however, Paul evidently uses the term to refer to the religion of the Law, represented in the immediate context by the practice of circumcision (6:12–13, 15). Despite the different *referential* meanings of the term in the two passages, they do bear a close relationship to one another at the level of soteriology. The soteriological connection between them is to be found in Paul's understanding of the cross of Christ as an apocalyptic event that destroys previous religious practices and beliefs, clearing the way for a new creation of "faith becoming effective through love" (Gal 5:6).

Chapter 6, "Paul's Use and Interpretation of a Justification Tradition," illustrates how Paul uses and adapts a received tradition for his own

---

42. This is the strand adhered to by Paul's Jewish conversation partners in Romans. (I use the terms "tracks," "patterns," and "strands" interchangeably to refer to Jewish cosmological and forensic apocalyptic eschatologies, as outlined in chapter 1).

43. The essay is the revised version of an invited paper presented to the Pauline Theology study group of the Institute of Biblical Research, Boston, MA, November 17, 2017, just prior to the Annual Meeting of the Society of Biblical Literature.

christologically focused apocalyptic agenda.[44] I argue that Paul cites a known formula in Gal 2:16a, which means that the three key terms used here (*erga nomou, pisteōs Iēsou Christou,* and *dikaioutai*) have not been coined by Paul himself nor introduced by him into the Galatian setting. The terms have been introduced by those opposing his work in Galatia and they understand them within the framework of traditions indebted to the *forensic* strand of Jewish apocalyptic eschatology. In Gal 2:15–21, Paul begins a process of contextually redefining their forensic understanding of justification with categories derived from *cosmological* Jewish apocalyptic eschatology. Justification comes to encompass not only God's forensic justification of the believer in the future but also, and more importantly in the Galatian context, God's dynamic rectification of the believer in the present—through Christ.

Chapter 7, "Justification in Paul: From Galatians to Romans" (previously unpublished),[45] asks how justification appears in Romans when looked at through the lens provided by knowledge of justification in Galatians. What does one see when one starts with Galatians and only then goes to Romans, instead of the other way around? I argue that Paul's thought in Romans has gone further and more clearly in the direction of a cosmological-apocalyptic understanding of God's act of justification in Christ than is the case in Galatians.

Chapter 8, "Apocalyptic and Salvation History in Galatians," addresses the issue of salvation history in Galatians, as raised in treatments of the issue by Bruce W. Longenecker and Jason Maston.[46] Both question, though in different ways, the apocalyptic interpretation of the letter as championed by me and J. Louis Martyn. Their views can be taken as representative and my response to them thus has a wider application and relevance. Salvation history involves a claim of continuity between the Law given at Sinai and the gospel Paul preaches, and thus also between the historical people of Israel and the empirical church. I argue that Paul at least in Galatians[47] has no

44. An early version was presented to the Paul Seminar of the British New Testament Conference in Edinburgh, Scotland, in September 2004. The substance of the article was subsequently incorporated into my commentary on Galatians (de Boer, *Galatians,* 139–65). The version presented here includes some small corrections and modifications that make it consistent with the treatment in the commentary and suitable for inclusion in this collection.

45. The chapter included here is a revision of the paper I delivered at the Annual Meeting of the Society of Biblical Literature, San Diego, CA, November 2014. I use this essay to clarify and to supplement the discussion of justification in my commentary on Galatians (de Boer, *Galatians*) and in chapter 6 above.

46. Longenecker, "Salvation History in Galatians," and Maston, "Salvation History in Galatians."

47. Romans may be a different matter.

interest or stake whatsoever in explicitly (or even implicitly) attributing the origin of the Law to God. For the same reason, he is also not interested in articulating a notion or theory of salvation history with respect to the people of the Law, Israel. His rhetorical agenda in Galatians is to emphasize *discontinuity* between the Law and the gospel, between works and faith, and thus also between the historical people of Israel and those who belong to Christ. He uses apocalyptic categories to articulate that discontinuity.

Chapter 9, "Christ and the Authority of the Old Testament in Galatians," complements chapter 8. It investigates the status of the OT *text* for Paul in Galatians as well as the value, or the authority, of the (salvation) *history* found in the OT documents. I argue that since the gospel of Christ has absolute authority for Paul, the Old Testament text cannot have this authority, nor then the (salvation) history to which this text bears witness. Christ's absolute authority allows Paul to appeal to the OT, or portions thereof, whether as Scripture or as (salvation) history, whenever it serves his proclamation of the gospel as he understands it—and to ignore it when it does not.

Chapter 10, "Paul's Quotation of Isaiah 54:1 in Galatians 4:27," is a case study in Paul's use of a text from the OT to advance his own understanding of the gospel as an apocalyptic event that liberates from slavery. Paul uses the oracle of Isa 54:1 with its picture of two women symbolizing two cities (for Paul, these are the present Jerusalem and the Jerusalem above) to give the Genesis account of Sarah and Hagar, and their respective sons by Abraham, an allegorical-typological interpretation that serves his eschatology, which is both christological and apocalyptic.[48]

Chapter 11, "Paul's Use of LXX Psalm 142:2 in Galatians and Romans,"[49] is another case study in Paul's use of an OT text for the proclamation of the gospel. LXX Ps 142:2 (= MT Ps 143:2) is the only Psalm text that Paul cites in two places, Gal 2:16 and Rom 3:20. Paul uses this text in both places to highlight the human inability to receive justification from God on the basis of keeping the Law, and thus to *illustrate* his understanding of the human condition "under Sin" as the problem for which Christ provides the solution.

Chapter 12, "Apocalyptic as God's Eschatological Activity in Paul's Theology,"[50] is a retrospective defense of my work on Paul as an apocalyptic theologian. It points out that in one long-standing tradition of scholarship of ancient Judaism and Christianity, apocalyptic concerns the (ancient Jewish) expectation of God's own eschatological activity whereby God will

---

48. As already indicated, for Paul, the two are inseparable.

49. A translation and revision of the original Dutch article.

50. A revision of an invited paper presented at the SBL Annual Meeting in San Diego, CA, November 2014.

put an end to the present evil order of reality ("this age") and replace it with a new, transformed order of reality ("the age to come"). With the crucial christological modification, Paul is an apocalyptic theologian in this sense: The coming of Christ represents God's apocalyptic-eschatological invasion of the human world whereby God has begun to wage a war of cosmic proportions against evil cosmological forces that have oppressed and victimized all human beings and brought about their separation from God and from life; this war will end in God's sure triumph at Christ's Parousia. The chapter may be regarded as both a conclusion to and as a summary of the essays included in this volume.[51]

51. Though the essays have been edited for inclusion in this volume, they for the most part retain their original contents and form. This means that there is some inevitable overlap in the essays, particularly in connection with the controversial matters of genre and definition. Aside from the fact that repetition with respect to these matters is often warranted by the context and the need for clarity, the overlap also allows each chapter to be read and understood independently of the others, as was the case when they were first published or presented.

Chapter 1

Paul and Jewish Apocalyptic Eschatology

Introduction

The Problem

THE IMPORTANCE OF JEWISH apocalyptic eschatology for understanding Paul's theology was first fully articulated by Albert Schweitzer in his own distinctively systematic way early in the twentieth century.[1] Rudolf Bultmann acknowledged its importance but argued that Paul had in fact begun a process of existentially reinterpreting ("demythologizing") received apocalyptic traditions with its talk of cosmological powers and future cosmic transformation, a process that Bultmann sought to bring to fruition in his own existentialist reinterpretation of Paul (and other NT writings).[2] Ernst Käsemann sought in the early 1960s to refute Bultmann's approach with a series of powerful essays reasserting the central significance of apocalyptic eschatology in the New Testament, Paul's letters in particular.[3] A vigorous debate followed the publication of Käsemann's essays,[4] one that continued in the decades the followed,[5] and has continued up to the present day.

Particularly in its early stages, the debate revolved around the terms "anthropology" and "cosmology," terms that acquired certain distinct,

1. Schweitzer, *Paul and His Interpreters*; Schweitzer, *Mysticism of Paul*. See also Wrede, *Paul*; Kabisch, *Eschatologie des Paulus*.

2. See his programmatic essay, "New Testament and Mythology," and further, Bultmann, *Theology*, 1.185–352.

3. Käsemann, "Beginnings of Christian Theology" (German 1960); "Primitive Christian Apocalyptic" (German 1962); "Paul and Early Catholicism" (German 1963).

4. See Bultmann, "Ist Apokalyptik die Mutter der christlichen Theologie?"; Käsemann, "Paul's Anthropology." Käsemann responded to many of his critics in the footnotes of the articles cited in the previous note.

5. Cf. Baumgarten, *Paulus und die Apokalyptik*; Beker, *Paul the Apostle*; Keck, "Paul and Apocalyptic Theology"; Martyn, "Apocalyptic Antinomies"; Branick, "Apocalyptic Paul?" Roughly speaking, Beker, Keck, and Martyn are in Käsemann's corner, Baumgarten and Branick in Bultmann's.

quasi-technical meanings with the context of the debate. The former, used to sum up the interpretation of Paul by Bultmann and his followers, referred to the *individual* as he or she is addressed by the gospel message in the *present* and confronted with the *decision* of faith. The latter, shorthand for Käsemann's apocalyptic interpretation of Paul, seemed to denote *God's* destruction in the *future* of the *cosmic forces* that now enslave the creation, a creation from which the individual human being cannot be isolated. Each, it may be noted, nevertheless sought to come to grips with the dialectic of "already" and "not yet" evident in Paul's thought. Both sides largely agreed that whereas "cosmology" was properly apocalyptic, "anthropology" (as defined above) was not.

Careful attention to the dispute between Bultmann and Käsemann over Paul's theology of justification (or rectification),[6] an aspect of Paul's thought that provided the larger debate with its focal point, causes one to begin to doubt, however, whether *only* the cosmological reading of Paul has the right to be deemed the apocalyptic one.

Bultmann and Käsemann

In the first volume of his *Theology of the New Testament*,[7] Bultmann had argued that there was "complete agreement" between Paul and first-century Jews "as to the formal meaning of *dikaiosyne*: It is a forensic-eschatological term."[8] The event of Christ's death and resurrection, however, caused Paul to make two key modifications in the Jewish view:

1. *Present not future*: "what for the Jews," Bultmann wrote, appealing to Rom 5:1, "is a *matter of hope* is for Paul a *present* reality—or, better, is also a present reality."[9] Thus, through the Christ-event, "God already pronounces His eschatological verdict (over the person of faith) in the present; the eschatological event is a present reality, or, rather, is

6. Whether the Greek words *dikaioō* and *dikaiosynē* are best translated "justify/justification" or "rectify/rectification" (for the latter, see Keck, *Paul and His Letters*, 118–23; Martyn, "Apocalyptic Antinomies," 418) is partly what is at issue: the former seems closer to Bultmann's views, the latter to Käsemann's. The Greek noun is also frequently rendered "righteousness." See chapter 7 below.

7. The following citations are from Volume I of this work.

8. Bultmann, *Theology*, 273, emphasis removed. Bultmann appeals to Rom 2:13; 4:3, 5, 6, 22; Gal 3:6. Righteousness as a forensic term implies the imagery of the law court and thus means "the favorable standing" one has in such a court (272). It does not mean "the ethical quality of a person" (272), but "his relation to God" (277).

9. Bultmann, *Theology*, 279, emphasis original.

beginning in the present."[10] Christ's death and resurrection was "the eschatological event by which God ended the old course of the world and introduced a new aeon [N.B.]."[11] Through that event "God's acquitting decision"[12] has been declared, a verdict that become a reality for the individual "hearer of the gospel."[13]

2. *Faith not works*: Whereas "the pious Jew endeavors . . . to fulfill the conditions which are the presupposition" of God's eschatological justifying verdict (at the Last Judgment), namely, "keeping the commandments of the Law and doing good works,"[14] the Christian does not seek justification by works of the Law but receives it by faith: "Righteousness then," Bultmann wrote, "cannot be won by human effort, nor does any human accomplishment establish a claim to it; it is sheer gift."[15] The "righteousness of God" (*dikaiosynē theou*) is thus "God-given, God-adjudicated righteousness."[16]

It is evident from this brief summary of Bultmann's views that he assumed that Paul's "anthropological" understanding of "the righteousness of God" was—apart from the two modifications discussed—essentially the same as that found in Jewish *apocalyptic* eschatology. The agreement pertains not only to the forensic-eschatological character of righteousness but, as the discussion of the second modification bears out, also to its concern with the *individual*.

In his essay, "'The Righteousness of God' in Paul" (originally 1961), Käsemann in turn argues that the expression *dikaiosynē theou* (Rom 1:17; 3:5, 21, 22; 10:3; 2 Cor 5:21) was a unified one, not to be subsumed (à la Bultmann) under the general heading of "righteousness" and furthermore not created by Paul.[17] It was a technical expression, derived from the Old Testament (Deut 33:21), that found a home in Jewish apocalyptic thought (1QS 11:12; *T. Dan* 6:10).[18] This unified expression denoted God's eschatological saving action and power. Paul, Käsemann argued, retained this meaning in his appropriation of the expression. For Käsemann, then, the

10. Bultmann, *Theology*, 276.

11. Bultmann, *Theology*, 278.

12. Bultmann, *Theology*, 279.

13. Bultmann, *Theology*, 275.

14. Bultmann, *Theology*, 273.

15. Bultmann, *Theology*, 280–81.

16. Bultmann, *Theology*, 285.

17. Käsemann, "'The Righteousness of God,'" 172.

18. Käsemann, "'The Righteousness of God,'" 172.

undoubted character of righteousness as a forensic-eschatological gift (a concession to Bultmann) cannot be separated from its character as God's saving power: "God's saving activity . . . is present in his gift"; the righteousness of God "partakes of the character of power, insofar as God himself enters the arena with it"[19] God's righteousness is a gift only insofar as it also signifies submissive obedience to God's saving power.[20]

In the process of establishing his thesis, Käsemann also attacked the two modifications Bultmann attributed to Paul:

1. According to Käsemann, what made Paul's use of the expression unique over against the Jewish apocalyptic use of it was not, as Bultmann maintained, the present reality of righteousness. The Thanksgiving Hymns from Qumran show that its present reality was also stressed in one stream of apocalyptic Judaism.[21] But Käsemann's basic point was not that Bultmann had misunderstood Jewish apocalyptic eschatology but that he had misunderstood *Paul*: Though Käsemann conceded that "Paul lays the strongest stress on the present nature of salvation,"[22] he emphasized that Paul's "present eschatology cannot be taken out its context of future eschatology . . . Paul remained an apocalyptist."[23]

2. Similarly, in attacking Bultmann's second modification, Käsemann asserted that "the righteousness of God does not, *in Paul's understanding*, refer primarily to the individual and is not be understood exclusively in the context of a doctrine of man."[24] The Bultmannian anthropological/individual constriction occurs when exclusive emphasis is laid on the gift-character of righteousness and the latter is interpreted in terms of the contract between faith and works.[25] *Paul's* theology of God's righteousness is not "essentially concerned with anthropology,"[26] but with God's own redemptive action in and for the world. It is here that the uniqueness of Paul's appropriation of the expression "the righteousness of God" lies, according to Käsemann. Over against Jewish apocalypticism as well as pre-Pauline Jewish Christianity, the disclosure of God's righteousness in Christ can no longer signify only

---

19. Käsemann, "'The Righteousness of God,'" 174.
20. Käsemann, "'The Righteousness of God,'" 182.
21. Käsemann, "'The Righteousness of God,'" 178.
22. Käsemann, "'The Righteousness of God,'" 178.
23. Käsemann, "'The Righteousness of God,'" 181.
24. Käsemann, "'The Righteousness of God,'" 180, emphasis added.
25. Käsemann, "'The Righteousness of God,'" 172–73, 176.
26. Käsemann, "'The Righteousness of God,'" 181.

covenant faithfulness but also, and primarily, his faithfulness toward the whole creation. It is "God's sovereignty over the world revealing itself eschatologically in Jesus"[27] through whom, contrary to the Jewish view, God justifies not the godly but the ungodly.[28]

Thus, while Käsemann was busy claiming that his cosmological interpretation of Paul's *dikaiosynē theou* found support in Jewish apocalyptic eschatology and that Bultmann had misunderstood Paul, he did not show that Bultmann's basic assumption was unwarranted, namely, that an anthropological interpretation of Paul's *dikaiosynē theou* also finds support in Jewish apocalyptic eschatology. We may thus begin to ask—leaving aside for the moment whether Käsemann or Bultmann gave the more compelling account of *Paul's* thought—on what grounds it is legitimate or accurate to label Paul's thought "apocalyptic," particularly in relation to the alternative "cosmology" and "anthropology." And that question in turn prompts us to ask about the nature of the Jewish apocalyptic eschatology that is the presumed background to the apostle's own views.

The Intention of this Essay

My intention in this essay is not, however, to undertake a new investigation of some discrete element in Jewish apocalyptic eschatology (least of all righteousness since that has been sufficiently done elsewhere, largely in support of Käsemann's theses)[29] in order to determine the relevance for "apocalyptic Paul." Rather, in the spirit of J. Louis Martyn, for whom this essay was originally written, I shall be bold and seek to demonstrate that Jewish apocalyptic eschatology took two distinct forms, or "tracks," in the New Testament period. One of these tracks, to be sure, provides support for Käsemann's "cosmological" reading of Paul, but the other provides some measure of support for Bultmann's "anthropological" reading.

---

27. Käsemann, "'The Righteousness of God,'" 180.

28. Käsemann, "'The Righteousness of God,'" 178. Bultmann and Käsemann defended their views in subsequent publications. See Bultmann, "ΔΙΚΑΙΟΣΥΝΕ ΘΕΟΥ." Käsemann responded to Bultmann in footnotes included in the republication of his original article ("The 'Righteousness of God,'" 168, 169, 173).

29. See Müller, *Gottes Gerechtigkeit*; Kertelge, *'Rechtfertigung' bei Paulus*; Stuhlmacher, *Gerechtigkeit Gottes bei Paulus*. These works provided support for Käsemann's position. A significant defense of Bultmann was the essay by Conzelmann, "Die Rechtfertigungslehre des Paulus." See Käsemann's response "Justification and Salvation History," 76 n.27. See further the discussion by Sanders, *Paul and Palestinian Judaism*, 474–511, and the appendix in the same work by Brauch, "Perspectives."

The Two Tracks of Jewish Apocalyptic Eschatology

Preliminaries

It is useful to begin by making explicit what has been implicit thus far, namely, the phrase "apocalyptic eschatology" does not occur in the literature we are about to discuss nor in the letters of Paul. It is a construct of scholars that purports to epitomize certain phenomena discernible in the sources. It has been used in Pauline scholarship because students of Paul perceive certain conceptual affinities between Paul's thought and Jewish eschatological expectations that also labeled "apocalyptic."

Such eschatology is usually associated with a genre of works known as "apocalypses" of which the canonical books of Daniel and Revelation (The Apocalypse to John) are notable examples. Recent scholars, however, such as Paul D. Hanson and John J. Collins, have sought to distinguish "apocalyptic eschatology" from the literary genre. Thus Collins characterizes apocalyptic eschatology "as a set of ideas and motifs that may be found in *other literary genres* . . . "[30] The point is of obvious importance since it means that apocalyptic eschatology, though it may find its most vivid expression in apocalypses, is not confined to such works.[31] The point is also of particular importance for any assessment of Paul's supposed apocalyptic eschatology since the apostle wrote letters not apocalypses.[32]

Most students of Jewish apocalyptic eschatology will agree with Vielhauer's assertion that "the essential characteristic of Apocalyptic" is what he labels "the eschatological dualism" of the two ages, "this age" and "the age to come."[33] The dualism is "eschatological" because it concerns the final, definitive replacement of "this age" by the new one. This basic definition of apocalyptic is presupposed by Pauline scholars as well.[34]

30. Collins, *The Apocalyptic Imagination*, 2, emphasis added. See Hanson, "Apocalypticism," 29–31.

31. In any event, Collins (*Apocalyptic Imagination*, 3) points out that it is dubious whether we can really speak about the genre "apocalypse" prior to the second century CE. He nevertheless proceeds as if we can.

32. For this reason, Paul's apocalyptic eschatology need not necessarily be confined to the scenarios found in, e.g., 1 Thess 4:14–18 or 1 Corinthians 15. See, for instance, Bornkamm, *Paul*, 199, or Baumgarten, *Paulus*, 130.

33. Vielhauer, "Introduction," 588–89. Similarly, Hanson defines apocalyptic eschatology as "a religious perspectives" whose "essential characteristics" are two ages separated by "a great judgment" (*Dawn of Apocalyptic*, 431, 440). D. S. Russell writes that the "dualistic view of the world, which is characteristic of apocalyptic eschatology, finds expression in a doctrine of two ages" (*Method and Message*, 269). The specific terminology need not be used for the motif to be present.

34. See e.g., Schweitzer, *Mysticism*, 55; Bultmann, *Theology*, 1.278; Käsemann,

Though Jewish apocalyptic eschatology finds, as is to be expected, its focus in God's covenantal relationship to Israel, the scope of the two ages is nevertheless cosmic in the sense that they involve two self-contained and all-embracing worlds.[35]

In accordance with the etymology of the term "apocalyptic" (from the Greek *apokalyptō*, to unveil), apocalyptic eschatology is "revealed" (from the Latin *revelare*, also to unveil)[36] eschatology—revealed, that is, *by God*.[37] Since it is only through the disclosure of the coming age that the present can be perceived as "*this* age," the notion of revelation in fact encompasses *both* ages. The point has been formulated with characteristic clarity and precision by Martyn: Apocalyptic, he writes, involves "the conviction that *God* has now given to the elect true perception *both* of present developments (the real world) and of a wondrous transformation in the near future."[38] As we shall see below, the perception of one age bears a complementary relationships to the perception of the other.

With these necessary introductory comments, it is now possible to outline the two tracks of Jewish apocalyptic eschatology.[39]

Romans, 150; Beker, *Paul,* 136.

35. The two ages can thus also be labeled "this world" and "the world to come." For the terminology and the motif, see *1 En.* 71:15; *4 Ezra* 7:50, 112, 119; *2 Bar.* 44:8–15; 83:4–9; Mark 10:30; Matt 12:32; Luke 18:30; Eph 1:21; 2:7; Heb 6:5; *m. 'Abot* 4:1; *m. Sanh.* 10:1; *b. Ber.* 9:5. In Paul, see Rom 12:2; 1 Cor 1:20; 2:6, 8, 18; 3:19; 5:10; 7:31; 2 Cor 4:4; Gal 1:4. Paul employs the expressions "this age" and "this world" interchangeably. He does not employ the expression "the age/the world to come," but as Keck ("Paul and Apocalyptic Theology," 234) points out, the idea is implied when the present world is characterized as "*this* age/world." Besides, such expressions as "the kingdom of God" (Rom 14:17; 1 Cor 4:20; 6:9–10; 15:24, 50; Gal 5:21; 1 Thess 2:12), "eternal life" (Rom 2:7; 5:21; 6:22, 23; Gal 6:8), and "new creation"(2 Cor 5:17; Gal 6:15) are surely other ways of speaking about the age to come.

36. See Martyn, "From Paul to Flannery O'Connor."

37. Apocalyptic eschatology is thus not simply the kind of eschatology found in apocalypses (contra Collins, *Apocalyptic Imagination,* 9), as if the genre defines the phenomenon. What joins the eschatology found in the apocalypses with the apocalyptic eschatology found in other literature is (among other things) the notion of the revelation (*apokalypsis*) of two world ages.

38. Martyn, "Apocalyptic Antinomies," 424n28 (emphasis added). For this reason, as Martyn points out here, a central concern of apocalyptic is epistemology, "the birth of a new way of knowing both present and future," one that is God-given. See already his earlier essay, "Epistemology at the Turn of the Ages." See also the comments of Rowland, *Open Heaven,* 113.

39. Unless otherwise noted, English citations from Old Testament apocryphal and pseudepigraphical works are indebted to *The Apocrypha: Revised Standard Version* and to Charlesworth, *Old Testament Pseudepigrapha.*

Track 1

In Track 1, "this age" is characterized by the fact that evil angelic powers have, in some primeval time (namely, the time of Noah), come to rule over the world.

The story of this angelic fall is found or alluded to in much of the literature (*1 En.* 6–19; 64:1–2; 69:4–5; 86:1–6; 106:13–17; *Jub.* 4:15, 22; 5:1–8; 10:4–5; *T. Reub.* 5:6–7; *T. Naph.* 3:5; CD 2:17–3:1; *2 Bar.* 56:12–15; *LAB* 34:1; Wis 2:23–24; cf. Jude 6; 2 Pet 2:4). The basic story, one that also lies behind Gen 6:1–6, is that some of God's angels descended to the earth and married beautiful women, thereby begetting giants. Though there was a preliminary judgment of the angels themselves in the time of the Flood, the giants they begot left behind a host of demonic spirits who continue to pervert the earth, primarily by leading human beings, even God's own people, astray into idolatry. Furthermore, it is evident that Satan (Mastema, Belial, the devil) and his angels continue to wreak havoc on the earth.

To illustrate this track we may turn to the first section of *1 Enoch*, the so-called "Book of the Watchers" (chs. 1–36).[40] In this section of *1 Enoch*, all sin and evil are attributed to the fallen angels (the Watchers) and their demonic progeny (cf. 9:1, 6–9; 10:7–9; 15:8–16:2; 19:1–2); "they," we are told, "have transgressed the commandments of the Lord" (21:6; cf. 18:15). When they descended to the earth where human beings dwell, they led them "astray" from God (19:1–2; cf. 5:4–5) and "revealed to them every (kind) of sin" (9:8; cf. 10:9; 16:3). The fallen angels imparted to human beings knowledge that is detrimental to their wellbeing, e.g., the making of weapons of war (8:1), with the result that "the whole earth was filled with blood and oppression" (9:9). It is thus the evil angels who are actually, or at least ultimately, responsible for the multiplication of "evil deeds upon the earth" by human beings (16:3; cf. 5:4–5). By leaving their proper heavenly abode, these angels have caused cosmic disorder (15:3, 9–10), bringing about the pollution, corruption, and perversion of both nature

40. Milik (*Books of Enoch*, 25) surmises on the basis of the Aramaic fragments from Qumran that "the Book of the Watchers had essentially the same form as that in which it is known through the Greek and Ethiopic versions." This "Book of the Watchers" is but one of five major sections of the *1 Enoch* and I treat it as a distinct unit because it may be doubted whether the five-book *Enoch* (now extant only in Ethiopic) existed as such prior to the second century CE. Black (*Book of Enoch*, 10–11), for instance, believes that the idea of an Enochic Pentateuch may have been the work of Christian scribes, writing in Greek, who completed their work in the second century CE. Milik (*Books of Enoch*, 31) has argued that the Enochic version of the fall of the angels may have influenced Gen 6:1–6 rather than the reverse. See also Black, *Book of Enoch*, 14, 124. Collins (*Apocalyptic Imagination*, 34) thinks that Gen 6:1–6 is prior.

and history. In the midst of "this age," however, there is a small group, God's righteous elect, who bear witness to the Creator, the God of Israel, and who know that this situation was not intended by God and will not be tolerated by him for very long (cf. 1–5).

When "this age" is perceived in this way, in terms of subjection to suprahuman angelic powers, it is understandable that the Last Judgment, the juncture at which "this age" is replaced by "the age to come," is depicted as a cosmic confrontation, a war between God and the Watchers. Thus we read in 1 En. 1:4–5: "The God of the universe . . . will come forth from his dwelling. And from there he will march upon Mount Sinai and appear in his camp emerging from heaven with a mighty power. And everyone shall be afraid, and the Watchers shall quiver." The arena of the coming eschatological war is the physical universe that God created to be the human habitat. The earth is to be delivered from those alien powers that have come to oppress it (cf. chs. 5, 10, 16, 19, 21). In the new age, Satan and his demonic spirits will be no more. They shall have been defeated and eternally banished from the world (cf. chs. 16, 19). The righteous elect will be vindicated and allowed to live on a purified earth (cf. 1:9; 5:7; 10:17–22).

We may label this track "cosmological apocalyptic eschatology."

Track 2

In Track 2, "this age" is characterized by the fact that human beings willfully reject or deny the Creator, who is the God of Israel, thereby bringing about death and the perversion and corruption of the world. Adam and/or Eve are the primal ancestors who set the pattern for all subsequent human beings.

The fall of Adam and/or Eve is mentioned in a number of works (see 1 Enoch 69:6; Jub. 3:17–25; 4:29–30; LAB 13:8–9; Sir 25:24; Wis 10:1; cf. 2 Cor 11:3; 1 Tim 2:13–14; 1 Cor 15:21–22; Rom 5:12–21), but is particularly prominent in two, 4 Ezra and 2 Baruch (4 Ezra 3:5–7, 20–21; 7:118–19; 2 Bar. 17:2–3; 23:4; 48:42–47; 54:14, 19; 56:6). *Evil angelic powers are absent from both works.*

To illustrate this "track" we may refer to 2 Baruch. In 54:14, 19, we read that while "Adam sinned first and . . . brought death upon all . . . *each* of us has become his own Adam." This sin of Adam (and of Eve, who is mentioned in 48:43) and each of his descendants is that they "did not recognize you [God] as their Creator" (48:46; cf. 14:15–19). God has, however, graciously given the Law as a remedy for this situation whereby each person's ultimate destiny is in his or her own hands: "each of them who has been born of him [Adam] has prepared for himself the coming torment . . . each of them has *chosen* for himself the coming glory" (54:15; cf. 51:16; 85:7). To choose the coming glory is to choose the Law: The righteous are those who devote themselves to God and His Law (cf. 17:4; 38:1–2; 48:22; 54:5), the wicked are those who do not (cf. 41:3; 51:3; 54:14). Thus, as W. Harnisch has suggested, while "this age" is the all-embracing time of transgression and thus death, it is also the time of *decision*.[41]

When "this age" is understood in this way, in terms of willful human rejection of God and of accountability vis-à-vis the Law, the turn of the ages is depicted accordingly. The Final Judgment is not a cosmic war against cosmological, angelic powers but a courtroom in which all humanity appears before the bar of the Judge (chs. 49–51). The righteous, those who have acknowledged the claim of God by choosing his Law, are rewarded with eternal life; the wicked are condemned to eternal punishment. The sentence of death that fell on Adam and Eve and all their descendants is reversed at the Last Judgment for those who chose the Law, and permanently confirmed for those who did not (cf. 51:16). The basis of God's judgment, not surprisingly, is "works" (51:3, 7; cf. 14:12; 46:6; 57:2).[42]

We may label this track "forensic apocalyptic eschatology." Free will and individual responsibility are emphasized in this track, unlike Track 1 where there is no exhortation to choose the Law. The emphasis in Track 1 falls rather on God's election (see above on *1 Enoch* 1–36). The righteous are not those who have exercised free will as individuals, but those whom God has collectively elected to be his witnesses to his rightful claim on the world in the midst of the old age where evil cosmological rulers hold sway.

The Two Tracks as Heuristic Models

By isolating and describing two distinct "tracks" in Jewish apocalyptic eschatology, I do not wish to suggest that the various Jewish documents that to one degree or another bear witness to the eschatological dualism of the two ages can be assigned simply to one of the two tracks. Rather, I present the two tracks as *heuristic models* that may be used as interpretive tools to understand the dynamics of the various texts, including of course the letters of Paul. Nevertheless, the two tracks *are* found in nearly "pure" form in *1 Enoch* 1–36 and *2 Baruch* and I have outlined the two tracks on the basis of these two works.

Other documents indicate that the two tracks can, like those of a railway, run side by side, crisscross, or overlap in various ways, even in

41. Harnisch, *Verhängnis*, 241.

42. See further Desjardins, "Law in 2 Baruch and 4 Ezra."

the same work. In the Dead Sea Scroll, to cite the most notable instance of this combining of the two tracks, we find both cosmological subjection and willful human transgression, both elections and human control of personal destiny, both predestination and exhortation to observe the Law (as interpreted by the community), both God's eschatological war against Belial and his cohorts and God's judgment of human beings on the basis of their "works" or deeds (see e.g., 1QS 1–4; 1QM; CD). According to the Scrolls, the community as a whole as well as the individual believer are under constant threat from evil cosmological powers (Belial, the Angle of Darkness, the Spirit of Falsehood or Deceit). To choose the Law is thus to choose to stand in the protected sphere of God's own power (as represented by Michael, the Angel of Light, the Spirit of Truth). The Law is God's powerful weapon whereby God enables the righteous believer to withstand the suprahuman power of the demonic forces (cf. CD 16:1–3). Present existence is thus marked by a struggle between two contending groups of cosmological powers or spirits that seek to lay claim on human beings. This struggle does not manifest itself only in the sociological separation of the righteous (the covenant community) from the wicked (the world outside), but also in the choice that the individual, especially the member of the community, must make each day for God and His Law. The struggle penetrates the heart of the individual (cf. esp. 1QS 3–4).[43]

Much the same could be said for the book of *Jubilees* and the *Testaments of the Twelve Patriarchs*, two works that exhibit numerous similarities to the Dead Sea Scrolls with respect to the ways in which "cosmological" and "forensic" (or "anthropological") elements run side by side or overlap, thought it might be argued that they do not keep the same balance between the two tracks as do the Dead Sea Scrolls.[44]

The Heuristic Value Demonstrated

For the purpose of the present essay, the heuristic value of the two tracks described above can perhaps best be seen not in connection with works that exhibit both tracks but in connection with those that qualify or reject, sometimes quite explicitly, Track 1.

43. See Sanders, *Paul and Palestinian Judaism*, 237–321, esp. 295.

44. Cf. e.g., Collins, *Apocalyptic Imagination*, 111: "The Testaments lack the strong deterministic note" of the Dead Sea Scrolls. "T. Asher emphasizes that men are free to choose between the two ways. The Qumran community Rule suggests that humanity is already divided into two lots, although in practice a choice would still seem to be required."

The author of 2 *Baruch*, for instance, knows the myth of the fallen angels (56:11–15), but he reports that they were definitively punished in the past: "At that time they who acted this were tormented in chains." Nothing is said about a demonic legacy nor about evil angelic powers in the author's own present. Furthermore, according to the author of 2 *Baruch*, it was in fact Adam who was responsible for the fall of these angels: "For he who was a danger to himself was also a danger to the angels!" It is human transgression, not angelic rebellion, that has brought about and continues to bring about cosmic disorder.

The qualification or rejection of Track 1 is in fact much earlier than 2 *Baruch* (ca. 100 CE). In the fifth section of 1 *Enoch*, the so-called "Epistle of Enoch" (chapters 91–105),[45] there is a notable polemic against cosmological apocalyptic eschatology, against blaming evil cosmological forces for human sinfulness. In 98:4, the author explicitly affirms that human beings are themselves responsible for sin:

> I have sworn to you, sinners: In the same manner that a mountain has not become a servant, nor shall a hill (ever) become a maidservant of a woman; likewise *sin has not been sent into the world. It is the people who have themselves invented it.*

Similarly, a Greek portion of 98:5 (not found in the Ethiopic text) reads: "lawlessness was not given from above but from transgression (παράβασις)."[46] For the author of the "Epistle of Enoch," then, personal accountability is central. He writes as a wise man (98:1) instructing his children to seek righteousness and walk in its paths (cf. 91:19; 94:1–4). He exhorts them to "*choose* righteousness and the elect life" (94:4) and thus to avoid "the ways of injustice and of death" (94:2). That choice determines one's destiny at the Last Judgment (cf. 91:7–8; 93:3; 94:7, 9; 96:8; 97:3, 5; 98:8, 10; 99:15; 100:4, 5; 103:8; 104:3, 5). The "Epistle of Enoch" has in effect adapted the idea of the Two Ways (cf. OT Ps 1) to the dualism of apocalyptic eschatology, *forensic* (Track 2) apocalyptic eschatology.

The same is true of the *Psalms of Solomon* (first century BCE), a work which makes no mention of evil cosmological powers in opposition to God. In these Psalms, too, there is a considerable emphasis on personal accountability and choice:

> Our works (are) in the choosing (*en eklogē*) and power of our souls, to do right (*dikaiosynē*) and wrong (*adikia*) in the works

45. Dated by Milik (*Books of Enoch*, 48–50) to the second century BCE.

46. For the Greek text, see Bonner, *Last Chapters*. See also the argument of Milik (*Books of Enoch*, 52–53) with respect to 1 *Enoch* 100:4.

of our hands . . . the one who does what is right (*dikaiosynē*) saves up life for himself with the Lord, and the one who does what is evil causes his own life to be destroyed (9:4–5).

Those who "live in the righteousness of his commandments, in the Law" (14:2) shall by God's mercy receive the reward of eternal life (3:12) at the Last Judgment when sinners shall be eternally punished (15:12–15).

4 *Ezra* (late first-century CE) and 2 *Baruch* also make use of the motif of Two Ways, a motif that finds its most notable expression in Deut. 30:19: " . . . I [Moses, speaking for God] have set before you life and death, blessing and curse; therefore, choose (LXX: *eklexai*) life, that you and your descendants may live . . . " This text is paraphrased by both 4 *Ezra* (7:129; cf. 7:48) and 2 *Baruch* (19:1; cf. 46:3; 54:15; 84:2). In both works, the exhortation to choose life, i.e., the Law (cf. 4 *Ezra* 14:30; 2 *Bar.* 38:2), has an individual focus, unlike Deut. 30:19 itself, where Moses addresses "all Israel" (29:1; 31:1) gathered for instruction as a people prior to their entry into the promised land.

4 *Ezra's* use of Deut 30:19 is particularly interesting since it occurs at the end of a passage that echoes the kind of modified cosmological apocalyptic eschatology we have observed in Qumran, namely, the violent struggle in the present between two spirits (cf. also *T. Jud.* 20:1).[47] An *angelus interpres*, who probably represents the views of the author,[48] speaks to the seer, "Ezra" (7:127–29):

> This is the meaning of the context which every man who is born on earth shall wage, that if he is defeated he shall suffer what you have said, but if he is victorious he shall receive what I have said. For this is the way of Moses, while he was alive, spoke to the people, saying, "*Choose* for yourself, that you may live!"

And yet, as previously noted, there are no cosmological powers present in 4 *Ezra*. The creative balance between the two tracks found in the Dead Sea Scrolls has been dissolved in the direction of Track 2: In 4 *Ezra* the cosmological struggle between two spirits is transmuted into a struggle in the human heart between a mysterious and unexplained "evil root" and the Law (3:20–22).[49] And the "evil root," though powerful, cannot serve as an excuse for evading the choice of Deut 30:19. The angel tells the seer that though it may be difficult to observe the Law, it is possible to do so. In 8:38, the

47. See Brandenburger, *Adam und Christus,* 33n6.

48. See Harnisch, *Verhängnis,* 48–50, 60–67.

49. Numerous interpreters see in the reference to the "evil root" (or the "grain of evil seed" in 4:30–31 and "evil thought" in 7:92) an analogue to the rabbinic notion of the Evil Impulse (or Inclination). This notion could be fruitfully investigated in terms of the two tracks I have outlined. See Cohen Stuart, *Struggle in Man Between Good and Evil.*

seer is told that God will not concern himself with the "death, judgment, or damnation" of sinners since "though they received freedom . . . they despised the Most High, and were contemptuous of his Law, and forsook his ways" (8:55–56; cf. 8:59; 9:11–12; 2 Bar. 85:7). Those who choose the Law, who will have "a treasure of good works laid up with the Most High" (7:7; cf. 8:33, 36), will be saved (cf. 7:13, 97, 113). In 4 Ezra, as in 2 Baruch, the future will bring a general resurrection in which all people will be judged on the basis of their observance of the Law and thus their "works" (7:33–39; 9:7–8).

It is worth noting that the qualification or even outright rejection of cosmological apocalyptic eschatology need not be confined to documents that exhibit the marks of forensic apocalyptic eschatology. Sirach, a work that like the "Epistle of Enoch" comes from the second century BCE, contains an evident polemic against attributing human sinfulness to cosmological powers. Thus is 21:27, the author writes: "When an ungodly person curses Satan, he is actually cursing himself" (my translation). You cannot blame the devil for human transgression. For the author, sin has a human origin: "From a woman sin had its beginning, and because of her we all die" (25:24; cf. 15:14). In this work too, then, the emphasis falls on personal responsibility and choice: "If you will, you can keep the commandments, and to act faithfully is a matter of your own choice (eudokias)" (15:15). In 15:17, Sirach echoes the Deuteronomic choice: "Before a man are life and death and whichever he chooses (eudokēsai) will be given to him." In Sirach, too, a person chooses life by choosing the Law (cf. Sir 15:1; 17:11), but, in contract to the "Epistle of Enoch," the Psalms of Solomon, 4 Ezra, and 2 Baruch, this choice has no evident eschatological significance.

Summary of the Two Tracks

We may summarize the two tracks of Jewish apocalyptic eschatology outlined in this section as follows:

1. Cosmological-apocalyptic eschatology: The world has come under the dominion of evil, angelic powers. God's sovereign rights have been usurped and the world, including God's own people, have been led astray into idolatry. But there is a righteous remnant, chosen by God, which by its submission to the Creator, the God of Israel, bears witness to the fact that these evil cosmological powers are doomed to pass away. This remnant, the elect of God, awaits God's deliverance. God will invade the world under the dominion of the evil powers and defeat them in a cosmic war. Only God has the power to defeat and to

overthrow the demonic powers that have subjugated and perverted the earth. God will establish his sovereignty very soon, delivering the righteous and bringing about a new age in which he will reign unopposed.

2. Forensic apocalyptic eschatology: This is a modified form of the first track. In this view, the notion of evil, cosmological forces is absent, recedes into the background or is even explicitly rejected. Instead, the emphasis falls on free will and decision. Thus we find a kind of legal piety in which personal responsibility and accountability are dominant. Sin is the willful rejection of the Creator God (the First Commandment) and death is punishment for this fundamental sin. God has, however, provided the Law as a remedy for this situation and a person's posture toward this Law determines one's ultimate destiny. At the Last Judgment, God will reward those who have acknowledged God's claim and chosen the Law, whereas He will punish those who have not.[50]

Track 1 is consistent with Käsemann's "cosmological" understanding of apocalyptic eschatology, Track 2 with Bultmann's "anthropological" understanding, particularly in terms of its emphasis on individual decision vis-à-vis the Law. With an eye on Bultmann, we may observe, first, that Track 2, like Track 1, is cosmic in scope, in contrast to Bultmann's individualistic constriction of Paul's thought., which had arguably more in common with modern existentialism than with Paul himself or first-century Judaism.[51] Secondly, Track 2, like Track 1, is theocentric, not anthropocentric. Both tracks are fundamentally concerned with the revelation of God's claim on the world God has created and its rectification. Whereas Track 1 underscores the human need for God's help and action, Track 2 underscores human accountability to God for sin and its terrible consequences.

---

50. The two tracks as I have outlined them do not pretend to account for all that may be important in Jewish apocalyptic eschatology, e.g., messianism, national disaster and restoration, the Temple, repentance, atonement, covenant.

51. In his essay, "New Testament and Mythology," Bultmann wrote that myth, with its talk of cosmic powers and forces controlling human life, "does not want to be interpreted in cosmological terms but in anthropological terms—or, better, in *existentialist* terms" (9, emphasis added). Bultmann's descriptive account of Jewish apocalyptic eschatology, however, is quite close to Track 2. For example, he writes: "In the apocalyptic view the individual's future is responsible for himself only . . . and the individual's future will be decided according to his works. And this is a judgment of the whole world" (*The Presence of Eternity*, 31). In *Primitive Christianity* (80–86), Bultmann relies primarily on 4 *Ezra* for his account of Jewish apocalyptic eschatology, while in his *Theology* (1.230), he attributes talk of cosmological powers in Paul to the influence of "the cosmological mythology of Gnosticism," rather than to the influence of Jewish apocalyptic eschatology.

The two tracks of Jewish apocalyptic eschatology as I have outlined them are meant to be heuristic models, each one seeking to describe an internally coherent or consistent configuration of motifs. These models are, of course, based on evidence provided by the primary sources. The two tracks are found in nearly "pure" form in *1 Enoch 1–36* and *2 Baruch*. Elements proper to one track can, and frequently do, run side by side or overlap with elements proper to the other, most notably in the Dead Sea Scrolls as we saw above. Furthermore, there is considerable evidence to indicate that there were Jews who specifically rejected motifs proper to what I have labeled "cosmological apocalyptic eschatology" in favor of what I have labeled "forensic apocalyptic eschatology" (see above). In addition, the evidence indicates that Track 2 overtook and displaced Track 1 completely after the disaster of 70 CE, when the Temple was destroyed by the Romans (cf. *4 Ezra, 2 Baruch*).[52]

Paul and the Two Tracks of Jewish Apocalyptic Eschatology

Paul lived in a time when both tracks of Jewish apocalyptic eschatology were still prominent and the discussion of the debate between Bultmann and Käsemann over Paul's theology of justification (or rectification) at the beginning of this chapter is a sufficient indication that the traces of both, *christologically appropriated and modified,* are present in Paul, much as in the Dead Sea Scrolls.[53] It is not possible to explore this claim in detail here; I must confine myself to a few pertinent observations and conclusions:

The Letter to the Romans indicates that Paul can isolate the two tracks to some extent. In Rom 1:1—5:11, the elements of forensic apocalyptic eschatology clearly dominate. In Rom 6:1—8:38, however, the elements of cosmological apocalyptic eschatology are notably prominent (e.g., sin, death, righteousness, the flesh, and the Spirit as cosmological powers). In Rom 5:12–21, where Paul appeals to Adam, the figure prominent in Track 2 Jewish apocalyptic eschatology, and sets him in contrast to Christ, the two tracks completely interpenetrate, though the passage itself marks the shift from predominantly forensic to predominantly cosmological categories in Paul's

---

52. Track 2 finds its fruition in Rabbinic Judaism. See Saldarini, "The Uses of Apocalyptic in the Mishna and Tosephta"; Hayman, "The Fall, Freewill and Human Responsibility in Rabbinic Judaism"; Schäfer, "Die Lehre von den zwei Welten."

53. I do not mean to imply that I necessarily agree with either Bultmann or Käsemann on all points.

argument.[54] That shift finds its anticipation in 1:16–17 and 3:9, two texts that occur at crucial junctures in Paul's argument in the first three chapters. Thus while such texts as 8:1 and 8:33–34 indicate that forensic categories have hardly been given up or left behind, the structure and progression of Paul's argument in Romans 1–8 suggest that motifs proper to Track 1 circumscribe and, to a large extent, overtake motifs proper to Track 2.

If this assessment of Romans is correct, then the question is: Why are motifs proper to Track 2 present at all? The answer, we may properly assume, has something to do with what Martyn liked to call Paul's "conversation partners." If one of those partners in Romans was "Judaism" (as interpreters of Romans have often claimed), then it was also a Judaism embracing Track 2 apocalyptic eschatology. It is not without interest to note that, in 2:5–8, Paul reproduces a nearly pure specimen of Jewish forensic apocalyptic eschatology with its characteristic adaptation of the Two Ways:[55]

> But by your hard and impenitent heart you are storing up wrath for yourself on the day of wrath when God's righteous judgment will be revealed. For he will render to every man according to his works; to those who by patience in well-doing seek for glory and honor and immortality, he will give eternal life; but for those who are factious and do not obey the truth, but obey wickedness, there will be wrath and fury (RSV; cf. 2:13).

Since Paul is writing to Christians in Rome, it is also quite possible (probable, in my estimation) that these particular conversation partners, whether of Jewish or Gentile birth, had appropriated Track 2 Jewish apocalyptic eschatology. For such Christians, Christ's death would have been understood as a sacrifice atoning for past sins or trespasses (Rom 3:25–26; 4:25; cf. 1 Cor 15:3; Gal 1:4). This sacrificial death did not put an end to Law observance, but quite to the contrary, obligated those so forgiven to obey it all the more (cf. Matt. 5:17–20).

---

54. I give detailed treatment of Rom 5:12–21 and the parallel passage in 1 Cor 15:20–28 in *Defeat of Death*.

55. Sanders argues that, apart from the "tag" of 2:16, there is nothing in Rom 1:18–2:29 that is peculiarly Christian (*Paul, the Law, and the Jewish People*, 123–35, esp. 231). The passage, he maintains, is "a synagogue sermon" whose "point is to have its hearers become better Jews on strictly non-Christian Jewish terms . . . the entire chapter is written from a Jewish perspective" (129). Sanders makes this claim even though he "can adduce no proof" for Paul's assertion in 2:12–15 that "all humanity will be justified or condemned according to the same law" (130–31). He might perhaps have considered such texts as 4 Ezra 7:37, 72 and 2 Bar. 15:5; 48:40. The motif of a general resurrection for judgment on the basis of "works," found in both 4 Ezra and 2 Baruch, is predicated on the universal applicability of the Law, the heart of which is the First Commandment (cf. 4 Ezra 8:60; 2 Bar. 48:46–47, with Rom 1:19–23).

Throughout Rom 1:18—3:19, Paul embraces the presuppositions of Track 2 Jewish (and/or Jewish-Christian) apocalyptic eschatology, most notably in its understanding of the role and function of the Law, only to claim that by the standard of the Law, through which "the whole world may be held accountable to God" (3:19; cf. 2:12–16), the human situation is in fact hopeless (cf. 3:10–20; 4:15; 8:1). It is hopeless because, for Paul, everyone is "under the power of Sin" (3:9), a claim that presumes what is made abundantly clear later in Romans, namely, the inability of the Law to provide deliverance from Sin and thus Death (cf. 7:7—8:8).

Reliance on "works of the Law" (3:20, 28), therefore, is quite literally a dead-end (cf. 4:15a) and, in any event, is ruled out of court by the justifying death of Christ (3:21–30; cf. 5:1–11), good news indeed. Faith is the appropriate human posture to this event, replacing (as Bultmann rightly claimed) "works of the Law." But Paul's cosmological understanding of God's righteousness (1:16–17) and of sin (3:9) indicates that faith is not, as Bultmann thought, analogous to what it replaces, i.e., it is precisely not a matter of human "choice," "decision," or, as Americans might say, "action" (cf. 10:17). It is in fact a matter of being initially passive and grateful beneficiaries of God's gracious, liberating power revealed in the death and resurrection of Jesus Christ (cf. 5:11). Thus, while Paul speaks of faith (or of justification by faith) primarily when he is combating the claim (among both Jews and Christians) that "works of the Law" provide the righteousness that will lead to eschatological acquittal and thus to life, the meaning of faith is actually determined by the cosmological-apocalyptic disclosure of God's righteousness and of sin in the death (crucifixion) of Christ. Christ's death cannot be understood in exclusively forensic terms, since it marks God's triumphant invasion of the world "under sin" (3:9) to liberate human beings (the ungodly) from its deadly power.

Much the same may, I think, be said about Paul's Letter to the Galatians, particularly in light of the highly illuminating article by Martyn, "Apocalyptic Antinomies in the Letter to the Galatians." Pointing to Paul's polemically ironical use of conversion terminology in Gal 4:9, Martyn observes that the circumcising, Law-observant "Teachers" whose gospel Paul combats in Galatians believed "that the advent of Christ introduced a new religion."[56] Paul accordingly "causes the letter to be focused" on this issue, at least in part.[57] For Paul, however, the gospel is not "about the better of two ways,"[58] nor then is the letter "designed to convert its readers from one

56. Martyn, "Apocalyptic Antinomies," 243n25.

57. Martyn, "Apocalyptic Antinomies," 243n25.

58. Martyn, "Apocalyptic Antinomies," 414.

religion to another."[59] Rather, the gospel, and the subject of Galatians, is the apocalypse of Christ and his cross,[60] an event that marks "the death of one world and the advent of another"[61] and inaugurates a cosmic warfare, most notably between Flesh and Spirit (Gal 5:19–23). Thus, the world in which the Galatians now live is "the scene of antinomous warfare on a cosmic scale."[62] Paul's use of such "pairs of opposites" as Flesh and Spirit in Galatians "does not fall in the line of the wisdom traditions, with its marriage of pairs to the doctrine of the Two Ways."[63] In short, the advent of Christ is *not* about making a choice between the better of two ways, two religions, but concerns God's redemptive invasion of the human world.

Martyn labels Paul's cosmological views "apocalyptic" and rightly so, but it seems to me that the views of the Teachers were also "apocalyptic," albeit in a different way: In line with forensic Jewish apocalyptic eschatology found in such works as the "Epistle of Enoch," the *Psalms of Solomon*, *4 Ezra*, and *2 Baruch*, they had not only married pairs of opposites to the doctrine of the Two Ways but had also adapted (with their own christological slant) the latter to the dualism of the two ages.[64] Paul circumscribes the forensic apocalyptic eschatology of the Galatian Teachers with a cosmological apocalyptic eschatology of his own. If the fact that Martyn begins his argument for apocalyptic antinomies in Galatians with the epistle's final paragraph is not coincidental, it may perhaps be said that by the end of the epistle the forensic apocalyptic eschatology of the Teachers has been decisively overtaken and neutralized by Paul's cosmological apocalyptic eschatology.

59. Martyn, "Apocalyptic Antinomies," 420.

60. Martyn, "Apocalyptic Antinomies," 421.

61. Martyn, "Apocalyptic Antinomies," 414.

62. Martyn, "Apocalyptic Antinomies," 421.

63. Martyn, "Apocalyptic Antinomies," 423n25.

64. That the gospel of "the Teachers" had an eschatological component (informed by the dualism of the two ages) is implied by Martyn's account of the Teachers' gospel in "A Law-Observant Mission to Gentiles," 307–24, esp. 322–23.

Addendum to Chapter 1

A Response to Jörg Frey
and N. T. Wright

N. T. WRIGHT AND Jörg Frey both give an extensive critique of my proposal,[1] as first worked out in the original publication of chapter 1 above and in *Defeat of Death*.[2] Frey regards the latter as "a step forward" because of my "detailed analysis of Jewish texts," as does Wright who congratulates me for doing what had not previously been done, namely, "an investigation of the Jewish 'apocalyptic' literature deemed relevant to the quest for an 'apocalyptic' understanding of Paul."[3] However, both Frey and Wright go on to criticize my proposal on the same two grounds, even if they formulate and support them differently. First, they maintain that my understanding of Jewish apocalyptic eschatology as fundamentally characterized by the dualism of two world ages is unsound. Second, they claim that my distinction between forensic and cosmological forms of ancient Jewish apocalyptic eschatology has actually been imposed on the ancient sources.[4]

With respect to the first point, Frey thinks that my characterization of apocalyptic as the dualism of the two world ages is not only "outdated" but also based on "handbook knowledge" (that of Vielhauer), a charge he also levels at Käsemann. The eschatological dualism of the two ages, regarded by Vielhauer as the essential characteristic of apocalyptic, is for Frey "only a feature of some later Jewish apocalypses (e.g., *4 Ezra* and *2 Baruch*)."[5] In

1. Frey, "Demythologizing Apocalyptic?," 508–10; Wright, *Paul and His Recent Interpreters*, 155–67. Frey's article is primarily a critique of Wright's *Paul and the Faithfulness of God* and he charges Wright with basically "neutralizing" apocalyptic (Frey, "Demythologizing Apocalyptic?," 490–502). I agree with this assessment.

2. The original article was written during the same period (the fall of 1986) that I was revising my dissertation for publication. The latter provided the basis for the former.

3. Frey, "Demythologizing Apocalyptic?," 509; Wright, *Paul and His Interpreters*, 156–57.

4. Since both Frey and Wright, despite their differences, make these same two criticisms, I presume that they may be more widely shared. See in particular Davies, *Paul Among the Apocalypses?*, 105–7, 192–93.

5. Frey, "Demythologizing Apocalyptic?," 509.

other words, according to Frey, the definition of apocalyptic as the dualism of the two ages does not do justice to the great variety of Jewish apocalyptic texts and their development over time. Frey goes on to insist that "the full range of texts" must be taken into account in defining and discussing Jewish apocalyptic. Frey himself, however, discusses only a selection (*1 Enoch* in particular) and, more problematically, does not even indicate on what basis particular texts falls under the heading "apocalypses or related texts."[6] What is an "apocalypse"? And what constitutes "a related text"? What exactly is "a Jewish apocalyptic text"?[7] The reader searches in vain for answers. The basis on which Frey compiles his long list of such texts[8] is nowhere articulated or explained.

Wright takes another approach to the same issue: "The two-age scheme, "he writes, "is simply a widespread feature of Jewish thought throughout the second-Temple period and on into the high rabbinic period," one that Paul "took . . . for granted." There is thus nothing particularly "apocalyptic" about it, since it characterized "the Jewish world in general."[9] In the manner of Rowland,[10] Wright links the use of the term "apocalyptic" to "a literary genre" containing "revelations,"[11] something which Frey also effectively seeks to do.

As I have noted in several places, also in this volume, the expression "apocalyptic eschatology" is a construct of scholars that purports to epitomize certain phenomena discernible in the primary sources, so that any definition of the term is partly a matter of scholarly tradition and convenience even though it is based, as of course it should be, upon the data of the available sources, primarily Revelation but also such conceptually related works as (parts of) Daniel, *1 Enoch*, and *4 Ezra*. There may be ancient apocalypses that contain no eschatology or an entirely different one, or that use the language of revelation outside the framework of apocalyptic eschatology, but that is of no consequence for the soundness of the definition since there is enough data to support it—as Frey seems to concede. For when Frey comes to discuss "apocalyptic thought," he seems to presuppose precisely the

6. Frey, "Demythologizing Apocalyptic?," 519.

7. Frey, "Demythologizing Apocalyptic?," 518.

8. Frey, "Demythologizing Apocalyptic?," 512.

9. Wright, *Paul and His Recent Interpreters*, 158. According to Wright, "a far more accurate indicator of 'apocalyptic' than the 'two ages' (which as we have seen are prominent in a much wider sphere) would be the way in which 'apocalypses' regularly concern themselves with telling the story of Israel and the world in a way that leads the eye up to the eventual moment of divine rescue" (160).

10. Rowland, *Open Heaven*. See chapter 2 below.

11. Wright, *Paul and His Recent Interpreters*, 140.

two-age dualism he earlier disparages as failing to do justice to "apocalyptic." For example, he refers to the "final removal" of evil and "the final defeat of the evil powers."[12] At the end of his discussion, Frey writes the following: "Apocalyptic thought is basically a reaction to the experience of tension, related to the faithfulness of God or to the belief that God still reigns, but longing for a new act of deliverance—a purified, renewed, or even 'freshly' created world, proportional to the insight into the depth of corruption of the present world."[13] This summary statement presupposes precisely the dualism of the two world ages, i.e., apocalyptic eschatology, as defined by Vielhauer and others. Evidence for apocalyptic eschatology, so defined, can be found in a range of literary genres, including the letters of Paul.

Wright's claim that the dualism of the two ages was a "widespread" idea in the Jewish thought of the period under scrutiny effectively posits that apocalyptic *eschatology* was in fact a widespread phenomenon in early Judaism,[14] and furthermore thereby concedes that this world-view is not limited to "apocalypses," however these may be defined.[15] The issue, however, is whether some distinctions are in order with respect to this evidently well attested phenomenon, one that crosses literary genres.

That brings me to the second point of their critique. Frey regards my "taxonomy" of forensic and cosmological forms of Jewish apocalyptic eschatology as questionable because it was "inspired from elsewhere," namely, "by Pauline issues and the Bultmann-Käsemann debate about the forensic and ontological [sic] views of justification."[16] Wright pursues the same argument but goes further, suggesting that I have anachronistically imposed "one very specific and highly contingent mid-twentieth-century debate," namely, that between Bultmann and Käsemann as outlined in chapter 1 above, onto the ancient texts. He regards my proposal as "a projection into the first century of a twentieth-century (and highly culturally conditioned) German discussion."[17]

12. Frey, "Demythologizing Apocalyptic?," 517.

13. Frey, "Demythologizing Apocalyptic?," 526.

14. Wright may however overstate the case, given the wisdom tradition.

15. I note at several places in this volume that the definition of the genre apocalypse for works prior to the second century is highly problematic. It may also be irrelevant for interpreting Paul who was a writer of letters.

16. Frey, "Demythologizing Apocalyptic?," 508. I do not use the term "ontological" in this connection, but "cosmological," as did Käsemann. I use the term "ontological" in connection with the eschatological *transformation* of the created (material) order, as found in 2 *Baruch* and 1 Cor 15:35–58 (*Defeat of Death*, 126-38, esp. 132, 137-38).

17. Wright, *Paul and His Recent Interpreters*, 167; also 159.

For the record, I developed the distinction between the forensic and cosmological tracks of ancient Jewish apocalyptic eschatology on the basis of a close analysis of the relevant Jewish material.[18] The fact that I did so in conversation with the issues posed by the Bultmann-Käsemann debate, which others had already framed in terms of "anthropology" (Bultmann) and "cosmology" (Käsemann),[19] does not necessarily make it wrong, or anachronistic. My distinction between "cosmological" and "forensic" apocalyptic eschatologies was based primarily on taking seriously the remarkable differences between *1 Enoch* 1–36 and *2 Baruch* (and *4 Ezra*).[20] The validity of my proposal, therefore, is finally to be judged in relation to this primary source material, and not in relation to the contours of the Bultmann-Käsemann debate.

Two other points are worth noting. First, I regard the forensic pattern in its relatively pure form as a weakened or qualified form of the cosmological pattern, so that one can see a rough development from *1 Enoch* 1–36 to *2 Baruch* (and the rabbis). Both patterns, including mixed forms, antedate Paul. I therefore cannot agree with Frey's claim that the forensic pattern with its explanation of sin and evil in terms of the transgression of Adam occurs "for the first time"[21] in Paul. It has older roots as Genesis 1–3 itself shows (cf. Wis 10:1); *4 Ezra* and *2 Baruch* attest these earlier understandings. And Paul's own views are rather different from the views of the latter when all is said and done.[22]

Second, Frey and Wright commonly refer to my "cosmological" track of Jewish apocalyptic eschatology as the "cosmic" track.[23] I understand their use of the term in this connection, and I have probably done so myself, though I have increasingly had difficulties with it, since I believe that the forensic track (or pattern) is also cosmic (universal, i.e., affecting all human beings as well as the cosmos in which they live).[24] To formulate the distinction between the two tracks as "forensic" versus "cosmic" thus risks distortion of the forensic pattern. Ironically, Frey and Wright's

18. See chapter 3 of *Defeat of Death*.

19. See chapter 2 of *Defeat of Death*.

20. I regard *2 Baruch* as the best representative of the forensic pattern, not *4 Ezra*, as Frey repeatedly maintains.

21. Frey, "Demythologizing Apocalyptic?," 509.

22. See chapters 3, 4, 7, and 12 below.

23. Frey, "Demythologizing Apocalyptic?," 508; Wright, *Paul and His Recent Interpreters*, 163.

24. A problem is that that Greek term *kosmos* as used by Paul can refer to the physical universe but also to the world of human beings in its entirety in distinction from the physical universe.

formulation of the distinction reflects the use of the terms "anthropological" and "cosmological" in the aforementioned Bultmann-Käsemann
debate. In this debate, the term "anthropological" was used to sum up
Bultmann's interpretation of Paul, referring to the autonomous *individual*
who is addressed by the gospel of justification in the present and confronted with an autonomous decision to have faith or not. The *cosmic* element
present in Käsemann's "cosmological" interpretation of Paul was notably
missing from Bultmann's "anthropological" interpretation.[25] But, as I have
repeatedly argued, including in Chapter 1 above, the cosmic element is
decisively present in Jewish forensic apocalyptic eschatology, as it is in the
cosmological variety. Wright writes: "Just because *4 Ezra* and *2 Baruch* do
not ascribe responsibility for evil to fallen angels, that does not mean they
are not thinking 'cosmically.'"[26] Exactly my point.[27]

25. See de Boer, *Defeat of Death*, 25, and chapter 4 below.

26. Wright, *Paul and His Recent Interpreters*, 162. For some reason, Wright makes
this point as a criticism of my proposal. Wright makes a number of other claims about
apocalyptic which Frey subjects to a trenchant critique in his article ("Demythologizing
Apocalyptic?"). These will not be repeated here. See also my critique of Wright in de
Boer, "N. T. Wright's Great Story."

27. See p. 29 above and e.g., chapters 3 and 12 below.

Chapter 2

Paul, Theologian of God's Apocalypse

Introduction

IN HIS MAJOR AND influential study of ancient apocalyptic, Christopher Rowland strenuously argued that apocalyptic is more than a matter of eschatology.[1] Indeed, in his view, the term "apocalyptic" ought to be used only in connection with what, according to him, is truly distinctive about apocalypses, namely their interest in the revelation of "divine mysteries."[2] "Apocalyptic," he asserts, "seems essentially to be the revelation of the divine mysteries through visions or some other form of immediate disclosure of heavenly truths."[3] According to Rowland, such divine mysteries can include not only the future ("eschatology" as commonly understood), but also "the movement of the stars, the heavenly dwelling of God, angelology, the course of human history, and the mystery of the human plight." All of these "fall within the category of the mysteries which can only be solved by higher wisdom through revelation."[4] He concludes: "To speak of apocalyptic . . . is to concentrate on the theme of direct communication of the heavenly mysteries in all their diversity."[5] For Rowland, then, "The use of the word apocalyptic to describe the literature of Judaism and early Christianity should . . . be confined to those works which purport to offer disclosures of the heavenly mysteries, whether as the result of vision, heavenly ascent or verbal revelations."[6] Apocalypses are not the only works which purport to offer disclosures of heavenly mysteries, according to Rowland, even though

---

1. Note the full title of his major study: *The Open Heaven: A Study of Apocalyptic in Judaism and Early Christianity.*

2. Rowland, *Open Heaven*, 1–3, 29–37, 70–72.

3. Rowland, *Open Heaven*, 70.

4. Rowland, "Apocalyptic," 34. See Hengel, *Judaism and Hellenism*, 1.202.

5. Rowland, *Open Heaven*, 14.

6. Rowland, *Open Heaven*, 70–71.

"it cannot be denied that apocalyptic frequently finds expression in a particular genre," which in "Judaism . . . is usually the apocalypse . . ."[7]

Rowland applies these insights to Paul: Paul is an apocalyptic thinker to the extent that he is the beneficiary of divine mysteries, mysteries which he imparts to his readers. The key text for Rowland is thus not those passages where Paul speaks about the Parousia of Christ or the resurrection of the dead (see especially 1 Corinthians 15 and 1 Thess 4:13–18) but 2 Cor 12:1 where Paul writes about "visions and revelations of the Lord" which he personally had received. Barry Matlock, in an extensive survey and critique of scholarship on Paul as an apocalyptic thinker, has followed Rowland's lead and commended his approach.[8]

In my view, Rowland has made a significant contribution in his insistence that apocalyptic is not only concerned with future events:

> Apocalyptic is as much involved in the attempt to understand things as they are now as to predict future events. The mysteries of heaven and earth and the real significance of contemporary persons and events in history are also the dominant interests of the apocalypticists. There is thus a concern with the world above and its mysteries as a means of explaining human existence in the present.[9]

Thus, if "the essential characteristic" of apocalyptic eschatology is the dualism of two world ages, cosmically conceived,[10] the notion of revelation in "apocalyptic" eschatology encompasses *both* ages, not just the one to come, since it is only through the disclosure of the coming age that the present can be perceived as "*this* (evil) age," as one which is destined to be brought to an end by God. Along similar lines, J. Louis Martyn has written that apocalyptic involves "the conviction that God has now given to the elect true perception both of present developments (the real world) and of a wondrous transformation in the near future." A central concern of

---

7. Rowland, *Open Heaven*, 71. For an influential definition of this genre, see Collins, *Morphology*, 9. According to Collins, an apocalypse is "a genre of literature with a narrative framework, in which a revelation is mediated to a human recipient, disclosing a transcendent reality which is both temporal, insofar as it envisages eschatological salvation, and spatial insofar as it involves another, supernatural world."

8. Matlock, *Unveiling Apocalyptic Paul*, 258–62, 282–87.

9. Rowland, *Open Heaven*, 2.

10. So Vielhauer, "Introduction," 588–89 (Vielhauer and Strecker, "Introduction," 549–50). Similarly, as pointed out in the Introduction above, Russell, *Method and Message*, 269, and Hanson, *The Dawn of* Apocalyptic, 432, 440. Cf. *1 En.* 71:15; *4 Ezra* 7:50, 112, 119; *2 Bar.* 44:8–15; 83:4–9.

apocalyptic is "the birth of a new way knowing both present and future."[11] The knowledge granted of the future, of the Last Judgment, and of the new age beyond the Judgment, thus bears *a close and reciprocal relationship* to the knowledge granted of "this age"—which is to say that the promised solution ("the age to come") must address the problem ("this age"). In apocalyptic eschatology, then, the notion of revelation applies not only to the Last Judgment and the coming age but also to "this age": the true nature and destiny of the latter are also disclosed.

In some respects, however, Rowland's proposal contains difficulties. Let me mention four. First, the definition of apocalyptic eschatology is partly a matter of scholarly tradition and convenience even though it is based, as it ought to be, upon the data of the available sources, namely, such books as Revelation, Daniel, *1 Enoch*, *2 Baruch*, and *4 Ezra*.[12] It really makes no difference to this definition if there are apocalypses which may contain no eschatology or an entirely different one. Nor does the fact that the language of revelation is used outside the framework of apocalyptic eschatology affect the soundness of the basic definition of "apocalyptic eschatology" as essentially the revealed dualism of the two world ages.

Second, John J. Collins asserts against Rowland that "the essential role" eschatology plays in the Jewish apocalyptic works ought not to be underestimated.[13] It is not just one element among others.[14] In Rowland's account,

11. Martyn, "Apocalyptic Antinomies," 424n28. See also Collins, "Introduction," xiii, where he supplements his earlier definition of the apocalypse genre (n. 122 above) with the observation of Yarbro Collins that such writings are typically "intended to interpret present earthly circumstances in light of the supernatural world and of the future, and to influence both the understanding and behavior of the audience by means of divine authority" (Yarbro Collins, *Early Christian Apocalypticism*, 7).

12. The use of the term "apocalyptic" (an adjective that is commonly used as a noun) to characterize a certain understanding of reality is due primarily to the book of Revelation where the term *apokalypsis* occurs in the opening verse. This book has thus always formed the touchstone for any understanding of apocalyptic, whether Jewish or Christian. See also the Introduction above and chapter 12 below.

13. Collins, *Apocalyptic Imagination*, 8. Apocalyptic eschatology refers in the first instance to the type of eschatology found in the book of Revelation (see previous note). "Apocalyptic" eschatology wherever it occurs is normally assumed to bear at least a "family resemblance" to the eschatology found in the book of Revelation. The eschatology found there is strongly indebted to Jewish antecedents and traditions, even it goes far beyond them its extensive use of (frequently lurid) imagery and symbolism.

14. Rowland says that there is "great variety not only in the contents of the apocalypses, but also in their eschatology. Consequently the contents are not easily reduced to terse summaries which encapsulate apocalyptic eschatology in a sentence or two" (*Open Heaven*, 29). I would disagree: the dualism of the two world ages, which is an eschatological dualism, captures the essence of apocalyptic eschatology and can accommodate a diverse array of views about the future, about salvation, and about the

the mysteries disclosed about contemporary persons or events, about the human plight, about angels, and much else are implicitly divorced from the expected future events, from eschatology, when such mysteries should perhaps be understood only (or at least primarily) in relation to this eschatology. The divine mysteries disclosed are arguably of no interest apart from the expectation of God's cosmic act of rectification.[15]

Third, and most importantly, in Rowland's account, apocalyptic is reduced to something mystical and individualistic. Rowland's view that apocalyptic literature is more concerned with secret knowledge and revelatory experience than with eschatology explains why he regards 2 Cor 12:1–4 as the key "apocalyptic" text in Paul.[16] The peculiar constriction of apocalyptic in Paul's thought and experience to his personal journey to the heavenly realm in 2 Corinthians 12 (an ecstatic experience Paul recounts only in order to devalue its importance) is in stark contrast to what is normally understood by apocalyptic, in Paul or elsewhere, and cannot, I think, be substantiated by Paul's own use of the language of revelation in a number of other passages (to which I return below). For Rowland, apocalyptic becomes curiously focused on the human experience of the divine world, rather than on God's own revelatory action of rectifying a world gone awry.

Fourth, the revelation which is an integral element of apocalyptic *eschatology* as I have defined and understood it does not refer, as in Rowland's proposal, to the mere disclosure of information, whether it be about the past, present, and/or the future, to a seer who is to pass it on to others (in an apocalyptic writing, for example).[17] On the contrary, it refers primarily to God's expected eschatological activity itself. That is, *the final events themselves*, when they occur, will constitute God's eschatological revelation (*apokalysis*) of himself, of his justice or righteousness, and of his sovereign claim

---

heavenly world.

15. See VanderKam, "Messianism and Apocalypticism," 196. There are some notable works, such as *Jubilees*, the *Testaments of the Twelve Patriarchs*, and the Community Rule (1QS) and the War Rule (1QM) from Qumran which assume a clearly apocalyptic-eschatological perspective (the dualism of the two world ages). Rowland, however, claims that the *Testaments of the Twelve Patriarchs* and the War Scroll, as well as the *Assumption of Moses*, are not apocalyptic because they do not contain anything which fits his basic definition of apocalyptic as the revelation of divine mysteries (*Open Heaven*, 17, 39–42).

16. See Matlock, *Unveiling Apocalyptic Paul*, 286–287, pointing to Rowland, *Open Heaven*, 374–86. Along similar lines Segal, *Paul the Convert*, 34–71, and "Paul's Thinking about Resurrection."

17. Rowland writes: "In Judaism this is usually an apocalypse granted to some great figure from Israel's past who then reveals to subsequent generations the secrets which have been disclosed to him and gives advice about the sort of life which God expects of the righteous" (*Open Heaven*, 71).

on the whole created world. The word "apocalyptic" in scholarly discussion (at least since the work of J. Weiss, A. Schweitzer, and E. Käsemann)[18] properly evokes this idea of God's own eschatological and sovereign *action* of putting an end to this world-age and replacing it with the new world-age (the kingdom of God).[19] To speak of apocalyptic, therefore, is to concentrate not on the theme of direct communication of heavenly mysteries to a human being (even if such can be involved) but on the theme of God's own visible eschatological activity, activity which will constitute the actual revelation, what we may call the Apocalypse of God.[20]

But a question remains: how does Paul himself use the language of revelation, what we may call his "apocalyptic language," the noun *apokalypsis* and the verb *apokalyptō*? Does his usage support Rowland or the alternative outlined above?

Paul's Apocalyptic Language

Paul uses the term "apocalypse" or "revelation" (*apokalypsis*) in several passages. Needless to say, Paul does not use the term as a genre designation.[21] However, it cannot be assumed in advance that the term as used by Paul in his letters is a technical one for his apocalyptic-eschatological understanding of Christ as the effective and definitive disclosure of God's rectifying action whereby this evil world or age is destroyed and brought to an end. Paul uses the Greek terms in three basic senses.

First of all, Paul employs the Greek term in connection with *Jesus' future or second coming*, the so-called *parousia*. In 1 Corinthians 1, Paul describes believers as those who are eagerly waiting for the *apokalypsis* of our Lord Jesus Christ" (1 Cor 1:7; cf. Rom 2:5; 8:18–19; 1 Cor 3:13). God "will strenghthen" the Corinthian Christians "to the End" (1:8; cf. 15:24) so that they "may be blameless on the day of our Lord Jesus Christ" (1:8). This

18. See further, chapter 12 below.

19. Apocalyptic often has a very negative and lurid connotation in common parlance, vividly described by Rowland, *Open Heaven*, 23: "pessimistic prognostications about the cataclysmic demise of a hitherto ordered society and the move from the predictable to the bizarre and chaotic. In these circumstances moral norms disappear and superstition triumphs over rational explanation. The human mind is allowed free reign to indulge in wild and fanciful speculations about an imminent disaster in which abnormal and superhuman forces will be involved." But the scholarly use must not be confused with the popular use.

20. Cf. Martyn, *Galatians*, 97–105.

21. The term is first used to denote a literary genre in the second century CE (Collins, *Apocalyptic Imagination*, 3).

passage clearly points forward to chapter 15 where Paul refers explicitly to Christ's Parousia (= "the day of our Lord Jesus Christ"):

> all will be made alive in Christ. But each in his own order: Christ the first fruits, then at his coming (*parousia*) those who belong to Christ. Then is the end, when he hands over the kingdom to God the Father, after he has destroyed every ruler and every authority and power. . . . The last enemy to be destroyed is death . . . . We will not all die, but we will all be changed, in a moment, in the twinkling of an eye, at the last trumpet. For the trumpet will sound, and the dead will be raised imperishable, and we will be changed . . . (1 Cor 15:23–24, 26, 51–52).

In 1 Cor 1:7, then, Paul's use of the term *apokalypsis* conforms to what most Christians take the word "apocalyptic" to signify: Jesus' Parousia as a future, cosmic event. The "revelation"—apocalypse—of Jesus Christ concerns his visible eschatological appearance at his Parousia and this is clearly an apocalyptic *event*, whereby this evil age is finally and irrevocably destroyed "so that God may be all in all" (cf. 1 Cor 15:24–28). The Corinthians are not to wait for the direct communication of heavenly mysteries, of divine information, in a dream, a mystical trance, or a moment of spiritual ecstasy, but for the visible re-appearance on the world scene of Jesus himself. 2 Thess 1:7 speaks similarly and more clearly of "the revelation (*apokalypsis*) of the Lord Jesus from heaven with his angels of power" (cf. also 2 Thess 2:3, 6, 8). The "revelation" here referred to is no mere disclosure of previously hidden heavenly secrets, nor is it simply information about future events, but is actual eschatological activity and movement, an invasion of the world below from heaven above, which is also in a sense an invasion of the present by the future.

Paul uses the word *apokalypsis* and the cognate verb *apokalyptō* in other passages (Rom 2:5; 8:18; 1 Cor 3:13) in a similar way, that is, in connection with a *future* apocalyptic-eschatological event.

Secondly, however, Paul also uses these same terms in connection with *the gospel that he preaches in the present*. This gospel is fundamentally oriented to and surely based upon an event in the past, the death and resurrection of Jesus, and thus not on an event in the future, the Parousia. The question is whether Paul's use of such "apocalyptic language" in connection with the gospel that he preaches in the present and with an eye on the current situation of Christians in the world, has to do with the visible, eschatological action and movement of God, that is, with the invasion of "this (evil) age" by God Himself.

There are expressions by the apostle which suggest that we must give an affirmative answer to this question. In Romans 1:16–17, Paul claims that in the gospel "the righteousness of God *is being revealed* from faith for faith." This gospel is "the power of God (*dynamis theou*) for salvation." Paul here relates the verb *apokalyptō* (reveal) directly to the notion of "the power of God." The gospel evidently involves an apocalyptic-eschatological event in the present: The righteousness of God becomes visible and powerful, or powerfully visible, in the gospel itself and for that reason within the sphere of faith. Faith is elicited or created by the gospel of God's powerful righteousness.[22] Faith (*pistis, pisteuō*) is evidently for Paul a form of sharing in God's eschatological revelation, that is, in God's eschatological activity and movement.[23] Through the gospel a believer is taken up into this eschatological activity in order to participate in it, to become a part of it. Faith thus means for Paul that a believer can truly see and perceive this action, this movement, of God *into* (and then *in*) the world. The movement and presence of God are to be seen in the crucified and risen Christ. Further, that this activity and movement of God involves judgement upon "this world" is evident in Rom 1:18ff.: The revelation of God's righteousness "through faith for faith" also means that "the wrath of God," normally associated with the Parousia (cf. Rom 2:5; 5:9; 1 Thess 1:10), "is [now also being powerfully] revealed from heaven upon all ungodliness and wickedness of those who by their wickedness suppress the truth" (Rom 1:16–18). The creation of something eschatologically new in the world, faith, also entails God's judgment of a world marked by its absence before and apart from Christ.

In Gal 3:23, Paul characterizes faith itself as something which is "revealed." "Now before faith came [on the scene], we were being held in custody under the Law, being confined until faith should be revealed (*apokalyphthēnai*)."[24] Faith "was revealed" and "came" onto the world stage, just as Christ himself did,[25] in order "to liberate those under the Law" (4:4–5). Christ entered a world in subjection to inimical enslaving powers (4:3, 8), in this case the Law (3:25), in order to liberate human beings from their subjugation (cf. 5:1). The context thus indicates that Paul

22. In Rom 3:21–22, he writes: "But *now* apart from the Law the righteousness of God has been revealed [*phaneroo*, a synonym of *apokalypto*] . . . the righteousness of God through the faith of Jesus Christ for all who believe . . . ."

23. This eschatological activity and movement are a sign and a confirmation of God's liberating love: cf. e.g., Rom 5:8. Further, faith itself "works through love" (Gal 5:6: cf. 1 Cor 13).

24. For more detail about the passages from Galatians discussed in this essay, see de Boer, *Galatians*.

25. Cf. 3:19: " . . . until the seed [Christ] should come."

here understands faith to be a metonymy for Christ himself (cf. 1:23).[26] The "Law was our custodian until Christ [came on the scene], so that we might be justified by faith [i.e., by Christ]. But now that faith [i.e., Christ] has come (on the scene), we are no longer subject to a custodian" (3:24). By identifying faith with Christ himself in this way, Paul makes clear that faith as a human activity does not involve an innate or natural human possibility but an apocalyptic-eschatological possibility (and thus a *novum*) which becomes a reality only when elicited by the proclamation of the gospel whose content is Christ as God's apocalyptic-eschatological act.[27] Faith is "new creation" (Gal 6:15),[28] an apocalyptic-eschatological reality inseparable from Christ as God's Apocalypse.

It would seem from Paul's usage of the language of revelation, of apocalypse, that any understanding of Paul as an apocalyptic theologian cannot be limited to scenarios devoted to the future, to the Parousia and the resurrection of the dead and the like. Paul applies "apocalyptic language" not only to the Parousia (and the End), but also to the gospel he now proclaims and the faith it newly creates. The gospel and faith, which take their point of departure from Christ's death and resurrection, are also part and parcel of Paul's apocalyptic eschatology, not just the Parousia.

Thirdly, in a number of passages, particularly in the Corinthian correspondence, Paul uses the term *apokalypsis* in connection with *the communication of heavenly or divine mysteries to those who are already believers.* "When you come together," the apostle writes to the Christians in Corinth, "each one has a hymn, a lesson, a *revelation*, a tongue, or an interpretation" (1 Cor 14:26; cf. 1 Cor 2:10; 14:6, 30; 2 Cor 12:1, 7; Phil 3:15; Gal 2:2; Eph 1:17). These instances of Paul's use of the noun *apokalypsis* (and of its cognate verb, *apokalyptō*) seem to approximate Rowland's linking of the term with the disclosure of heavenly secrets or information to an individual (who mediates what he or she has seen and heard to others). In 1 Corinthians 14, Paul

---

26. Earlier in the letter, Paul twice refers to "the faith *of* (Jesus) Christ" (2:16) and once to "the (faith) of the Son of God" (2:20). It is true of course that these phrases are often translated as "faith *in* (Jesus) Christ/the Son of God." Nevertheless, it is possible to understand the construction to mean Christ's own faith (i.e., his faithfulness or obedience), an interpretation supported in turn by Paul's use of "faith" as a metonym for "Christ" in Gal 3:23–25. The faith which Christians have in Christ ("we have believed in Christ Jesus," Gal 2:16), is bound to and derives from Christ's own faith, i.e., his faithful death (2:20–21). Cf. Martyn, *Galatians*, 271.

27. See Martyn, *Galatians*, 363: "Paul envisions, then, a world that has been changed from without by God's incursion into it, and he perceives that incursion to be the event that has brought faith into existence."

28. Note the parallel between "faith working through love" in Gal 5:6 and "new creation" in Gal 6:15.

makes a close connection between revelation and prophetic speech; visionary experiences as such play no discernible role and are not mentioned (cf. 14:6, 29–31; 2:10; also Phil 3:15). These prophetic revelations during the gatherings of the community in Corinth are caused by the Holy Spirit and this Spirit represents for Paul the *apocalyptic-eschatological* presence and activity of Jesus Christ and thus of God himself in the life of believers.[29]

In 2 Cor 12:1–4, a key passage for Rowland as for others, Paul juxtaposes (in vs. 1) the term "revelations" (*apokalypseis*) with the term "visions" (*optasiai*). Indeed, the terms seem here to be roughly synonymous (cf. 12:7). Together they point to the visionary and auditory disclosure of heavenly secrets to an individual, in this case Paul himself. But this passage is the exception that proves the rule, partly because Paul seeks here utterly to relativize the importance of such visionary, revelatory experiences (cf. 12:5–7), much as he does glossolalia in 1 Corinthians 14 or the revelation from an angel in Gal 1:8. He uses the word "revelation" in 2 Cor 12:1 (also vs. 7) in a sense which is not typical of him elsewhere. Apart from 2 Cor 12:1–4, a revelation is not for Paul a private matter; it has communal implications and is placed in a communal context, as 1 Corinthians 14 shows. Nevertheless 2 Cor 12:1–4 does indicate that the literary and the rhetorical context is a crucial consideration in determining the meaning and the import of the term.

We need in this connection to pay some attention to Gal 2:2 because Paul's use of the term "revelation" is often considered the same as his use of the term in the Corinthian letters. Paul employs the term here in a different sense, however. He maintains that he together with Barnabas "went up [to Jerusalem] *kata apokalypsin*." The latter phrase is commonly understood to mean "prompted by" or "as a result of" a special revelation.[30] Paul says nothing explicit, however, about the circumstances or the content of this supposed revelation.[31] A neutral rendering of the phrase yields the ambiguous translation "in accordance (conformity, line) with (a) revelation" or even "with respect to (a) revelation."[32] The context must be considered to determine what Paul wants to say.[33] The function of the expression in his argument is in any case clear. Paul thereby indicates that

---

29. Fee, *God's Empowering Presence.*

30. KJV, RSV: "by revelation"; NIV, NRSV: "in response to a revelation"; REB: "in response to a revelation from God"; NJB: "inspired by a revelation"; Martyn, *Galatians*, 190: "because God revealed to me that I should go" (appealing to *BAGD* II.5.d).

31. One can (dubiously) use Acts to fill in some of the details (cf. Acts 11:28–30).

32. See *BAGD*, B.5d.

33. The meaning of the preposition *kata* (with the accusative) has a diverse range of meanings, depending on the context. It can, for example, also mean "for the purpose of" (*BAGD*, B.4).

he had not gone to Jerusalem because the apostles who were resident there had summoned him or called him on the carpet. And he also makes it plain that he had not gone to Jerusalem because he felt a personal need to have their official stamp of approval (or that of the church there) for his gospel and his apostleship to the Gentiles. In the foregoing chapter of Galatians Paul has already made it clear that his gospel and his apostleship have God's approval and backing; he needs no other. According to Paul, then, the purpose of his visit to Jerusalem was something else. He went there so that the apostles could "see" (*idontes*)—and according to Paul they did in fact see (2:7)—that his proclamation of the gospel to the uncircumcised had been entrusted to him by God, and so that they could "recognize" (*gnontes*)—and according to Paul they did in fact recognize (2:9)—the grace which had been granted to him by God.

Everything here turns on *the action of God* in the life and work of Paul, including his visit to Jerusalem. This visit as a whole, not just the initial decision to go, was a matter of God's revelation, of God's apocalyptic-eschatological activity in Christ.[34] Through the visit of Paul to Jerusalem the apostles were granted the opportunity, *by God*, to see and to recognize God's presence and the activity in the preaching of Paul. "For," Paul writes, God "who worked through Peter for the apostleship to the circumcised also worked through me for the Gentiles" (Gal 2:8). According to Paul, then, his visit to Jerusalem functioned as a revelation to the apostles and the church there, because this visit had granted them new insight into the one and only gospel (1:7), and thus into the activity of God in the world, especially among the Gentiles. His visit to Jerusalem was part and parcel of God's apocalyptic-eschatological activity to save the world through Jesus Christ.[35]

The Revelation—Apocalypse—of Jesus Christ to Paul in Galatians 1

Gal 2:2 is not the first time that Paul uses the word "revelation" in his Letter to the Galatians. He makes use of this noun and its cognate verb in the first chapter of this letter. The instances in Galatians 1 are disputed. In this chapter, as in Galatians 2, Paul attempts to defend the gospel which he had preached to the Galatians (and other Gentiles). He insists with all emphasis

---

34. If one understands the Greek verb *anebēn* ("I went up") in Gal 2:2 as a complexive aorist (a series of actions retrospectively regarded as a whole; BDF #332), Paul could be understood to mean: "my journey to Jerusalem, including my stay there, was a matter of God's revelatory activity and intention."

35. Along similar lines, Martyn, *Galatians*, 200–203.

that the gospel he had preached to them "is not of human origin." He did "not receive it from a human source," nor was he "taught it." Rather he received it "through a revelation—an apocalypse—of Jesus Christ" (1:12). He writes a few verses later that he began to proclaim God's Son among Gentiles "when God . . . was pleased to reveal his Son in me, so that I might proclaim him among the Gentiles" (1:15–17). We have here an unmistakable allusion to the cataclysmic and visible appearance of the risen Christ to Paul near Damascus (cf. 1 Cor 9:1; 15:8–10; Phil 3:7–9).

Much has been written about these verses, especially in connection with the nature of Paul's experience of the risen Christ. The stories of Paul's encounter with the risen Christ are described in much more detail in the book of Acts (9:3–9; 22:6–11; 26:12–18) than in Paul's own letters. Even if we confine ourselves to the report of Paul himself we can say that the "apocalyptic language" Paul uses in Galatians 1 certainly can imply a visual experience of some sort. That surmise is confirmed through the use of the verb "to see" (*horaō*) that Paul uses in 1 Cor 9:1 ("I have seen the Lord") and 1 Cor 15:9 (Christ "appeared to me," *ōphthē*). But, many have asked, is Paul here speaking of a subjective, even mystical experience or an objective one, or perhaps some combination of the two? An answer is not easy to find in the language of Galatians 1 itself.

Interpreters often seek an explanation for the expression found in Gal 1:12 ("an apocalypse of Jesus Christ") in 1 Cor 1:7 where, as we saw above, Paul describes the Parousia as "the apocalypse of our Lord Jesus Christ." Given 1 Cor 1:7, "the apocalypse of Jesus Christ" in Gal 1:12 could be regarded as an anticipation of the future, objective revelation of the Lord at his Parousia (so, e.g., Rowland). The difficulty with this interpretation is among other things that Paul wants in Galatians 1 to say something about the origin of the gospel which he now, in the present, proclaims among the Gentiles (1:16). This gospel does not have its origin in the future apocalypse of the Lord at his Parousia. Other interpreters seek an explanation in the reference to "the visions and apocalypses of the Lord" in 2 Cor 12:1. In that light, "the apocalypse of Jesus Christ" in Gal 1:12 could be regarded as a *revelatio specialissima*, a personal, very special revelation for Paul himself. But these "revelations of the Lord" are rather different from the *one* "revelation of Jesus Christ" in Gal 1:12. The latter gave Paul the content of his gospel and changed his life completely, whereas the former did not do that at all. This difference is in my view a decisive feature of "the revelation of Jesus Christ" in Gal 1:12. The revelations of 2 Corinthians 12 (just as those of 1 Corinthians 14) are the experiences of people who are already believers, already Christians. But that is not the case in Gal 1:12. The Law-observant Pharisee, the persecutor of the church of God, the zealot for the traditions of his fathers (Gal 1:13–14), was not waiting for a revelation during a worship service of Christians in Corinth or elsewhere! He also did not ask for this revelation or seek it out. On the contrary, this apocalypse of Jesus Christ, of God's Son in his life, was according to Paul a completely unexpected and unwanted event.

It is also of importance that Paul does not in Gal 1:16 use the term "to see" (*horaō*), but the verb "to reveal" (*apokalyptō*). The context contains a strong contrast between human experiences or learning processes and God's sovereign activity in the life of Paul. God is the subject of the verb *apokalyptō*, not Paul (as he is of the verb "to see" in 1 Cor 9:1). What Paul saw is not at issue, but what God revealed. God, who set him apart before he was born and called him through his grace, "was pleased to reveal his Son in" Paul (1:16). Paul thus makes immediately clear that he wants to give full attention not to his own human experience, but to the activity and movement of God. The focus of his thought does not lie in *his* human experience, not in *his* vision of the risen Lord to which he makes no formal appeal, but in *God*'s decision and deed to which he does here make an emphatic appeal.

In this connection, the meaning of the prepositional phrase *en emoi* ("in me") in 1:16 needs to be discussed: "God was pleased to reveal his Son *in me*." Commentators give three rather different interpretations of this phrase.

(1) *en emoi* has the same meaning as the simple dative *emoi*, "to me." This interpretation fits well with the idea of an objective revelation to Paul. The problem with this interpretation, however, is that Paul could very easily and clearly have used a dative, as he does elsewhere when using the same verb (Phil 3:15; 1 Cor 2:10; 14:30; cf. Matt 16:17).

(2) *en emoi* means "through me." According to this interpretation, the first part of 1:16 ("reveal his Son in/through me") looks forward to the following subordinate clause ("in order that I might proclaim Him among the Gentiles"). This interpretation means that God reveals his Son among the Gentiles through the proclaiming work of Paul. Rom 1:17 could support this interpretation: The righteousness of God is revealed "in" (*en*), and thus through, the gospel that Paul preaches. But the syntax of Gal 1:15–16 can scarcely support this interpretation. The revelation of God's Son "in" Paul took place in the past (God *was pleased* to reveal). The present preaching activity (*euangelizomai*) of Paul among the Gentiles was the purpose and thus the *consequence* (*hina*) of the revelation of God's Son "in" Paul, not a part of that revelation.

(3) *en emoi* is to be taken literally. In this case, we would be dealing with an inner, subjective revelation and experience. This interpretation seems the most natural. The context, however, lays no emphasis on a subjective

(mystical or inner) experience by Paul. There is in Paul's very concise report about "the revelation of Jesus Christ" no trace of a journey to heaven during a dream, a vision, or a trance whereby he received his gospel or came into contact with the risen Christ. The subjective explanation can only appeal to the phrase *en emoi* itself. That might be sufficient, except that there is another (and, in my view, more convincing) possibility.

(4) *en emoi* means "in my former manner of life." This phrase refers to Paul's earlier life in what he here calls "Judaism" (1:13–14; Phil 3:5 makes clear that this was the Pharisaic variety in Paul's case). The revelation of God's Son "in" Paul stands in direct relation to his previous manner of life (*anastrophē*) in Pharisaic Judaism (1:13–14) when, according to his own report, he persecuted "the church of God" (cf. Phil 3:6) and "advanced in Judaism beyond many among my people of the same age," being "more zealous [than they] for the traditions of my ancestors." As noted previously, "the revelation of Jesus Christ" about which Paul here writes took place in the past and had as its result that Paul became a preacher of the gospel among the Gentiles. The context suggests then that phrase "in me" must mean "in my former career as a zealous Pharisee who persecuted the church of God." The action of God brought this career to an end. We can paraphrase 1:15–16 as follows: God invaded my life as a zealous Pharisee and persecutor of the church with his Son, thereby bringing this life to an end, so that I could subsequently proclaim God's Son among the Gentiles, as I now do.

The context confirms that "the revelation of Jesus Christ" and the revelation of God's Son "in" him must mean that God entered into the life of Paul, the persecutor of God's church and an extremely zealous, Law-observant Pharisee, in order to bring that manner of life to a complete and irrevocable end. Through this act of God, a radical discontinuity came into being between Paul the persecutor of God's church and Paul the apostle to the Gentiles. The action of God in his own life is interpreted by Paul as an apocalyptic-eschatological event, or to put it somewhat more carefully, as Paul's participation in an apocalyptic-eschatological (thus cosmic) event, that of Jesus Christ. The revelation of Jesus Christ "in" Paul was no private, merely personal event but a public one: Paul's public life was never the same (cf. Gal 1:23–24).

Later in this Letter to the Galatians (2:19–20), Paul does indeed describe his experience of this event in his life and he uses there the language of crucifixion to characterize the break with his past: "I have been crucified with Christ," that is, the Pharisaic I, zealous for the traditions of his ancestors and persecutor of the God's church, was crucified with Christ. In 6:14, he writes that this "I" has been crucified to "the world," and further that "the world has been crucified to me," probably referring here to the well-ordered and familiar world determined by one's posture to the Mosaic Law.[36] The nomistically determined I and the nomistically determined world were both crucified (put to death) in relation to each other, so that a radical disjunction between them and the "new creation" occurs (6:15). "The life I now live in the flesh" is a life characterized "by faith, the faith of the Son of God who loved me and gave himself up for me." The result is that "I no longer live, rather Christ lives *in me*" (2:20). As in 1:16, Paul here also uses the phrase *en emoi*. In this case, the phrase concerns Paul's new manner of life: Christ lives "in" Paul, that is, in the activity of Paul the apostle, in his public proclamation of the gospel to the Gentiles. In short, Paul personifies in his own life the radical discontinuity between the two ages (this one and the one to come) characteristic of all apocalyptic eschatology whether Jewish or Christian. For Paul in his Letter to the Galatians this discontinuity does not primarily concern a subjective, inner reality, but an objective, visible reality. The life of Paul was totally changed, as everyone, friend or foe, believer or opponent in Galatia, could see and confirm (cf. 1:23–24). One manner of life had been utterly destroyed and a new one had taken its place.

From his description of this break with his past as a crucifixion with Christ, it becomes clear that Paul did not understand the revelation, the apocalypse, of Jesus Christ in his life as an anticipation of the return of Jesus at his Parousia, as frequently argued, but as his direct participation in a cosmic event, the cross (and resurrection) of Jesus Christ, an event of the recent past. Participation in this singular apocalyptic event is in principle valid for every believer, because in the faith which the gospel of Jesus Christ creates, the righteousness of God is repeatedly disclosed anew, that is, it becomes eschatologically effective and visible on the world stage (Rom 1:16–17; 3:20–25; 5:1–11).

We can ask in closing how Paul's understanding of Jesus changed through the "apocalypse of Jesus Christ" in his life. Presumably Paul came to understand that the crucified Jesus whose followers he persecuted had been raised and thus vindicated by God. Paul realized for the first time that the crucified Christ was also the risen Christ. It is however noteworthy that in his proclamation of the gospel Paul announced precisely the reverse. Not: the crucified Christ is also the risen Christ. But: the risen Christ is also the crucified Christ. When Paul first went to Galatia, he did not speak about his personal vision of the risen Christ. On the contrary, according to 3:1, he placarded the crucified Christ before the eyes of the Galatians, the Christ who on the stage of human history was hung and died on a cross. In Gal 2:20, Paul defines "the Son of God" who was revealed to him (1:16) as "the one who

36. See chapter 5 below.

loved me and gave himself up for me." In the heading of the letter (1:1–4), Paul defines the "Jesus Christ" (1:3) who was revealed to him (1:12; cf. 3:1) as "the one who gave himself for our sins." He adds a revealing phrase: "in order to rescue us from the present evil age according to the will of God." The death of Jesus clearly has here an apocalyptic-eschatological import.

For Paul, though not for him alone, the death and resurrection of Christ are together regarded as the apocalyptic-eschatological, thus definitive incursion of God into the world. The expected Parousia is the complete working out and the confirmation of the revelation—the eschatological, visible, liberating action of God—which has already taken place and which determines the present situation. The radical dimension of Paul is that he consistently and even in provocative ways (witness his opponents in Galatia) makes the violent death of Jesus on the cross the starting point of the gospel. He does that especially in his Letter to the Galatians where the Parousia is not explicitly mentioned, and even the resurrection of Jesus is mentioned explicitly only once, in the opening verse of the letter. In his Letter to the Galatians Paul appeals to the "revelation" of the crucified Christ in his life in order to validate his gospel and his apostleship.

Conclusion

The apocalyptic perspective of Paul cannot be reduced to a personal, mystical experience of the heavenly world nor to the reception of heavenly secrets. It has substantially little or nothing to do with travel up to heaven in a visionary experience or something similar (dream, trance), but everything to do with the invasive action of God in this world in order to deliver human beings from this present evil age (cf. Gal 1:4).

Paul uses "apocalyptic language," i.e., the words *apokalysis* and its cognate verb *apokalyptō*, in a number of places in order to characterize the action of God in Jesus Christ (in the past, present as well as the future) as an apocalyptic-eschatological event. Paul's apocalyptic is not only discernible in his future expectation, a common view in writing on Paul. What happens between Jesus' resurrection and Parousia, e.g., the call of Paul himself, the proclamation of the gospel, faith and the working of the Spirit, can be placed under the rubric of apocalyptic. The whole of God's eschatological saving activity in Jesus Christ is from beginning to end apocalyptic. This event thus involves a cosmic drama that God has begun and that God shall bring to a conclusion at the Parousia.

The focus of Paul is the redemptive or liberating action of God in Christ, the Christ who is now proclaimed in the gospel. Apocalyptic eschatology in

Paul thus has little or nothing to do with a decision human beings must make, but everything to do with a decision God has already made on their behalf. According to Paul, God has done this in the apocalyptic-eschatological event of Jesus Christ who (so Paul claims) died for human beings and was raised by God. Paul presents himself primarily as a theologian of this revelation, this Apocalypse, of God.

Chapter 3

Paul's Mythologizing Program in Romans

Introduction

MY TITLE CONTAINS AN obvious allusion to Rudolf Bultmann's well-known program of demythologization.[1] I want to argue in this paper that Paul's concern in Romans is not *de*mythologization but *mythologization*, if the word can be allowed. One of the main reasons Paul programmatically mythologizes in these chapters is to explain why the Law is not, or no longer, a viable option for those who have come to believe in Christ.

Paul's concern with the Law is evident throughout the first eight chapters, indeed the first ten chapters (cf. esp. 2:12–17; 3:19–31; 4:1–25; 5:13, 20; 6:14–15; 7:1—8:4; 9:31—10:5; 13:8–10). This focus on the Law in Romans reflects its unique occasion. Briefly, the Letter appears to have a triple occasion: (1) Paul has received information about differences, even conflicts, among believers in Rome (evident especially in chapters 14–15); (2) as Christ's apostle to the Gentiles, Paul has made plans to go on to new missionary territory in Spain by way of Rome (15:20, 24–25, 28); and (3) before going to Rome, he plans to go to Jerusalem with a collection of funds from the Gentile churches he had founded (15:23–33). Paul hopes that this collection will be accepted by "the saints" (15:31) in Jerusalem and he fears that he will receive a hostile reception there from those he calls "the unbelievers in Judea" (15:31). At issue for Paul on all three fronts are the status and the role of the Law now that Christ has come on the human scene. Closely related to the issue of the Law is the question of "the righteousness of God" and justification. Again, this theme pervades much of Romans (cf. 1:17; 2:12; 3:4–30; 4:1–25; 5:1–21; 6:7, 13–20; 8:10, 30, 33; 9:30—10:10; 14:17), especially the first four chapters, but also chapter 5 (and chapters 9–10).

---

1. See Bultmann, "New Testament and Mythology." The essay was first published in 1941, in Germany during World War II!

In my view, one of Paul's major aims in this letter is to remind the believers in Rome that they are not "under the Law" (*hypo nomon*)[2] but "under grace" (*hypo charin*), as he puts it in 6:14 (cf. 6:15). "The Law" and "grace" constitute the overarching polarity in Romans 5–8. The other major polarities in these chapters—sin and righteousness, death and life, flesh and Spirit—are largely brought into the service of explaining the fundamental polarity of the Law and grace. Paul wants to bring out the implications and advantages of being under grace rather than being under the Law. One of these implications is to see the world as it really is now that Christ has appeared on the human scene and another is to redefine the status and the role of the Law in the light of this event.

It will also be relevant to take note here of the broader context of chapters 5–8. In chapters 9–11, Paul's concern is explicitly with unbelieving Israel—put otherwise, with a form of Judaism in which Christ has no place, whether that be in Jerusalem or in Rome. In these chapters Paul returns to the issues of justification and the Law (especially in chapters 9 and 10) that were prominent in the first four chapters, using similar terminology and formulations. In that light, it seems to me probable that in chapters 1–4 Paul also has unbelieving Israel in view. That is to say, Paul is here in dialogue with a form of contemporary Judaism embracing a certain understanding of sin, justification and the Law, one in which Christ has no place. It will be my working assumption that 4 *Ezra* and 2 *Baruch* are representative of the views with which Paul is in dialogue in the opening chapters of Romans, including chapter 5.[3] Both works stem from the late first or early second century, it is true, but scholars also maintain that they mediate traditions that go back to the early and middle of the first century, when Paul was active.[4] Paul is in dialogue with these views in his Letter to the Romans evidently because, so Paul assumes, the believers in Rome will hear and read his letter with these views in the backs of their minds.[5]

2. Lit., "under Law," but the absence of the article after prepositions is common in Paul and appears to be a matter of style. Cf. BDF #258.2.

3. The analysis below will indicate whether this working assumption is indeed sound.

4. For translation and discussion, see Metzger, "The Fourth Book of Ezra"; and Klijn, "2 (Syriac Apocalypse of) Baruch." Both 4 *Ezra* and 2 *Baruch* were written in Hebrew in Palestine. Both were subsequently translated into Greek and then a third language (Latin in the case of 4 *Ezra*, Syriac in the case of 2 *Baruch*) which have provided the basis for the existing English translations (the original Hebrew versions of both as well as the Greek translations have unfortunately been lost). 4 *Ezra* comprises chapters 3–14 of the work known as 2 Esdras in the Apocrypha of English Bibles such as KJV, RSV, and NRSV.

5. Paul may also be in dialogue with *Jewish-Christian* views on sin, justification, and

Bultmann's Proposal and Käsemann's Reaction

Bultmann argued that one must attempt to understand "the mythical world picture" of the NT[6] "in terms of its real intention," and that is to give expression to "how we human beings understand ourselves in our world. Thus," he claimed, "myth does not want to be understood in *cosmological* terms but in *anthropological* terms."[7] The point is to get "to the understanding of [human] existence" contained in the mythological or cosmological language.[8]

In his demythologizing program, Bultmann saw himself as following in the footsteps of John and Paul. For our purposes what Bultmann says about Jewish apocalyptic eschatology with respect to Paul is particularly pertinent. Jewish apocalyptic eschatology is defined by Bultmann as a "basic dualistic view according to which the present world and the people living in it are under the dominion of demonic, satanic powers and in need of redemption, a redemption that they themselves cannot provide and that can be given them only through divine intervention."[9] For Jewish apocalyptic eschatology, that divine intervention is an imminently future event whereby God "puts an end to this old age and ushers in the new one through God's sending of the Messiah."[10] Paul has demythologized this Jewish apocalyptic eschatology in at least two ways according to Bultmann:

1. Jewish apocalyptic eschatology is "demythologized insofar as the day of salvation has already dawned for believers and the life of the future has already become present"[11] (18). In other words: present eschatology.

---

the Law, which (apart from the Christology) were similar to those of Paul's presumed Jewish conversations partners. See de Boer, *Defeat of* Death, 154; and de Boer, "Paul and Jewish Apocalyptic Eschatology," 169–90, esp. 183 (see chapter 1 above). I leave that issue aside here though inclusion would not change the substance of my argument.

6. Bultmann, "New Testament and Mythology," 1–3.

7. Bultmann, "New Testament and Mythology," 9 (emphasis added). Bultmann problematically added here: "or, better in *existentialist* terms" (emphasis added). His proposal can be evaluated, however, apart from the existentialist hermeneutic, which he derived from Heidegger. If we leave the Heideggerian turn aside, the point is that cosmological statements give expression to anthropological realities and thus may be interpreted, and appropriated, in that light.

8. Bultmann, "New Testament and Mythology," 10.

9. Bultmann, "New Testament and Mythology," 14. He also attributes this view to "the Gnostic myth of redemption." See p. 29 n. 51 above for Bultmann's ambivalence on this point, which has its origin in what I have outlined as the two distinct tracks of Jewish apocalyptic eschatology.

10. Bultmann, "New Testament and Mythology," 14.

11. Bultmann, "New Testament and Mythology," 18.

2. Paul emphasizes individual responsibility and "decision" (*Entscheidung*). Talk of cosmic powers lording it over human beings serves to indicate that "we can in no way free ourselves from our factual fallenness in the world, but are freed from it only by an act of God."[12] That point is crucial for Bultmann for it distinguishes faith from philosophy which can pose the problem of inauthentic existence but cannot provide the needed solution.[13] Nevertheless, for Bultmann, there is "never any doubt about our responsibility and guilt" or that "God is also the Judge before whom we are responsible."[14]

With respect to Paul, then, Bultmann's demythologization of Paul came down to what may be described as a de-apocalypticized Paul, a Paul with no future eschatology and no cosmological powers.[15]

In response to Bultmann, his former student, Käsemann, argued for the following two points:

1. Despite the new emphasis on the present reality of salvation in Paul's thought, "Paul remained an apocalyptist" in that a "future eschatology" remained a crucial element of his thinking.[16]

---

12. Bultmann, "New Testament and Mythology," 26. On this page and elsewhere, Bultmann refers constantly to what "the New Testament" says, but he supports his claims exclusively with references to Paul's letters.

13. Bultmann, "New Testament and Mythology," 27. See also his follow-up essay "On the Problem of Demythologizing," in Ogden, ed., *New Testament and Mythology*, 95–130, esp. 110–23.

14. Bultmann, "New Testament and Mythology," 15. Bultmann observes that "the New Testament" contains "a peculiar contradiction": "on the one hand, human beings are cosmically determined, and, on the other hand, they are summoned to decision (*Entscheidung*); on the one hand, sin is fate, and, on the other hand, it is guilt. . . . In short, human beings are understood, on the one hand, as cosmic human beings and, on the other hand, as independent persons who can win or lose themselves by their own decisions" (11). Bultmann gives the preference to the second of these alternatives, allowing this second alternative to provide the clue for interpreting the first: "the issue" he writes, "is whether the New Testament offers us an understanding of ourselves that constitutes for us a genuine question of decision" (15).

15. Congruent with this is Bultmann's understanding of the Spirit ("New Testament and Mythology," 20): The Spirit is not "a natural force" for Paul but represents "the possibility of life," one that a human being "must take hold of by resolve (*Entschluss*)." "We are not relieved of decision," Bultmann emphasizes when he cites such passages as Gal 5:16 with its imperative: "Walk by the Spirit" (RSV). The decision for faith, for authentic existence, must be taken every day anew: "So it is," Bultmann concludes, "that the concept of the 'Spirit' is demythologized."

16. Käsemann, "'The Righteousness of God' in Paul," 181; see further "On the Subject of Primitive Christian Apocalyptic," 131–33.

2. Bultmann's interpretation of Paul's cosmology in terms of an individualistic anthropology is untenable. Paul's use of the Greek term *sōma* ("body") belies Bultmann's claims. Bultmann rightly saw that Paul used this term to designate the whole person,[17] but he failed to see that the body signifies for Paul the creaturely solidarity of human beings with one another and with the rest of creation. The Pauline understanding of *sōma*, Käsemann argued, signifies that the individual cannot isolate herself from the world to which she belongs and that the human being is subject to "the rule of outside forces" that determine his existence, identity, and destiny.[18] So for Käsemann, "The world is not neutral ground; it is a battlefield, and everyone is a combatant. Anthropology must then *eo ipso* be cosmology."[19] Or, as he puts it elsewhere: Since a human being's life is "from the beginning a stake in the confrontation between God and the principalities of this world," it "can only be understood apocalyptically."[20]

Käsemann thus offered what we may call a "cosmological-apocalyptic" reading of Paul.[21]

The difference between Bultmann and Käsemann was also evident in their different interpretations of Paul's theology of justification. For Bultmann," the righteousness of God," *dikaiosynē theou* (Rom 1:17; 3:5, 21, 22; cf. 2 Cor 5:21) is a gift for the individual, the "favorable standing" a believer

17. Cf. Bultmann, *Theology*, 1.192–95.

18. Käsemann, "Primitive Christian Apocalyptic," 135–36; Käsemann, "Anthropology," 19–22); Käsemann, *Commentary on Romans*, 176.

19. Käsemann, "Anthropology," 23.

20. Käsemann, "Primitive Christian Apocalyptic," 136. From the previous discussion, it will have become evident that for Käsemann the term "apocalyptic" can be used for both Paul's future eschatology and his cosmology (the suprahuman forces that determine human existence, identity, and destiny). This is so despite Käsemann's occasional formal definition of apocalyptic as the expectation of the Parousia and the like. For discussion of this issue, see de Boer, *Defeat of Death*, 15–16, 29–30.

21. Congruent with these two points is Käsemann's understanding of the Spirit in Paul. The Spirit is not, as it is for Bultmann, the "possibility of life" to be "taken hold of by resolve" (see n. 15 above), but God's eschatological power already present in the world (cf. "Anthropology," 28): When Paul talks about the spiritual warfare between the Spirit and the Flesh, as he does in Romans 8 (as also in Galatians 5), he does not refer to the individual but to realities "which, as the power either of the heavenly or the earthly, determines him from outside, takes possession of him and thereby decides into which of the two dualistically opposed spheres he is to be integrated" ("On the Subject of Primitive Christian Apocalyptic," 136). The dialectic between indicative and imperative reflects this situation in the present. The powers remain an ongoing threat, and that explains the need for the imperative: the struggle is not yet over.

has in God's court.[22] The righteousness of God is "God-given, God adjudicated righteousness."[23] For Käsemann, the formulation "the righteousness of God" actually refers to God's own righteousness and concerns God's re-establishing his sovereignty over the world. Thus, "the righteousness of God does not, in Paul's understanding, refer primarily to the individual and is not to be understood exclusively" as anthropology.[24] Because "the righteousness of God" refers first and foremost to God's own saving action, effective in the Lordship of the crucified Christ, the justifying action on behalf of the ungodly not only "declares righteous" (is not simply a forensic-eschatological pronouncement, as it is for Bultmann) but also actually "makes righteous."[25] It does so by coming on the human scene to liberate human beings from cosmological forces and powers that have enslaved them.

Now, it is interesting to observe that Bultmann predicated his forensic-eschatological understanding of justification and God's righteousness largely on Romans 1–4, whereas Käsemann based his cosmological-apocalyptic reading of Paul largely on Romans 6–8.[26] Romans 5 is contested territory in that the views of both Bultmann and Käsemann can find support in this passage (see below). The Bultmann-Käsemann exchange allows us to see, or at least to suspect, that Romans 5 marks a shift from predominantly forensic-eschatological categories (focused on the individual) to predominantly cosmological-apocalyptic ones in Paul's argument in Romans.[27] The question this phenomenon of course raises is: Why is this the case and what does it signify?

The Cosmic Context of the Gospel

Paul begins chapter 5 with a summary of the preceding argument: "Since, then, we have been justified on the basis of faith [rather than on the basis of the Law], we [now] have peace with God through our Lord Jesus Christ, through whom we have obtained access into this grace in which we [now] stand" (1:1–2a). This emphasis on the present (cf. Bultmann), on what has been attained, is certainly retained throughout the first eleven verses. The opening paragraph concludes in vs. 11 with the words: "We rejoice in God through our Lord Jesus Christ through whom we have *now* received

22. Bultmann, *Theology*, 1.273.

23. Bultmann, *Theology*, 1.295.

24. Käsemann, "The 'Righteousness of God,'" 180.

25. Käsemann, "The 'Righteousness of God,'" 176.

26. Cf. Käsemann, *Romans*, 163.

27. See above, chapter 1.

reconciliation" (5:11). The result of justification is peace or reconciliation with God.

At the same time another note may be heard, one that points to the future (cf. Käsemann): Because "we" have been justified and thereby obtained peace with God and access to the grace in which "we" now stand, "we" can also "boast in the *hope* of the glory of God" (5:1–2). Or as Paul expresses it later in the passage: "having been justified, how much more *shall* we be saved through him from wrath" (5:9), and "having been reconciled how much more *shall* we be saved in his life" (5:10). Hope indeed "does not disappoint, since the love of God *has been* poured into our hearts through the holy spirit that *has been* given to us" (5:5). God's love becomes manifest in the justifying and reconciling death of Christ (5:8–10) and this fact of faith provides the basis for hope—hope for the future, not only for the long term (the Parousia) but also for the lives of believers from now on.

These new accents are continued in the second paragraph of chapter 5, vss. 12–21, but Paul now also places Christ's work within an explicitly cosmic framework. By "cosmic" I mean simply "pertaining to the whole human world"; Paul uses the term *kosmos* in vs. 12 to refer to "the whole human world"—not the universe or the earth, two possible other meanings of the term (cf. 1:8 ["the whole world"]; 3:19 ["the whole world"]; 4:13; 2 Cor 5:19). If in vss. 1–11 he repeatedly uses the first person plural "we" ("*we* have peace with God," "*we* boast," and so forth), limiting his discussion to believers, he now uses a third person construction (until the very end of vs. 21 when he reverts back to the first person plural as a transition to chapter 6). Paul widens the scope as it were, from the new situation in which believers find themselves, the realm of God's grace, to the whole human cosmos:

> [5:12a]Just as through one human being [i.e., Adam] sin came into the world and through sin death [came into the world] . . . [5:21b]so also grace might reign through justification[28] for eternal life, through Jesus Christ our Lord.

Romans 5:12a and 5:21b stand respectively at the beginning and at the end of the paragraph. Just as sin came into the world through one human being, along with death, so also grace came to reign through justification for life, through Jesus Christ "our Lord." That is the literary frame of the second

---

28. By translating the instance of *dikaiosynē* in 5:21b not with "righteousness" but with "justification" the *inclusio* with 5:1 ("having been *justified* [*dikaiōthentes*] on the basis of faith") becomes immediately evident. Notice also the mention of "grace" (*charis*) in 5:2 and 5:21. See chapter 7 below.

paragraph and the intervening verses may be regarded as annotations and explications of this central claim.[29]

Rom 5:12–21 is not the first time Paul has used a cosmic frame of reference in Romans, particularly in connection with the human condition before and apart from Christ. From 1:18 onward there is an account of human wrongdoing that is universal in scope as is the account of God's wrath against this wrongdoing. We may refer in particular to 3:23: "for all have sinned and fall short of the glory of God," which contains an allusion to Adam's lost glory (cf. *Ap. Mos.* 20:2; 21:6; 39:2–3; *4 Ezra* 7:122–25; *2 Bar.* 51:3; 54:15, 21; 1QS 4:23; 1QH 17:15; CD 3:20). Rom 5:12–21, however, is the first time Paul refers explicitly to Adam whereby the cosmic context of Paul's understanding of Christ's work also becomes explicit. Adam is here called "the type" of "the coming one," that is to say, of Christ (vs. 14). Christ is thus Adam's antitype. As Adam's antitype Christ is "the one human being" (vss. 15, 19) who stands over against the other "one human being," Adam, undoing what Adam brought about. And Christ does so on a correspondingly cosmic scale, as vss. 18–19 make plain: "So then, as through one trespass there was for *all people* condemnation, so also through one act of justification (*dikaiōma*) there is for *all people* justification (*dikaiōsis*) of life. For just as through the disobedience of the one human being *the many* [= all] were made sinful (*hamartōloi*),[30] so also through the obedience of the one [human being] *the many* [= all] will be made just (*dikaioi*)."[31]

Paul, then, places Christ and his saving work in a cosmic context and he does so by contrasting Christ with the figure of Adam. Paul has made this move earlier, in 1 Corinthians 15, where the resurrection of Christ is placed in a cosmic context against some believers in the Corinthian church who were denying the resurrection of the dead:

> [15:21]Through a human being, death,
>
> also through a human being, resurrection of the dead.
>
> [15:22]For just as in Adam, *all* die,
>
> so also in Christ, *all* will be made alive.

Just as Adam stands at the head of the old world or age *for all*, so Christ stands at the head of the new world or age *for all*. This cosmic frame of reference is one of the distinguishing marks of an apocalyptic perspective, as is the implicit notion of two world ages. Again, by placing Christ over

29. See de Boer, *Defeat of Death*, 162–63.

30. Or "sinnners."

31. Or "just ones."

against Adam Paul makes plain that Christ's work is as cosmic (= pertaining to all human beings) in its implications and consequences as Adam's initial trespass or disobedience. If all died because of Adam, all will be made alive because of Christ. Verse 22 makes explicit the universal implications of vs. 21—for both Adam and Christ.

In 1 Corinthians 15, then, Paul's interest in Adam is limited to two things: (1) his agency in causing death to come into the world (through a human being = in Adam), and (2) the cosmic consequences of this agency (death = all die). Furthermore, Paul's appeal to Adam functions primarily as a foil for Christ. Just as Adam determined universal human destiny, so also Christ does. Christ's saving role is analogous to, even as it also surpasses, Adam's destructive role, particularly in terms of its (1) agency (through a human being = in Christ) and (2) the cosmic consequences of this agency (resurrection of the dead = all will be made alive).[32]

Much the same may be said about Paul's recycling of the Adam-Christ typology in Romans 5; it is a matter of agency and of the cosmic consequences of this agency. But there are some differences.

Adam and Christ, Death and Life

In Romans 5, the issue is not the resurrection of the dead but "life," *zōē* (vss. 17, 18), or "eternal life," *zōē aiōnios* (vs. 21). Those "who receive the abundance of grace, i.e., the free gift of justification, will reign in *life*" (vs. 17). The "one act of justification for all people is for justification of *life*" (vss. 18). Grace "more than abounded" (vs. 20) so that it "might reign through justification for *eternal life*" (vs. 21). The mention of grace in vs. 21 indicates that the issue in Romans 5 is the status and the function of the Law, which Jewish sources refer to as "the Law of life" (*4 Ezra* 14:30; *2 Bar.* 38:1: "Your Law is life"; cf. Sir 17:11; 45:5). Grace is for Paul the antithetical correlate of the Law, as 6:14 shows (see Introduction above). That explains why Paul explicitly mentions the Law in vss. 13 and 20 of chapter 5. Christ and his saving work—"life"— are, then, placed not only in opposition to Adam and his trespass but *also* to the Law as the presumed remedy for the trespass.

Because the issue here is "(eternal) life" rather than the resurrection of the (physically) dead as in 1 Corinthians 15, the primary referential meaning of the term "death" (*thanatos*) in Romans 5 is not physical death, as it is in 1 Corinthians 15. Paul works with at least three referential meanings for "death" as an anthropological reality of the present world: physical death (bodily demise), moral or spiritual death (sinful behavior as a form of

32. de Boer, *Defeat of Death*, 109–12.

death), and eternal death (perdition, damnation). The close association of death with sin and the dualistic contrast of death with (eternal) life in Romans 5 as well as the chapters that follow indicates that the last two meanings are at the forefront. What binds these various referential meanings to one another is the notion of separation from God and from life before God. That, for Paul, truly is death.

In Romans 5, in contrast to 1 Corinthians 15, sin is explicitly brought into the equation (though it may be implicit in 1 Corinthians 15 as well; cf. 15:3, 17). And that brings us to the much discussed verse 12.

Corporate Destiny or Individual Culpability?

Many interpreters have noted the evident tension between the first half of the verse (vs. 12a) and the second half (vs. 12b):

> 5:12aJust as through one human being sin came into the world and through sin death,
>
> 5:12band so death spread to all human beings, since all sinned.

The tension between the two halves of the verse has usually been described in terms of the contrast between corporate destiny in the first half (Adam caused the fatality of death to come upon all people) and personal responsibility in the second (since everyone sinned, everyone is also responsible for their own death). Bultmann argued that Paul in effect corrects the former motif with the latter.[33] The Adam motifs to which Paul is here indebted have of course ultimately been derived from Genesis 3, but then as interpreted in a certain strain of Jewish apocalyptic eschatology, as witnessed to by *4 Ezra* and *2 Baruch*. These books, though written some decades after Paul wrote Romans, clearly make use of earlier and commonly available traditions and do so independently of each other.[34] In both works, the destruction of Jerusalem in 70 CE and the gift of the Law are placed against the cosmic backdrop of Adam's transgression and its disastrous consequences for the world, for all humanity.

In *2 Baruch*, we read: "Adam sinned and death was decreed against those who were to be born" (23:4) and "when he [Adam] transgressed, untimely death came into being" (56:6; cf. Gen 2:17; 3:19). It is also said, however, that "Adam is . . . not the cause, except for himself, but each of us has become our own Adam" (54:19). Adam may have "sinned first"

---

33. Bultmann, "Adam and Christ According to Romans 5," 153.

34. For a recent treatment, see Henze, "*4 Ezra* and *2 Baruch*," esp. 197–98.

(54:15) but he was not the last! The death that Adam brought into the world is justifiably imposed on those who are descended from him. In 4 *Ezra*, there is a very similar tale. God "laid one commandant" upon Adam, we read in 3:7, "but he transgressed it, and immediately you [God] appointed death for him and his descendants." But we also read: "O Adam, what have you done? For though it was you who sinned, the fall was not yours alone, but ours also who are your descendants. For what good is it to us, if an eternal age has been promised to us, but we have done deeds that bring death?" (7:118–20)

The figure of Adam thus has a double function in both works: to give expression to the all-embracing reality of death in the present world and to assign responsibility for the reality of death to the willful and thus accountable repudiation of God by human beings. The logically irreconcilable tension between corporate destiny and personal culpability discernible between the two halves of Romans 5:12 is thus part and parcel of the Adam tradition as it occurs in these Jewish apocalyptic texts. The figure of Adam functions as both a corporate personality who determines all subsequent human destiny and as the paradigmatic human being who sets the pattern for his descendants. It thus seems unlikely that the motif of personal culpability in the second half of vs. 12 is to be construed as Paul's 'correction' of the motif of corporate destiny in the first half. They belong together in the tradition about Adam in Jewish thought of the period.

It may also be noted here that in both *4 Ezra* and *2 Baruch* the fundamental sin of Adam and his descendants is the refusal to acknowledge and to worship God the Creator (cf. *4 Ezra* 7:118; 8:60). As *2 Baruch* puts it: God "knew the number of those who are born from him [Adam] and how they sinned before you [God], those who existed and who did not recognize you as their Creator" (48:46; cf. 14:15–19; 54:18). Paul shows his deep familiarity with such conceptions in chapters 1–3 of Romans. To cite an example, Rom 1:28–32:

> And since they did not see fit to acknowledge God, God gave them up to a base mind and to improper conduct. They were filled with all manner of wickedness, evil, covetousness, malice. Full of envy, murder, strife, deceit, malignity, they are gossips, slanderers, haters of God, insolent, haughty, boastful, inventors of evil, disobedient to parents, foolish, faithless, heartless, ruthless. Though they know God's decree that those who do such things deserve to die [lit. are worthy of death, *axioi thanatou*] they not only do them but approve those who practice them (RSV).

We would not blink an eye or raise an eyebrow if we had come across this passage in either *4 Ezra* or *2 Baruch*. Paul is in dialogue with such views in the early chapters of Romans. But that then raises the question of Paul's distinctiveness.

Paul's Distinctiveness

What is distinctive in Paul's use and application of the story of Adam in 5:12–21 is his characterization of sin and death as cosmological forces that have invaded the human cosmos as alien intruders: "Sin [capital S] came into the world, and through Sin, Death [capital D] [came into the world]." In short, Paul personifies and thereby "mythologizes" the notions of sin and death, which is to say, he talks about them as he elsewhere does about Satan (cf. Rom 16:20; 1 Cor 5:5; 7:5; 2 Cor 2:11; 11:14; 12:7; 1 Thess 2:18; cf. 2 Cor 4:4; 6:14; 1 Thess 3:5), evil angels (cf., e.g., Rom 8:38; 1 Cor 4:9; 6:3; 2 Cor 11:14; 12:7) or demons (cf. 1 Cor 10:20–21), i.e., as inimical powers or beings that victimize and enslave human beings,[35] and that do so contrary to God's intention for the world.[36] Paul is not interested in cosmological speculation for its own sake, but in giving an account of the *human* condition or plight. Put otherwise, Paul's cosmological language about Sin and Death as malevolent powers represents an attempt to account for anthropological realities and experiences. Behind *human* sinning and *human* dying, Paul discerns cosmological powers at work which he calls Sin and Death. He thus mythologizes with what Käsemann called "anthropological relevance."[37]

In Paul's mythologization of death, death is not thought of as the punishment for sin (as in 1:32, cited above),[38] but as the ineluctable result or outcome of sin (6:16b; 6:21b; 6:23a; 7:5b). Sin came into the world with Adam, and the ineluctable result was Death. And that means, then, that where the one is, the other also is. Paul's appropriation of the Adam tradition places the motif of personal accountability or culpability in a new context, a cosmological-apocalyptic one (cf. Käsemann). For Paul, the fact

35. On Sin as a power in Romans, see Gaventa, "The Cosmic Power of Sin."

36. For parallels in Jewish apocalyptic literature, see the useful survey on angels and demons provided by Russell, *Method and Message*, 235–62.

37. Cf. Käsemann, "On Paul's Anthropology," 27. See further de Boer, *Defeat of Death*, 179.

38. Rom 1:32 contains the only instance of the noun *thanatos* ("death") before 5:12–21 (apart from the instance in 5:10 referring to the death of Jesus). In contrast to the five instances in 5:12–21, the instance in 1:32 has a forensic-eschatological meaning (death as punishment) and is equivalent to "wrath" (*orgē*, a term Paul uses seven times before 5:12–21 (1:18; 2:52; 2:8; 3:5; 4:15; 5:9).

that "all sinned" (5:12d; 3:23) signifies that all human beings since Adam have been and are, as he has already asserted in 3:9, "under (the power of) Sin." The second half of vs. 12 ("And so Death spread to all people, since all sinned") is to be interpreted accordingly. The power of Death came upon all people, since all, by being under the power of Sin, sinned. Sinning is not the result of a bad choice made by an autonomous individual; it is the result and the mark of a cosmological force that has come into the world and has reigned over human beings since the time of Adam, bringing death in its wake (vs. 21a; cf. 7:17).[39]

Paul's mythologization of Sin and Death has particular pertinence for what he says about the Law, or the observance of the Law.

The Status and the Role of the Law

As I have noted, grace, which is mentioned several times in 5:12–21, is the antithetical correlate of the Law (cf. 6:14–15). Paul's mention of the Law in verses 13 and 20 is therefore no accident. Before we look at what precisely he says and why, it will be useful to return here briefly to 2 Baruch and 4 Ezra to see how they regard the Law as the divinely given solution to the human condition since Adam. According to 2 Baruch, God has graciously given the Law as the remedy for the world determined by the sentence of death imposed on Adam and his progeny. By giving the Law, God also allows each person to determine her or his ultimate destiny. In 19:1, God tells the seer that he had made a covenant with the people in the time of Moses and confronted them with a choice: "Behold, I appoint for you life and death" (cf. 44:3; 84:2), a partial citation of Deut 30:19: "I have set before you life and death, blessing and curse; therefore, choose life that you and your descendants may live." In 2 Baruch, the terms life and death from Deut 30:19 have not only moral connotations as they do in Deuteronomy itself but also eschatological ones (cf. also 46:3). Observance of the Law in the present determines whether the sentence of death passed on Adam and all his descendants will be the ultimate rather than the penultimate destiny of Adam's offspring, i.e.. whether this death will in fact be eternal or overcome with the gift of "life" in the world to come (cf. 42:7–8; 44:7–15; 51:3, 7–8). Each person can freely choose to obey the Law (51:16), whereby the claim of the Creator is acknowledged (48:47), and thus inherit "that world which has no end" (48:50). "For the Judge will come and will not hesitate. For each of the inhabitants of the earth [note the cosmic framework and the individualism here!] knew when he acted unrighteously, and they did not know my

39. See further chapter 4 below.

Law because of their pride" (48:40). "For although Adam sinned first and has brought death upon all who were not in his own time, yet *each of them* who has been born from him [again, note the individualism and the cosmic framework] has prepared for himself the coming torment. And further each of them has chosen for himself the coming glory"(54:15–16). Your destiny is in your own hands now that God has given the Law (cf. 48:38–40)! For those destined to be "saved because of their works," "the Law is now a hope" (51:7). The present is a time of *decision*—for or against the Law, which is a decision for or against life.

In 4 *Ezra*, a primary concern is what is called "the evil heart" (*cor malignum* in 3:21, 26; 4:4; or *cor malum* in 7:48) and the ability of the Law to counter its effects. The seer, called Ezra, wonders whether the Law is sufficient to overcome the problem: "For the first Adam, burdened with an evil heart, transgressed and was overcome, as were also all who were descended from him. Thus the disease became permanent." He then adds the following interesting observation: "the Law was in the people's heart along with the evil root, but what was good departed, and the evil remained" (3:21–22). Thus Ezra complains that when God gave the Law to Israel he did "not take away from them the evil heart, so that your Law might bring forth fruit in them" (3:20; cf. 7:48; 9:36). This sounds almost Pauline. The angel (Uriël) sent to converse with Ezra about such matters, who speaks for God and thus probably represents the views of the author of the book,[40] responds that though the number of those saved will indeed be few, those who have kept the Law "perfectly" (7:89) will receive the award of "immortality" (7:13, 97, 113). It is "for this reason, [that] the Most High has made not one world but two" (7:50), to give people the opportunity to prove themselves in this age and to receive their proper reward in the age to come: "This is the meaning of the contest which *every human being* who is born on earth [again, note the cosmic framework and individualism] shall wage, that if he is defeated he shall suffer what you [Ezra] have said, but if he is victorious he shall receive what I [the angel] have said" (cf. 2 *Bar.* 15:8). The angel then goes on to cite from Deut 30:19: "For this is the way of which Moses, while he was alive, spoke to the people saying, 'Choose for yourself life, that you may live!'" (7:127–29). The angel thereby affirms that the Law is indeed the remedy for the "disease of the evil heart," the observance of which is the condition for participation in the coming age (cf. 7:17, 21, 45, 92). The Law is after all "the Law of life" (14:30). Those with "a treasure of good works laid up with the Most High" (7:77; cf. 8:33, 36) will be saved. For the author of 4 *Ezra* it is possible to "choose life" in the midst of the present evil age of death.

---

40. Cf. Harnisch, *Verhängnis*, 48–50, 60–67.

Again, in the first part of Romans, Paul exhibits his deep familiarity with this theology of the Law. Take 2:5–8:

> But by your hard and impenitent *heart* you are storing up wrath for yourself on the day of wrath when God's righteous judgment will be revealed. For he will render to every one according to their works: to those who by patience in well-doing seek for glory and honor and immortality, he will give eternal life; but for those who are factious and do not obey the truth, but obey wickedness, there will be wrath and fury (RSV, modified).

Or 2:13: "For it is not the hearers of the Law who are righteous before God, but the doers of the Law who will be justified"! Or 3:19: "We know that whatever the Law says it speaks to those in the Law, that every mouth [individualism!] may be stopped and the whole world [cosmic scope!] may become accountable to God." In the first three chapters, through 3:19, Paul adopts this perspective in order to undermine it, concluding in 3:20: "Therefore, no one shall be justified before Him as a result of works of the Law, for through the Law comes [only] knowledge of Sin."

In 3:21, Paul goes on to maintain that in any case the Law has been overtaken by events, or rather by an event, that of Jesus Christ, whereby "the righteousness of God" has become manifest "apart from the Law." But Paul's argument is not simply that believers in Christ are now justified on the basis of faith rather than as a result of "works of the Law" (3:20, 28). In 5:12–21, Paul goes on to place the Law within a cosmological-apocalyptic context: "For [the power of] Sin was in the world prior to the Law," i.e. before the Law could "register" it (vs. 13). If Sin was in the world prior to the Law, so of course was Death: "Death reigned from Adam to Moses," just as Sin did. Death reigned "also over those who did not commit sin in the likeness of the transgression (*parabasis*) of Adam" (vs. 14). No, those who lived prior to the Law did not transgress a specific divine commandment as did Adam. There was no Law to transgress, since "where there is no Law there is no transgression" either (4:15)! Nevertheless, those who lived prior to the coming of the Law did sin, did all commit the fundamental "trespass" (*paraptōma*) of Adam in that they repudiated the Creator (cf. 1:28). Paul seems to use the word *paraptōma*, of which there are five instances in 5:15–20, to mean a "falling away" from God, a repudiation or rejection of God (cf. 4:25; 11:11, 22; Wis 10:1). It is for this reason that Death "reigned" (5:14) from Adam onward, also before the Law came on the scene, when of course Sin also reigned (5:21) even if there was no Law to transgress. The significance of these claims about a bygone period of human history becomes evident in vs. 20, where Paul writes that "the Law came in alongside (*pareisēlthen*)," that is to say, came into a situation already fully determined by these twin powers. In other words, the Law has been—and still is—no match for the power of Sin and its partner Death (cf. 8:3). "The Law came in alongside, so that the trespass might increase," and that means for Paul that "[the power of] Sin increased" (vs. 20b), intensified and solidified its death-dealing grip over human beings, so that "Sin reigned in Death," which is to say, in the realm of total separation from God and life.

But now it is interesting to observe that 2 Baruch and 4 Ezra, which James D. G. Dunn has labeled "the two classic Jewish apocalypses,"[41] do not support Paul's cosmological-apocalyptic construal of Sin and Death. The absence of cosmological powers from these two works is striking. [42] 2 Baruch and 4 Ezra represent a Jewish apocalyptic worldview in which such malevolent forces play no role.[43] The emphasis falls on choice and on personal accountability and culpability (cf. Bultmann's interpretation of Paul). Paul, I have argued, has introduced the cosmological understanding of sin and death into the Jewish Adam traditions—and he has done so to show that the Law, instead of being the solution for sin and thus death as in 2 Baruch and 4 Ezra, only solidified the hold of Sin and thus Death on human beings: Alas, the Law has nothing to do with obtaining the requisite righteousness nor with justification nor, then, with (eternal) life. Nothing.

Paul's appraisal of the Law's status and the role of the Law in the light of Christ, hinges in part on his understanding of Sin and Death as cosmological powers. The Law is their plaything and tool. It is no more than "the Law of Sin and Death," as he writes in 8:2. The Law itself may be holy, good, and spiritual (7:12–14), but Christ's death has unmasked the terrible fact that the (observance of the) Law is not—in fact, cannot be—the remedy for sin and does not—in fact, cannot—bridge the yawning chasm of death that, because of Sin, separates human beings from God and life. In the face of the powers of Sin and Death, those who predicate their hopes on Law observance live under an illusion. The Law does not and cannot, in Paul's view, liberate human beings from the deadly orb in which Sin rules, cannot

41. Dunn, *Theology of Paul*, 88.

42. *4 Ezra* and *2 Baruch* show, therefore, that not all apocalyptic eschatology is necessarily cosmological, even though both Bultmann and Käsemann appear to work with that assumption (see the section titled "Bultmann's Proposal and Käsemann's Reaction" above). For the two patterns (or "tracks") of Jewish apocalyptic eschatology, see chapter 1 in this volume and *Defeat of Death*, 85–88. For a summary and restatement of my views, see *Galatians*, 31–35, 79–82.

43. In a survey article, Wright has asked for "evidence of the split between two types of 'apocalyptic' theology" for which I have argued (Wright, "Paul in Current Anglophone Scholarship," 367–81). The evidence is available in my earlier publications (see previous note) as well as in this chapter.

rectify their broken relationship with God, cannot grant or assure eternal life (cf. Gal 2:21; 3:21). The Law only "came in alongside" the powers of Sin and Death, and, as the crucifixion of Christ has revealed, increased Sin's lethal hold on human beings (cf. 7:7—8:8).[44]

Paul's Aim

Paul's mythologizing agenda in Rom 5:12–21 and beyond seems, then, to mark a major shift in Paul's argument in Romans. However, as pointed out in chapter 1 above, that shift finds its anticipation in at least two verses in chapters 1–4. In 1:16–17 Paul personifies "the righteousness of God" as God's saving power (if Käsemann is right and I think he is) and in 3:9 he personifies sin as a cosmological, subjugating power, anticipating the material extending from 5:12–8:3 where he speaks of sin as a cosmological power some forty times. These two texts—1:16–17 and 3:9—occur at crucial junctures in Paul's argument in the first three chapters. The first arguably states the fundamental theme of the epistle, while the second summarizes the multifarious sins of both Jews and Gentiles, catalogued in the preceding discussion, as proof that they are all "under (the power of) Sin." His mythologizing program, therefore, is anticipated in the earlier chapters.

Now, one can regard Paul's mythologizing of Sin and Death merely as a rhetorical ploy, determined by the need to exclude the Law, or "works of the Law," as the solution to the problem of the human condition among the Roman Christians.[45] However, Paul has made similar moves in earlier letters. In 1 Corinthians 15, he ranges the death that came into the world through Adam with the principalities and powers that Christ must put under his feet; Death is "the last enemy" (15:24–26). In Galatians, he has argued that "the Scripture shut all things [including even the Law] under [the power of] Sin (*hypo hamartian*)" (3:21), using the same expression that he uses in Rom 3:9: "all people, both Jews and Greeks, are under [the power of] sin (*hyph' hamartian*)."[46] Paul's mythological/cosmological understanding of Sin and Death appears to belong to his primary convictions

44. As Gaventa writes, Sin is "a cosmic terrorist. Sin not only entered the cosmos with Adam; it also enslaved, it unleashed Death itself, it even managed to take the law of God captive to its power" ("Cosmic Power," 130–31; emphasis removed).

45. For other possible objections (Paul's personification of Sin is a mere metaphorical device; modern people cannot share Paul's worldview), see the instructive discussion of Gaventa, "Cosmic Power," 133–35. See further chapter 4 in this volume.

46. The slight difference in the spelling of the preposition is not significant. More important is the fact that this is the first time Paul uses the word *hamartia* in Romans and he uses it to personify Sin as a cosmic power.

as an apostle of the crucified and risen Christ. As the coming of Christ has shown, the human predicament is much worse than it appears before or apart from that event.

Paul is not a preacher of bad news, however. His focus is finally not the terror of the human predicament, but the miracle of God's grace that has invaded the human cosmos in the "justifying work" (*dikaiōma*) of the one human being, Jesus Christ. Just as Paul thinks of sin and death as cosmological powers, so also, in Rom 5:20–21, does he characterize God's grace as tantamount to a cosmological power in the world. If Sin and Death are said to reign, so also does Grace (hence the capital G) in 5:21. Grace is not simply the divine favor, it is also the divine saving activity and as such the sphere within which believers are repeatedly granted life (5:1–2).[47] "Where Sin increased, Grace more than abounded," was more than sufficient to meet the challenge.[48] In Christ, God himself has entered the human cosmos and God's powerful Grace, in contrast to the weak and ineffectual Law, is more than equal to the task of putting an end to the reigns of Sin and Death.

47. See M. Winger, "From Grace to Sin," 154–55.
48. Cf. Gaventa, "Cosmic Power," 131–32, 134.

Chapter 4

Sin and Soteriology in Romans

Introduction

As is well known, Paul tends to use the noun *hamartia* in the singular in Romans, some forty-five times.[1] There are only four such instances in his other undisputed letters.[2] By contrast, the plural occurs only three times in Romans (4:7; 7:5; 11:27) of which two are in OT quotations (4:7; 11:27). The remaining undisputed letters contain but four more instances of the plural.[3] It is clear from the raw data that the singular can be regarded as Paul's characteristic usage, certainly in Romans.

Also relevant is the fact that aside from the forty-five uses of the singular noun *hamartia* in Romans there are only twelve instances of cognate terms: the verb *hamartanō*, "to sin" (Rom 2:12 [2x]; 3:23; 5:12, 14, 16; 6:15),[4] the noun (or adjective), *hamartōlos*, "sinner (sinful)" (Rom 3:7; 5:8 pl.; 5:19 pl.; 7:13),[5] and the noun *hamartēma*, "sinful deed" (Rom 3:25 pl.).[6]

---

1. 3:9, 20; 4:8; 5:12 [2x], 13[2x], 20, 21; 6:1, 2, 6[2x], 7, 10, 11, 12, 13, 14, 16, 17, 18, 20, 22, 23; 7:7[2x], 8[2x], 9, 11, 13[2x], 14, 17, 20, 23, 25; 8:2, 3[3x], 10; 14:23.

2. Gal 2:17; 3:22; 1 Cor 15:56; 2 Cor 11:7.

3. 1 Cor 15:3, 17; Gal 1:4; and 1 Thess 2:16. The instance in 1 Cor 15:3 ("Christ died for our sins") is clearly part of a tradition that Paul is citing and that is probably the case in Gal 1:4 as well ("having given himself for our sins").

4. There are only six more instances in the remaining undisputed letters: 1 Cor 6:18; 7:28, 36; 8:12 [2x]; 15:34.

5. Also Gal 2:15 pl.; 2:17 pl.

6. Also 1 Cor 6:18. There are also conceptually related words, such as *parabasis*, "transgression" (Rom 2:23; 4:15; 5:14; cf. Gal 3:19 pl.), *paraptōma*, "trespass" (Rom 5:15, 15, 16 pl., 17, 18, 20; 11:11, 12; cf. Gal 6:1; 2 Cor 5:19 pl.), *anomia*, "iniquity/ lawlessness" (Rom 4:7 pl. OT quotation; 6:19; cf. 2 Cor 6:14), *adikia* , "wickedness/ unrighteousness" (Rom 1:18, 29; 2:8; 3:5; 6:13; 9:14; cf. 1 Cor 13:6; 2 Cor 12:13), *akatharsia*, "impurity" (1:24; 6:19; cf. 2 Cor 12:21; Gal 5:19; 1 Thess 2:3; 4:7), and *asebeia*, "ungodliness" (Rom 1:18; 11:26 OT quotation; cf. *asebēs*, "ungodly," in Rom 4:5; 5:6).

The noun *hamartia* in the singular dominates Paul's discourse on sin and does so particularly in Romans.[7]

Sin as a Cosmic Power in Romans[8]

The first occurrence of the term *hamartia* in Romans occurs in 3:9. In this verse Paul arguably sums up (much of) his previous argument,[9] which began in 1:18, by writing how he has established that all people, "both Jews and Greeks" are "under sin," *hypo hamartian*. Joseph A. Fitzmyer writes that Paul here "personifies it [sin] as a master [*kyrios*] who dominates a slave; it holds human beings in bondage to it."[10] Fitzmyer thus paraphrases the phrase "under sin" as "under *the power* of sin," as do many other commentators and translations (e.g., NRSV).[11] It is this personification of *hamartia* as an enslaving power that characterizes Paul's use of the singular—for which reason the English translation is normally capitalized: Sin. Though perhaps not every singular in Romans can be regarded as a personification of *hamartia* as an enslaving power (cf. 3:20; 4:8; 14:23),[12] that does appear to be the case regularly and consistently in Romans 5–8: forty-one of the forty-five

7. Simon Gathercole's recent attempt to minimize the significance of Paul's use of the singular and to shift the emphasis to the plural goes against the evidence: Gathercole, *Defending Substitution*, 48–50; and Gathercole, "'Sins' in Paul."

8. This essay is primarily exegetical. For particularly helpful treatments that go beyond exegesis, see Gaventa, "Cosmic Power of Sin"; Eastman, *Paul and the Person*; Croasmun, *Emergence of Sin*.

9. Barclay has recently argued that 1:18—3:20 is not to be construed as a unit "whose *single* theme is the sinfulness of all humanity" (*Paul and the Gift*, 466), since there are also passages (2:7–10, 14–15, 26–29 in particular) that concern believers, both Gentile and Jewish, who "have been *transformed* in their inmost being ('the hidden things' of 'the heart') by divine power" (467). Emphasis original in both quotations. For a critical survey of previous scholarship on this issue and a different treatment of the evidence, see Mininger, *Uncovering*.

10. Fitzmyer, *Romans*, 331. See chapter 3 above.

11. Paul has used the expression "under Sin" earlier, in Gal 3:22. It was, therefore, already part of his thinking. He did not come up with the notion in composing Romans, which can be read as a further articulation of his thinking on this score. Indeed, according to Mininger, the force of the verb *proētiasametha* ("we have already established") in Rom 3:9 "is best understood, not with respect to what Paul has said previously in this letter, but with respect to what he has previously in his ministry in general, the very ministry which was just assailed in 3:8" (*Uncovering*, 320). Surprisingly, Mininger does not support this claim with a reference to Gal 3:22.

12. Mininger argues strongly for regarding the instance in 3:20 as a reference to Sin as a power (*Uncovering*, 310–12). It is in any event also the case that where Sin (as a power) is mentioned, sinning (as a human activity) is implied. Sin does not exist apart from sinning (see further on this point below).

instances of the singular in Romans are to be found in these chapters, beginning at 5:12 and extending to 8:10.[13]

In Romans 5–8, the personification of *hamartia* as an evil power introduced in 3:9 is further developed and emphasized. That is true quantitatively (there are a large number of instances) but also qualitatively (its nature and significance come to the fore in various ways). In 5:12, Paul writes that "through one human being [identified as Adam in 5:14], Sin came into the world (*kosmos*) . . ." At the beginning of time, we could say, Sin came into the human world as an intruder and as an alien force, conquering territory that belonged to someone else (God). Sin invaded and, like an ancient potentate, came to "reign/rule" (5:21; cf. 6:12: *basileuein*) or "lord it" (6:14: *kyrieuein*) over the human world in all its dimensions, individual as well as social. It is thus not only a lord/master (*kyrios*) of slaves but also a ruler (*basileus*) with a domain. The residents who make up this domain, the world (*kosmos*) under Sin, are expected to be obedient (6:16) to their lord and king, and thus to do what it[14] requires and demands.[15] In fact, as slaves and thus as part of a given and fixed hierarchical structure of relationships, they have little or no choice. Perhaps in theory they have some choice but not in actual fact, not in practice, any more than slaves (in the ordinary, social sense of the term) did in the ancient world. Disobedience was theoretically *possible* but in practice *impossible*—a possible impossibility, as it were.

Hence, apart from Christ, human beings are, as Paul twice puts it in Romans 6, "slaves of Sin," *douloi tēs hamartias* (6:17, 20). In 7:14, he describes the (Adamic[16]) self as "sold [like a slave] under [the power of] Sin," *pepramenos hypo tēn hamartian*. It does not belong to itself, but to something else. Sin has control; it has the power and the hegemony. In 7:16–17, Paul writes: "if I do what I do not want . . . it is no longer I that do it, but Sin which dwells within me." He uses the same language in 7:20. Sin causes someone to do what they do not want to do. Sin, then, is evidently not to be

13. Aside from the instance in 3:9, the remaining instances of the singular are to be found in 3:20; 4:8 (an OT quotation); and 14:23.

14. Given the fact that the Greek noun *hamartia* is grammatically feminine, the feminine personal pronoun "she" could be appropriate here. But the grammatical gender of the term seems to play no evident role in Paul's exposition any more than the grammatically masculine gender of the Greek term for death, *thanatos*, does.

15. See 6:13 ("yielding our members [*melē*] to Sin as instruments of wickedness"), 19 ("yielding your members [*melē*] as slaves to impurity and increased iniquity"), and 12 ("obeying the desires [*epithymiai*]" of "our mortal body"; cf. 7:5 [*pathēmata*], 8 [*epithymia*]; 8:13 [*praxeis*]). For Paul, "our old human being" (*ho palaios hēmōn anthrōpos*) and "the body of sin" (*to sōma tēs hamartias*) (6:6) are characterizations of human beings, both individually and collectively, under the power of Sin.

16. Cf. de Boer, *Defeat of Death*, 242n66; Meyer, "Worm at the Core."

identified with the human self who wills to do what is good (as stipulated and determined by the Law) but cannot achieve it (7:18b). Sin is evidently not something intrinsic to the being and identity of human beings. The descendants of Adam are here being portrayed as the victims and pawns of an alien force that compels them to do things that they know they should not do.[17] As a power, Sin causes or effects "sinful deeds" (*hamartēmata*, 3:25), turning human beings into "sinners" (5:8, 19)[18] who actively "commit sin" (2:12; 3:23; 5:12; 6:15).[19] Sin is here understood to be an alien force that has invaded the individual human being with, as 5:12 suggests, an enormous and deleterious impact on the collective or social world of human beings, i.e., on interpersonal relationships.[20]

As a ruler, Sin has a domain which can be understood as an orb or sphere into which every human being is born—which means that every human being has entered (and enters) at birth a world in which Sin already reigns or rules. For this reason, each and every human being is born a slave to Sin and will as a matter of course behave in a way that reflects this situation, which is one of bondage requiring conformity to the wishes of the master.[21] Or as Paul puts it: "all sinned" in 5:12, and earlier in 3:23: "all sinned and [for that reason] fall short of the glory of God." Using the past tense in both cases (an aorist in Greek: *hēmarton*), Paul looks at the history of the world retrospectively, as it were, from the eschatological Christ event. In 3:9, where, as I noted earlier, he has written that both Jews and Greeks, in other words "all people," are "under Sin," he cites from Scripture to illustrate the concrete implications: "for it stands written: 'no one is righteous, no not one'" (3:10; cf. Gal 3:22). No one meets God's standard of what is good and right ("righteousness"). Paul goes on to cite a whole list of similar passages to drive the point home (3:11–18).[22] The domain of Sin

17. See further on Romans 7, Eastman, *Paul and the Person*, 109–125.

18. The personification of Sin as inimical power cannot be dismissed as a merely metaphorical, literary, or rhetorical device. See Gaventa, "Cosmic Power of Sin," 133–34; Croasmun, *Emergence of Sin*, 8–11 and *passim*. The personification reflects something about reality as experienced by human beings.

19. Sin (as a power) thus always implies sinning (a human activity). Gathercole's critique ("'Sins' in Paul") that those who highlight Sin as a power in Paul's theology thereby neglect sins (sinful human actions) is thus misplaced. There is no Sin without sinning. See Furnish, *Theology and Ethics*, 163.

20. Cf. Eastman, *Paul and the Person*, 121: "There is no freestanding self capable of watching itself; it is already invaded by a personified power that radically compromises its agency."

21. The offspring of a slave in the ancient world was also a slave. On slavery in the Greco-Roman world, see the helpful overview of Bartchy, "Slavery."

22. See the discussion of Mininger, *Uncovering*, 305–9, and chapter 11 below.

is our collective destiny. And this domain is a *factual* reality, whatever the explanation of its origin may be.[23]

Sin and Death

The ineluctable result of the rule of Sin is deliverance to the realm of Death.[24] When Sin came into the world, Death did too: "through the one

23. The traditional explanation of its origin is the notion of "original sin" in the sense attributed to or associated with Augustine: sin as a genetic defect that beginning with Adam has been transmitted from one human being to another through "concupiscence" (sexual desire and union), as if the propensity to sin were an inherited condition. See the critical review in Croasmun, *Emergence of Sin*, 133–37, who also discusses the common alternative, namely the *social* transmission of sin (attributed to Friedrich Schleiermacher, Albert Ritschl, Walter Rauschenbusch, and "liberationist" theologians). He cites in this connection the words of Monika Hellwig as a good summary of this explanation: "The complex structures of our societies set limits to what we can see, understand, and choose to do. We are caught in a web of relationships, expectations, economies, cultural activities, acculturation to particular contexts political and administrative arrangements which seem to take on a life of their own, larger, more enduring, and more resistant than the efforts of any individual or group of individuals to change or act in opposition to such forces. Here, then, is the concrete presence of original sin or the sin of Adam, the force of evil that precedes the choices of those who appear to be choosing, preempts the actions of those who appear to be acting, and tends to crush out of existence any who persist in acting in critical opposition" (from Croasmun, *Emergence of Sin*, 135). Croasmun sees value in both theories of transmission and himself adds to them "a theory of *mythological* transmission" (136; emphasis added), which is that of Paul: "Generation after generation is bound to sin because each generation is bound—that is, enslaved—to *Sin*. It is the dominion of this cosmic tyrant that accounts for the persistence of human sin" (136; emphasis original). Croasmun writes that "we can make sense of Paul's language about Sin as a cosmic power by understanding Sin as a mythological person emergent from a complex system of human transgressions" (177), both individual and social (105). That could also, according to Croasmun, be said for Satan, for which reason Sin and Satan might in fact be different names for "the same entity" (189). For Croasmun, the mythological explanation does not mean that such transmission is any less biological or social. In his view "the tyrant, Sin, owes its longevity through the ages to the stability of its biological and social bases." In other words, "the sinful sociocultural environment shapes the bodies of individuals" and together allow Sin as a cosmic tyrant to emerge and persist (136). It takes on a life of its own, as it were. Along similar lines Eastman writes that "Paul narrates sin as both external and internal, and as both environmental and agential: human beings are 'in sin' and 'under sin' as a kind of relation environment, yet also indwellt by sin personified as an agent acting in and through the self" (*Paul and the Person*, 122). According to Eastman, "Sin is not a decision made by self-determining individuals, but rather a socially mediated power greater than human beings yet operative through human thought, words, and deeds" (177).

24. This receives too little attention in the works of Barclay, Croasmun, and Eastman and its significance is therefore missed. See de Boer, *Defeat of Death*, 143–44 and

human being, Sin came into the world and through Sin Death [came into the world]. And so Death [subsequently] spread to all people because [of course, as the evidence indicates][25] all people sinned."

Death too is personified by Paul as a cosmic power. Even though Paul does not use the expression "under Death," nevertheless, Death, like Sin, has "reigned" (*basileuein*; 5:13, 17) and "lorded it" (*kyrieuein*; 6:9) over the world, over all humanity. It too, like Sin, is as an orb, realm, or domain. The inextricable link between Sin and Death is given expression repeatedly in the chapters 6–8 (cf. 6:16, 21; 7:5, 9–11, 13, 23, 24; 8:6, 10–11). Where there is Sin, there is also Death. Or as Paul puts in 5:21: "Sin reigned in Death." Death is the distinguishing mark, and result, of Sin's reign.

A comparison with 1 Corinthians 15, Paul's treatise on the resurrection of the dead, i.e., of those who have physically died, would suggest that *thanatos* in Romans 5:12–21 concerns physical, bodily demise, what we could call natural or biological death: "through a human being death . . . in Adam all die" (1 Cor 15:21–22; cf. Gen 2:17; 3:3–4, 19; *4 Ezra*; *2 Baruch*).[26] That understanding of death can certainly not be excluded here, given the references to the Christ's resurrection from the dead in the opening verses of chapter 6 (6:4, 5, 9) or the subsequent references to the "mortal body" (6:12) and the "mortal bodies" (8:12) of human beings (cf. 7:24; 8:10, 13, 23; 1 Cor 15:55–44). But, as noted in chapter 3 above, in contrast to 1 Corinthians 15, physical death is surely not where Paul's focus lies in Romans 5:12–21 or in the three chapters that follow. Paul here uses the term *thanatos* primarily in a metaphorical sense to signify the irremediable separation of human beings from God and thus their removal from life, i.e., life in God's presence and in accordance with the divine will. This metaphorical understanding of *thanatos* as separation from God applies also to those who are still physically alive but find themselves "under the power of Sin," as all human beings do. Death thus has a profoundly theological significance for Paul since it indicates something about the relationship of human beings to God, namely, *the end and the absence* of such a relationship.[27] When Paul refers to *thanatos*

---

the last chapter of this volume.

25. This represents my interpretation of the debated subordinating conjunction *eph' hō*. See de Boer, *Defeat of Death*, 158, 161, 236–37n42.

26. See chapter 3 above.

27. See Furnish, *Theology and Ethics*, 136. Barclay unfortunately for all intents and purposes reduces Paul's discourse concerning death in Romans 5–8 to physical demise: "It is not for nothing that Paul emphasizes several times in these chapters the mortality of the body . . . [N]ew creation life begins" in the case of believers "not on the other side, but on this side of death," which is "a residue of their Adamic heritage"; "they are dead to sin (6:11), but not to death," i.e., physical demise (*Paul and the Gift*, 501; cf. 502–3). The nuanced analysis Barclay applies to *charis* is absent from his discussion of *thanatos*.

as "the wages" of Sin (6:23), he has this primary theological significance of death in view. Death is the total absence of life, life before God in particular, and it thus signifies the end of all human possibilities and hopes. And that in turn means that prior to or apart from God's intervention in Christ, there was and is no remedy for the human plight since to be "under Sin" is also to be in the realm of Death, the realm of absolute and (from a human point of view) irremediable separation from God. It is only God who can bring life out of *thanatos*, something out of nothing (cf. Rom 4:17b). Only God can undo the ineluctable and utterly disastrous effect of Sin, that effect being *thanatos* (total separation from God and from life before God).

The reign and the realm of Sin completely coincide with the reign and the realm of Death, for where the one rules the other rules as well. Since that is the case, it is also the case that God in doing something about Death must do (and does do) something about Sin. A moral appeal to change one's ways (to repent) seems to make no sense in this context, and Paul does not make such an appeal.[28] Only God can rectify this situation (and, of course, Paul believes God has done so).

Sin and the Law

As pointed out in chapter 3 above, much of Romans seems to be concerned with making plain that the Law cannot be regarded as God's remedy for Sin.[29] According to 5:20, the Law "came in alongside" a situation determined not by willful, autonomous human transgression but by the twin powers of Sin and Death. The Law's effect was not to ameliorate that situation but to make it worse: the Law came in alongside "so that the trespass might increase." And that means that "Sin increased," which is to say, intensified and solidified its Death-dealing grip over human beings.[30] Paul continues

---

See also further below on the distinction maintained by Paul between mortality and actual physical dying, a distinction that is also absent from Barclay's analysis.

28. The single reference to repentance in Rom 2:4 is not an appeal to repent but part of Paul's indictment of the human being for presuming on "the riches and the forbearance and the patience" of God in the face of wrongdoing: Paul points out that "God's kindness" is supposed to "lead" someone "to repentance (*metanoia*)," which alas it has not done. Paul uses the Greek noun (*metanoia*) or verb (*metanoeō*) elsewhere in his genuine letters only in 2 Cor 7:9–10 (noun) and 2 Cor 12:11 (verb). By contrast these two terms occur some twenty-five times in Luke-Acts, for which repentance is thus a key theme. That is not the case in Paul's letters.

29. See now also Schnelle, "Auseinandersetzung," 86, 92–93.

30. Cf. already 3:20: "through the Law comes knowledge of Sin." See Mininger, *Uncovering*, 314–17.

along this line in chapter 7 of Romans. As "the Law of God" (7:22), the Law itself is "holy" and "spiritual" (7:12, 14) and thus not the culprit (Paul thereby *exonerates* the Law from all blame), but it is also an instrument of the power of Sin. Sin uses the Law or "the commandment," which is "holy and righteous and good" (7:12), as its "base of operations" (*aphormē*; 7:8–11), and does so to lethal effect. As the instrument of Sin, the Law not only cannot (cf. 8:3; Gal 3:21) deliver the righteousness and thus the eternal life it promises, it ironically also brought about what it was meant to overcome and prevent, namely, Death understood as permanent separation from God and thus from life. Sin perverted the Law's promise of life (7:10) by turning it into an instrument, perhaps more accurately, *the* instrument of Sin's Death-dealing hegemony (7:5, 8–10). To emphasize the point, Paul can go so far as to say here that "apart from the Law, Sin is dead" (7:8) and that the "coming" of the Law (the commandment) caused Sin to "come to life" (7:9).[31] For this reason, to be "under (the) Law" (6:14–15) is tantamount to being "under Sin" (3:9; 7:14).[32] That implicit equation seems to underlie much of the argument found beginning at 6:1 and extending into chapter 7. The Law, regrettably and lamentably, constitutes a dead end.

A presupposition of this argument about the inefficacy or weakness of the Law (8:3a) is that Sin is not a matter of the Law's transgression. Paul divorces Sin (and thus sinning) from the matter of Law observance. A transgression (*parabasis*) concerns a willful breaking (lit. a stepping over) of a given and recognized commandment. Transgression is what Paul calls "transgression *of the Law*," in 2:24. That in turn means that "where there is no law there is no transgression" either (4:15). Adam himself transgressed a specific divine commandment, as the account in Genesis indicates (Gen 2:16–17; 3:11), and for this reason Paul refers to "the transgression of Adam" (Rom 5:14). According to 5:13–14, however, "Death reigned from Adam to Moses"—thus, as Paul says, "*prior* to the Law"—because, as he continues, "Sin was in the world" during that time too. That means that those who lived in the pre-Mosaic period ("prior to the Law") had no divine commandment to transgress. By asserting that Sin was in the world prior to the giving of the Law, Paul in effect indicates that Sin is not a matter of the willful transgression of the Sinaitic Law. Because Sin was in the world prior to Moses, Death also reigned "even (*kai*) over those who did not sin" in the same way that

31. This passage shows how Paul can play with the terms life and death. Sin's "coming to life" actually effects "death" for human beings.

32. The phrase "under (the) Law," also used by Paul in Gal 3:23; 4:4–5, 21; 5:18, implies that just like Sin the Law is an enslaving power. See Mininger, *Uncovering*, 314–17 (on Rom 3:20).

Adam did (5:14), that is, by transgressing a given divine commandment.[33] The human condition is much more dire in Paul's view than the limitation of Sin/sinning to the transgression of God's Law would imply.

The Primal Sin and its Consequences

How then is Sin, and the sinning which results, to be regarded?[34] If not transgression of the Law, or of God's commandment, what then?

It is significant, I think, that Paul avoids the term "transgression" (*parabasis*) after 5:14 when referring to Adam and his descendants.[35] Instead, he resorts to the term "trespass" (*paraptōma*). *Paraptōma* signifies a falling away (cf. *parapiptein*)—a falling away from God is evidently in view (cf. 1:19–23). The real sin of Adam in transgressing God's commandment in Eden was that it constituted a *trespass*, a term used in Wisdom of Solomon 10:1 in connection with Adam's fall.[36] The trespass of Adam, his signature "disobedience" (5:19), is a falling away from God, i.e., his rejection and repudiation of God. This is the sin, in the sense of "sinful deed" (cf. 3:25), that was and is repeated by each and every human being in turn, also those who lived before Moses and thus before the Law could "register" it. "All sinned" (3:23; 5:12d) and "fall short of the glory of God" (3:23) because all *trespassed*, thereby producing the aggregate "many trespasses" referred to in 5:16. According to 4:25, where Paul cites what appears to be a traditional formulation, Christ died for this cosmic accumulation of trespasses by Adam's descendants: he "was handed over on account of our trespasses" (cf. 2 Cor 5:19; Col 2:13; Eph 1:7; 2:1, 5). In 5:20, the statement that "the trespass increased" is interpreted to mean that "Sin increased." Paul's point appears here to be that the vast increase or accumulation of trespasses led to the increase or wide extension of Sin's hegemony: Sin reigned in the universal domain of Death. And "so Death spread to all people, because all sinned," that is, because all repudiated God. This is the primary sin that characterizes and informs all subsequent misbehavior. Sin is the failure to acknowledge God, a failure with disastrous consequences for human life on earth (1:18ff.)[37]

33. Note that in 2:12, Paul refers to Gentiles "sinning" outside of the Law or apart from the Law.

34. There is no Sin without sinning for Paul. See nn. 12 and 19 above.

35. See de Boer, *Defeat of Death*, 165–67. Also chapter 3 above.

36. NRSV, e.g., unfortunately translates the term here as "transgression."

37. See Käsemann, "God's Image and Sinners," 114–15 ("Idol worship is original sin").

One issue about which Paul is not as clear as we might wish is whether Adam's trespass and its repetition by each of his descendants is being regarded as the *result* or as the *cause* of Sin's hegemony. "Through one human being, Sin came into the world" (5:12a). Does Paul mean that the rule of Sin is the result of Adam's trespass? Or that the trespass itself was caused by Sin? And what would be the answer for Adam's descendants who repeat his trespass: Is the rule of Sin the result of their trespasses or are their trespasses the result of Sin's hegemony?[38] This dilemma reflects the old debate between corporate destiny and individual responsibility, between determinism and free will. Put otherwise: are human beings merely victims of powers beyond their control or can they (also) be held accountable for what they do?[39] Paul's answer seems ultimately to be both-and rather than either-or.

Some would read 5:12 as Paul's correction of the idea of corporate destiny in the first half of the verse with the notion of individual responsibility in the second. Adam's transgression caused the fatality of death to come upon all people (cf. 1 Cor 15:21–22) but since "all sinned" all are actually individually responsible for their own deaths. That is one notable way of reading 5:12.[40] As indicated in the chapter 3 above, a comparison with the appeals to Adam in such Jewish apocalyptic texts as *4 Ezra* and *2 Baruch* shows that this interpretation is unlikely. To cite from *2 Baruch*: "Adam sinned and death was decreed against those who were to be born" (23:4); "when he [Adam] transgressed, untimely death came into being" (56:6; cf. Gen 2:17; 3:19). Along with such passages, there are others, however: "Adam is . . . not the cause, except for himself, but each of us has become our own Adam" (54:15). Similar passages are found in *4 Ezra*. In these Jewish apocalyptic works Adam functions both as a corporate personality whose trespass determines all subsequent human destiny (all die because of Adam's fall) *and* as the paradigmatic human being whose sinful deed sets the pattern

38. In chapter 3 above, I have written: "The power of Death came upon all people, since all, by being under the power of Sin, sinned. Sinning is not the result and the mark of a choice made by an autonomous individual; it is the result and the mark of a cosmological force that has come into the world and has reigned over human beings since the time of Adam, bringing Death in its wake" (from "Paul's Mythologizing Program in Romans 5–8," 14; also earlier in *Defeat of Death*, 161). See also on Rom 5:12d, Schnelle, "Auseinandersetzung," 88–89 (Sin leads to or causes sinning). While this interpretation may on the whole be a correct reading of 5:12–21 insofar as this passage provides a description of the *factual* situation apart from Christ, I now think that this formulation may need some nuancing in light of the fact in view of Paul's total argument. See further below on the primal sin of Adam and subsequent humanity.

39. Bultmann wrestles with this issue in *Theology*, 1.249–58 (see chapter 3 above), as does Croasmun, *Emergence of Sin*.

40. See in particular, Bultmann, "Adam and Christ." See also Bultmann, *Theology*, 1.249–58.

for his descendants (all die because all repeated Adam's fall). That seems logically inconsistent, to us at any rate, but Paul seems to adopt it in Rom 5:12. As in *4 Ezra* and *2 Baruch*, Adam's two functions go together.[41] Where Paul deviates from the treatment of Adam as found in *2 Baruch* and *4 Ezra* is in his conception of Sin and Death as cosmic tyrants that reign and rule over human beings whereby the Law, which is the God-given solution to the problem of Adam's fall in *4 Ezra* and *2 Baruch* (and in Jewish thought generally), is excluded by Paul as the remedy. It is merely a tool in the hands of Sin and brings death (Death) rather than life.

Looking back at chapter 1 of Romans we see that Paul reproaches humanity for having "exchanged the glory of the immortal God" for idols (1:23). They are, however, "without excuse" since "what can be known about God is plain to them. . . . Ever since the creation of the world his invisible nature, namely, his eternal power and deity, has been clearly perceived in the things that have been made" (1:19–20). It is "because they exchanged the truth about God for a lie and worshiped and served the creature rather than the Creator" (1:25) that God "gave them up (*paredōken*) in the lust of their hearts to impurity" (1:24) and also "gave them up (*paredōken*) to dishonorable passions" (1:26). God's handing over of humanity to such forms of sinful behavior is evidently the revelation of God's wrath mentioned in 1:18. Paul goes on to repeat the point a third time: "since they did not see fit to acknowledge God, God gave them up (*paredōken*) to a base mind and improper conduct" (1:28), which are catalogued in 1:29–31. Those who do such awful things are "worthy of death" he concludes (1:32). Death here again means eternal separation from God and from life, but now clearly as a punishment for sinful behavior (cf. *2 Baruch*; *4 Ezra*). Eternal death so understood will be their lot "on the day of wrath when God's righteous judgment will be revealed" (2:5).[42]

One could thus say that as a result of repudiating God and exchanging God for idols—which, I have suggested, is the trespass (or primal sin) referred to in chapter 5:12–21—God handed the human world over to Sin's

---

41. Cf. de Boer, *Defeat of Death*, 161. Also noted by Wedderburn, "The Theological Structure," citing a number of texts, including *4 Ezra* 3:7–11; 7:116–19 and *2 Bar.* 48:42–47; 54:14, and concluding that "the balance of an apparent determinism with a stress on individual responsibility and guilt is a pattern of thought well attested in Judaism" (439); Käsemann, *Romans*, 148, citing *2 Bar.* 54:15, 19.

42. See the further references to "wrath" in 1:18; 2:8; 3:5; 4:15; 5:9 (cf. 9:22; 12:19; 13:4–5). Evidently Paul sees a distinction between God's present wrath and his future wrath. See Mininger, *Uncovering*, 175: "Taking 1:18 and 2:5 together, one can therefore say that Paul describes a two stage unfolding of the display of God's wrath, *now* upon some who have already been handed over and *not yet* upon hypocrites presently experiencing God's temporary patience" (emphasis original).

reign (and thus Death's as well). The terrible human condition is the result of an initial human act, Adam's trespass, which is also repeated by each and every human being after him. This trespass is the conscious, deliberate repudiation of God and the result is a world ruled by Sin and Death. The joint rule of Sin and Death constitutes the realm of the repudiation of God, on the one hand, and irremediable separation from God, on the other. These two go hand in hand. The first leads ineluctably to the second. When Paul illustrates (or supports) his claim in 3:9 that all people are under Sin with scriptural citations, his catena of passages from Scripture concludes in 3:18 with a slightly modified citation from Psalm 36: "There is no fear of God before their eyes" (LXX Ps 35:2, which has "his eyes"). They have rejected and repudiated God (cf. Deut 6:5–6). That is the basic problem (godlessness), the basic sin that leads to the hegemony of Sin (and thus Death) over the human world, causing all sorts of iniquity, wickedness, and impurity. It seems, therefore, that the hegemony of Sin is the result of the original, primal sinful act of rejecting or repudiating God, i.e., exchanging God for false gods, exchanging the truth for a lie.[43] Every human being repeats this primal sin, thereby becoming a slave of Sin with its terrible consequences for human life, which for this reason ends in Death (the realm of definitive and irremediable separation from God and from life before God). Or as Bultmann famously put it: "sin came into the world by sinning."[44]

We see something similar in chapter 7. Paul can here say that he was "once alive apart from the Law, but when the commandment came, sin came to life and I died" (7:9). Paul evidently here suggests with polemical intent that the situation of Adam's descendants to whom the universally applicable Law came is analogous to the situation of Adam to whom the commandment came (the "I" is probably Paul playing the role of the Adamic self, looked at from the vantage point of Christ).[45] Paul evidently thinks that "the commandment" of the Mosaic Law functioned in a way similar to the commandment given to Adam. The commandment caused Sin to come to life and thus paradoxically to bring about the fatal result it sought to prevent (7:9–10). It "deceived me," Paul writes, with a clear allusion to the story of Adam, and "it

43. See Gaventa, "Cosmic Power of Sin," 233: "Paul's depiction of humankind opens with an action taken by humanity rather than by another power . . . humanity's refusal of God's lordship meant that God conceded humanity for a time to the lordship of another."

44. Bultmann, Theology, 1.251. On the one hand, Bultmann writes, "the sin of humanity after Adam is attributed to Adam's sin and . . . it therefore appears as the consequence of a curse for which mankind is not itself responsible"; on the other hand, while the human situation is one of "an enslavement to powers," it is nevertheless one for which the human being "is himself responsible" (Theology, 1.257).

45. See n. 16 above.

killed me" (7:11). This way of looking at the matter of the coming of the Law seemingly cannot be logically reconciled with 5:13–14 where Sin and Death are in the world prior to the coming of the Law. According to chapter 7, when the Law came, the result was the same as when the commandment not to eat of a certain tree came to Adam: Sin came into the picture, intensified its grip on human beings, bringing Death in its wake.

From what I have sketched, then, one could argue that for Paul human beings *in principle* had and have the ability not to sin, i.e., not to repudiate God (cf. Augustine's *posse non peccare*, able not to sin), but also that *in actual fact* they were, and are, *unable* not to sin (*non posse non peccare*).[46] The principle (able not to sin) makes it possible to call human beings to account for their sinful actions, their complicity in (the establishment and ongoing reality of) the reigns of Sin and Death,[47] whereas the *factual* reality of enslavement to Sin's power (not able not to sin) makes divine intervention necessary, or better, explains why God has indeed invaded the world under the dominion of Sin and Death in order to replace their reign with the reign of his Grace as revealed and made effective in Christ.

The issue is then this *factual* reality and why it is what it is and why (ever since Adam) it is inevitable.

The Weakness of the Flesh

In 5:6–10, Paul summarizes in passing the human condition under Sin. Paul here lists those for whom Christ died: the ungodly (5:6), sinners (5:8), and enemies (5:10). The ungodly, sinners, and enemies—these are descriptions of Adamic human beings, i.e., those who have repudiated God and thus come to be slaves of Sin. (That is probably the reason why "ungodly" is the first term used). Christ dies for them, i.e., "for us," and did so "while we were weak." This phrase, which stands at the beginning of 5:6, is not to be construed as a reproach but as a neutral description of human beings as created beings. Weakness is closely associated with life "in the flesh," something that

46. Augustine, "Nature and Grace," 137–38 (par. 57).

47. Eastman, *Paul and the Person*, 111: "Within this situation human actors are not simply passive victims, but rather are both captive and complicit," so that it is possible to speak of "humanity's collusion" with Sin. See also the extensive analysis of Croasmun on this point (*Emergence*, 109–11, 137–39, 175–77). His book is an attempt "to synthesize Bultmann's account of personal responsibility for sin, Käsemann's account of Sin's tyranny, and the liberationist phenomenology of unjust structural coercion" (176). See further on the notion of complicity, Martyn, "Afterword," 163. Ziegler, *Militant Grace*, xv, xvii, 59 ("women and men subjected to Sin are not merely its passive victims; they also become its active servants," summarizing the work of Käsemann).

is picked up in chapters 7 and 8.[48] So Paul refers to "the weakness of your flesh" as a given in 6:19 (the first time Paul refers to the flesh in chapters 5–8). That weakness of the flesh makes it an easy prey for Sin: "I am fleshly, sold under Sin" (7:14; cf. 7:5).[49]

When Paul remarks that "Sin dwells in me" in 7:17, he goes on to say, "I know that nothing good dwells in me, that is, in my flesh" (7:18). It is Sin that dwells in his flesh. Indeed, in 8:3, he refers to "Sin in the flesh" and can even virtually equate the two when he writes here of "the flesh of Sin." To "walk" or "live according to the flesh" (8:4, 12–13) then describes life under the power of Sin, with as result a "mindset of the flesh" (to phronēma tēs sarkos) that "is hostile to God" (8:7). It is for this reason, then, that "those who are in the flesh cannot [as a matter of fact] please God" (8:8).

If the weakness of the flesh makes human beings an easy prey for Sin, that then also counts for Death. Here the terms "mortal body" (6:12) and "mortal bodies" (8:11) are relevant. "Mortal" does not mean "dead" but "subject to Death" or, perhaps more accurately, "susceptible or vulnerable to Death," for that is what the human body as weak, i.e., as fleshly, is.[50] The body is "the body of Death" (7:24), the body that is "dead (nekron) on account of Sin" (8:10), for which reason it can also be called "the body of Sin" (6:6), i.e., the body ruled by Sin. The mortal body has inherent desires (epithymiai) that are exploited by Sin (6:12; cf. 7:8: "Sin wrought in me all desire"). The "members (melē)" of the body can be co-opted by Sin to serve as "weapons of wickedness" (6:13), thereby becoming "slaves to impurity and iniquity" (6:19), what Paul in 8:13 summarizes as "the practices/deeds (praxeis) of the body" (cf. 7:5).

So to return to 5:6: "while we were weak," i.e., while we were "in the flesh," while we were in our "mortal bodies," and thus vulnerable to the dual

48. See Eastman, Paul and the Person, 121: "Sin is here [7:14] depicted as something that takes over ownership of the ego through its fleshly existence." The self is "invaded by a personified power that radically compromises its agency," which means that "the porous fleshly body, understood both as individual and as communal corporeal existence, is taken over by sin." Along similar lines, Croasmun, Emergence of Sin, 112–24.

49. See Timmins, Romans 7, 88: "'The weakness of the flesh' is an anthropological condition, linked to the present age determined by Adam, with its characteristic corruption and moral impotency. In a context dominated by both implicit and explicit references to the body, this is the most plausible understanding of the term."

50. See de Boer, Defeat of Death, 132 (on 1 Cor 15:50–57). Paul's uses the term "body (sōma)" in two, overlapping ways, to designate the mortal, fleshly body of an individual human being and the collective social body. It is not always possible, or perhaps necessary, to distinguish them (e.g., "the body of Sin" in 6:6 or "the body of Death" in 7:24). Cf. Eastman, Paul and the Person, 120–25; Croasmun, Emergence of Sin, 112–22.

rule of Sin and Death, with the result that we became "ungodly," "sinners," and "enemies" of God, Christ died "for us."

God's Remedy

Particularly as God's enemies human beings need peace or reconciliation with God. And that is what they receive through the death of Christ "for us" (5:8): "we have peace with God" (5:1), "we have now received reconciliation" (5:10). On the basis of faith, through the justifying death of Christ (5:1, 9), believers are given the righteousness (Christ's) that makes them (morally) acceptable to God (5:15–21). They are no longer regarded by God as ungodly people, as sinners (in the primal sense of the term: repudiators of God), or as enemies of God. Through faith they have come to acknowledge God's claim on their lives and attention spans.

These stirring assertions would perhaps not amount to much if Christ's death did not also involve deliverance from Sin's deadly rule, which is the realm of the rejection and repudiation of God. That is the theme of the opening paragraphs of chapter 6. Here Christ's death is spoken of not in terms of "dying for us," but in another way, which is to be found in 6:10: "the death he died he died to Sin." Paul here uses the expression "to die to something." This metaphorical expression means "to become completely separated from something." Christ quite literally died of course, but in so dying "he died to Sin" (cf. 6:2, 11; 7:6), i.e., Christ became completely separated from the power of Sin. He was "under Sin," like the rest of humanity, but he did not commit sin, did not succumb to Sin's hegemony (cf. 8:3; 2 Cor 5:21; Phil 2:6–11). He refused to be complicit in Sin's hegemony but remained faithful to God to the very end, the very bitter end. And that was his victory, one validated by his resurrection. For this reason, it can also be said that "Death no longer lords it over him" (6:9). At one level, this claim is understood quite literally, in terms of "Christ having being raised from the dead" (6:9; also 6:4) and his "resurrection" (6:5), but at another level it is also understood metaphorically to signify that he no longer abides, as does Adamic humanity before and apart from Christ, in the realm of separation from God, which is what Death signifies. Because Christ died to Sin, he lived and lives to God (6:10; cf. Gal 2:19).

Believers share in Christ's death to Sin (6:2); that is what Paul wants to emphasize here with his rhetorical question: "How can we *who died to Sin* still live in it?" (6:1b). He uses the tradition and language of baptismal initiation, a bodily event, as a way of giving expression to participation in Christ's death to Sin: "all of us who have been baptized into Christ Jesus, have been baptized into his death," that is, his death to Sin. "Our old human being was crucified with him," i.e., was put to death, metaphorically speaking, so that "the body of Sin," which is the body ruled by Sin, "might be destroyed," and that means that it is "no longer a slave of Sin" (6:6). "For someone who has died [with Christ to Sin], has been freed [lit. justified, *dedikaiōtai*] from Sin" (6:7), a claim which Paul repeats in 6:18 and 22, using the expression *eleutheroun apo*, to set free or liberate from (cf. 6:20; 7:3; 8:2, 21). Slaves need to be freed or liberated and that is what has happened to those have been baptized into Christ. On the other side of that death to Sin lies "newness of life" (6:4), which is a participation in Christ's resurrection life, not just in the future but also now, and is characterized by righteousness, the polar opposite of sin.[51] Believers are to consider themselves "dead to Sin and living to God in Christ Jesus" (6:11). "If Christ is in you, [although] the body is dead (*nekron*, a corpse) on account of Sin, the Spirit is life on account of righteousness" (8:10).[52]

It is then as liberated human beings, living by the power of God's grace (5:21; 6:14–15), that Paul exhorts the believers in Rome: "Let not Sin therefore reign in your (pl.) mortal body so that you obey its desires" (6:12). It is Christ's liberating action that for the first time makes the human being truly morally addressable and accountable. "Do not yield your members (limbs, organs) to Sin as instruments of wickedness, but yield yourselves to God as people who have been brought from death to life, and your members as weapons of righteousness. For Sin will not rule over you, since you are not under Law but under grace" (6:13–14).[53] Believers in other words have been brought into the sphere of God's powerful, redemptive grace (5:2, 21; cf. 3:24). They are "under Grace," rather than "under (the) Law" (6:14–15) where Sin can exert its lethal control. If to be under Law is tantamount to being under Sin, to be under Grace is tantamount to being under Righteousness, here also personified as a power and a name for God (6:18, 19, 20). Believers are now, paradoxically, "slaves of Righteousness" (6:18; cf. 6:13), which is to say "enslaved to God" (6:22; cf. 6:13). They are not free in the sense of people who have no accountability to God; they are not autonomous, i.e., free to do whatever they want. Rather, they find their freedom

51. Cf. Eastman, *Paul and the Person*, 177: "Redemption is therefore . . . a matter . . . of liberation from one realm of power to another, from the rule of sin and death to life in Christ. In both cases, the person is constituted by participation in realities larger than the self or than merely human relationships."

52. Cf. Käsemann, *Romans*, 224: "in the context of the antithesis *dikaiosynē* cannot refer to the sentence of justification. . . . It is rather walking by the Spirit in bodily service in a way which is pleasing to God."

53. Martyn, "Epilogue," 180–81.

in the reign and realm of God's powerful, redemptive Grace. In obedience (6:16) to God, believers are given back their true humanity, for they have been liberated from Sin and from Death, being given righteousness and thus life in their stead. This new life is "the impossible possibility" (Barth) created by God's intervention in Christ.

If Sin leads to or brings Death, God's redemptive righteousness leads to or grants life, not just in the future but also now, whenever believers stop being complicit in Sin's lethal reign and yield themselves to God (5:21; 6:8, 11, 22, 23). After all, as Ernst Käsemann has emphasized, baptism marks a change of lordship.

Conclusion

Paul's position can perhaps be summed up as follows: Though victims of Sin, human beings cannot entirely escape responsibility for the wrong that they do (cf. 1:20: "they are without excuse"),[54] and if they become believers who put their trust in Christ, they cannot claim full credit for the good that they may subsequently do, for they cannot achieve or do what is right without the Spirit which "dwells" in them (cf. 8:9, 11; cf. 8:10, 13, 14). In human action before and apart from Christ, there is another actor besides human beings, namely, Sin. By the same token, for believers in Christ there is another actor who cannot be ignored, namely, the Spirit of God and Christ.[55] If sinful deeds are never simply actions by autonomous human beings for Paul (Sin as an alien power with a domain must also be taken into account), the good works of believers are never simply the achievements of human beings autonomously deciding to do what is right (the role of the Spirit must also be acknowledged).

---

54. See Martyn, "Afterword," 163: "Paul emphasizes his apocalyptic view of Sin as an enslaving power without altogether eclipsing his view of sin as a human act."

55. See Martyn, "Epilogue"; "Afterword"; "The Gospel Invades Philosophy."

Chapter 5

Cross and Cosmos in Galatians

Introduction

PAUL USES THE TERM *kosmos* in two passages of Galatians and these shall be the focus of this chapter. First, in 4:3, while looking back to the common past of believers in Christ, Paul writes that "when we were children, we were enslaved under the *stoicheia* of the *kosmos*." Second, in 6:14, where the term occurs twice, Paul writes about "the cross of our Lord Jesus Christ, through which to me the *kosmos* has been crucified and I to the *kosmos*."[1]

At issue here is the precise reference of the term *kosmos* in the two passages. Does the term refer to the same reality in 4:3 and 6:14? A second question naturally follows when we take into account that in both passages the *kosmos* being referred to belongs to the past of believers: To what extent are the two passages related to one another at the level of soteriology?

I shall argue that in 4:3 the *kosmos* in view is evidently the physical universe which is comprised of certain elements; in 6:14, however, the *kosmos* in view pertains to the religion of the Law, represented in the immediate context by the practice of circumcision (6:12–13, 15). On this point I differ from a number of exegetes who argue that the term has the same referent in the two passages.[2] I shall also argue, however, that despite the different *referential* meanings of the term *kosmos* in the two passages, they do bear a close relationship to one another at the level of soteriology.

---

1. Translations of passages from Galatians follow those defended in my commentary: de Boer, *Galatians*. Beverly Gaventa has convincingly reminded us that "the governing theological antithesis in Galatians" is actually not "between Christ and the law and between the cross and circumcision" but "between Christ/new creation and cosmos" (*Our Mother*, 103, 108). "The theology reflected in Galatians" she points out, "is first of all about Jesus Christ and the new creation God has begun in him (1:1–4; 6:14–15), and only in the light of that christocentrism can Paul's remarks concerning the law be understood" (*Our Mother*, 102).

2. Cf. esp. on different grounds, Adams, *Constructing the World*, 229; Martyn, *Galatians*, 405–6.

Before I turn to an exegetical analysis of Gal 4:3 and 6:14 a very brief word about the rhetorical situation of the letter is in order. Paul addresses his Galatian readers in 4:21 as "you who want to be under the Law." This characterization of the Galatians reflects the fact that after Paul founded the churches in Galatia (cf. 1:2, 8–9, 11; 3:1; 4:13) new preachers (Christian Jews who have a close relationship with the mother church in Jerusalem) have come into the Galatian churches and have been putting pressure on the new believers in Galatia to adopt the practice of circumcision (1:6–9; 3:1; 4:17; 5:2–4, 7–12; 6:12–13).[3] The practice of circumcision is a communal and a family matter, pertaining not simply to individuals or men. By adopting the practice of circumcision, the churches in Galatia, consisting of both women and men, will be incorporated into God's people, also known as the offspring of Abraham (3:29), and as a result will be under obligation to observe the remainder of the covenantal Law. Among that remainder is, e.g., the obligation to observe feast days such as the Sabbath and Passover. Paul writes in 4:10 about the Galatians "observing days and months and seasons and years." His consternation about this turn of events is palpable. The Letter to the Galatians represents Paul's passionate attempt to prevent this turn to the Law in Galatia from going any further, indeed to reverse it, and to announce to the believers in Galatia that as the recipients of what was promised to Abraham, namely, the Spirit of God's Son (3:14, 18, 22, 29; 4:6–7), they *are* the offspring of Abraham apart from any observance of the Law (2:15–16; 3:1–5, 29).

Finally, I should note that in this chapter I shall refer to what I call Paul's "negative soteriology" and his "positive soteriology." What I mean by these terms can perhaps best be illustrated by what Paul says in 2:19–20: "I . . . died to the Law" (negative soteriology) "so that I might live to God" (positive soteriology). "It is no longer I who live" (negative soteriology) "but Christ who lives in me" (positive soteriology). They are two sides of the same coin for Paul, the positive presupposing the negative.

Galatians 6:14

Because the occasion of the letter finds its clearest expression in the letter closing in 6:11–18, I begin with 6:14, which is part of that closing. In this passage, Paul's focus is on those who would seek to impose the Law on the Galatians, beginning with the rite of circumcision, whereas in 4:3 his

---

3. For more detail and support, see Excursus 4 in de Boer, *Galatians*, 50–61. An earlier version of this excursus is de Boer, "The New Preachers in Galatia."

focus is on the believers in Galatia, former Gentiles who now want to be under the Law.

Apart from the final benediction in verse 18, the closing constitutes a recapitulation of the argument of the letter, which Paul writes in his own hand (vs. 11). In verses 12 and 13, Paul offers a final rebuke of the new preachers in Galatia, focusing on their central demand for circumcision. Verses 14–15 emphasize the significance of the cross of Christ and provide a final contextualized summary of the gospel as preached by Paul. The closing thus places over against one another two central topics of the epistle: circumcision and the cross.[4] The former (circumcision) encompasses the primary aim of the new preachers in Galatia, to get the Galatians to adopt the practice of circumcision and then, as the necessary result of that first step, to observe the remainder of the Law; the latter (the cross) encapsulates Paul's theology with respect to circumcision and the Law and does so in a particular way.

In Galatians 6:12–13, Paul provides a catalogue of accusations against the new preachers active in Galatia. These accusations are a mix of historically plausible facts about the new preachers (vss. 12b, 13b) and unprovable assumptions about their supposed motivations and aims (vss. 12a, 12c, 13a, 13c). Historically plausible is certainly the charge that the new preachers are "putting pressure" on the Galatians "to practice circumcision" in vs. 12, a charge repeated in vs. 13 in slightly different words: "they are wanting you to practice circumcision." Although the nature of the pressure being exerted is not elaborated, neither the new preachers nor the Galatians will disagree with what Paul says here. With respect to the new preachers' supposed motivation and aims in insisting on the practice of circumcision in the Galatian churches, Paul makes two related but unprovable accusations: the new preachers, he writes, "want to make a good showing in the flesh" (vs. 12) and they "want to boast" in "the flesh" of the Galatians (vs. 13). The term "flesh" is here surely an allusion to their demand for circumcision (cf. LXX Gen 17:9–14: circumcision involves removing "the flesh of your foreskin"). Paul virtually accuses the new preachers of counting the number of foreskins severed with the circumcision knife. They are, he suggests, after trophies, presumably (so Paul intimates) in order to impress their fellow Jews, perhaps especially Law-observant Christian Jews such as James and the circumcision party in Jerusalem (cf. 2:12).

A deeper meaning may be that Paul accuses the new preachers of wanting to make a good showing "in the realm of the Flesh," with a capital F, rather than in that of the Spirit (5:13—6:10; cf. 3:3). In 5:13—6:10, Paul presents the

4. See Weima, "Gal 6:11–18."

fleshly circumcision being recommended by the new preachers as an indication of a greater problem, that of "the Flesh."[5] In that earlier passage, Paul
widens the scope as it were, moving from the particular instance of the fleshly circumcision being demanded by the new preachers to a consideration of
"the Flesh" as a cosmic power equivalent to and interchangeable with "Sin"
(1:17; 3:22). Only the Spirit of Christ is sufficient to counter its attacks on human life, i.e., its destructive impact on relations between human beings. The
coming of the Spirit has unmasked this power in all its malignancy and at
the same time inaugurated a victorious apocalyptic struggle against it. Those
"wanting to make a good showing in the Flesh" (capital F) do not know that
there has been a change of regimes (3:25); they still orient their lives to the
Flesh instead of to the Spirit of God's Son (cf. 4:6; 6:8), with all the dangers
for communal life that involves, as given expression in 5:13-24 ("works of
the Flesh"). The Flesh threatens to undo what Paul's initial preaching of the
gospel in Galatia had brought about (3:1; 4:13-14). Thus, the accusation that
the new preachers "want to make a good showing in the flesh" in the letter
closing could be a reference to "the Flesh" with a capital F. However, it must
also be said that Paul himself does not connect the dots explicitly; he leaves
it up to his readers/hearers in Galatia to do that. But that may well be his
intent and, if so, there are consequences for how he wants the Galatians to
understand the *kosmos* referred to in 6:14.

Paul also charges that the new preachers insist on circumcision "only
in order that they not be persecuted for the cross of Christ" (vs. 12). This
charge recalls 5:11, where Paul has also linked what he there calls "preaching circumcision" to the avoidance of persecution for the sake of the cross:
"if I am still preaching circumcision, why am I still being persecuted? Then
the offense (*skandalon*) of the cross has been destroyed (*katērgētai*)," i.e.,
devoid of all significance (cf. 3:17; 2:21). In both passages "circumcision"
and "the cross (of Christ)" stand in stark opposition to one another; to reject
the former (preaching circumcision) is to incur persecution for the sake of
the latter (preaching the cross). In Paul's view, then, the new preachers are
advocating circumcision for the believers in Galatia not from altruistic mo-
tives (the presumed salvation of the Galatians through their incorporation
into Israel as a first and necessary step) but from selfish concerns—they
want to avoid persecution for the cross of Christ. It is impossible to know
whether Paul is right in this charge against the new preachers (the word
"only" in any event points to a polemical exaggeration of this charge) or
whether he is here merely extrapolating from his own experience, both as
a former persecutor of the church and as the persecuted apostle of Christ

5. Cf. de Boer, *Galatians*, 329-32, 335-39, 403.

(cf. 6:17). However that may be, in 6:12, as in 5:11, Paul effectively accuses the new preachers of being unwilling to discern and to accept the radical implications of the cross of Christ for the observance of the Law (2:16, 21), beginning with the rite of circumcision (2:3; 5:2–4), implications that he himself has painfully experienced in his own body (6:17 referring to "the *stigmata* [scars] of Jesus" he carries on his own body). It remains for them "an offense." In 1 Cor 1:23, Paul writes that "we preach Christ crucified, an offense (*skandalon*) to Jews." In Galatians, the proclamation of the crucified Christ, the cross (cf. 1 Cor 1:18), is evidently an offense to Christian Jews such as the new preachers active in Galatia because, so Paul claims, it has brought about the end of the Law as the reliable basis for righteousness and life (cf. 1:13–16; 2:16, 21; 3:1, 13–14, 21, 23–25; 4:4–5).

Paul's charge in 6:13 that the new preachers have as their goal to "boast in the (circumcised) flesh" of the Galatians provides a rhetorical foil for his articulation, in 6:14, of what in his view legitimate boasting entails: "But let it not be for me to boast except in the cross of our Lord Jesus Christ, . . . " Paul becomes personal here ("me"), as he had been in chapters 1–2, which suggests that Paul is here contrasting two forms of evangelism, one carried out by the new preachers (vss. 12–13), the other carried out by Paul (vss. 14–17; cf. 5:11). Whereas they (according to Paul's perception) aim to boast in the number of converts they have made (cf. 6:4) and then on the basis of a theology that in Paul's view, "turns the gospel of Christ into its opposite" (so 1:7), Paul aims, in his preaching of the gospel (2:2; 3:1), "to boast . . . [only] in the cross of our Lord Jesus Christ." The reference to "*our* Lord Jesus Christ" is notably confessional and solemnly calls attention to the one who is the Lord not only of Paul but also of the Galatians and the new preachers among them. By using the word "our," he calls the Galatians and the new preachers to his side. Their common Lord has a cross and this fact cannot be ignored or evaded.

As I have already intimated, "the cross" (5:11), which is "the cross of Christ" (6:12) or "the cross of our Lord Jesus Christ" (6:14), is Pauline short-hand for "the crucifixion of Christ" and, in the context of the Letter to the Galatians, all that event entails with respect to circumcision and the Law.[6] In that sense, the cross—the crucifixion—is also a matter of soteriology. The soteriology of "the cross" represents, however, what I have called "the negative side" of Paul's soteriology as we see on the basis of what Paul writes in the remainder of 6:14. The cross "of our Lord Jesus Christ" has effected a double crucifixion, that of the *kosmos* and that of Paul himself, each in

6. Paul here uses the figure of metalepsis, or double metonymy (cf. Bullinger, *Figures of Speech*, 608–11). The "cross" stands for the very real, literal crucifixion of Christ but also for the soteriological effects of this event.

relation to the other: Through the cross, "the *kosmos* has been crucified to me and I [have been crucified] to the *kosmos*" (vs. 14b). Paul's language of crucifixion is here metaphorical and hyperbolic, yet also realistic and serious. It is not just a figure of speech, but a vivid interpretation of a truly painful and real experience. Paul here articulates the "negative" soteriological consequences of Christ's faithful death on the cross (cf. 2:16, 19–21; 3:1). In other places and contexts Paul can use the expression "to die to [something]" to articulate these negative soteriological consequences, as in 2:19 where as we have seen he writes "I . . . died to the Law" (cf. e.g., Rom 6:2). To be crucified "to" someone or something, i.e., with respect to someone or something, is an intensification of this "dying to" language. It suggests a violent and painful death with respect to someone or something. Paul uses the language of crucifixion in this context to underscore the destructive soteriological effects of Christ's death by crucifixion.[7]

Paul announces, first, that with respect to himself ("to me," *emoi*) the *kosmos* has been crucified, violently put to death. What is this *kosmos*? The word carries the strong nuance of "order."[8] A (or the) *kosmos* is assumed to be an orderly, coherent whole. Consistent with contemporary usage,[9] furthermore, Paul uses the term elsewhere to refer to "the (whole) human world" (e.g., Rom 5:12), "planet earth" (e.g., Rom 1:8), or "the physical universe in its entirety" (e.g., Rom 1:20).[10] None of these meanings easily applies here. Given the immediate context, the *kosmos* to which Paul here refers is most probably the religion of the Law, what he has earlier in this letter characterized as "Judaism," *Ioudaismos* (1:13–14), and as "works of the Law," *erga nomou* (2:16; 3:2, 5, 10), which includes circumcision (2:3; 5:2–12; 6:12–13).[11] That particular *kosmos*, the *kosmos* structured by the practice of circumcision and the observance of the Law, has been utterly destroyed, in any case, for Paul himself as a believer in Christ (cf. Rom 6:6).[12] He is probably not here simply giving his personal, subjective opinion ("As far as I am concerned . . . ") but describing what he takes to be an objective situation, the effect of Christ's death on an objective cross and (the effect of) his own experienced participation in that objective death. That world of the

7. See de Boer, *Galatians*, 172, on 3:1.

8. Cf. LSJ, 985.

9. BAGD, 561–63.

10. It is not always possible to distinguish clearly between these three meanings in all instances. Especially the first two can overlap.

11. For this reason the omission here of the definite article with the word *kosmos* may be significant, though it may also be purely stylistic (cf. 1 Cor 3:22; 2 Cor 5:19). See BDF #253:4.

12. Burton, *Galatians*, 354.

Law no longer exists "for him." For that reason, he can go on to say that with respect to the world of the Law that he himself has also been crucified ("and I to the *kosmos*"), a claim that echoes 2:19, where he writes: "I died to the Law. . . . I have been crucified with Christ," i.e., to the Law. Faith *in* Christ is participation in "the faith *of* Christ" (2:16), that is to say, in Christ's faithful death (2:20–21).[13] For this very reason Paul can speak of this participation as crucifixion *with* Christ—in this case, to the Law. In both 2:19 and 6:14, then, Paul has in view his nomistic "I," the "I" whose existence and identity were given shape and direction by the (communal) practice of circumcision and the (communal) observance of the Law. Paul's "previous, cherished and acknowledged identity" was put to death and separated from the ordered nomistic *kosmos* into which he was born, in which he was nurtured, and in which he grew up.[14] That *kosmos* still exists of course, but not for Paul as a participant in the crucifixion of Christ.

In 6:14, as in 2:19, Paul employs a perfect tense, indicating a past action with continuing effect on the present (cf. 3:1). In both passages, Paul refers to himself ("I") not in an exclusive sense but as a paradigm for all believers who take their bearings from "the cross of *our* Lord Jesus Christ." Both Paul's nomistic self and the nomistic world he once inhabited have been put to death by his participation in the crucifixion of Christ. The two crucifixions are two sides of the same coin, as it were; his crucifixion with Christ also involves the crucifixion of the world in which he had found his identity and his bearings. This is Paul's way of emphasizing the complete break with his past as a devotee of the Law and the pain this break caused him. For him, a world has been destroyed and he has suffered the loss of that world.

Does the crucified *kosmos* include the Flesh, with a capital F? We have seen that Paul's accusation that the new preachers want to make a good showing "in the flesh" (6:12) may refer to the realm of "the Flesh" as a malevolent, cosmic power against which the Law is ineffectual (3:21; 5:23). Back in 5:24, Paul has written that "those who belong to Christ (i.e., all believers who have received the Spirit) have crucified the Flesh with its desires," here again using the language of crucifixion. Given the implicit link Paul establishes between fleshly circumcision and the realm of the Flesh, the *kosmos* crucified in 6:14 seems also to encompass "the Flesh with its passions and desires" (5:24). The word *kosmos* in 6:14 then has a much broader reference than the religion of the Law and comes (more emphatically) to signify a realm that is hostile to God and inimical to human life before God (cf. *ho kosmos houtos* in 1 Cor

13. Cf. de Boer, *Galatians*, 148–50.
14. Martyn, *Galatians*, 564.

3:19; 5:10a; 7:31b). Again, Paul himself does not connect the dots explicitly; he leaves it up to his readers to do that.

Whatever the case may be, the extreme language of crucifixion with Christ in 2:19 or crucifixion to the world in 6:14 gives expression to a key element of participation in Christ's faithful death, the end or the permanent loss of a previous manner of life (cf. 5:24; Rom 6:6), in this case one determined by fleshly circumcision and the Law. Crucifixion with Christ represents for the individual believer the destruction of his or her participation in the old age where the Law functions as a cursing, imprisoning, and enslaving power on a cosmic scale (3:10, 13, 19–23; 4:4–5).[15] A crucifixion with Christ is thus also a crucifixion to this world of Law observance. This is Paul's soteriology of the cross in Galatians, and it is a negative soteriology.

It must also be said, however, that when Paul says that he has been "crucified with Christ" or "to the world," he also means that he has been rescued from the present evil age (1:4) or redeemed from the curse of the Law (3:13; cf. 4:4–5; 5:1). On the other side of the crucified religion of the Law lies a new creation: "For neither circumcision is anything nor uncircumcision but [only] a new creation."[16] Where there is circumcision, there is also uncircumcision.[17] The Law also implies, and in a sense encompasses, the not-Law.[18] So, when circumcision (the rite and the condition) becomes irrelevant, so of necessity does uncircumcision (the absence of the circumcision rite and the presence of the foreskin). The religious, ethnic, and social distinctions caused by a world divided into circumcision and uncircumcision have in Paul's view been violently replaced by "a new creation" (kainê ktisis), a new reality brought into being by the action of God in Christ. That "world" of religious, ethnic, and social differentiation came to an end in the cross, i.e., in the crucifixion of Christ, at least for those who are "in Christ." What matters now is the new creation that has replaced a world divided by circumcision and uncircumcision.[19] The

15. For the Law as a cosmic power before and apart from Christ, see de Boer, *Galatians*, 35, 201, 209–10, 264. For those "in Christ" that is no longer the case.

16. Adams rightly remarks: "With the terms *kosmos* and *ktisis*, Paul is invoking the apocalyptic spatio-temporal dualism of 'this world' and 'the world to come/new creation'" (*Constructing*, 227).

17. "Circumcision" can here refer both to the practice of circumcision (cf. Rom 4:11) and to the condition of being circumcised. "Uncircumcision" (*akrobustia*, lit. "foreskin") can in turn refer both to the absence of the practice of circumcision and to the condition of being uncircumcised (cf. 1 Cor 7:19). In 2:7–9, Paul uses the two terms metonymically for groups of people practicing ("Jews") or not practicing ("Gentiles") circumcision.

18. Martyn, *Galatians*, 571.

19. Cf. Adams, *Constructing*, 227–28.

new creation represents the positive side of Paul's soteriology. This positive soteriology has a negative soteriology as its foundation.

Galatians 4:3[20]

The meaning of the phrase *ta stoicheia tou kosmou* has been debated since antiquity. Commentators on the passage routinely discuss the four meanings proposed in the English versions of the standard Greek lexicon of Walter Bauer, i.e., BAG (1957) and BAGD (1979):

1. Elements (of learning), fundamental principles.

2. Elemental substances, the basic elements from which everything in the natural world is made, and of which it is composed, namely, earth, air, fire, and water.

3. Elemental spirits which the syncretistic religious tendencies of later antiquity associated with the physical elements (cf. RSV; NRSV).

4. Heavenly bodies (as in "the twelve *stoicheia* of heaven," the 12 signs of the Zodiac).

In the most recent English edition of Bauer, that of Danker (BAGD 2000), the first of these meanings is given preference. It approvingly cites the translation "elementary ideas belonging to this world," taken from a footnote of the NEB. This interpretation of the phrase follows in the footsteps of the commentators Lightfoot and Burton, both of whom translate: "elementary teaching" (cf. Heb 5:12).[21] Longenecker continues this tradition of interpretation in his commentary ("the principles of the world").[22] In this line of interpretation *kosmos* evidently means "the human world."

The research carried out by three scholars, Blinzler (1963), Schweizer (1988), and Rusam (1992),[23] has shown conclusively, however, that the full Greek phrase *ta stoicheia tou kosmou* was a common, technical expression, derived primarily from Stoic thought, designating the four elements from which the ancients thought the physical universe was composed: earth,

20. For the next several pages, see de Boer, *Galatians*, 251–58, which incorporates a previous article: de Boer, "The Meaning of the Phrase *ta stoicheia tou kosmou* in Galatians."

21. Lightfoot, *Galatians*, 167; Burton, *Galatians*, 517.

22. Longenecker, *Galatians*, 165.

23. Blinzler, "Lexikalisches"; Schweizer, "Slaves of the Elements"; Rusam, "Neue Belege."

water, air, and fire.[24] These three scholars show that this is by far the most common referential meaning of the term *stoicheia* and the *only* referential meaning attested for the full expression *ta stoicheia tou kosmou* in Paul's time. The word *kosmos* in this full expression refers to the physical universe. Now, Paul's concern in 4:3 is certainly not to expatiate on the nature of the physical universe when he writes that "we were [all once] enslaved under *ta stoicheia tou kosmou*." Something more is surely involved in Paul's use of the term. The question is: What?

In 4:8–10, Paul mentions the *stoicheia* a second time and in this passage it becomes clear that the *stoicheia*, the "elements," lay at the basis of the religion of the Galatians before they became believers in Christ:

> Then, when you did not know God, you served[25] beings not gods by nature. But now having come to know God, or rather having become known by God, how can you be turning again to the weak and impotent *stoicheia* which you are wanting to serve[26] once more? You are observing days and months and seasons and years!

Paul here works from two assumptions: (1) The *stoicheia* have something to do with the gods the Galatians once venerated.[27] Paul is telling the Galatians something about the *stoicheia* that they already know. (2) The veneration of the *stoicheia* by the Galatians involved calendrical observances.[28] Here too Paul is telling the Galatians something they already know.

---

24. Cf. e.g., Philo, *Aet.* 107, 109–10: "there are four elements (*stoicheia*), earth, water, air and fire, of which the world (*kosmos*) is composed . . . all these have transcendent powers. . . . For just as the annual seasons circle round and round, each making room for its successor as the years ceaselessly revolve, so, too, the elements of the world (*ta stoicheia tou kosmou*) in their mutual interchanges seem to die, yet, strangest of contradictions, are made immortal as they run their race backwards and forwards and continually pass along the same road up and down. . . ." (trans. F. H. Colson, LCL).

25. The verb here is *douleuō* which means "to serve (as a slave)" or "to be a slave." Paul's choice of this word to signify veneration or worship is probably rhetorically motivated. See de Boer, *Galatians*, 272.

26. See previous note.

27. Cf. Philo, *Contempl.* 3–4: "Can we compare those who revere the elements (*ta stoicheia*), earth, water, air, fire, which received different names from different peoples who call fire Hephaestus . . . , air Hera . . . , water Poseidon . . . , and earth Demeter . . . ? Sophists have invented these names for the elements (*ta stoicheia*) but the elements themselves are lifeless matter incapable of movement of itself and laid by the Artificer as a substratum for every kind of shape and quality" (trans. F. H. Colson, LCL).

28. Cf. Wis 7:17–19: 17: "For it is he [God] who gave me unerring knowledge of what exists, to know the structure of the world (*kosmos*) and the activity of the elements (*ta stoicheia*): the beginning and end and middle of times, the alternations of the solstices and the changes of the *seasons* (*kairoi*), the cycles of the *year* (*eniautos*) and the

Paul also tells them something that they do not already know: to turn to the Law and its calendrical observances is to return to the *stoicheia* and the calendrical observances associated with them. I will come back to this startling equation below.

If we bring what Paul writes in 4:8–10 to bear on the full phrase *ta stoicheia tou kosmou* in 4:3—which as I have indicated was a common, technical expression referring specifically to the four constituent elements of the physical universe—then we may conclude that the full phrase is being used by Paul as *a summary designation* for a complex of religious beliefs and practices at the center of which were the four elements of the physical cosmos to which the phrase concretely refers. In Paul's usage, the full phrase is an instance of *metonymy*, whereby an aspect or attribute stands for a larger whole of which it is a part. In this case *ta stoicheia tou kosmou*—the four elements of physical reality—stand for the religious beliefs and practices of the Galatians associated with the *stoicheia* prior to their becoming believers in Christ. Calendrical observances and the physical phenomena associated with such observances—the movements of sun, moon, stars, and planets— were an integral part of these religious beliefs and practices. The gods the Galatians worshiped were so closely linked to the four *stoicheia* that the worship of these gods could be regarded, at least by Paul, as tantamount to the worship of the *stoicheia* themselves.[29] The sense of Gal 4:3 can be captured with the following paraphrase: "we were [all once] enslaved under the religious beliefs and practices associated with the four elements of the universe (earth, water, air, and fire)."

One of the difficulties presented by 4:3 is Paul's use of the first-person pronoun "we" (*hēmeis,* emphatic in the Greek) in vs. 3. This "we" must include Jewish believers such as Paul himself. Yet that seems strange, since Jews, for whom God was "one" (Deut 6:4; cf. Gal 3:20), certainly did not as a rule venerate the *stoicheia* as gods, as did the Galatians before they came to believe in Christ (cf. Wis 13:1–3). How, then, can Paul claim that Jewish believers and not only Gentile believers were once enslaved under the *stoicheia* when these *stoicheia* evidently concern pagan religious beliefs and practices? The answer to this question probably lies in the fact that Paul has the calendrical

---

constellations of the stars, . . . " (NRSV). Also Wis 19:18–20.

29. It is for this reason that the phrase is frequently taken to mean "elemental spirits" or the like. But that is not the *referential* meaning of the phrase. On the relationship between worship of gods and worship of the four elements, see Wis 13:1–3: "For all people who were ignorant of God . . . 2 . . . supposed that either fire or wind or swift air, or the circle of the stars, or turbulent water, or the luminaries of heaven were the gods (*theoi*) that rule the world. 3 If through delight in the beauty of these things people assumed them to be gods (*theoi*), let them know how much better than these is their Lord, for the author of beauty created them" (NRSV).

observances related to these four elements of the *kosmos* particularly, even exclusively, in view, as indicated by 4:8–10, where, as we have seen, Paul reproaches the Galatians for "returning again to the . . . *stoicheia* which you want to serve once more: You observe days and months and seasons and years!" Calendrical observances, therefore, were for the Galatians an integral part of the religious beliefs and practices associated with the *stoicheia* prior to their becoming believers in Christ. Calendrical observances (e.g., Sabbath, Passover) linked to the primal elements and associated phenomena (the movements of sun, moon, planets, stars) were also an integral part of Jewish belief and practice (cf. *Jub.* 2:8–9; *1 En.* 82:7–9; Wis 7:17–19). In this particular, limited sense both Gentile and Jewish believers in Christ were once "enslaved [together] under *ta stoicheia tou kosmou*," under the religious beliefs and practices connected to the four elements that make up the physical universe and determine its specific character.

This also explains how Paul can in the verses preceding and following 4:3 refer to all believers in Christ as once having been "under the Law (*hypo nomon*)" (3:23–25; 4:4–5; cf. 3:10–14). To be under the Law is evidently to be under *ta stoicheia tou kosmou* as well. For this reason, to place oneself under the Law (as the Galatians are wanting to do) is to place oneself once again under *ta stoicheia tou kosmou*. Paul has introduced a reference to *ta stoicheia tou kosmou* into his argument at this point precisely because he wants the Galatians to realize that there is a conceptual and functional overlap between being under the Law and being under *ta stoicheia tou kosmou*, i.e., between the religion of the Law and the religion of *ta stoicheia tou kosmou*. That conceptual and functional overlap may be found in calendrical observances related to the four elements of the universe found in both forms of religion.[30] It hardly needs to be said that this equation between the two situations supports Paul's rhetorical agenda, which is to prevent the believers in Galatia from becoming observers of the Law, beginning with the rite of circumcision. He wants to make plain to the Galatian believers, who are tempted to observe the Law as the new preachers in Galatia are insistently recommending, that their liberation from the *stoicheia* (and the calendrical observance associated with these *stoicheia*) was also, at the same time, their liberation from the Law (and the similar calendrical observances associated with that Law).

Paul's reference to *ta stoicheia tou kosmou* occurs, then, in connection with the religious beliefs and practices once adhered to by the Galatians.

---

30. In 4:1–7, Paul says that the religion of the *stoicheia* which the Galatians left behind is equivalent to the religion of the Law from which Christ delivered human beings; in 4:8–10, however, he says the reverse: the religion of the Law the Galatians are in the process of adopting is equivalent to the religion of the *stoicheia* they had left behind.

The term *kosmos* in the phrase refers to the physical universe. There is no indication that the *kosmos* so understood has come to an end. It continues to exist. The physical *kosmos* does not disappear; nor then do the *stoicheia* that comprise this physical *kosmos*. What has come to an end is the religion of the *stoicheia* that make up the *kosmos*. Put otherwise: What has changed is the *relationship* of the Galatians to this *kosmos*. We can see that in 4:8–10. Paul here calls the gods the Galatians had once worshiped "beings not gods by nature." These "gods" (*theoi*) are not here specified; they are simply distinguished from the singular one "God" (*theos*) who by implication *is* God "by nature." "By nature" (*physei*) here means simply "in reality" or "in fact": the Galatians had worshiped beings that were not in fact gods at all. Upon becoming believers in Christ, the Galatians had come to see, following Paul, that the gods they had been worshipping were not really gods. He reminds them of this fact, that the gospel has removed the aura of divinity from the beings they had once worshiped, reducing the *stoicheia* to the merely natural phenomena they in fact always were.

The *stoicheia* became gods in Paul's view, and can become gods once again, only if and whenever human beings venerate them as such. It is evidently Paul's view that once human beings begin venerating the *stoicheia* they in effect become enslaved to the gods they have created for themselves (4:3). The gospel liberates human beings from such enslaving delusions. For such reasons Paul characterizes the *stoicheia* as "weak and impotent" (*asthenē kai ptōcha*), which is what they actually are apart from the power human beings grant them. This characterization of the *stoicheia* is part of Paul's rhetorical strategy of dissuading the Galatians from becoming observers of the Law: The *stoicheia* are just as ineffectual for salvation as the Law, which is unable to give life (3:21).[31]

Is Paul's "demythologization" of the gods behind the *stoicheia* a consequence of his theology of the cross as it comes to expression elsewhere in Galatians? One sign that this is the case is 3:1 where Paul claims that when he came to Galatia he portrayed Christ as "having been crucified" before their very eyes. As Paul's reference to his crucifixion with Christ in 2:19 indicates, the appeal to Christ's crucifixion here instead of merely to his death (as in 2:20c–21) calls attention to the manner of Jesus' death as an apocalyptic event, i.e., as an event that announces and effects the end of the world (cf. 1 Cor 1:18–19), in this case the world of Law observance (cf. 2:16, 19; 3:25; 4:4–5; 6:14–15), which is the point at issue in 3:1–5 and, in fact, throughout Galatians. In Christ's crucifixion a world has been destroyed and that is what Paul wishes to emphasize in this context by characterizing

31. Cf. Martyn, *Galatians*, 412.

Jesus Christ as "having been crucified" (cf. 1:4; 2:19–20; 5:11; 5:24; 6:14). For the Galatians to take up Law observance as part of their new Christian identity would thus be tantamount to returning to that world from which Christ has delivered them (4:8–11). Paul here already assumes (perhaps only subconsciously) an equation between the religion of the Law and the religion of the *stoicheia*. For when he came to the Galatians with the gospel he did not preach Christ crucified in connection with the religion of the Law but in connection with their religion of *ta stoicheia tou kosmou*. The cross has put an end both to the religion of the Law and to that of the *stoicheia* for those who "came to believe in Christ" (2:16b). In fact, Paul makes it appear as if there is in essence and in practice no difference between these two religions whatsoever. So when Paul says in 6:14 that "the *kosmos* has been crucified to me and I to the *kosmos*," he could in principle be including the religion of *ta stoicheia tou kosmou*.[32]

That is Paul's *negative* soteriology with respect to the *stoicheia*. For the *positive* side, we return briefly to 4:3 in its context. Paul's claim that "we were enslaved under *ta stoicheia tou kosmou*" is followed in vs. 4 by what may well be the central theological announcement of the letter: "When the fullness of time came, God . . . " God did something. In Christ a new time has begun—the time of faith, the time of the Spirit, succeeding the time of the Law (cf. "no longer" in 3:25 and 4:7). The contrast prominent in 4:1–2 (between childhood and adulthood, or between immaturity and maturity) gives way in vss. 4–5 to a contrast between a situation of enslavement "under the Law" before Christ and a situation of adopted sonship for believers after "the fullness of time" has come. Adopted sonship has as its presupposition liberation from (the religion of) the Law and from (the religion of) *ta stoicheia tou kosmou*. The "fullness of time" thus signifies a clean break with the past and may be regarded as an apocalyptic assertion on Paul's part: the fullness of time signals the end of "the present evil age" (1:4) and the beginning of the "new creation" (6:15). In Christ, God has destroyed a world, the world of the religion of the Law and that of *ta stoicheia tou kosmou*, which amounts to the same thing, and given human beings another one to live in, the new creation, which in this context is represented by the Spirit of God's Son, whereby a believer knows him or herself to be "no longer a slave, but a son, and if a son, also an heir" (4:7) of the promise God made to Abraham. Paul's positive soteriology here presupposes a negative soteriology, the end or destruction of a previous, familiar "world," in this case one determined by *ta stoicheia tou kosmou*.

32. Exegetical honesty requires us to note, however, that Paul does not himself explicitly say this.

Three Concluding Observations

Paul uses the term *kosmos* with two different referential meanings in the two passages analyzed. In 4:3, it refers to the physical universe composed of certain elements (earth, water, air, and fire). In 6:14, it refers first and foremost to (the religion of) the Law, which effects a dichotomy between circumcision and uncircumcision, thus also between those who practice circumcision and those who do not (cf. 2:7–9). At the level of soteriology there is a connection between the two uses of the term, though Paul does not make this connection explicit. In 4:1–5 and 8–11, he establishes a functional and a conceptual similarity between (the religion of) the Law and (the religion of) *ta stoicheia tou kosmou*. For this reason, we can say that the end (the crucifixion) of the *kosmos* of the religion of the Law in 6:14 is also the end (the crucifixion) of the religion of *ta stoicheia tou kosmou*. In that sense, Martyn is right when he insists that the new creation replaces "not Judaism as such, but rather the world of *all* religious differentiation."[33] We can extend that claim, as Martyn does, to the pairs of opposites in Galatians 3:28: The dichotomies of the present world (Jew/Greek, slave/free, male/female, circumcision/uncircumcision) have been abolished, or at least relativized, for those who have come to believe in Christ.[34]

Second, in the hortatory section of the letter (5:13—6:10), Paul casts the human conflict over fleshly circumcision, the explicit topic of both the preceding and following passages (5:2–12; 6:12–13), as an instance of a cosmological conflict between the Spirit and the Flesh. He informs the Galatians at one point that they "have crucified the Flesh with its passions and desires" (5:24). The *kosmos* crucified in 6:14 can then also be understood to encompass the realm of the Flesh. Paul does not, however, make this (seemingly probable) link between the *kosmos* of 6:14 with the realm of the Flesh explicit in the closing. Paul has not thought through, or at least not fully or systematically articulated, all the possible ramifications of his assertions.[35]

Finally, it may be significant that Paul does not use the word *kosmos* for the new creation. For him the new world, the new *kosmos*, for which he does not use this term, carries such descriptive labels as "the kingdom of God" (5:21), "eternal life" (6:8), and, of course, "new creation" (6:15). Perhaps the main indicator of its character is to be found in 5:6, where Paul uses a formulation that is quite similar to that found in 6:15:

33. Martyn, *Galatians*, 565, emphasis original.

34. Cf. Gaventa, *Our Mother*, 72.

35. He has thereby de facto left room for believers in general and systematic theologians in particular to make their own contributions to the discussion.

5:6a for in Christ Jesus neither circumcision avails anything nor uncircumcision,

5:6b but faith becoming effective through love

6:15a for (in Christ Jesus)[36] neither circumcision is anything nor uncircumcision,

6:15b but a new creation.

Gal 5:6a and 6:15a describe the crucified *kosmos* in similar terms. This parallel between the two verses suggests that "new creation" in 6:15b is to be equated with "faith becoming effective through love" in 5:6b (cf. 2:20; 5:13–14, 22).[37] The new creation is both God's newly creative act in Christ[38] and the result of this newly creative act, a community of mutual love and service in the Spirit of Christ (cf. 4:6–7; 5:13–24).[39]

36. This phrase is missing from important manuscripts and may have been included under the influence of 5:6. See discussion in de Boer, *Galatians*, 394, 403n498.

37. For the interpretation of this compact phrase, see de Boer, *Galatians*, 317–19, 403, where I argue that the phrase has both a christological dimension and an anthropological one.

38. As Gaventa has written in a comment based on Gal 6:15: "The good news Paul proclaimed to the Galatians is that the release that could not be secured by human effort of any sort has come about through the action of God in Jesus Christ" (*Our Mother*, 74).

39. See Adams (*Constructing*, 226–28) for a nuanced discussion of the possible cosmological, anthropological, and ecclesiological dimensions of the "new creation" for Paul. The various dimensions are not necessarily mutually exclusive. On the use of the term *ktisis* in Romans 8, see the helpful discussion of Gaventa, *Our Mother*, 53–55. She rightly questions the tendency to limit the reference of the term to the non-human parts of the (old) creation, and convincingly argues that the term includes a reference to all humanity as well.

Chapter 6

Paul's Use and Interpretation of a Justification Tradition in Galatians

Introduction

GAL 2:15–21 CONCLUDES THE first major section of Galatians (1:11—2:21)[1] and is a contextualized summary of "the gospel" (1:6–7, 11; 2:2, 5, 7, 14), that is, Paul summarizes "the gospel" in a manner that addresses the situation in "the churches of Galatia" (1:2).[2] Paul here, for the first time in this letter,[3] pursues an expressly theological argument against "a different gospel" being proclaimed to the Galatians by a new group of evangelists (1:6–9).[4] These new preachers in Galatia are seeking to persuade the Galatians that they need to observe the Mosaic Law, beginning with circumcision, in addition to believing in Christ (5:2–4; 6:12–13; cf. 3:1–3; 4:10–11, 17, 21; 5:1, 7–8).[5]

1. Others begin this major section with 1:6, 10, 12, or 13. Betz claims that Gal 2:15–21 "conforms to the form, function, and requirements" of the *propositio*, summing up the preceding *narratio* (1:12–2:14) and providing a transition to the *probatio* in chapters 3 and 4 (*Galatians*, 114). One does not have to agree with Betz's specific rhetorical analysis to recognize the importance of the passage within the structure and argumentation of the letter.

2. On the problem of the connection between this passage and the preceding one where Paul gives an account of his confrontation of Cephas (Peter) in Antioch (2:11–14), see below.

3. According to Martyn, Gal 2:15–21 "consists of a concerted argument, the first one of its kind in the letter" (*Galatians*, 246). There is no mention of justification in what appears to be Paul's earliest letter, 1 Thessalonians.

4. Paul denies that the "different (*heteron*) gospel" (1:6) of the new preachers can be regarded as "another (*allo*) gospel" (1:7), i.e., another beside the one preached by him to the Galatians (cf. 1:11: *to euangelion to euangelisthēn hyp' emou*, "the gospel which was preached by me") when he founded the churches in Galatia (4:13).

5. The recent attempt of Nanos (*The Irony of Galatians*), followed by Walker ("Paul's Opponents?"), to revive the theory that Paul's opponents were (non-Christian) Jews is in my view unconvincing, especially given 1:6–9 where Paul labels the message of the new preachers "a different gospel" (*euangelion*). See de Boer, Review of *The Irony of Galatians*.

In 2:15–16, Paul asserts with great emphasis that "someone is justified (*dikaioutai*)" not "as a result of works of the Law" (*ex ergōn nomou*)—as the new preachers in Galatia are evidently claiming—but only "through/as a result of the faith of (Jesus) Christ" (*dia pisteōs Iēsou Christou*). Works of the Law are thus *completely irrelevant* for justification; the only thing that matters (for Paul) is "the faith of Christ." This is for Paul "the truth of the gospel" (2:14) in the Galatian situation.

Ever since the Reformation and more recently in "the new perspective on Paul,"[6] there has been considerable discussion about Paul's theology of justification as it comes to expression in this passage (and elsewhere in Paul's letters, particularly Romans). The debate has revolved around the precise meaning of the verb *dikaiousthai* (to be justified) in vs. 16.[7] In its simplest and most traditional form, this issue comes down to the following: Does the verb mean "to *declare* just (righteous)" or "to *make* just (righteous)"?[8] In addition to the verb *dikaiousthai*, the meanings of the two expressions that accompany it have also been at issue, namely, *erga nomou* (what are these works and what is the problem with them?)[9] and *pistis Iēsou Christou*, literally "(the) faith of (Jesus) Christ," which can be understood to refer to "(a human being's) faith in Christ" (an objective genitive) or to "Christ's own faith(fulness)" (a subjective genitive).[10] A decision on this point obviously affects one's understanding of Paul's theology of justification in the passage. The purpose of this chapter is to make a contribution to the clarification of these terms and thus to the clarification of Paul's theology of justification in this passage. It argues (a) that Paul, in vs. 16a, cites a Jewish-Christian

6. "The New Perspective on Paul" was the title of Dunn's programmatic Manson Memorial Lecture, given at the University of Manchester in November 1982, and published the following year. References below are to the reprint from 1990. The new perspective was given its decisive impulse by Sanders, *Paul and Palestinian Judaism* (1977); cf. Dunn, "New Perspective," 183–88. See the overview and critique of the new perspective by Westerholm, *Perspectives Old and New*.

7. Gal 2:16 plays a major role in Dunn, "New Perspective," 188: "This is the most obvious place to start any attempt to take a fresh look at Paul from our new perspective. It is probably the first time in the letters of Paul that his major theme of justification by faith is sounded" and thus "may tell us much, not only about the theme itself, but about why it meant so much to Paul."

8. For instructive yet diverse discussions of justification, see Westerholm, *Perspectives Old and New*, 141–50; Dunn, *Theology of Paul*, 334–89; Sanders, *Paul*, 44–76; Bultmann, *Theology of the New Testament*, 1.270–85; Wright, *What Saint Paul Really Said*, 95–133.

9. The issue was posed most sharply by Dunn in "New Perspective" and "Works of the Law."

10. It can also be understood as a genitive of authorship (the faith that comes from Christ, is created by him) or as a genitive of quality (Christ-faith).

formula (tradition) containing all three terms (*dikaiousthai, erga nomou, pisteōs Iēsou Christou*),[11] (b) that the point at issue between him and the new preachers in Galatia is in the first instance not the referential meanings of the three terms in question but the relationship between them,[12] and (c) that Paul begins to redefine the meaning of justification in the remainder of the passage (i.e., in vss. 19–21), though he does so only indirectly and by implication, i.e., contextually.

The Tradition Cited in 2:16a

In the preceding passage (2:10–14), Paul gives an account of his confrontation with Cephas (Peter) in Antioch where he rebuked him for not behaving correctly with respect to "the truth of the gospel." His account of his short but telling rebuke of Cephas in 2:14 turns imperceptibly (for us) into a rebuttal of the new preachers in Galatia in 2:15–16. Paul may have said something similar to Cephas in Antioch, but these words are now primarily directed to the new preachers in Galatia, who are Christians of Jewish birth like Cephas and Paul himself (and unlike the Galatians who are Gentiles; 4:8–10).

Gal 2:15–16 is one long sentence (also NRSV)[13] consisting of three subordinate clauses (vss. 16a, c, d), all of which contain a reference to, and a firm rejection of, justification on the basis of works of the Law. The main sentence, which has a positive thrust, is to be found in vss. 15 and 16b, in italics below:

(15) *We Jews by birth*[14] *and not sinners from the Gentiles,*

---

11. This hypothesis came about through reflection on the analyses of Gal 2:16a by Dunn, "New Perspective," 188–91, and by Martyn, *Galatians*, 263–75; cf. Martyn, "On Hearing the Gospel."

12. The referential meanings of terms are to be kept distinct from the theological ones (what are the deeper theological implications of the realities to which the terms refer?). The former are matters of description, the latter, which have to do with the "sense" or the "significance" of concepts, are matters of theological evaluation and insight. Two parties can agree on the former, yet disagree sharply about the latter.

13. There are, however, other ways to punctuate the Greek. Verse 15 could in fact be regarded as an independent sentence ("We ourselves [are] Jews by birth and not Gentile sinners. Because we know . . . ."). In support of this division is the conjunction *de* ("and, but") at the beginning of vs. 16 in some important manuscripts (a, B, C, D* among others), though there are also very good manuscripts that omit this word (including p46, A, Y, 33, 1739, 1881), for which reason the word has been placed between brackets by Nestle-Aland[28].

14. Lit., "by nature," *physei*.

(16a) because we know that someone is not justified on the basis of works of the Law but through the faith of Jesus Christ,

(16b) *we too came to believe in Jesus Christ,*[15]

(16c) so that we might be justified on the basis of the faith of Christ and not on the basis of works of the Law,

(16d) because on the basis of works of the Law shall all flesh not be justified.

Paul has to repeat the "we" (*hēmeis*) in vs. 16b because of the long intervening subordinate clause (vs. 16a). The main sentence, a *captatio benevolentiae*, represents the starting point in his theological rebuttal of the new preachers and their attempt to impose circumcision and other works of the Law on Paul's Galatian converts. Paul begins by pointing out what he and the new preachers have in common: He and the new preachers—all of them "Jews by birth" like Cephas—also (*kai*), i.e., just like the Gentiles in Galatia (or Antioch), "came to believe in (*episteusamen eis*)[16] Jesus Christ." In the main sentence, Paul is completely silent on the matter of the Law and its observance; the only relevant point is that he and other Jewish Christians "came to believe in Jesus Christ."

As part of his *captatio benevolentiae*, Paul contrasts "We Jews by birth" and "(those) sinners from the Gentiles" at the beginning of the sentence (vs. 15). He could simply have said: "We Jews by birth . . . we too have come to believe in Jesus Christ." In Antioch, however, Cephas, Barnabas, and the other Jewish believers who had fallen under the influence of the emissaries from James and the circumcision party in Jerusalem had been telling Gentile believers that Gentiles, being without the Law, are by definition sinners according to that standard. In Galatia, the new preachers, spiritual relatives of the circumcision party in Jerusalem, are now telling the Gentile Galatians (4:8) the same thing: Gentiles who had come to believe in Christ without also becoming Law-observant Jews nevertheless remain sinners. Paul momentarily adopts this perspective of the new preachers in order to point out

15. Here, as in vs. 16a, there is also good manuscript support for the reading "Christ Jesus." The difference in meaning and implication is not discernibly great.

16. The verb *episteusamen* is an ingressive, or inceptive, aorist. Paul uses the verb *pisteuō* with the meaning "believe" only three times in the letter (see 3:6, 22); only here does he use the construction with the preposition *eis*, "believe in" (cf. Rom 10:14a; Phil 1:29). In 3:6, a quotation from Gen 15:6, the construction is *pisteuō* plus the dative, which normally means "believe something to be true, give credence to," whereas in 3:22, the verb is used absolutely, with no object, "those who believe," though "in (*eis*) Christ" is probably to be mentally supplied. The nuance of the construction "believe in" is trust or reliance upon (BAGD, 817).

to them that "we Jews by birth," and thus *not* Gentile "sinners," *still* came to believe in Christ, whereby "we" implicitly conceded that "works of the Law" were inadequate for "justification," a point driven home in the latter part of vs. 16. In vs. 21, Paul will point out that if justification were indeed possible through the Law, Christ would have died, i.e., performed a justifying act, for no evident reason (see further on vs. 21 below).

The three subordinate clauses in vs. 16 make Paul's agenda with respect to "works of the Law" explicit. They are closely related to one another in terms of wording and content. Whereas the main sentence has a positive thrust ("we too have come to believe in Jesus Christ"), the subordinate clauses all contain a sharp negation: *Works of the Law are irrelevant for justification.* That the emphasis falls on this negation is further indicated by the structure of these clauses in relation to one another. The first clause begins with the negation of works of the Law as the source of justification and the third clause ends emphatically with that negation. The second clause has been structured to provide a transition to the last clause. It is also the case, however, that over against the threefold rejection of justification on the basis of works of the Law, Paul twice places justification through (*dia*) or on the basis of (*ek*) "the faith of (Jesus) Christ."

In the first subordinate clause, Paul gives the reason why "we Jews by birth" came to believe in Jesus Christ (vs. 16b): "because we know that someone (*anthrōpos*) is *not* justified on the basis of (*ek*)[17] works of the Law but (*ean mē*) through (*dia*) the faith of Jesus Christ" (vs. 16a). He appeals here to knowledge shared by believers who like himself and Peter are Jews by birth ("because we know that . . . ," *eidotes hoti . . .*). *To what extent, then, is Paul making use of already existing views and formulations in this clause?* Is everything after the phrase "because we know that" in vs. 16a a quotation from a formula? There are no certain answers to these questions. Nevertheless, there are good reasons for concluding that Paul cites a known formula in vs. 16a and—this is the crucial point—that three key terms in vs. 16, namely, *erga nomou, pisteōs Iēsou Christou,* and *dikaioutai,* have not been coined by Paul himself nor introduced by him into the Galatian setting. If so, some important building blocks of his theology of justification in this letter (and subsequently in Romans) have been given him by those opposing his work in Galatia.

At least five considerations speak in favor of regarding vs. 16a as a quotation the content of which was known to, and perhaps even given its specific formulation by, the new preachers in Galatia: (1) As already

---

17. One can also translate the preposition "as a result of" or "by means of," without substantially altering the meaning.

indicated, the introductory words "because we know that" (*eidotes hoti*) suggest that what follows may be a quotation, in whole or in part. (2) The preposition "through" (*dia*) in the phrase "through the faith of Jesus Christ" is remarkable, given the fact that in vs. 16c, where Paul clearly and unmistakably stakes out his own position, he uses the preposition *ek* ("from, on the basis of") instead of *dia*: "from (*ek*) the faith of Christ" in antithetical contrast to "from (*ek*) works of the Law."[18] (3) Paul does not pause to explain or to define the meaning of the verb *dikaioutai*. That the verb was being used in the proclamation of the new preachers in Galatia and thus known to the Galatians is indicated by its occurrence in 5:4 where Paul warns the Galatians: "you who are trying to be justified (*dikaiousthe*)[19] in the Law" as the new preachers want (cf. 5:8–12) have been "separated from Christ" and "have fallen from grace." It occurs further only in 2:17 and in 3:8, 11, and 24, where Paul seeks to undermine the theology of the new preachers. (4) Without introduction or elaboration, Paul employs two crucial expressions in vs. 16a: *erga nomou* and *pisteōs Iēsou Christou*. At issue in vs. 16 is not the basic referential meanings of these terms (the realities to which they refer)[20] but the substantive *relationship* between them in connection with the matter of "justification."

Finally (5), the conjunction *ean mē*, translated as "but" above, literally and normally means "if not" and thus "except" or "unless."[21] It has only this latter meaning elsewhere in Paul (Rom 10:15; 11:23; 1 Cor 8:8; 9.16; 13:1; 14:6–7, 9, 11, 28; 15:36).[22] With this meaning the conjunction could be taken to imply that someone is not justified as a result of works of the Law *unless* by way of "the faith of Jesus Christ." In other words, "the faith of Jesus Christ" is compatible with, or complements, works of the Law in the matter of justification.[23] Given vs. 16c, where works of the Law

18. The preposition *dia* itself is not un-Pauline (cf. 3:14, 26; Rom 3:22; Phil 3:9), but in combination with the other considerations its presence here indicates that it may be part of the quoted formula.

19. A conative present tense, signifying an attempt; cf. BDF #319.

20. See n. 12 above.

21. BAGD, 267; Burton, *Galatians*, 121; Dunn, "New Perspective," 195–96, 212.

22. See Das, "Another look," 530–31. The related conjuction *ei mē* in 1:7 and 19 also appears to have an exceptive meaning, but the key point is that for Paul *ean mē* is always exceptive.

23. The question of the import of the conjunction was first sharply posed by Dunn, "New Perspective," 195–96. According to Dunn, Paul pushes an initial "qualification of covenantal nomism" shared by him and other Jewish Christians into an outright antithesis" in the remainder of the verse. Dunn evidently does not think Paul is actually quoting a formula but only articulating in his own words what is "common ground" between him and other Jewish Christians. Dunn's approach prompted vigorous objections; see

and the faith of Christ are regarded as mutually exclusive in the matter of justification, *ean mē* must mean "but" for Paul himself, despite the pattern of his usage elsewhere (so most interpreters).[24] But Paul's interpretation of vs. 16a in vs. 16c also indicates that if he had been composing freely he would have avoided the ambiguous *ean mē* in favor of the unambiguous adversative *alla*, of which there are twenty-three instances in Galatians alone.[25] In vs. 16a, then, Paul is apparently appealing to a formula stemming from Christian Jews in which "works of the Law" and "the faith of Jesus Christ" were regarded as compatible and complementary. Christian Jews, including the new preachers in Galatia, would have understood the ambiguous *ean mē* as exceptive in the sense outlined above.[26] Under the tutelage of the new preachers in Galatia, the churches there would also have so understood it. Paul is out to correct this reading of the shared formula; he does so in the latter half of vs. 16.

In sum, it appears that everything in vs. 16a after the introductory phrase "because we know that" is a direct citation of a formula.[27] Paul and his dialogue partners in this passage, the new preachers in Galatia (like other Jewish believers), thus agree on the referential meanings of the three key expressions in vs. 16a: *erga nomou, pistis Iēsou Christou* (which Paul abbreviates in vs. 16c to *pistis Christou*) and the verb *dikaiousthai*. A question now arises: What are the referential meanings of these terms in the formula? We treat each in turn.

Dunn, "New Perspective," 206–14 (where he responds to his critics).

24. See Räisänen, "Galatians 2:16," 547. For other interpretations of *ean mē* as exceptive also for Paul, yet consistent with the meaning "but," see Lightfoot, *Galatians*, 115; Burton, *Galatians*, 121; Fung, *Galatians*, 115; Longenecker, *Galatians*, 83–84; Walker, "Translation." This solution interprets the exceptive clause in one of two complementary ways: (1) as limiting only the principal clause ("someone is not justified . . . except through the faith of Jesus Christ") or (2) as being elliptical ("someone is not justified as a result of works of the Law; [someone is not justified] except through the faith of Jesus Christ").

25. 1:1, 8, 12, 17; 2:3, 7, 14; 3:12, 16, 22; 4:2, 7, 8, 14, 17, 23, 29, 30; 5:6, 13; 6:13, 15.

26. Das, "Another look," 537–39.

27. Martyn brings some weighty arguments against this conclusion (*Galatians*, 264n158): In comparable justification formulas used by Paul (in Rom 3:25; 4:24; 1 Cor 6:11), there is according to Martyn, "no hint of a polemical antinomy that would place opposite one another Christ's faithful deed in our behalf and our observance of the Law" (268). Martyn thus attributes all the negatives in 2:16 to Paul's hand (with the third borrowed from LXX Ps 142:2). In his view (270), Paul has also coined the expression *pistis Christou*. Since Paul does not, however pause to explain the three key terms he uses, it seems plausible to conclude that they were also part of the formula on which he here relies. Furthermore, in the interpretation of the new preachers in Galatia, or in that of other Christians of Jewish birth, vs. 16a does not contain the antinomy that Paul discerns in it.

Works of the Law

As we have seen above, Paul gives the distinct impression that he is citing a Jewish-Christian formula in Gal 2:16a and that the expression "works of the Law" (*erga nomou*) was an integral part of that formula. He appears to assume that the meaning of the expression is evident to other Christians who were Jewish by birth as well as to the Gentile Christians in Galatia, who had undoubtedly been instructed in this matter by the new preachers who had come there (1:6–9). Paul uses the expression two more times in Gal 2:16. It also occurs in Gal 3:2, 5, 10. In each case Paul is refuting the "different gospel" (1:6–7) of the new preachers in Galatia.

Apart from the two instances in Rom 3:20 and 28,[28] the expression is curiously absent from the remainder of the NT as well as from the LXX. The Hebrew OT also contains no precise equivalent. The only exact parallel is to be found in a document from the Dead Sea Scrolls known as 4QMMT, which is part of a letter. In one fragment of this document (4Q398, frg. 14–17, col. 2.2–4), the author writes: "we have written to you some of *the works of the Law* (*ma'aśê ha-torah*) which we think are good for you and for your people, for we saw that you have intellect and knowledge of the Law."[29] Here the expression seems to mean "the precepts (commandments) of the Law." M. Bachmann[30] has argued that this is what the expression *erga nomou* also refers to in Paul's letters: The "works of the Law" are the commandments of the (Mosaic) Law preserved in the Pentateuch (cf. 3:10–21) irrespective of whether these commandments are actually done.

There are other texts among the Dead Sea Scrolls, however, where the term *ma'aśim* ("works, deeds") must refer to the actual observance or doing of the precepts of the Law:

> And when someone enters the covenant to behave in compliance with all these decrees, enrolling in the assembly of holiness, they shall examine their spirits in the community, one another, in respect of his insight and *his deeds in the Law* (*ma'aśê ba-torah*) . . . (1QS 5:20–21).[31]

---

28. Rom 3:20 is a slightly rewritten version of Gal 2:16d and Rom 3:28 a slightly rewritten version of Gal 2:16a. It is noteworthy that the two instances of the expression in Romans sandwich manifestly traditional Jewish-Christian material in Rom 3:24–26; see e.g., Fitzmyer, *Romans*, 342.

29. Translation García Martínez and Tigchelaar, *Scrolls*, 2.803, slightly altered.

30. Bachmann, "4QMMT."

31. Translation García Martínez and Tigchelaar, *Scrolls*, 1.83, slightly altered. The same formulation occurs in 1QS 6:18.

In the following lines, "his deeds in the Law" become simply "his deeds" or "their deeds" (5:23–24; cf. 1QS 4:25; 6:17). Further, the section of 4QMMT quoted above (4Q398) ends with the statement: "And it shall be reckoned to you as justification when you do (ăśa) what is upright and good before him, for your good and that of Israel."[32] The verb ăśa ("do") is from the same root as the noun ma'ăśim ("works"). The ma'ăśê ha–torah, then, clearly are precepts to be done, so that the expression can also be taken to mean "the works/deeds required by the Law."

In the Hebrew OT, furthermore, the term ma'ăśeh (pl., ma'ăśim) means "deed(s)" or "work(s)" (BDB 795; cf. e.g., Gen 20:9; 44:15; Ex 23:12).[33] In Ex 18:20, Moses must teach the people "the statutes and instructions and make known to them the way they are to go and *the work that they shall work*" (NRSV, modified). The last phrase means the same as "the deed that they shall do." Here we find the noun ma'ăśeh with the cognate verb ăśa in a context pertaining to Law observance, as in 4QMMT and 1QS above. The LXX changes the singular to a plural, using *erga*: "You [Moses] shall testify to them the ordinances of God and his Law, and you shall show them the ways in which they shall walk in them and the works (*erga*) that they shall do (*poiēsousin*)."

In Gal 3:10–12, where the topic is "those who live by works of the Law (*erga nomou*)" (3:10), Paul twice quotes passages from the LXX in which the verb "do" (*poieô*) occurs, as it does in Ex 18:20 above: The point of all the things written in the book of the Law is "to *do* (*poiēsai*) them" (Deut 27:26), for "the one who *does* (*poiēsas*) them shall live in them" (Lev 18:5).[34] If in Rom 3:20, 28, Paul refers to "works of the Law" (*erga nomou*), he refers in Rom 3:27; 4:2, 6 simply to "works" (*erga*) without the qualification "of the Law" (*nomou*), similar to 1QS above. The context and the subject matter, which is justification on the basis of "works," indicate that "works" here are primarily, though perhaps not exclusively, "works of the Law," especially circumcision (Rom 4:10–12). Further, given what Paul writes in Rom 4:4, the "works" referred to must be "deeds" performed by human beings: "Now to the one who works (*tō ergazomenō*), his wages are not reckoned as a gift but as his due" (NRSV). For Paul, then, as for the formula he cites in vs. 16a, *erga nomou* are the actions performed or carried out in obedience to the many commandments of the Mosaic Law as preserved in the Pentateuch. The phrase *erga nomou* thus refers to the actual "observance (doing) of the Law."

---

32. Translation García Martínez and Tigchelaar, *Scrolls*, 2.803, slightly altered.

33. *BDB* 795.

34. The corresponding Hebrew passages use the verb ăśa.

In the interpretation of Paul, two questions have commonly been posed in connection with his rejection of "works of the Law" as the source of justification: (1) Is Paul's rejection of "works of the Law" actually a rejection of "legalism"? (2) Do "works of the Law" refer to the observance of all the commandments or only of some selection of them? These questions can now also be posed to the formula Paul takes over in Gal 2:16a.

(1) The claim that Paul does not reject the Law as such but only "legalism" arises in part from the positive things he says about the Law in Romans (cf. 7:12: "the Law is holy, and the commandment is holy and just and good"). "Legalism" can be understood in at least three different ways, though it always implies a wrong attitude toward the Law and thus a sinful misuse of it: (a) The Law is observed in order to achieve or to earn salvation ("works righteousness"); the works done can then be construed as an attempt to "bribe" God. (b) The Law is observed in such a way as to lead to self-righteousness or boasting in one's achievements and good works, either before God or before others. (c) The Law is observed in a purely formal, external way, according to the letter and not according to its spirit. There is not a shred of evidence that legalism in any of these forms is at issue in Galatians. For both Paul and the cited formula, works of the Law refer simply to the observance of the Law, whether that observance be "legalistic" or not.

(2) The view that Paul has only a particular selection of works of the Law in view arises in part from his seeming embrace of a portion of the Law later in Galatians (the commandment to love one's neighbor as oneself from Lev 19:18 in 5:14; 6:2) and again in Romans (13:9). There are two primary variations on this approach: (a) Paul rejects the cultic, ceremonial sections of the Law (e.g., circumcision, food laws), but not the moral law (cf. Rom 13:8–10 where some of the Ten Commandments in addition to the love commandment are quoted with approval). (b) Paul rejects those portions of the Law that set Jews apart from Gentiles, i.e., circumcision, food laws, and special feast days, especially the sabbath.[35] "Works of the Law" are these "badges" of Jewish identity,[36] "Paul's way of describing in particular the identity and boundary markers" in which "the typical Jew placed his confidence," whereby he "documented his membership of the covenant" and distinguished himself and his people from the Gentiles.[37] In favor of

35. Dunn, "New Perspective," 191, 196.

36. Dunn, "New Perspective," 194, 196. See also Hays, "Galatians," 239.

37. Dunn, "Works of the Law," 220, 221, 224. In Dunn's view, such covenantal identity markers also led to a wrong "attitude to the law as such . . . The law as fixing a particular social identity, as encouraging a sense of national superiority and presumption of divine favour by virtue of membership of a particular people—that is what Paul is attacking" ("Works of the Law," 224). But such an attitude is one thing, the definition

this interpretation is the contrast between "we Jews by birth" and "sinners from the Gentiles" in 2:15 and the fact that Paul in Galatians specifically mentions circumcision (2:3, 7–9, 12; 5:2–3, 6, 11; 6:12–13, 15), alludes to food laws (2:11–14), and names feast days (4:10). That "works of the Law" cannot be limited to these three, however, becomes clear when Paul in 5:3 warns the Galatians that everyone who practices circumcision is "obligated to do the whole Law."[38] As Westerholm writes, Paul places "the particular issue [of circumcision] in the broader context of a discussion of the origin, nature, and function of the Mosaic law as a whole."[39] The warning found in 5:3 explains why Paul can use the term *nomos* as a synonym for *erga nomou* in 2:21, as in 3:11 and 5:4 where justification *en nomō* is rejected, just as justification *ex ergon nomou* is rejected in 2:16 (cf. the juxtaposition of *erga nomou* and *nomos* in Rom 3:20). In 4:5, Paul claims that those whom Christ was sent to redeem were *hypo nomon*, not then under some portion of it.[40] These considerations also apply to the view that Paul draws a distinction between the ritual Law and the moral Law. The "works of the Law" apply to any and all deeds required by the Law.

In sum, for Paul as for the formula he cites *erga nomou* are the actions or deeds demanded by the Law without distinction and without regard to the manner in which these deeds are performed.

---

of "works of the Law" as badges of identity another. The limited definition of "works of the Law" would presumably be valid apart from the presence or absence of the attitude of covenantal, nationalistic pride, which is a form of "legalism" (see previous point). Cf. Dunn, *Theology of Paul*, 354–59.

38. Gal 5:3 could be read to indicate that Paul is newly informing the Galatians about the link between the practice of circumcision and the observance of the whole (Mosaic) Law. It is more probable, however, that Paul here emphasizes the "*whole*" Law, which in 5:1 he has characterized as a "yoke of slavery," to underscore the far-reaching, burdensome consequences of beginning with circumcision. Just like the Christian Jews in Acts 15:5, the new preachers in Galatia believe that the practice of circumcision obligates the practitioners to do "the (undivided) Law," but they do not present this obligation as a terrible burden as Paul here does.

39. Westerholm, *Israel's Law*, 118.

40. In his commentary on Galatians, Dunn appears to take a more nuanced view of the issue: "'Works of the law' would mean in principle all that the faithful Israelite had to do as a member of the chosen people, that is, as distinct from 'Gentile sinners'. But in practice there were a number of test cases, several specific laws . . . boundary markers where the distinctiveness of Jew from Gentile was most at stake" (*Galatians*, 136); cf. *Theology of Paul*, 358: "the phrase 'the works of the law' does, of course, refer to all or whatever the law requires, covenantal nomism as a whole. But in a context where the relationship of Israel with other nations is at issue, certain laws would naturally come more into focus than others."

The Faith of Jesus Christ

The expression *pistis Iēsou Christou* in vs. 16a seems to have been part of a formula Paul cites (if the argument above is correct).[41] The same or similar expressions occur in vs. 16c ("the faith of Christ"), vs. 20 ("the faith of the Son of God"); 3:22 ("the faith of Jesus Christ"); Rom 3:22 ("the faith of Jesus Christ"), 26 ("the faith of Jesus"); and Phil 3:9 ("the faith of Christ"). Does Paul mean "(a human being's) faith in Jesus Christ" (objective genitive) or "Jesus Christ's (own) faith(fulness)" (subjective genitive)? A mediating position would be to render "faith effected by Christ" (genitive of authorship) or "Christ-faith" (genitive of quality), though these two options are like the first in that the faith of believers is in view. The issue continues to be a matter of sharp debate.[42]

Among the arguments in favor of the first interpretation (faith *in* Jesus Christ), which is common and traditional (NRSV, RSV, NIV, NJB, NAB), are the following: (1) The expression *pistis Iēsou Christou* is parallel to the phrase "we came to believe (have faith) in (*episteusamen eis*) Christ Jesus" in vs. 16b and must then mean "faith in Jesus Christ." (2) A similar parallelism between the noun *pistis* and its cognate verb *pisteuō* occurs in 3:6–7 where Paul glosses the citation from Gen 15:6 (Abraham "believed [*episteusen*] God and it was reckoned to him as justification") with the words: "Know therefore that those from faith (*hoi ek pisteōs*), these are the sons of Abraham."[43] (3) If *erga nomou* refers to a human activity, *pistis Iēsou Christou* does as well; faith is the human response to God's act of grace. (4) Christ never appears in Paul as the subject of the cognate verb *pisteuō* as one might expect if Christ's own faith(fulness) were meant.

In favor of the second interpretation (Jesus Christ's own faith or faithfulness) are the following arguments:

41. Moving in a similar direction is Longenecker, *Triumph*, 105.

42. For an overview of the debate, with extensive bibliographies, see Hays, "Πίστις"; Dunn, "Once More"; Rusam, "Was versteht Paulus?"; and Matlock, "'Even the Demons Believe.'" Hays argues for the subjective genitive, as do e.g., the commentators Martyn and Longenecker; also B.W. Longenecker, *Triumph*, 95–103; Campbell, "The Story of Jesus," 120–23; Foster, "First Contribution." Dunn argues for the objective genitive, as do Matlock and e.g., the commentators Burton and Betz. Rusam pleads for a genitive of authorship and Williams argues that it is both Christ's faith and the "answering faith" of human beings (*Galatians*, 70), what he also calls "Christ-faith" ("*Pistis Christou* Again," 446), i.e., a Christian's faith is like that of Christ's; thus aside from being the creator of the believer's faith, Christ also functions as its "exemplar." I limit myself here to a presentation of what appear to be the strongest arguments in favor of the two main possibilities.

43. The prepositional phrase *ek pisteōs* is here taken to be an abbreviation of the full phrase found in 2:16c and 3:22, *ek pisteōs (Iēsou) Christou*. The expression *hoi ek pisteōs* then means "those (whose identity comes) from (their) faith (in Jesus Christ)."

1. In 3:22, Paul refers once again to *pistis Iēsou Christou*, as he does in 2:16a; in the verses that immediately follow (3:23–25) Paul speaks of *pistis* in a personified way, as a virtual synonym for Christ (3:24): Faith "came" onto the world stage at a certain juncture in time (3:23, 25), as Christ himself did (3:19). As a result "we are no longer under a custodian" (3:25), i.e., "under the Law" (3:23), which was "our custodian until (*eis*) Christ" (3:24), i.e., "until (*eis*) faith (*pistis*) should be revealed" (3:23). Faith is not here an intrinsic human possibility nor even a human activity. In these verses "faith" functions as a metonym for Christ.[44] "Faith" here is thus something that belongs to or defines Christ himself.

2. Gal 3:22 shows that the phrase *pistis Iēsou Christou* is probably to be construed as a subjective genitive: " . . . that the promise [of the Spirit; cf. 3:14] be given on the basis of the faith of Jesus Christ (*pistis Iēsou Christou*) to those who have faith [in him] (*tois pisteuousin [eis auton]*)." To translate the phrase here as an objective genitive would produce a tautology: " . . . that the promise be given on the basis of faith in Jesus Christ to those who have faith [in him]."

3. If Paul had wanted to say "faith in (Jesus) Christ," he would have used an expression such as *pistis eis Christon* (found in Col 2:5; cf. Acts 16:18),[45] corresponding to the verbal construction *pisteuein eis*, "to believe in," in vs. 16b.[46]

4. The formulation *pistis Iēsou Christou* has an exact parallel in *pistis Abraam* in Rom 4:16; the latter undoubtedly means "the faith of Abraham," not "faith in Abraham" (also 4:12, "the faith of our father Abraham").[47]

---

44. Not for "the gospel," as e.g., Hays, "Πίστις," 296.

45. See also Acts 20:21.

46. Put otherwise, the case for construing *pistis Iēsou Christou* as an objective genitive would carry more weight if the corresponding verb, *pisteuō* had the meaning "have faith *in*, believe *in*, rely *upon*" in its transitive usage (i.e., when taking an accusative direct object). In its transitive usage, however, the verb (with a double accusative) means "to entrust (someone with something)," as in Gal 2:7. The meaning "to believe *in*, have faith *in*, rely *upon*" can only apply to the construction *pisteuō eis* used in Gal 2:16b (or to the construction *pisteuō* plus dative, as in Gal 3:6), i.e., when the verb is intransitive. Cf. Meyer, "Pauline Theology," 115n82; BDF #163.

47. Cf. Rom 3:3: "the *pistis* of God," where the genitive is also subjective. There are no parallels to the objective genitive interpretation of *pistis Christou* in Paul's own letters, and there is only one relatively clear instance of an objective genitive after *pistis* in the whole New Testament (Mark 11:22: "Have faith in God," *echete pistin theou*).

5. In Gal 1:1, Paul posits an antinomy between human activity and God's action in Christ ("Paul, an apostle not from human beings nor through a human being, but through Jesus Christ and God the Father"), as he does in 1:11–12 (his gospel is "not of human origin" but came "through an apocalyptic revelation of Jesus Christ"); he probably does the same here, setting over against one another a human activity, the observance of the Law, and God's own gracious, justifying act, "the faith of Jesus Christ" (cf. vs. 21: "the grace of God").

6. In Rom 1:5, Paul describes faith as obedience, in the phrase *hypakoē pisteōs*, "the obedience which is faith"; in Rom 5:19, he refers to the *hypakoē* of Christ, which can then also be described as his *pistis*, as perhaps in Rom 1:17 ("from [Christ's] faith to [our] faith").

7. The parallel with vs. 21 indicates that *pistis Iēsou Christou* probably refer to Christ's death (his "obedience" in Rom 5:19):

vs. 16a	*vs. 21*
Justification (*dikaiousthai*) from works of the Law (*ex ergōn nomou*)	Justification (*dikaiosynē*) through the Law (*dia nomou*)
contrasted with	contrasted with
justification through the faith of Jesus Christ (*dia pisteōs Iēsou Christou*)	(justification because) Christ died (*Christos apethanen*)[48]

The argument for the second interpretation seems stronger than the argument for the first and is thus to be preferred.[49] In the formula from which Paul cites, and for Paul himself, *pistis Iēsou Christou* refers in the first instance to Christ's faithfulness to (and thus also his trust in or reliance upon)

---

48. Cf. Christ as "faithful" (*pistos*) in his death in Heb 2:17; 3:2; Rev 1:5; 3:14; 19:11.

49. This conclusion would then also apply to the expression *hoi ek pisteōs* found in 3:7 (see n. 42 above), where the prepositional phrase *ek pisteôs* is an abbreviation of *ek pisteōs (Iēsou) Christou* (2:16c; 3:22): The expression *hoi ek pisteōs* means "those (whose identity comes) from (the) faith (of Christ)" (subjective genitive). If Paul had wanted in 3:7 to refer straightforwardly to human believing (as a parallel to Abraham's believing) he could have written *hoi pisteuontes* ("those who believe, have faith"), as he does in 3:22. Naturally those whose identity comes from Christ's faithful death in 3:7 have in fact "come to believe (have faith) in Christ Jesus" (2:16b) and for this reason the expression *hoi ek pisteōs* can rightly be understood to include or to signify, at a secondary level, such human believing (having faith) in Christ. The primary or referential meaning of the expression, however, is "those who derive their identity from Christ's faithful death." See next note.

God, as this faithfulness came to concrete, visible expression in his death.[50] Christ's *pistis* does not, then, refer so much to a subjective attitude on the part of Christ as to an objective event, namely, his atoning death on a cross. In 1:4 ("he gave himself for our sins"), Paul has cited and modified a formula concerning this atoning death, namely, the formula preserved and designated as such in 1 Cor 15:3: "Christ died for our sins" (cf. Rom 3:21–26; 4:25). This formula was probably also known to the Galatians and to the new preachers who have taken up residence among them. Paul adapts this formula again in vs. 20, referring there to "the faith of the Son of God," who is defined specifically as "the one who loved me and gave himself up for me."

In sum, it seems highly probable that for Paul and for other believers who are Jews by birth, *pistis Iēsou Christou* is "a summary description of Christ's faithful death."[51] Such is the referential meaning of the phrase for both Paul and the new preachers in Galatia.

Paul's Interpretation of the Formula with Respect to Justification

In Gal 2:16, "justification" (*dikaiousthai*) is the particular point at issue between Paul and the new preachers. The latter, to whom Paul specifically directs this passage, understand the formula quoted in vs. 16a as follows:

> We know that "someone, i.e., a Jew or an Israelite, is not justified (*dikaioutai*) on the basis of the observance of the Law except through (by means of) the faithful death of Jesus Christ.

The present tense of the verb *dikaioutai* in the cited formula of vs. 16a is timeless and thus indicates that a basic principle is involved. The passive voice is probably to be construed as a circumlocution for God's activity (a divine passive): It is God who "justifies" (cf. 3:8: "God justifies . . . "). It is thus misleading to speak of "justification *by* works (of the Law)" or of "justification *by* faith." In both cases, the question at issue is justification *by* God.[52] The issue is the basis on which God justifies. Given the formulation, the formula was probably originally used in missionary activity by Christian

---

50. That Paul distinguishes between Christ's own *pistis* and human believing in him is also clear from 3:22, discussed under point 2 above. In this way, a human being's "believing (having faith) in Jesus Christ," in both 3:22 and 2:16b, constitutes participation in Christ's own faithfulness to (trusting reliance upon) God in his death, with the soteriological benefits thereof (the gift of the Spirit). See also Sanders, *Paul and Palestinian Judaism*, 447; Longenecker, *Triumph*, 105–6.

51. Hays, "Πίστις," 287.

52. See Meyer, "Pauline Theology," 115n82.

Jews (led by Cephas) among their fellow Jews (cf. Gal 2:7–9). The framework is and remains "covenantal nomism," i.e., God's gracious covenant with the people of Israel entailing observance of the Law as the people's response and responsibility within that covenant relationship.[53] Christian Jews were convinced, however, that the observance of the Law does not bring justification apart from God's intervention in the faithful, atoning death of Jesus Christ for the sins of the nation (cf. the formula cited in 1:4). That was the burden of their message to their fellow Jews. The formula would apply to Gentiles only to the extent that they also became part of Israel, which is what the new preachers in Galatia have been telling the Gentile Christians there (5:2–4; 6:12–13). For this reason, for the new preachers, the word "someone" in the formula must refer to a Jew or an Israelite.

As the remainder of vs. 16 indicates, Paul reads the formula in vs. 16a in the following way:

> We know that "someone, i.e., a Gentile as well as a Jew, is not justified on the basis of the observance of the Law but only through (by means of) the faithful death of Jesus Christ.[54]

Paul here takes over the key terms of the formula, retaining their referential meanings with the exception of "someone" (*anthrōpos*): Justification is not just for Jewish believers but also for Gentile believers (cf. Rom 3:28). In Paul's interpretation, the observance of the Law and the faithful death of Jesus Christ are mutually exclusive rather than complementary when it comes to justification. That Paul reads the formula in this way becomes polemically clear in vs. 16c:

> [we Jews by birth too came to believe in Christ Jesus, just like the Gentiles] so that (*hina*) we might be justified on the basis of the faith of Christ and *not* on the basis of works of the Law.

The point is driven home by vs. 16d: "because (*hoti*) on the basis of works of the Law all flesh shall *not* be justified (*ou dikaiōthēsetai*)," and that means that *no one* shall be so justified. The language is largely borrowed from LXX Ps 142:2: "because everyone living shall not be justified (*ou dikaiōthēsetai*) before you," meaning that no living being shall be justified

---

53. Cf. Sanders, *Paul and Palestinian Judaism*, 75, 180, 236.

54. If the conjunction *ean mē* is still to be regarded as exceptive, then Paul understands it to modify not the whole of the preceding clause, as the new preachers do, but the verb *dikaioutai*, "someone is not justified . . . except through the faith of Jesus Christ. The same result is achieved if the exceptive clause is regarded as an ellipsis: "Someone is not justified on the basis of Law observance, [someone is not justified] except through the faith of Jesus Christ." See n. 24 above.

before God. Paul weaves into the words of the Psalm the phrase *ex ergōn nomou*, as he also does in Rom 3:20 ("therefore, *ex ergōn nomou* all flesh shall not be justified before him"). In both places, he (or his LXX text?) also substitutes the words "all flesh" (a Hebraism) for "everyone living" (cf. e.g., LXX Pss 64:3; 135:25; 144:21), probably to emphasize the collective vulnerability and weakness of human beings (see vs. 20). Paul does not indicate in any way that he is relying upon or quoting from the Scripture, as he does later in chapters 3–4. The words from Scripture are simply incorporated into what amounts to a declaration.[55]

The cited formula in vs. 16a assumes that *before and apart from Christ,* "someone (a Jew or an Israelite)" could expect to be justified by God purely "on the basis of observing the Law." The imagery behind the verb is that of a law court in which God functions as a judge, as in Ps 142:2 LXX (= Ps 143:2) whose language Paul borrows in vs. 16c, as we saw in the previous paragraph (cf. LXX Mic 7:9; Isa 43:9, 43:26, 50:8; 53:11). The term "justify" is thus here forensic, or judicial: The person who observes the Law is justified, or approved, by God; he or she is declared to be righteous, that is, in the right.[56] In this scheme God declares righteous those who by observing the Law "are" righteous and thus also in terms of their relation to God (cf. Ps 119:1–8). They have in effect proved themselves to be righteous and deserving of their vindication (cf. Deut 25:1): Well done, good and faithful servants! In the apocalyptic Judaism of Paul's time justification had come to have a distinctly eschatatological dimension; Paul articulates this view when he writes in Romans that "the doers of the Law shall be justified (declared right, vindicated)" (Rom 2:13), i.e., by God at the Last Judgment, when "sinners" or "the wicked" will be condemned (cf. Rom 2:5–8; Matt 12:36–37; *Pss. Sol* 2:34–35; 13:11–12; 14:1–3, 9–10; 15:12–13; *4 Ezra* 7; *2 Bar.* 14:12; 38:1–2; 46:6; 48:22; 51:3, 7; 54:5; 57:2). This understanding of justification is at home in one particular strand of Jewish apocalyptic eschatology in Paul's time, namely, the *forensic* pattern in which personal accountability and the obligation to choose the Law are paramount considerations.[57]

This understanding of justification is essentially also that of the new preachers now active in Galatia. The latter are telling the Gentile Christians

---

55. Paul perhaps does not let on he is quoting because he knows that the new preachers (1) could point out that the words *ex ergōn nomou* do not occur in Ps 142:2, and (2) could interpret the passage to mean that "no one shall be justified before God *apart from* works of the Law"!

56. The verb (like its cognate noun *dikaisynē*) has a range of meanings (cf. LSJ 429; BAGD, 247–49). Paul's use of language from LXX Ps 142:2 provides a clue to the meaning it has in this context. See chapters 7 and 11 below.

57. See chapter 1 of this volume.

there that even as believers in Christ they need "to do" the Law (3:10, 12; 5:3), beginning with circumcision (5:2–3; 6:12), if they want "to be justified" (5:4) when Christ returns for judgment. Only so do they have "the hope of justification (*dikaiosynē*)" (5:5), i.e., of divine approval and vindication. By turning to the "different gospel" (1:6) of the new preachers, the Galatians are wanting "to practice Judaism" (2:14) and, as a result, are also "trying to be justified (*dikaiousthe*)[58] in the Law" (5:4). In the view of the new preachers, then, justification is something that will occur for the Law-observant believer in the future. They understand Christ's faithful death not as a justifying act (an act of vindication and approval) but as an atonement for the past sins of the nation against God and his Law (1:4; 1 Cor 15:3).[59] This faithful death did not put an end to Law observance for Jewish believers, but obligates those so forgiven now to obey it all the more, to reach a level of Law-based righteousness (*dikaiosynē*) surpassing that of other (non-believing, non-Christian) Jews (cf. Matt 5:17–20). Applied to the Gentile Christians in Galatia, the traditional missionary formula Paul cites in vs. 16a is being interpreted by the new preachers in Galatia to indicate that Gentile believers in Christ also have to become part of the Law-observant covenantal people of Israel in order "to be justified" in the future, at Christ's return.

Especially in vs. 16c ("so that we might be justified on the basis of the faith of Christ and not on the basis of works of the Law"), Paul rhetorically dissociates justification from Law observance and associates it exclusively with the faithful death of Christ. Both steps are equally important and have far-reaching theological consequences. The subordinating conjunction *hina* probably does not point to Paul's own purpose or to that of other Christian Jews in coming to believe in Christ; the purpose is probably God's: "so that, as God wills (cf. 1:4), we might be justified . . . " It is unclear, however, whether the temporal reference of vs. 16c (*dikaiōthōmen*, aor. subj.) is future ("so that we might be justified by God in the future . . . ") or present ("so

58. A conative present tense, signifying an attempt. Cf. BDF #319.

59. The notion that Gentiles, being without the Law, are by definition "sinners" (vs. 15) does not mean that "those who live (*hoi poreuomenoi*) in the righteousness (*dikaiosynē*) of his commandments, in the Law," as *Pss. Sol.* 14:2 refers to the righteous, do not themselves ever transgress. In the *Psalms of Solomon*, where there is a recurrent contrast between "the righteous" and "the sinners," "the discipline of the righteous (for things done) in ignorance is not the same as the destruction of the sinners" (13:7): God "will forgive . . . those [righteous ones] who have sinned" (9:7) and "will wipe away their mistakes with discipline," but "sinners shall be taken away to destruction" (13:10–11; cf. 3:3–12). Such forgiveness is not to be identified with justification (vindication), which occurs at the Last Judgment (cf. *Pss. Sol.* 15:12–13) and constitutes God's approval of the righteous for having chosen and observed the Law (despite occasional lapses), not his forgiveness for having transgressed it. (Translation R. B. Wright, in Charlesworth, *Old Testament Pseudepigrapha*, 2.639–70).

that we might be justified by God, as we now are, . . . ").[60] If the latter, the clause of vs. 16c is then best understood as signifying (God's intended) result whereby justification is coordinate with the coming to believe in Christ (*episteusamen eis Christon*), which is thereby also joined to, or made dependent on, Christ's faithful death (*pistis Christou*), just as justification itself is. In the next clause (vs. 16d), however, Paul uses a future tense ("shall be justified," *dikaiōthēsetai*, from LXX Ps 142:2), which is consistent with 5:5 where Paul speaks of "the hope of justification," *elpis dikaiosynēs*. Paul thus still refers to justification as a future expectation in line with the formula he cites and the views of the new preachers in Galatia. The same can be probably be said for vs. 17 where Paul refers to "seeking to be justified (*zētountes dikaiōthēnai*) in Christ (*en Christō*)." One seeks for something that is not to hand (cf. Rom 10:3; Acts 17:27; 1 Cor 1:22; Matt 6:33); hence Paul's formulation can be read to point to a future justification.

It is difficult not to read Galatians through the lens of Romans where Paul explicitly and unambiguously identifies Christ's faithful death as God's act of eschatological justification, whereby "having faith" and "being justified" are coordinate events in the present for the believer (cf. Rom 3:21–26; 4:1–8; 5:1–10; 8:30; 1 Cor 6:11).[61] That move also makes it possible for Paul to include the notion of forgiveness in the meaning of justification (Rom 3:25; 4:6–8; 5:8–9).[62] In the Jewish-Christian formula from which Paul cites in Gal 2:16a, "to justify" means "to declare righteous those who by observing the Law are righteous," or "to declare observers of the Law to be in the right." Justification here is not God's forgiveness for having transgressed the Law, but God's approval for having observed it (to a greater or a lesser extent).[63] By claiming in Galatians that justification occurs as a result of the faithful death of Christ and not as a result of Law observance, Paul intimates, but does not yet say in so many words, that justification occurs *now* for those who "have come to believe in Christ Jesus," not (just) in the future. Once justification is made exclusively dependent on Christ's faithful, atoning death, justification also comes to entail, and thus also to mean,

---

60. The remaining uses of the verb "to justify" in 3:8, 11, and 24 are just as ambiguous on this score, at least syntactically.

61. See chapter 7 below.

62. For a link between forgiveness and justification, cf. 1QS 11:11–15; LXX Mic 7:9; Isa 43:25–26.

63. In *4 Ezra* and the Dead Sea Scrolls, the demand is that the Law be kept "perfectly" (*4 Ezra* 7:89; 1QS 3:1–11; 4:22; 8:1; CD 2:15; 20:1–7). See Sanders, *Paul and Palestinian Judaism*, 416. For a more moderate view, see the *Psalms of Solomon*, discussed in n. 59 above.

forgiveness, as it clearly does in the passages in Romans.[64] Justification can then no longer be a matter of approving the righteous (those who do right by observing the Law) but of accepting sinners ("the ungodly" of Rom 4:5; 5:6), despite their sinfulness (cf. Rom 3:25; 4:6–8; 5:8).[65] Paul goes even a step further, however, since for him justification cannot mean only "to accept" sinners but also "to rectify" them, i.e., to make them righteous,[66] by freeing them from the powers of Sin and Death, as Rom 5:12–6:23 bears out.[67] In Gal 2:15–16 (and 17), however, this striking redefinition of justification as God's powerful rectifying action remains inchoate.[68]

Nevertheless, Paul appears to take the first steps to this new understanding of justification in Gal 2:19–21 of the passage under scrutiny. The theme of justification reappears explicitly once again in vs. 21 and this verse employs the ostensibly forensic language also discernible in vss. 15–16: "I do not nullify the grace of God [as the new preachers do with their "different gospel"],[69] for if justification is [in fact] through [works of] the Law [as the new preachers claim], then [let us be clear about this:] Christ died for

64. Martyn (*Galatians*, 266) discerns this meaning already in pre-Pauline tradition (1 Cor 6:11; Rom 3:25–26a; 4:25), as does de Boer, *Defeat of Death*, 235n35. It seems, however, that the equation of forgiveness through the atoning death of Christ with eschatological justification now is Paul's doing. See Bultmann, *Theology*, 1.276; Sanders, *Paul and Palestinian Judaism*, 471.

65. Paul's new use of the verb "to justify" has led to considerable confusion. The Greek verb in the LXX normally means "to declare someone righteous who is righteous from observing the Law," whereas Paul makes it mean "to declare the sinner righteous even though s/he is a sinner," providing the exegetical foundation for Luther's notion of justification as the imputation of (a fictional) righteousness (Luther, *Lectures*, 123, 132–33).

66. In this way, Paul avoids the implication that the justification of the sinner is merely a legal fiction, as Luther's interpretation suggests (see previous note).

67. See Käsemann, "'Righteousness of God'"; de Boer, *Defeat of Death*, 152.

68. See Martyn, *Galatians*, 272. According to Sanders (*Paul*, 48), the passive form of the verb *dikaioō* as used in Gal 2:16a "almost always means [for Paul] to be *changed*, to be *transferred* from one realm to another: from sin to obedience, from death to life, from being under the law to being under grace" (emphasis original). He bases this conclusion largely on Rom 6:7 however ("For the one who has died has been freed [*dedikaiōtai*] from sin"). Furthermore, Sanders here appears to confuse what the verb itself "means" for Paul with the soteriological result or implication of God's justifying action (God justifies/rectifies the sinner and the result is a change of lordships).

69. Verse 21a could be read to indicate that the new preachers are accusing Paul of nullifying God's grace, perhaps in the giving of the Law (cf. e.g., 2 *Bar.* 44:14; so Burton, *Galatians*, 140; Martyn, *Galatians*, 259), but the accusation probably runs in the other direction, especially if the reference to God's grace is meant to refer back to 1:15 and 2:9. By saying that he does not nullify God's grace in Christ, Paul implies that the new preachers with their Law-based gospel are doing precisely that (just as Cephas and other Jewish believers did earlier in Antioch).

nothing." "Justification (*dikaiosynē*) through the Law" seems to be simply another way of saying "to be justified (*dikaiousthai*) on the basis of works of the Law" (vs. 16a; cf. 5:4–5). The noun then can be taken to mean either "God's justifying pronouncement" ("justification") or "the status of having been justified by God" (the "righteousness" that comes from God); both can be in view at the same time (cf. LXX Mic 7:9) and both are forensic-eschatological (see on vs. 16 above). For the new preachers in Galatia, who have adopted and adapted the categories and perspectives of Jewish forensic apocalyptic eschatology, those who shall be justified (declared righteous) by God are in fact now "righteous," i.e., "living as God's people,"[70] and thus rightly related to God, by virtue of their observance of the Law (cf. *Pss. Sol.* 14:2). The eschatological verdict of divine justification will confirm their status and also eternalize it: the life of God's people in the new age beyond the Judgment will be characterized by the same righteousness (cf. 3:21). For the new preachers it is therefore a matter of urgency that the Galatians observe the Law, beginning with the practice of circumcision. In a substantive argument, Paul attempts to undermine this position, believing that the "different gospel" of the new preachers turns "the gospel of Christ" into its opposite (1:7): It effectively nullifies[71] God's grace. To paraphrase vs. 21b only slightly: If justification is indeed attainable through observing the Law, as the new preachers claim, then (*ara*) it must follow that Christ died for nothing, i.e., needlessly (*dōrean*, lit. "gratuitously").[72] The corollary to vs. 21b is thus that if justification occurs on the basis of Christ's faithful death, as Paul believes to be the case (vs. 16), works of the Law must be entirely superfluous and irrelevant. To rely on them is to "(seek to) nullify" God's grace in Christ (cf. 1:6). Paul here once again drives a wedge between the Law and justification, indeed between the Law and God (cf. 3:15–22).

The intervening material in vss. 19–20 indicates, however, that this forensic reading of vs. 21 is inadequate. The three verses together constitute Paul's (further) interpretation of his apostolic call as recounted in 1:13–16, except that he here clearly presents himself as a paradigm for all believers.[73] The following parallels between the two passages are particularly noteworthy:

---

70. Ziesler, *Galatians*, 30.

71. The verb *atheteō* ("to nullify") also used in 3:15 in connection with a testament, is a judicial (forensic) term meaning "to declare invalid" (BAGD, 24).

72. Paul uses the form of real condition here, though the sense for Paul is actually unreal (contrary-to-fact), as in vs. 18: If righteousness were through the Law (which it is not), then Christ died for nothing (which he certainly did not). Cf. BDF #360.

73. See B. Gaventa, "Galatians 1 and 2"; Schütz, *Anatomy of Apostolic Authority*, 114–58.

1:13–16	2:19–21
in me (*en emoi*)	in me (*en emoi*)
patriarchal traditions	the Law
his Son	the Son of God
his grace	the grace of God

Paul understands his call to preach the gospel among the Gentiles, and he wants the Galatians to understand this call, "apocalyptically," namely, as God's sovereign redemptive act whereby he effected a radical discontinuity between Paul the zealous Law-observant persecutor of God's church and Paul the apostle of Christ to the Gentiles, between who Paul was then and who he is now.[74] The apocalyptic discontinuity between "then" and "now" discernible in 1:13–16 is emphasized anew in 2:19a in a series of abbreviated, staccato claims:

(vs. 19a) For I through the Law, died to the Law, that I might live to God

(vs. 19b) I have been crucified with Christ

(vs. 20a) I no longer live, but Christ lives in me

"To die to something" (vs. 19b) is metaphorical and means to become separated from it (cf. Rom 6:2, 10, 11; 7:6): Paul became separated from the Mosaic Law. With respect to this Law, Paul's "I" (*egō*) has ceased to exist; it is thus his nomistically determined "I"—the "I" that finds its identity and its hope of justification (5:5) in (the observance of) the Law—that has died. This same "I" has been "crucified with Christ" (vs. 19b). Paul's language is metaphorical and hyperbolic, yet also realistic and serious (cf. 5:24; 6:14); it is not just a figure of speech, but a vivid interpretation of a truly painful and real experience. His dying, like Christ's dying, was also a painful crucifixion (cf. 3:1) whereby the nomistic "I" was put to death. This "I" therefore "no longer lives" (vs. 20a). In Paul's understanding of the gospel, everyone who "has come to believe in Jesus Christ" (2:16a) participates in, i.e., is joined to or taken up into, the cosmic, apocalyptic event of Christ's crucifixion (cf. Gal 5:24; Rom 6:6),[75] an event that spells the end of the old age where

74. See chapter 2 above.

75. Paul's "participationist" language is not here sacramental (as for many commentators who read Rom 6:1–10 into Gal 2:19), but informed and shaped by the categories and motifs native to Jewish cosmological apocalyptic eschatology (see chapter 1 above). The interpretation of this passage has been much hampered by the tendency to read it

malevolent powers hold sway over God's creation. The Law is one of those powers (cf. 3:13, 23; 4:4–5, 21; 5:18).

The other side of dying to the Law, however, is living "(in relation) to God" (RSV, NRSV) or, with little difference in meaning, "for God" (NIV, NAB). That was the purpose of Paul's dying to the Law, that (*hina*) he could "live to (or for) God (vs. 19a). When Paul says he has been "crucified with Christ" (vs. 19b) he also means that he has been rescued from "the present evil age" (1:4). Verse 20a makes the same point using other words: "Christ [now] lives in me." The death of Paul's nomistic "I" had left him, as it were, an empty container which Christ subsequently filled, creating a new "I."[76] That new "I" still lives "in the flesh" (*en sarki*) to be sure, but also "in faith (*en pistei*), namely, that *of* the Son of God who loved me and gave himself up for me" (vs. 20b).[77] Paul here refers primarily to himself, but he surely expects the new preachers and the Galatians to say it after him and to apply it themselves. Paul's point is that the believer's life in the sphere of the flesh is now being determined by life in the sphere of Christ's faithful death, giving life in the flesh a completely different character, one marked by God's grace (vs. 21a; cf. 1:15; 2:9).

The theme of justification that reemerges in vs. 21 is to be read through the lens provided by vss. 19–20. By referring explicitly to Christ's death (*Christo epethanen*), Paul alludes back to vss. 19–20, and the theme of dying to the Law and being crucified with Christ. Paul thereby implies that the new preachers' understanding of *dikaiosynē* in vs. 21 as a purely forensic-eschatological manner is insufficient. *Dikaiosynē* for Paul is evidently not merely a matter of God's forensic-eschatological acquittal of the righteous in the future but God's putting right (rectifying) what is wrong in the human world, in the present as well as in the future. God does so concretely now by joining believers to the death of Christ, thereby freeing them from the powers that enslave, namely, Sin (vs. 17; cf. 3:22) and the Law (cf. 2:4; 4:1–5). Back in 1:4, Paul has defined the "Jesus Christ" in whom "we (Jewish believers) too have come to believe" (2:16b) as "the one who gave himself for our sins, that he might rescue us from the present evil age according to the will of God and our Father." Paul has interpreted the atoning death of Jesus apocalyptically, as God's act of deliverance from an evil realm. For the sake

---

through the lens provided by Romans and thus to make it seem more complicated than it already is (see e.g., Betz, *Galatians*, 123–24). "Mysticism" (Longenecker, *Galatians*, 93) is also an inappropriate description of Paul's language unless one means what Schweitzer (*Mysticism of Paul*, 3) called "eschatological mysticism," being taken up into a cosmic event.

76. Cf. Barclay, "Paul's Story," 142–43: the self is "reconstituted."

77. *En pistei* is thus virtually equivalent to *en Christō* (vs. 17).

of argument, Paul adopts the language of forensic-eschatological justification (in the future), but the context in which he places it forces it to take on
a different meaning, that of God's rectifying power (in the present).[78] It must
be emphasized here that only the argumentative context points to this new
understanding of justification; no explicit redefinition occurs.

Conclusion

In Gal 2:15–21, Paul takes as his point of departure a Jewish-Christian
justification formula, which he cites in vs. 16a. Paul does not here contest
the basic referential meanings of the primary terms of the formula, namely,
dikaiousthai, erga nomou, and *pistis Iēsou Christou.* Paul limits himself in
vs. 16 (and vs. 17) to the rhetorical and theological dissociation of justification (*dikaiousthai*) from *erga nomou* and its exclusive association with *pistis
Iēsou Christou.* In the remainder of the passage, however, justification (for
which Paul uses the noun *dikaiosynē* in vs. 21) receives a new theological
meaning from the *context* in which Paul places it. It comes to encompass
not only God's forensic justification of the believer in the future but also,
and more importantly in the Galatian context, God's dynamic rectification
of the believer in the present. In Gal 2:15–21, then, Paul begins a process
of redefining the forensic-eschatological justification language of the new
preachers in Galatia (and other Christian Jews) with categories derived
from cosmological Jewish apocalyptic eschatology.[79]

Finally, we may ask: How important is the language of justification
for Paul's own theology in Galatians? The answer must be: Not very. In the
remainder of the letter the language of justification is almost exclusively
confined to chapter 3 (the verb appears in 3:8, 11, 24; the noun in 3:6, 21),
where Paul attempts to refute the so-called gospel of the new preachers exegetically.[80] Justification language disappears from the letter after 3:24, reap-
pearing only briefly in 5:4–5, where Paul makes a last-ditch attempt to keep
the Galatians from practicing circumcision and "trying to be justified in the
Law," as the new preachers want. The justification language is thus that of the
new preachers, not that of Paul (it is entirely absent from his earliest letter, 1

78. Martyn, *Galatians,* 272–73. Martyn sees this new definition of "justification"
clearly emerging in 3:6—4:7.

79. I have argued that Jewish apocalyptic eschatology exhibits two discernible patterns, the forensic and the cosmological. Paul's own views seem to be closer to the latter
than the former. See chapter 1 in this volume.

80. Furthermore, the two expressions introduced alongside the language of justification in 2:16, namely, "works of the Law" and "the faith of (Jesus) Christ," occur for the
last time in 3:10 and 3:22 respectively.

Thessalonians, which shows that he could preach the gospel to the Gentiles without it). He does not resort to it in 4:4–5, which is arguably "nothing less than the theological center of the entire letter."[81] These two verses form part of the paragraph (4:1–7)[82] with which Paul concludes his refutation of the so-called gospel of the new preachers (3:1—4:7). For the Paul of Galatians, the language of deliverance (1:4), crucifixion with Christ (2:19; 6:14), redemption (3:13; 4:5), liberation (5:1), and walking by the Spirit (5:16) is much more important to his own theological understanding of Christ's death and resurrection than is the language of justification.[83]

---

81. Martyn, *Galatians*, 388.

82. In the original article, I dubbed 4:1–7 Paul's *second* contextualized summary of the gospel in Galatians ("Paul's Use," 216). I changed my mind slightly in my commentary on Galatians, arguing that 4:4–5 (not 4:1–7) is Paul's *third* contextualized summary. See de Boer, *Galatians*, 15–18. The first two summaries are to be found in Gal 1:4 and 2:15–16, with a fourth and a fifth in 5:5–6 and 6:15, respectively.

83. This judgment applies to Galatians and makes no claims about Romans or about Paul's theology as a whole. It is important, however, for the exegete to let Galatians be Galatians and to resist reading it through the lens of Romans, which represents a more developed stage of Paul's theological thinking on the matter of justification. See chapter 7 below.

Chapter 7

Justification in Paul:
From Galatians to Romans

Introduction

JUSTIFICATION IN PAUL IS a complicated and controversial topic, one that has been the subject of intense and repeated debate since the Reformation among both New Testament scholars and systematic theologians.[1] The amount of literature produced on the topic is immense and can appear daunting to anyone who wants to look at the issue afresh.

From an exegete's point of view, one of the problems that plagues the discussion is the tendency to read Paul's letters synthetically on the issue, to assume that what Paul says about justification in, say, Romans must be what he means to say also in, say, Galatians.[2] It is frequently the case that the accents that are discerned in Romans are also assumed to be present, and then "found," in Galatians. That is all the more the case for those who want to produce a synthetic "theology of Paul." There is then—inevitably but also understandably—the tendency to ignore the differences between the two letters or to smooth them out, and also to take Romans as the guideline or template for the interpretation of Galatians. N. T. Wright's massive *Paul and the Faithfulness of God* is a good example of this,[3] as is J. D. G. Dunn's *Theology of Paul*.

An exegete or a commentator on one of these letters will want to give that letter its own distinctive voice. Still, for anyone writing on Galatians or Romans, even a commentary on one of them, a look at the other letter can hardly be avoided since justification is a prominent theme in the opening chapters of both (Gal 2:15—3:24; Rom 1:17—5:21), with some notable overlap in key terminology and themes. Aside from the terminology of

1. See Beilby and Rhodes, *Justification: Five Views*.

2. I limit myself to these two letters here, though there are also a small number of relevant texts in 1 Corinthians, 2 Corinthians, and Philippians.

3. See de Boer, "N. T. Wright's Great Story."

justification itself, there is the figure of Abraham, and the terms *erga nomou* and *pistis Christou*. And if you assume that Romans was written after Galatians, an assumption warranted by the scholarly consensus about the sequence in which they were written, how then do you read Romans on this issue? As "a clarification" of the views first articulated in Galatians? Or should we think more in terms of a "development" or even a "change" in Paul's thinking?

Here I want to limit my investigation to finding an answer to the following question: How does justification in Romans appear when looked at through the lens provided by knowledge of justification in Galatians? What was does one then see when one starts in Galatians and then goes to Romans, instead of the other way around? We can at least determine whether or not there are some noteworthy differences in Romans when compared with Galatians.

In what follows, I will use "just-" words to translate the relevant Greek words with the stem *dikai-*: *dikaios*, just (= righteous); *dikaioun*, to justify; and *dikaiosynē*, justification or justness (= righteousness).[4] By using "just-" words, the oral and aural connection between these words evident in the Greek remains discernible also in English translation. The translation with "just-" words is also meant to provide a baseline for further analysis and discussion.

Galatians

Gal 2:16 contains the first mention of justification in the letter. For me, a breakthrough of sorts in the interpretation of this verse occurred when I realized that the precise meaning and significance of justification were not all that important for understanding the thrust of Paul's argument. The thrust of Paul's argument in this verse is to dissociate justification (whatever it may entail or signify) from the Law and to associate it firmly with *pistis*, faith. More precisely, Paul dissociates justification from *erga nomou*, "works of the Law," and he associates it firmly *and indeed exclusively* with *pistis Christou*, "(the) faith of/in Christ." Whatever Paul may

---

4. "Justness" is regarded as a perfectly acceptable synonym of "righteousness" in the *Unabridged Random House Dictionary*. "Justice" could also be used, I suppose, but that term tends to have the negative connotations associated with *iustitia distributiva*, distributive justice, which the Greek term, at least in Paul's usage, does not seem to have. See further n. 9 below on the difficulty of translating *dikaiosynē* as either "justification" or "justness." On the problem of the translation of the Greek terms into English equivalents, using either "righteous" and its cognates (derived from Anglo-Saxon) or "just" and its cognates (derived from French), see Sanders, *Paul*, 45–47.

take justification to entail or to signify (we can argue about that), the most remarkable and controversial aspect of his argument here is this exclusive association of justification with *pistis Christou* and its complete and utter dissociation from the (Mosaic or Jewish) Law.

This rhetoric of association and dissociation is polemically motivated. That is evident from the fact that three times in 2:16 Paul emphatically denies that justification occurs *ex ergōn nomou*, "on the basis of works of the Law," which I understand to mean "the observance (or doing) of the Law" (cf. *poiēsai* in 3:10b, 12b; 5:3b).[5] The emphatic triple denial indicates that there are people known to Paul who evidently *do* think that justification is based on such works. These people are undoubtedly the new preachers who have come into the Galatian churches after Paul's departure and who have been telling the Galatians that they must become observers of the Law, beginning with the rite of circumcision, if they are to obtain justification (cf. 1:6–9; 3:1; 4:17; 5:2–12; 6:12–13).[6] The new preachers have somehow managed to turn (all or many of) the Galatian believers into people "who are seeking to be justified in the Law" (*hoitines en nomō dikaiousthe*[7]), as Paul puts in 5:4, with evident dismay. The whole issue of justification, then, is a matter that has been raised not by Paul but by his adversaries in Galatia.

Now, it is of course significant that in his indignant and vehement reaction to the work of the new preachers in Galatia, Paul does not reject justification as a legitimate concern or hope, as he at least theoretically could have done. Nor does he even contest what for the new preachers is the basic referential (lexical) meaning of the verb used here, *dikaiousthai* ("to be justified"). And as a consequence he also does not contest their assumption of the fundamental theological and soteriological importance of justification.

Let us look at this more closely.

The theme of justification is represented in 2:16 by Paul's threefold use of the passive verb *dikaiousthai*, "to be justified," thereby indicating that justification is an *event* that happens *to* someone. Someone "is (2:16a), might be (2:16c), or will be (2:16d) justified"—justified, that is, by God. That God is the justifier is a surmise confirmed by Gal 3:8, where the word "God" occurs as the subject of the active form of the verb: "God justifies . . . " (*dikaioi . . . ho theos*). Justification is thus a divine action of which human beings are the recipient. Paul shares this understanding of justification with his adversaries, the new preachers active in the churches of Galatia as he writes the letter.

---

5. See de Boer, *Galatians*, 145–48; chapter 6 above.

6. See de Boer, *Galatians*, 50–57.

7. The present tense of this verb is conative, indicating an attempt.

The imagery behind the verb *dikaiousthai* is that of a law court in which God functions as a judge, as in Ps 142:2 LXX (= Ps 143:2) whose language Paul borrows in the last clause of 2:16 (cf. LXX Micah 7:9; Isa. 43:9, 26; 50:8; 53:11). The term "justify" is thus evidently derived from the LXX and has here forensic, or judicial, connotations, as is commonly recognized.[8] Its basic lexical meaning here is "to declare just," that is to say, in a courtroom setting, "to declare just someone who is just." In LXX Deut 25:1, judging, *krinein*, involves "condemning the ungodly person" (*katagnōsin tou asebous*) on the one hand and "justifying the just person" (*dikaiōsōsin ton dikaion*) on the other. So in the event of justification, God declares the just person to be just. (In contrast to human judges, who might justify someone who is actually unjust, God does not make such mistakes). Put otherwise: God attributes justness (*dikaiosynē*) to someone who is in fact just (*dikaios*). God thereby vindicates, approves, and accepts the just person (cf. Pss 7:8–9; 9:4, 7; 11:7; 17:1–7, 15; 18:20–24). That is the view of both the new preachers in Galatia and of Paul. On this aspect of justification they do not appear to disagree. Where they differ is the basis on which this divine declaration of justness (*dikaiosynē*) occurs, that is, on what counts as "justness" before God. For one it is observance of the Law, for the other it is *pistis Christou*.

There is one more important point of agreement discernible in 2:16. Both the new preachers and Paul appear to think that justification is an event that will take place in the future, at Jesus' Parousia. In other words, justification is assumed to be an eschatological event. To establish this point we must look beyond the threefold use of the verb *dikaiousthai* in 2:16. The verb occurs a total of eight times in Galatians, four times in the present tense. That would seem to suggest that justification occurs in the present, at least for Paul. In three of the four instances, however, we are dealing with timeless presents indicating a generally valid principle. In Gal 2:16a, "someone is not justified (*ou dikaioutai*) on the basis of works of the Law," a principle repeated in slightly different words in 3:11: "in the Law no one is justified (*oudeis dikaioutai*) before God." And according to 3:8, "God justifies (*dikaioi*) the Gentiles on the basis of faith." The fourth instance, in 5:4, concerns a conative present tense: "For those of you who are seeking to be justified (*dikaiousthe*) in the Law have been separated from Christ."[9] These texts say nothing conclusive about the moment or time of justification, but only about the basis on which it can occur. That is the issue at

8. For a good discussion of the issue, see Prothro, "Strange Case of Δικαιόω." See also Seifrid, "Paul's Use."

9. In *Paul and the Gift*, Barclay disputes this conative reading at one point (375n65), but then appears to adopt it later, when he translates the construction as "you who would be considered righteous . . . " (392).

hand. In 2:16b, Paul uses the subordinate phrase "that we might be justified on the basis of *pistis Christou*," using the aorist subjunctive *dikaiōthōmen*, as he does in 3:24 where virtually the same phrasing occurs: "that we might be justified (*dikaiōthōmen*) on the basis of *pistis*." The temporal reference of *dikaiōthōmen* could be the present ("so that we might be justified by God, as we now are"), but it could also be the future ("so that we might at some future moment be justified by God"). In the next clause (2:16d), Paul uses a future tense, "shall be justified," *dikaiōthēsetai*, which to be sure has been taken from Ps 142:2 LXX, but Paul does not tell his (Gentile) readers that he is quoting. They will read the word as Paul's own. In the following verse, 2:17, he speaks of himself as "seeking to be justified in Christ," using an aorist infinitive (*zētountes dikaiōthēnai en Christō*). You don't normally seek something you already have. Moreover, in 5:5, Paul speaks of "the hope of justification/justness" (*elpis dikaiosynēs*), which implies a future justifying act of God.[10] And that is the last time he refers to justification in the letter. The verse represents a summary of his views on justification in Galatians: "we by the Spirit, on the basis of faith (*ek pisteōs*), are eagerly awaiting the hope of justification." So it seems that the Paul of Galatians thinks of the event of justification as something that will happen in the future, at the Parousia/Last Judgment, most probably in line with the views of the new preachers active in Galatia.

Neither the definition nor the moment of justification is Paul's *primary* concern in Galatians. His focal concern is to sever justification from the Law and to bind it exclusively to *pistis Christou*. For the sake of his primary goal—to sever justification from the Law and to bind it exclusively to Christ—he lets the understanding of justification of the new preachers pretty much stand without challenge or change.

That in any case could be our conclusion whenever we read 2:16 (and the other verses in which justification is explicitly mentioned) apart from their immediate or larger contexts. The theme of justification that was introduced in 2:16 and reemerges in vs. 21 is probably finally to be read through the lens provided by vss. 19–20, where Paul at least *implies* that the understanding

---

10. The Greek term *dikaiosynē* in Galatians (2:21; 3:21; 5:5) has diverse, overlapping meanings and implications: (1) justness as an ethical category or quality, closely linked to the observance of the Law, (2) justification in the sense of "the state of having being declared justified, or just, by God" (the term "justness" can also be used to indicate this state), and, as a consequence of the latter, (3) justification in the sense of "God's justifying act or declaration" (for which *dikaiōsis*, in Rom 4:25; 5:18, would be the better term). The phrase "the hope of *dikaiosynē*" in Gal 5:5 seems to involve all three (see de Boer, *Galatians*, 316). Note the parallelism between "to be justified (*dikaiousthai*) on the basis of works of the Law" in Gal 2:16 and "*dikaiosynē* from the Law" in Gal 2:21 (de Boer, *Galatians*, 163–64). On the usage in Romans, see below.

of justification as purely forensic-eschatological and future-oriented, good as far as it goes, does not reach for enough.[11] Verses 19–20 constitute Paul's further interpretation of his apostolic call as a paradigmatic event for the Galatians. That also counts for vs. 21, for when he there denies that he nullifies God's grace, he refers back, I think, to God's grace as demonstrated to him in God's calling him (1:15; 2:9; cf. 1:6). The "*apokalypsis* of Jesus Christ" (1:12c), whereby God "was pleased to *apocalypse* his Son in me" (1:16a), is understood by Paul to have brought about the end of his life as the persecutor of God's church and as the Law-observant Pharisaic zealot. God effected a radical discontinuity between Paul the zealous, Law-observant persecutor of God's church and Paul the apostle of Christ to the Gentiles, between who Paul was then and who he is now. Paul "died to the Law," having "been crucified with Christ." Everything had already changed![12]

My basic point here is the following: For the sake of argument, Paul does not call into question, at least not directly, the language of forensic-eschatological justification (in the future) of his adversaries in Galatia in 2:16 and elsewhere in Galatians, but the argumentative *context* in which he places it forces it to take on a much deeper meaning and significance, that of God's rectifying power (in the present) whereby human beings are delivered, freed, from evil powers (cf. 1:4; 3:13; 4:4–5) and brought into the sphere of Christ's Lordship ("in Christ"). For this reason, Martyn in his magisterial commentary on Galatians insisted on translating the verb in 2:16 as "rectify" and the corresponding noun in 2:21 as "rectification." But this translation involves an interpretive leap since Paul does not explicitly indicate that he is giving these terms a new meaning. In Galatians, Paul's seeming redefinition of justification as also involving God's powerful, apocalyptic rectifying action in the present remains inchoate.

Is that still true in Romans?

Romans

In Romans, the forensic-eschatological meaning and significance of justification is hardly abandoned. Indeed, as I have argued elsewhere, Paul's presumed primary conversation partners, Jews who reject the claim that Jesus is the hoped-for Messiah, seem to understand justification in pretty much the same way the new preachers in Galatians do, apart from the

11. I regard vss. 17–18 as parenthetical—vs. 19 picks up where vs. 16 left off. See de Boer, *Galatians*, 156–58.

12. See chapters 2 and 6 above.

christological modification.[13] It is a forensic event that is to take place in the future, at the Last Judgment, and will be based on the observance of the Law (cf. 2:13). Everyone will be called to account on that basis. To a large extent, just as in Galatians, Paul shares with his conversation partners the forensic meaning of the term and the theological and soteriological significance of the event of justification as divine vindication, approval, and acceptance (the result of which is the gift of "eternal life" in "the kingdom of God"). The just God will justify the just.

For Paul's conversation partners in Romans, the just are those who have devoted themselves to God and God's Law, as was the case in Galatians. In responding to this new yet similar challenge, Paul does not abandon the dissociation of justification from the Law and its exclusive association with *pistis Christou* that he formulated in Galatians. Rom 3:21–22 makes that clear: "But now the *dikaiosynē theou*—the justness of God—has been manifested apart from the Law, the *dikaiosynē theou* through *pistis Iēsou Christou* for all who believe." The difference between Paul and his conversation partners in Romans revolves around where and how "the justness of God," the *dikaiosynē theou*, becomes manifest, in and through the Law or in and through Christ. The dispute indicates that Paul did not invent the term *dikaiosynē theou*.

This expression does not occur in Galatians but it plays a significant role in the first three chapters of Romans, where it occurs six times (1:17; 3:5; four times in 3:21–26, twice in the form "his justness"; cf.10:3 for the only other instance in Romans). The first occurrence, in 1:16–17, gives an indication of what the expression signifies for Paul: "For we are not ashamed of the gospel, for it is the power of God for salvation to everyone who has faith (*panti tō pisteuonti*) . . . for in it [i.e., the gospel] the justness of God (*dikaiosynē theou*) is being revealed from faith (*pistis*) to faith (*pistis*) . . . " (cf. LXX Ps 97:1–2). God's power is here specified as God's justness which "is being revealed" or, perhaps better, "is being apocalypsed" (*apokalyptetai*). For the revelation of God's justness is not merely the disclosure that God is just, but the manifestation of God's eschatological saving power and action (as Käsemann has shown).[14] God is just in that he actively justifies and that justifying activity entails more than a forensic-eschatological declaration.

There are three further differences from Galatians. First, Paul explicitly and unambiguously identifies Christ's faithful, atoning death (cf. Gal 1:4) as God's act of eschatological justification, whereby "coming to faith" and "being justified" are coordinate events in the *present* for the believer

---

13. See chapter 3 above, and de Boer, *Defeat of Death*, 141–56.
14. Käsemann, "The 'Righteousness of God.'"

(cf. Rom 3:21–26; 5:1–10). In 10:6, he can speak of "the *dikaiosynē* that is from faith" (cf. 10:10). Six times in Romans 4, again appealing to Abraham as he had in Galatians 3, Paul emphasizes that faith is "reckoned" or "credited'" (*logizetai*) as *dikaiosynē*, as justness (4:3, 5, 6, 9, 11, 22). He twice uses here the expression "the *dikaiosynē* of faith" (4:11, 13; cf. 10:6), i.e., justification occurs on the basis of the *dikaiosynē* which is faith. That justification occurs now, as the first clause of 5:1, which functions as a summary of the foregoing argument, makes clear: "Having then been justified (*dikaiōthentes*) on the basis of faith (*ek pisteōs*) . . . " Here we may compare 5:10, where Paul writes: "having *now* been justified in his blood." Justification is now not an event that will take place in the future but an event that has happened to the believer in Christ in the past so as to determine the present. In Galatians, that is at best implied but never clearly asserted, and Gal 5:5 ("the hope of justification") speaks against it, as we saw above. Only in Romans does the presence of justification become a *clearly* expressed position. The believer in Christ *has been* justified, which means that he or she has been declared just on the basis of faith, *pistis* (i.e., *pistis Christou*) and so approved and accepted by God.

Second, the binding of the event of justification to Christ's atoning death in Romans (clearly in 3:21–26; 5:8–10) makes it possible for Paul to include the notion of *forgiveness* in the meaning of justification (Rom 3:25; 4:6–8; 5:8–9). For the new preachers in Galatia, as we saw, and for the Jewish conversation partners of Paul in Romans, "to justify" means "to declare just those who by observing the Law *are* just," or "to declare observers of the Law to be just, in the right." Justification, which in their view will occur at the Last Judgment, entails not God's forgiveness for having transgressed the Law, but rather God's approval for having observed it, to a greater or a lesser extent.[15] Paul now brings that expected final justification forward into the present, as we have seen. Once justification is understood to occur *now* and made exclusively dependent on Christ's atoning death "for our sins" (Gal 1:4; 1 Cor 15:3), justification also, almost inevitably, comes to entail, to encompass, and thus also seemingly to *mean*, forgiveness, as it evidently does in the passages in Romans.[16]

That move has significant theological and soteriological consequences for the Pauline understanding of justification. Justification now entails

15. I leave aside here the thorny issue of determining how strict an observer of the Law one had to be in order to be justified—views varied and there were means of atonement for transgressions of the Law.

16. It is I suppose for this reason that some exegetes tend to regard forgiveness as a forensic category, but forgiveness is for Paul and his conversation partners a cultic act, as Rom 3:25 seems to indicate.

accepting sinners ("the ungodly" of Rom 5:6; cf. 4:5), *despite* their sinfulness: "While we were yet sinners Christ died for us, how much more *now that we have been justified in his blood* shall we be saved through him from wrath!" (5:8–9; cf. Rom 3:25; 4:6–8). Paul articulates here a wholly new theological understanding of the meaning and significance of the event of justification. God justifies—forgives and accepts—sinners, those who have no justness of their own to bring, which is to say everybody (cf. 3:23; 5:12). Yet it must also be said that in Paul's understanding of justification God still justifies the just. The justification of the ungodly or sinners does not mean that God approves of ungodliness or sinful behavior. Forgiven sinners become just on the basis of *pistis*, i.e., *pistis Christou*, which I understand to refer primarily to Christ's faithful, atoning death for past sins and secondarily to the faith in him that is thereby elicited (cf. 1:17: "from [Christ's] faith to [our] faith"; 3:21–26).[17] Believers are forgiven sinners who acquire the desired and necessary justness from Christ, i.e., "the justness (*dikaiosynē*) of faith" (4:11, 13; 10:6). That justness is a free gift (5:17; cf. Phil 3:9). To paraphrase 4:5, using plurals instead of singulars as Paul does: "to those who do not work but rely on him [God] who justifies the ungodly *their faith* is credited to them as *dikaiosynē*, as justness" (cf. 3:26b).

Third, in 4:5, we can sense another, stronger meaning for the verb "to justify," especially since it has "the ungodly" as its object (singular in the Greek, probably referring in the first instance to Abraham; the plural is used in 5:6). It does not mean merely "to declare sinners or the ungodly just on the basis of Christ's faithful death" (cf. 3:26b) for Paul. It also means "to make them just" (cf. 5:19). We can call this making just *rectification* (cf. Martyn). Paul here continues on a trajectory begun in Galatians. What was there implicit here becomes explicit. God makes believers just by freeing them from the powers of Sin and Death, as Rom 5:12—6:23 bears out. In Rom 6:17–21, the term *dikaiosynē* is used three times as a metonym for God and thus functions as a virtual synonym for God (6:18, 19, 20). This function goes well with the meaning of the expression *dikaiosynē theou*, "the justness of God" (Rom 1:17; 3:21), as God's eschatological saving power and action: God's justness (his just way of acting) becomes visible in making human beings just (rectifying them). Justification in the sense of rectification comes down to liberation from the power of Sin in particular.[18] Rom 6:7 is most remarkable in this regard, for literally this verse reads: "for the one who has died [with Christ to

---

17. See above chapter 6.

18. In Romans 5–6, *dikaiosynē* consistently forms the polar opposite of *hamartia* (again, something only hinted at in Gal 2:17, 21b–22a). *Dikaiosynē* is therefore also a moral category or quality in Romans (cf. 14:17).

Sin][19] has been justified (*dedikaiōtai*) from Sin." As many have noted, including the translators responsible for N/RSV, the verb "has been justified" must here mean something like "has been freed," or "liberated": "the one who has died [with Christ to Sin] has been *freed* from Sin." In the previous verse, Paul claims that "the old human being has been crucified with" Christ (Rom 6:6, echoing Gal 2:19–20). In this way, the justification of the ungodly, which is based on *pistis Christou*, does not merely impute to the believer a fictional or an alien justness: "In Christ" the justness of the believer is, or perhaps better, becomes continually real through the presence and action of the Spirit (cf. 5:5; 8:10). As Paul probably could have written in Romans, and does in 2 Cor 5:21: In Christ, believers become the *dikaiosynē theou*—which is to say, along with Käsemann, "God's saving activity . . . is present in his gift. . . . God himself enters the arena with it."[20] Justification so understood is not static but dynamic, and its goal and completion is salvation (cf. 5:9–10). In God's good time, according to 5:19, "the many [= all] will be made just (ones) (*dikaioi*)," and thus saved, which is to say, fully delivered from the powers of Sin and Death (cf. Romans 8).

Conclusion

In Galatians, Paul's primary concern is to sever justification from works of the Law and to bind it exclusively to Christ. He does not call into question, at least not directly, the language of forensic-eschatological justification (in the future) of his adversaries in Galatia in 2:16 and elsewhere in Galatians. Nevertheless, the argumentative *context* in which he places it forces it to take on a much deeper meaning and significance, that of God's rectifying power (in the present) whereby human beings are delivered, freed, from evil powers and brought into the sphere of Christ's Lordship. In Romans, Paul does not abandon the dissociation of justification from the Law and its exclusive association with Christ he propounded in Galatians. There are, however, at least four points at which Romans differs *explicitly and significantly* from Galatians: (1) the use of the expression *dikaiosynē theou*, "the justness of God," along with its apocalyptic implications; (2) justification as a present reality for the believer in Christ; (3) justification as forgiveness of past sins; and (4) justification as rectification in God's ongoing battle on behalf of human beings against the malevolent, supra-human forces of Sin and Death. In short, in Romans, Paul makes justification language do a lot more work than it had to do in Galatians! Does Romans then represent a clarification

---

19. Cf. Rom 6:8 ("we died with Christ") and 6:10 ("he [Christ] died to Sin").

20. Käsemann, "The 'Righteousness of God'," 174.

of his thinking about justification in Galatians or does it represent a further development, perhaps even a change, in his thinking in response to a new challenge? It is probably a bit of both.

Chapter 8

Apocalyptic and Salvation History in Galatians

Introduction

IN THEIR ARTICLES ON Galatians, both Bruce W. Longenecker and Jason Maston[1] raise the issue of salvation history with reference to the apocalyptic interpretation championed by J. Louis Martyn[2] and myself.[3] It must be recognized at the outset that Paul does not use a Greek equivalent for the expression "salvation history" (or its common German counterpart, *Heilsgeschichte*) anywhere in his correspondence, including Galatians. In fact, Paul also does not use the language of "salvation" (*sōzō, sōtēria*) in Galatians (contrast Rom 1:16; 5:10; 10:10; 11:11; 2 Cor 6:2; Phil 1:19). The term "salvation" evidently functions for Longenecker and Maston as convenient shorthand for divine gifts and actions that are in some way beneficial to and for human beings, though they do not pause to explain the significance of the term or of the quasi-technical expression "salvation history." At issue in the use of the latter by scholars such as Longenecker and Maston is evidently the theological significance (if any!) Paul ascribes to the period of the Law between Abraham and Christ as well as the nature of the continuity (if any!) between that period of the Law and the coming of Christ, which among other things has put an end to the time of the Law for those who have come to believe in Christ (cf. Gal 3:17, 19c, 23–25). Both Longenecker and Maston argue that there is a form of salvation history discernible in Galatians, but they disagree markedly with respect to its nature. I will respond to each proposal in turn. I will begin in each case with a summary and critique of the basic thesis and then follow with a numbered list of critical comments on questionable exegetical decisions made by our authors.

---

1. Longenecker, "Salvation History in Galatians," and Maston, "Salvation History in Galatians." I summarize both articles in this response.

2. Martyn, *Galatians*.

3. De Boer, *Galatians*.

Bruce W. Longenecker

Longenecker's basic concern is to determine whether the implied understanding of salvation history discernible in the analogy of the olive tree
in Rom 11:17–24 is a "stable feature within Paul's theology." According to
Longenecker, the analogy of the olive tree conceptualizes Gentile believers
in Christ as being "grafted into" the long-standing and ongoing "salvation
history of the Jewish people." He calls this understanding of salvation history
"the expanded-covenant model." Does this model underlie Paul's theological discourse in Galatians? Longenecker comes to the convincing conclusion
that "not a trace" of this model of salvation history is to be found anywhere
in Paul's argumentation in Galatians (contrary to J. D. G. Dunn and N. T.
Wright). Paul, according to Longenecker, "in fact seems to devise strategies to
avoid it altogether." Does that mean there is no salvation history to be found
in Galatians? No, it does not. Longenecker discerns another form of salvation
history in Galatians, one which amounts to a middle way between Martyn
and myself on the one side and Dunn and Wright on the other.

The key passage for Longenecker is Gal 4:4–5. In opposition to Martyn and others (including myself), Longenecker maintains (with others) that
Paul's reference in 4:5a to "those under the law" concerns not "humanity in
general" but Jews. He finds support in Paul's use of "we" in 3:23 ("*we* were
kept in confinement under the law, being locked up") and "us" in 3:13 ("Christ
redeemed *us* from the curse of the law"). Longenecker recognizes that the
first person plural in 4:5b ("so that *we* might receive adoption as sons"), as
in 3:14 ("that *we* might receive the promise of the Spirit through faith"), is
all inclusive: it refers to all believers whether of Jewish or Gentile origin. This
twofold use of the first person plural by Paul signifies for Longenecker that
any universal implications of the gospel must be seen as "an immediate consequence of what God has done for the Jewish people." Put otherwise: "What
God has done in Christ has universal and cosmic significance *only in so far
as* it impacts *first of all* upon the Jews as a distinct people" (emphasis added).
Paul's theology in Galatians thus "includes a salvation-historical component,"
though this is different from the expanded-covenant model.

Longenecker sums up the results of his investigation as follows: "A
robust awareness of the covenant between God and the Jewish people must
lie behind all this, with a conviction about God's faithfulness to his covenant with the Jewish people *animating* Paul's discourse in 4:4–5a" (emphasis added).[4] It is not clear to me, however, what Longenecker is claiming

4. Longenecker also attributes an understanding of salvation history to Paul's opponents in Galatia. But since, in contrast to Paul, they insisted that gentiles observe
the Law and become part of Israel, their understanding of salvation history was not the

with the verb "animate" in this context. Presumably it means "govern" or the like. If so, I would demur. That Paul is aware, even robustly aware, of the discourse about the covenant between God and Israel cannot of course be doubted given his own background as a born Jew (cf. Gal 1:13–14; 2:15). The same can be said with respect to discourse about God's faithfulness to this covenant. But it cannot be said that this discourse about the covenant with Israel *governs* Paul's discourse about Christ in Gal 4:4–5 or anywhere else. The reverse is more probably true: It is the gospel that "animates" (governs) his discourse about the covenant with Israel.

In other respects, Longenecker makes a strong and carefully considered case for finding a particular two-step form of salvation history in Galatians, one reminiscent of Rom 1:16 ("to the Jew *first* and [then] to the Greek"). Given the ambiguities of Paul's formulations (especially in his use of the first person plural whether as an independent pronoun or as a verbal suffix), this thesis may be correct. I would like, however, to bring the following exegetical considerations to our common attention:

1. Longenecker attempts to find support for his interpretation of 4:4–5 with an appeal to 3:22 which he properly translates as "But the scripture has imprisoned *all things (ta panta)* under the power of sin" (emphasis added). But he then, without any explanation or justification, interprets the verse to mean that Scripture imprisoned *all people* under the power of sin. He goes on to interpret 3:23 to indicate "how that imprisonment works out for the Jewish people": Whereas all people were imprisoned "under sin" (3:22), Jews were imprisoned "under the Law" (3:23). In 3:22, however, Paul says "all things" (*ta panta*), not "all people" (*pantas*), and that needs to be taken seriously.[5] Given Paul's comment in 3:21 about the incapacity of the Law to make alive, 3:22 is probably to be interpreted as follows: "But the Scripture imprisoned all things, *including (the works of) the Law,* under the power of Sin."[6] The Law, like everything else, is a captive of Sin. That seems to be Paul's immediate point in 3:22. For this reason, then, existence "under the Law" in 3:23 is also presented by Paul as a matter of confinement and imprisonment for "us." In my view, the first person plural contained in the verb *ephrouroumetha* ("we were confined") refers in this context

---

expanded-covenant model found in Romans 11 but "a fairly straightforward form of 'covenantal nomism'" that characterized Judaism as such.

5. Paul uses the expression "all people" in Rom 3:9; 11:32. But it is then striking that he does not do so here.

6. See de Boer, *Galatians,* 234–35. Longenecker may disagree but he does not advance an argument for his disagreement.

not so much to "humanity in general" (to use Longenecker's phrasing) as to all believers in Christ, whether of Jewish or Gentile origin ("Before faith came we [believers] were [all] confined under the law . . . ").[7] The same is probably true in 4:3, a verse Longenecker ignores, where Paul claims that "*we* [both Jewish and Gentile believers] were [once] enslaved under the elements of the world." Putting 3:23 and 4:3 side by side shows that for Paul existence under the Jewish Law and existence under the pagan "elements of the world" are comparable and interchangeable conditions.[8] In Galatians, then, Paul arguably conceptualizes the Law as a *cosmic* enslaving power[9] that is part and parcel of "the present evil age" (1:4) to which Christ has now put an end for all those who have come to believe in him (cf. 2:16; 3:22b, 23, 25; 4:4–5).[10]

2. In his treatment of 3:15–18, Longenecker repeatedly refers to the "giving" of the Law, when Paul does not use this term in this particular passage. In 3:17, Paul says that the Law simply "came" or "happened" (*gegonōs*). He thus avoids the term "give" (*didōmi*). Consistently with this, he does *not* ask in 3:19a "Why then did God *give* the Law?" but simply "Why then the Law?" When Paul does use the verb *didōmi* in 3:21b, it is to emphasize in a contrary-to-fact construction that no life-giving law has been given: "For if a law had been given [by God] that could make alive"—Paul implies that God has never given such a life-giving law—"justification would indeed be on the basis of the law."[11] Gal 3:17 and 3:21b thus hardly support the claim that the covenant of God with Israel at Sinai "animates" Paul's argument in Galatians, including in 4:4–5. Longenecker's own fine interpretation of the term "covenant" in 3:17 also does not support his interpretation of 4:4–5: The promissory covenant of God with Abraham, he writes, "has nothing to do with the giving of the law and the establishment of a particular people; the salvific *diathēkē* that Paul heralds bypasses the history of the Jewish people, whose salvation history begins, in a sense, with their participation in the true offspring of Abraham, Jesus Christ" (cf. 3:16). Right. But then one must add what Paul writes in 3:28: in

---

7. On Paul's blurring of the distinction between Jew and Gentile, both before and "in" Christ, see de Boer, *Galatians*, 256–58.

8. De Boer, *Galatians*, 256–57.

9. I here use the term "cosmic" to mean "universal" or "applying to all people" (cf. Rom 5:12).

10. See de Boer, *Galatians*, 200–201, 209.

11. See de Boer, *Galatians*, 226, 233.

Christ, there is neither Jew nor Greek. The distinction is obliterated, also salvation-historically.

3. With respect to 3:21a, where Paul asks whether "the Law is against the promises of God," Longenecker simply declares that Paul "of course" does not want to claim that "the law and the promise are wholly at odds with each other"; they are, according to Longenecker's reading, "complementary, precisely because they serve different roles." The little phrase "of course" emerges from Longenecker's unexamined assumption that God's giving of the Law forms an integral part of Paul's argumentation and message in Galatians ("There were reasons why the law was given," Longenecker writes in this context). I would ask Longenecker to look at my arguments, and those of Martyn, for a rather different interpretation of Gal 3:21a, and then to engage those arguments one way or the other. I confine myself here to pointing out that Paul's question is *not*, as Longenecker and many others assume "Is the law *of God* against the promises of God?" but simply "Is the law against the promises of God?" God is explicitly named only in connection with the promises—and expressly omitted in connection with the Law. Paul continues here a process begun in 2:15–16, namely, the rhetorical association of God exclusively with the promise(s) to Abraham and the rhetorical *dissociation* of God from the Mosaic Law (cf. 2:19: "I . . . died to the Law so that I might live to God"!).

Jason Maston

Maston's primary concern is to find an exegetically sound alternative for the anti-*heilsgeschlichtlich* bias of the apocalyptic interpretation of Martyn (and myself), which he otherwise admires and accepts. The apocalyptic interpretation of Galatians of Martyn and de Boer, Maston points out, "centres on the invasive act of God in Christ and promotes a sharp break between the past of Israel and the present of Christ and his followers." The result is that "Martyn and de Boer strive to eliminate all traces of salvation history in Paul's argument in Galatians." This is a mistake, according to Maston. Focusing his attention on 3:15—4:7, Maston faults the apocalyptic reading for exegetically questionable interpretations of "difficult texts" and for a failure to take seriously Paul's temporal markers (3:17, 19, 24; 4:4). The latter indicate for Maston that Paul is working with a linear notion of salvation history. It is true, Maston concedes, that a form of salvation history within which the Law has a positive function is not attested in Galatians. But, so Maston argues, salvation history can also have a negative side, as Oscar Cullmann and Martin Hengel pointed out. That is the case in Galatians for Maston: the period of the Law represents for Paul a period of *Unheil* rather than one of *Heil*. Paul's apocalyptic understanding of the Christ-event has thus caused him to articulate "a completely reworked understanding of salvation history," one in which the Law plays an entirely negative role.[12] In Maston's interpretation of 3:15—4:7, that negative role is part of "the divine plan." For Maston, 3:21 indicates that the promise(s) to Abraham and the Law complement each other because they serve different purposes (one positive, the other negative) in Paul's new understanding of salvation history.

With respect to the issue of temporal markers, which play the central role in his argument for some notion of salvation history in Galatians, Maston points out that the images of *paidagōgos* in 3:24–25 and *epitropoi* and *oikonomoi* in 4:2 "serve to reinforce the temporal contrast being drawn in these verses," adding that "even de Boer acknowledges" this fact. According to Maston, "the anti-*Heilsgeschichte* reading struggles to account for these temporal markers." That is not the case, however. Martyn after all maintains that 3:25 ("Now that faith has come, we are no longer under a *paidagōgos*") can be said "to encapsulate the message of Galatians."[13] He has also regarded "the central question of the Galatian letter" to be: "What time is it?"[14] The temporal markers are thus taken seriously by those supporting an apocalyptic reading of Galatians.[15] But Martyn and I draw conclusions different from those drawn by Maston. Maston claims that the "historical line that Paul presents stands against Martyn's emphasis on the punctiliar." But the point for Martyn is that the *salvation brought by Christ* is punctiliar, i.e., it has no redemptive-historical antecedents: Christ is the one and only seed of Abraham and thus the only one to whom the promise applies (3:16). The Christ-event is for this reason understood to be punctiliar.

The crucial question Maston's thesis thus raises is whether we can still talk of "salvation history" when the Law itself is regarded as the source of *Unheil*. I doubt it, the work of Cullmann and Hengel notwithstanding (for those two scholars, as Maston points out, the *Unheil* of *Heilsgeschichte* concerned

12. Maston's attempt to marry apocalyptic with salvation history is reminiscent of Beker, *Paul the Apostle*. See Martyn's assessment in *Theological Issues*, 176–81.

13. Martyn, *Galatians*, 364.

14. Martyn, *Theological Issues*, 121–22; cf. Martyn, *Galatians*, 23, where he adds a second, closely related question: "In what cosmos do we actually live?" For Martyn, it is now the time "after the apocalypse of the faith of Christ (3:23–25), the time of things being set right by that faith, the time of the presence of the Spirit, and thus also the time of the war of liberation commenced by the Spirit" (*Theological Issues*, 122).

15. Time is arguably a central element of any apocalyptic worldview, but in the sense that time is divided into two monolithic epochs. See de Boer, *Galatians*, 31–35.

sin, not the Law). Maston's denial that the coming of the Law is construed by Paul to be a salvific event (a position consistent with that of Martyn and de Boer) means that there can be no question of *salvation* history between the promise to Abraham and the fulfillment of that promise in the coming of Christ and his Spirit. There were no acts of salvation in that period and the term "salvation history" cannot be applied to a period of *Unheil* in which no *Heil* occurs. Maston's use of "salvation history" with respect to the period the Law as *Unheil* can only be regarded as a contradiction in terms.

I would also like to make the following critical observations with respect to certain exegetical decisions made by Maston to support this thesis:

1. Maston recognizes that Gal 3:16 with its claim that Christ is the one offspring (seed) of Abraham is the lynchpin of the anti-*heilgeschichlicht* reading of Paul. Maston responds that "Paul is not indicating that God was not at work between Abraham and Jesus in the people of Israel. Rather, what Paul rejects is an interpretation that gives priority to Israel over Christ." According to Maston, the new preachers ("troublemakers") in Galatia have given "priority to the Torah over Christ," and Paul now "argues for the incorporation of his readers into Christ as the seed, rather than into Israel as the seed. He does not state or imply that God has not been at work through the nation of Israel, only that it was not the definitive point of his work." These are mere assertions and are not supported with an exegetical analysis of the verse in question. There is nothing in 3:15–18 about misplaced priorities. There is nothing in this passage about God's work in or through the nation of Israel before the coming of Christ. The Law is depicted as a third party that illegitimately tried to tamper with God's promise to Abraham 430 years after the promise had been made to Abraham. I have made an extensive case for this interpretation in my commentary and I will not repeat it here.[16] I will content myself with pointing out, as I have in connection with Longenecker's proposal, that Paul does *not* say in 3:15–18 that the Law "was given by God"; he says only that it "came" or "happened" (3:17). The word "God" is exclusively linked to or associated with the promise(s) to Abraham in 3:15–18 (as in 3:19–22), *never* with the Law (cf. again 2:19).

2. With respect to 3:19–20, Maston maintains against the anti-*heilgeschichtlich* reading that "there is no clear indication that Paul is ascribing the Torah solely to the angels and maintaining that God was not

16. See de Boer, *Galatians*, 218–25.

involved at all."[17] But the real exegetical issue here is that the opposite is the case, namely, that there is no clear indication that Paul is ascribing the Law to God or that God was in any way involved in it. That is remarkable to say the least. Maston himself grudgingly acknowledges that "the lack of a direct reference to God may be important," and he notes that "God is conspicuously absent" from 3:19 in connection with the coming of the Law. Right. The absence of the word "God" from Paul's formulations about the Law in 3:19 at the very least *implies* (i.e., raises the specter of) God's lack of involvement in the Law. Paul does nothing to discourage such a conclusion on the part of the Galatians. Indeed, everything he has said to this point, especially in 3:15–18, seems to lead inevitably to that conclusion. Moreover, Paul has continuously implied from 2:15–16 onward that God had (and has) nothing to do with the Law. When Paul wrote Galatians, he may actually have believed in his heart of hearts that the Law is in fact "the Law of God" (Rom 7:22, 25; 8:7). But that is not the point. The point is that he does *not* use this formulation in Galatians; in fact, he seems consciously to avoid it. Here it is important to remember once again the rhetorical situation of the letter: Paul wants to prevent the Galatians from becoming observers of the Law at all costs and, for that reason, he has no stake at all in saying anything explicitly positive about the Law, including its origin in God. To acknowledge that possibility, or even to imply it, would not help his rhetorical agenda in any way. Paul creates a huge chasm between God and the Law in Galatians and he does so intentionally since that chasm serves his immediate rhetorical agenda, which is to make the observance of the Law an unattractive, indeed an impossible option for the Galatians.

3. Maston's counterargument hinges largely on the interpretation of the preposition *dia*. On the basis of Paul's usage elsewhere, Maston maintains that it is "highly unlikely" that Paul is using the preposition to identify the angels as the originators of the Law. But he concedes that Paul can and does use this preposition in connection with "the ultimate agent," normally (though not exclusively) God or Christ (cf. e.g., Gal 1:1: "Paul, an apostle . . . through [*dia*] Jesus Christ and God"). That concession indicates that a decision about the use of the preposition in connection with the angels mentioned in 3:19 can only be decided on the basis of contextual considerations, namely, the flow and import of Paul's argumentation to that point. In any case,

17. God, Maston asserts, *was* involved for Paul, albeit indirectly, in contrast to the promise where God was directly involved, i.e., without mediation.

something that is generally true may not hold in a particular instance. It all depends. It still needs to be demonstrated or made plausible on the basis of contextual considerations. Again, Paul's failure explicitly to mention God in this context is significant and arguably brings the Galatians to the edge of Martyn's abyss, compelling them to contemplate "the vision of a godless law."[18]

4. In his discussion of mediation (3:19d–20), Maston mistakenly attributes to me[19] the view of Lührmann that the term "mediator" (mesitēs) can apply "only to groups, not to individual persons." In my commentary, I argue that Paul evidently assumes that "a mediator is needed only when the party initiating a transaction consists of a plurality. Whether the other party to the transaction is also a plurality is irrelevant; the issue is the plurality of the initiating party."[20] As I point out, Paul leaves it to the Galatians to draw the implicit conclusion: Since Moses was mediator of the Law for the angels (a plurality), he could not have been the mediator for God, since God is "one," not a plurality. Maston criticizes interpreters who are said to rely "on a skewed understanding of mediation which presumes that mediation must involve a multitude ('a many')." But they rely on such a skewed understanding because Paul himself arguably does so as well in 3:19d–20: the mediation of Moses implies a plurality on the initiating side, namely, the angels who, unlike God, are explicitly mentioned in this connection.

5. According to Maston, the question in 3:19 ("Why then the Law?") "assumes that the same person has given the promise and the Torah." "If Paul has already separated God and the law," he claims, "then there is no reason for him to provide an answer to the question of the law's purpose." That claim ignores the rhetorical situation: Paul is responding to those who are seeking to convince the Galatians that they must keep the Law, beginning with the practice of circumcision. It is for this reason that Paul must ask that question. The Law is a phenomenon for which the new preachers in Galatia are making grand claims, namely, that it represents a divine addition to, and an obligatory modification of, the promissory covenant God made with Abraham. Paul wants to counter those claims and he does so by consistently putting the Law in a bad light and creating a chasm between God and the Law.

---

18. Martyn, Galatians, 358.

19. Maston, "Salvation History in Galatians," 95n38.

20. De Boer, Galatians, 227–28 (emphasis original and parentheses removed).

6. With regard to the question "Is the law then against the promises of God?" in 3:21a, Maston places a great deal of weight on Paul's *mē genoito*. He maintains that "a correct interpretation" of Paul's answer in 3:21b–22 depends in the first instance on how Paul uses the phrase in his argumentation generally: "In his typical practice, he [Paul] uses the expression to deny a logical possibility that his argument has created." Maston illustrates the point with some passages from Romans 7 and he then applies what he has learned to Gal 3:21–22. In response I have two points to make. First, Paul's usage generally or elsewhere is not necessarily decisive for this particular instance; it also depends on the context and the form of the question, e.g., the import of the preposition *kata* ("against"). Maston does not engage my arguments, or those of Martyn, on this score. Second, Maston problematically assumes that Paul regards the promises and the Law as "two acts *of God*" (emphasis added). But that is precisely what is at issue! Paul's question arguably posits a contrast between "the Law" on the one hand (Paul pointedly does not say "the Law *of God*") and "the promises *of God*" on the other. Paul has prepared the way for this contrast in 3:15–18, indeed in his whole argument from 2:15–16 onward. In my view, Maston's exegesis founders on this highly questionable assumption, that Paul is referring to two acts of God in 3:21a. He thereby creates the problem of a potentially "schizophrenic God who works through different, conflicting means at different points in history." God is effectively made responsible for the Law's function as an enslaver, rather than Sin (cf. 3:22–23; Rom 5:20–21; 7:7–13). That does not seem to amount to an improvement on the specter of God's implied non-involvement with the Law, as in the interpretation of Martyn and myself.

7. Maston refers explicitly to "the giving of the law" with respect to Galatians, as does Longenecker, but he does not explain the origin of this conception any more than Longenecker does. It seems to be a presupposition brought to the text. Maston approvingly cites my statement that for Paul in Galatians "God did *not* give the law, certainly not as a life-giving instrument of justification."[21] Maston's position is actually quite different, however: God *did* give the Law, but it was not the life-giving instrument of justification. My statement was based on Gal 3:21b: "for if a law had been *given* (*edothē*) that is able to make alive, justification would indeed be on the basis of the Law." This contrary-to-fact sentence probably conceals in its form the standpoint of the new preachers in Galatia: "Since a Law has been given which is able to make

21. De Boer, *Galatians*, 226 (emphasis original).

alive—the one given by God through angels by the hand of the mediator Moses[22]—justification is on the basis of the Law."[23] They work from
the assumption that since God gave the Law it must have a life-giving
purpose. Paul's formulation clearly undermines this standpoint: He in
effect denies that such a life-giving law has been given, which means
that justification cannot occur on the basis of the Law.

8. It must be conceded to Maston, however, that the protasis of 3:21b ("if
a law had been given that is able to make alive") can in theory be taken
to contain the following presupposition: "God gave the Law, which
however is not able to make alive." This is evidently Maston's view
though he does not justify it with an exegesis of the protasis found
in 3:21b. But this protasis can also be read to contain the following
presupposition: "God did not give the Law, which is not able to make
alive." Given what Paul has written leading up to this verse in 3:15–21a,
this interpretation of the protasis probably represents Paul's intention,
i.e., this is how he hopes the Galatians will hear his words. The new
preachers in Galatia have been telling the Galatians all about God
giving the Law. Against this background, Paul's formulation in 3:21b
intentionally implies, and will be taken by the Galatians to imply, that
God may have had nothing to do with the genesis of the Sinaitic Law
and does not stand behind it or (and this is the immediate rhetorical
point) behind the Law-based gospel of the new preachers.

Conclusion

In his Letter to the Galatians, Paul has no interest or stake in saying positive
things about the Law. In this letter, he is attempting to keep the Galatians
from doing what the new preachers in Galatia want them to do, become
observers of the Law, beginning with the rite of circumcision. Saying positive things about the Law and/or explicitly (or even *implicitly*) attributing
the Law to God would undermine this rhetorical agenda in significant ways.
For the same reason, the Paul of Galatians also has no interest or stake whatsoever in articulating a notion or a theory of salvation history with respect
to the people of the Law, Israel. That issue falls entirely beyond the purview
of Paul's argument and intention in Galatians.[24]

22. Note that I here attribute to the new preachers in Galatia what Maston attributes
to Paul, that God gave the Law through angels by the hand of Moses, the mediator. Paul
has questioned the validity of this scenario in 3:19–20. See de Boer, *Galatians*, 229, 233.

23. See de Boer, *Galatians*, 232–33.

24. For Romans, see chapters 3 and 4 above.

Chapter 9

Christ and the Authority of the
Old Testament in Galatians

Introduction

IN AN ARTICLE ON the significance of the Old Testament in the Fourth
Gospel, Maarten J. J. Menken pointed out that scholars have often discerned a certain ambivalence in the Gospel of John with respect to the Old
Testament (henceforth OT).[1] On the one hand, passages from the OT are
cited positively as witnesses to Jesus; on the other hand, since Jesus is the
exclusive revelation of God, the OT cannot, it seems, function as a mode or
a source of God's revelation. Menken accepts this ambivalence as a characteristic of the Fourth Gospel and uses it as a starting point for posing the
following question: "If God reveals himself exclusively in Jesus, what value
does the OT retain as revelation?"[2] In seeking an answer to this question,
Menken finds it useful to posit a distinction between "the *text* of Scripture
and the *history* narrated in this text."[3] Whereas the text of Scripture may well
retain "a positive witnessing function" in the Gospel of John it is not so clear
that the history narrated in Scripture does.[4]

Menken's distinction between "the status of the *text* of Scripture," on
the one hand, and "the revelatory value of OT *history*," on the other,[5] informs the present investigation into Paul's use of the OT in his Letter to
the Galatians. My specific question is: What is the status of the OT *text* for
Paul in Galatians and what is the value, or the authority, of OT *history* for
him in this letter?[6] As for Menken, *history* is here understood not in the

1. Menken, "Observations."
2. Menken, "Observations," 156.
3. Menken, "Observations," 156.
4. Menken, "Observations," 157.
5. Menken, "Observations," 157.
6. I use the division and the translation of Galatians defended in my commentary:
de Boer, *Galatians*. I also rely on the exegesis presented in that commentary.

sense of "a critically reconstructed history" behind the text, but "the events as they appear in the OT," what is commonly referred to as "the OT history of salvation."[7] This "history of salvation" is in effect the *story* of Israel as it is recounted in the OT documents.[8]

Three assumptions inform this brief investigation of Galatians: (1) Paul is in dialogue about the interpretation of the OT, what he refers to as "the Scripture," *hē graphē* (3:8, 22; 4:30),[9] with new preachers who have become active in Galatia after he founded the churches there (cf. 1:6–9; 4:17; 3:1; 5:2–4, 7–12; 6:12–13). These new preachers are Christian Jews who seek to persuade Paul's converts in Galatia that it is necessary to observe the Mosaic Law, beginning with the rite of circumcision.[10] They find the warrants for their message in "the Scripture," which for them carries absolute authority. Gen 17:9–14, where God commands Abraham and his descendants to practice the rite of circumcision, probably plays a central role in their thinking and preaching of the gospel to the Galatians.

(2) Both Paul and the new preachers work from existing Greek translations of the OT, commonly and conveniently known as the Septuagint (LXX).[11]

(3) As a former, well-educated Pharisee (Phil 3:5–6; Gal 1:13–14), Paul has extensive knowledge of the Scripture. It comes as no surprise, therefore, that there are a number of places where he makes *unmarked* use of vocabulary and formulations from the LXX (cf. esp. 1:15–16 [Isa 49:1–6]; 2:16d [LXX Ps 142:2]; 3:11 [Hab 2:4]; 3:12 [Lev 18:5]).[12] Such unmarked use of material from the OT (LXX) says little or nothing about the authority of the OT *text* for Paul the apostle, only his—unsurprising—familiarity with, and his indebtedness to, its language and contents.

Galatians 3:6–18

Paul does not explicitly cite from the Old Testament in the first two chapters of Galatians, even if he is indebted to its vocabulary and formulations at

---

7. Menken, "Observations," 156.

8. To what extent this story can pass critical muster as history will not be addressed and is not relevant to the investigation.

9. Elsewhere he can also use the plural "the Scriptures" (cf. Rom 15:4; 1 Cor 15:3–4).

10. See de Boer, *Galatians*, 41–61.

11. For the problems with this designation, see Stanley, *Paul and the Language of Scripture*, 41n24.

12. In some cases, quotations that are unmarked in Galatians are marked in Romans (cf. Hab 2:4 in Rom 1:17; Lev 18:5 in Rom 10:5).

several junctures. In other words, an (explicit) appeal to the Old Testament (whether as text or as "history") plays no role in his argument in favor of "the truth of the gospel" (2:5, 14) that he initially preached to the Galatians (1:11; 4:13) and still proclaims among the Gentiles (2:2).[13] That changes in chapter 3 where there are several marked and unmarked citations (3:6, 8, 10, 11, 12, 13, 16). We here focus on the marked citations.

Many of these are related by Paul to the figure of Abraham who plays a crucial role in the passage, as he does in Genesis. He is mentioned seven times (3:6, 7, 8, 9, 14, 16, 18), with a further instance in 3:29 and another in 4:22. This focus on Abraham indicates that the Galatians have probably been hearing much about the founding patriarch of Israel from the new preachers. Emphatically citing Gen 17:9–14 and other relevant passages ("for it stands written . . . " *gegraptai gar* . . .), these new preachers have been telling the Galatians that by practicing circumcision as Abraham did and thereby committing themselves to observing the Law they will become "sons of Abraham" (3:7), thus heirs of "the promise(s)" (3:14, 16–18, 21–22, 29) God made to Abraham. In his response to this argument, it is significant that Paul does not deny the relevance of Abraham. Rather, he agrees with the new preachers (a) that the God of Jesus is also the God of Abraham, (b) that the gift of the Spirit which God has bestowed and still bestows (3:1–5) on those who "have come to believe in Christ" (2:16b) is the fulfillment of a promise God made to Abraham (cf. 3:14), and (c) that this gift is given to the "sons of Abraham" (3:8), i.e., to his "descendants" (*sperma*) and "heirs" (*klēronomoi*) (3:29).[14] For the new preachers, however, that Spirit is closely linked to Law observance, whereas for Paul the Spirit is exclusively linked to (the proclamation of) Christ's death (cf. 3:1); for Paul, the observance of the Law is entirely irrelevant to the Spirit's bestowal or reception (cf. 3:2–5). In 3:6–18, Paul enters into dialogue with the new preachers on their own turf, that of "the Scripture," in which they find the authoritative warrants for their demand that the Galatians take up the practice of circumcision and observe the remainder of the Law.

It is not clear whether the first quotation of an OT text, the one of Gen 15:6 in 3:6, is to be read as a marked citation. Literally translated Gal 3:6 reads

13. Cf. Harnack, "The Old Testament in the Pauline Letters" (German original from 1928). Paul's frequent explicit quotations from the OT in "the so-called main letters" (Galatians, 1 and 2 Corinthians, Romans), which are "missing completely" from 1 and 2 Thessalonians, Colossians, Philippians, Ephesians, and Philemon, "have been called for by special conditions. From this it follows that from the beginning Paul did not give the Old Testament to the young churches as the book of Christian sources for edification" (44).

14. For neither Paul nor the new preachers, then, does the promise of "the land" (Gen 12:7; 13:14–17; 15:7, 18–20; 17:8; 24:7) play any role.

as follows: "Just as (*kathōs*) Abraham believed God and it was reckoned to him as justification" (cf. KJV: "Even as Abraham believed God, and it was accounted to him for righteousness"). Ancient Greek manuscripts of the NT contain little or no punctuation. For this reason, it seems at first glance that only someone familiar with the text of LXX Gen 15:6 (or Rom 4:2, where Paul introduces the quotation of Gen 15:6 with the words "What does the Scripture say?") would know that 3:6 contains a quotation of that passage.[15] In favor of a marked quotation are (1) 3:7, which draws a conclusion (*ara*, "therefore") from the words about Abraham in vs. 6, and (2) 3:8a, which restates this conclusion as something foreseen by "the Scripture." The new preachers now active in Galatia in opposition to Paul will surely recognize Paul's words as a quotation, since they are undoubtedly well-versed in the Scripture, especially those sections pertaining to Abraham in the book of Genesis.

Some interpreters maintain that *kathōs* ("just as") is in fact an abbreviation for the introductory formula *kathōs gegraptai* ("just as it stands written"; cf. e.g., Rom 1:17; 1 Cor 1:31), and functions in the same way: "Just as [it stands written]: 'Abraham believed God and it was reckoned to him as justification.'" This would mean (a) that the Galatians as well as the new preachers would also recognize (or at least sense) that Paul is introducing a quotation with the simple word *kathōs*, and (b) that the word "Abraham" belongs to the text being cited from Gen 15:6.[16] The citation then seems to match the text of the LXX exactly, except that in the LXX the verb and the subject are reversed (*episteusen Abram* instead of *Abraam episteusen*, as Paul has in 3:6).[17] Paul follows the inverse word order of the LXX text when he cites Gen 15:6 again in Rom 4:2, which indicates that his failure to do so in Gal 3: 6 is probably intentional. That has caused other interpreters to maintain that the word "Abraham" belongs to the citation's introductory formula: "Just as Abraham: 'He believed God . . .'" (cf. RSV, NRSV, NIV, NAB). This introductory formula means "and so it was with Abraham,"[18] "take Abraham as the example,"[19] or "things were the same with Abraham."[20] If this interpretation is correct, the new preachers and the

15. Cf. NRSV: "Just as Abraham 'believed God, and it was reckoned to him as righteousness.'" Clearly, the translators of the NRSV know that Paul is quoting (hence the inclusion of the quotation marks), but would the Gentile Galatians have known this, at least at the first reading of the letter?

16. So Betz, *Galatians*, 140; Vouga, *Galater*, 71; Dunn, *Galatians*, 160.

17. There is also a slight difference in the spelling of Abraham's name. Paul's spelling reflects the change of the patriarch's name from Abram to Abraham in Gen 17:5.

18. Lighfoot, *Galatians*.

19. Longenecker, *Galatians*.

20. Martyn, *Galatians*.

Galatians would still be able recognize (or at least sense) that Paul is citing something from "the Scripture" of Israel. But as the peculiar introduction indicates ("Just as *Abraham*: . . ."), Abraham *himself* is being summoned as the authority here, not the Scripture (the text) as such. More precisely, the event of Abraham's believing God and God's justifying him as a result (declaring him to be in the right) is cited authoritatively by Paul. From this authoritative event, Paul will draw the conclusion in 3:7 that "those who are from faith" are in fact "the sons of Abraham," not "those who are from works of the Law" (3:10; cf. 2:16; 3:2, 5).[21] Gal 3:6 assumes what is made plain in 3:8, that in believing God Abraham actually believed a promise God made to him, that promise (according to Paul) being, "In you [Abraham] shall all the Gentiles be blessed," which is a quotation from Gen 12:3 with elements from Gen 18:18 (the phrase "all the Gentiles" of Gen 18:18 strategically replaces the phrase "all the tribes of the earth" of Gen 12:3). For the new preachers in Galatia, the phrase "in you [Abraham]" in Gen 12:3 probably means "in your offspring (*sperma*)," i.e., in Abraham's fleshly, Law-observant descendants down the generations, beginning with the patriarch Isaac and followed by Jacob (cf. Gen 28:14: "in you [Jacob] and in your offspring shall all the tribes of the earth be blessed"). In their interpretation of these passages, therefore, the new preachers in Galatia are probably telling the Galatians that "inasmuch as it is in Abraham that all the nations are to be blessed, the Gentiles to be blessed must be in Abraham, i.e., incorporated into his descendants by circumcision."[22]

Paul obviously reads the text of Gen 12:3 differently. He relates it to Gen 15:6. In the promise of Gen 12:3, Paul asserts, "the Scripture (*hē graphē*), having foreseen [in Gen 15:6] that God justifies the Gentiles on the basis of faith, preached the gospel in advance (*proeuēngelisato*) to Abraham." The intervening participial clause ("having foreseen . . . on the basis of faith") shows that Paul has his own understanding of the gospel in view (justification on the basis of faith rather than on the basis of the observance of the Law) in making this claim about "the Scripture" (cf. 2:16). Paul's personification of "the Scripture" (*hē graphē*), attributing to it foresight (of God's justification of the Gentiles on the basis of faith) and intentionality (preaching the gospel in advance to Abraham), is probably rhetorically motivated. The new preachers now active in Galatia attach great importance to the Scripture: it is undoubtedly *the* authority for them. Paul now solemnly summons this witness for his own theology, *against* the new preachers and their "different gospel" (1:6).

---

21. On the expression "works of the Law," see de Boer, *Galatians*, 145–48. It probably means "the observance of the Law." See above chapter 6.

22. Burton, *Galatians*, 159.

The personification is thus not to be unduly pressed, as if Paul is making some grand statement about the Scripture. It is probably a mere figure of speech,[23] serving a rhetorical purpose, which is to undermine the theology of the new preachers in Galatia on their own terms.[24] For Paul himself, the gospel is the final, in fact sole, authority, as the previous two chapters of the letter have repeatedly emphasized. In Gal 3:8, Paul means to say that God's justification of the Gentiles on the basis of faith, rather than on the basis of the Law, is actually attested in "the Scripture," i.e., "it stands written" (*gegraptai*) there (cf. 3:10, 13), as his quotation and interpretation of Gen 15:6 in 3:6–7 have just demonstrated and as his allusion back to the same passage in 3:9 ("faithful Abraham") will further underline (see below). As a matter of principle, and as foreseen by the Scripture the new preachers hold dear, God justifies the Gentiles on the basis of faith, *not* on the basis of Law observance. Paul thus solemnly subpoenas the Scripture so important for the new preachers' work in the churches of Galatia for his own understanding of the gospel as articulated especially in 2:16.

Paul's appeal to Scripture is clearly selective, since he simply ignores such inconvenient passages about Abraham as Gen 17:9–14. That selectivity once again becomes evident in 3:9, where he writes that "those who are from faith (*hoi ek pisteōs*, as in 3:7) are blessed with the faithful (*pistos*) Abraham." The latter part of the verse ("are blessed with the faithful Abraham") is (at one level) an allusion to the *story* of the near sacrifice of Isaac (Gen 22:1–19) and its interpretation in contemporary Jewish tradition. The promise that God makes to Abraham in LXX Gen 12:3 is reiterated in LXX Gen 22:18, where it is linked to Abraham's obedience: "in your offspring shall all the Gentiles/nations (*panta ta ethnē*) of the earth be blessed, *because you have obeyed my voice.*" Here "all the Gentiles" (or "nations") are blessed along with Abraham because of his obedience to God in connection with the near sacrifice of Isaac. In Sir 44:20–21, as in 1 Macc 2:52, Abraham is called "faithful" (*pistos*) precisely for having obeyed God's instructions in connection with Isaac (cf. *Jub.* 7:15–16); his faithful obedience provides the basis for the blessing of his offspring: "when he [Abraham] was tested [Gen 22:1–19] he proved faithful (*pistos*). Therefore the Lord assured him with an oath that the nations would be blessed (*eneulogēthēnai*) in his offspring [cf. Gen 22:18; 28:14]."

In Sirach too we see an appeal not to the Scripture as such but to the *figure* of Abraham himself as a unique figure of authority. It is entirely

---

23. Burton, *Galatians*, 160; R. N. Longenecker, *Galatians*, 115.

24. For the similar personification of Scripture in 3:22, see de Boer, *Galatians*, 234–35.

conceivable that the new preachers were doing the same, combining this appeal to the figure of Abraham with references to "what stands written" about him in "the Scripture." They would maintain that *those who are from works of the Law* (*hoi ex ergōn nomou*; cf. 3:10) are blessed with the faithful Abraham." The polemical nature of Paul's formulation in Gal 3:9 thereby becomes evident: "So then, *those who are from faith* (*hoi ek pisteōs*) are blessed with the faithful Abraham." The people who are "from faith" are the true offspring of Abraham, being heirs of the promise God made to Abraham. They are blessed with the promised Spirit (3:14) whose bestowal rests on faith, just as justification does, as the precedent provided by the patriarch himself demonstrates. The adjective *pistos* for Paul means "believing God and his promise," alluding back to 3:6 and its quotation from Gen 15:6, not "obeying God and his Law" (cf. LXX Gen 26:5; Sir 44:20), as in the Jewish tradition from which the new preachers take their bearings. Paul thereby dissociates "the faithful (*pistos*) Abraham" from Law-observance and associates him with "faith," specifically "the faith of Christ" (2:16).[25]

It is not the text of the OT as such that here functions as authoritative, but the figure of Abraham himself, at least as this figure is attested in Gen 15:6: the patriarch who believed God (God's promise) and it was reckoned to him as justification (God deemed him to be in the right, to be just). When Paul does explicitly cite an OT text, as he does in 3:8, it is in support of his own understanding of the gospel as the fulfillment of God's promise to Abraham by which the Gentiles are justified by faith and not by works of the Law (cf. 2:16). Other texts not supporting this view of the gospel (as Paul understands it) are simply ignored.

What then about 3:10 and 3:13 where Paul twice introduces a citation from the LXX with the solemn words "because (*gar/hoti*) it stands written (*gegraptai*)"? In both cases, Paul seeks to support an assertion concerning the existence of a curse with a citation from the LXX; in both cases, the citation begins with the words: "Accursed [= under a curse] is everyone who . . . " (*epikataros pas ho . . .*). In 3:10, he supports the claim that "those who are from works of the Law are under a curse" with a (modified) citation from LXX Deut 27:26: "Accursed (*epikataros*) is everyone who does not remain in all the things written in the book of the Law so as to do them."[26] In 3:13 he in turn supports the claim that "Christ became a curse [=

---

25. I am of the view that the genitive here is subjective, though taking the genitive as objective would not affect my argument in this chapter. See de Boer, *Galatians*, 148–50, and chapter 6 above.

26. LXX Deut 27:26 reads: "Accursed is every human being who does not remain in all the words of this Law so as to do them." On the significance of Paul's changes, see de Boer, *Galatians*, 199–201.

accursed/under a curse][27] for us" with a (modified) citation from LXX Deut 21:23: "Accursed (*epikataros*) is everyone who hangs on a tree."[28] A curse is the opposite of a blessing (cf. Gen 12:3; Deuteronomy 27–30); the two are mutually exclusive. With respect to 3:10, therefore, to be "under a curse," i.e., under "the curse of the Law" (3:13a), is to be deprived of a blessing, in this case the blessing of the promised Spirit, which is called "the blessing of Abraham" in 3:14 (cf. 3:8–9). For Paul, to be "under the Law" (3:23; 4:4–5, 21) is to be under its curse, as shown by the parallelism between 3:13 ("Christ redeemed [*exēgorasen*] us from *the curse of the Law*") and 4:4–5 ("God sent forth his Son . . . so that he [the Son] might redeem [*exagorasē*] *those under the Law*"). Christ's "having become (*genomenos*) a curse for us" in 3:13 then also means the same as Christ's "having become (*genomenos*) under the Law" in 4:4. In short, in both 3:10 and 3:13, Paul solemnly cites an Old Testament text to support his own understanding of the gospel and to undermine that of his opponents in Galatia (the new preachers active there), using what they hold most dear (the Scripture) against them. According to the Scripture they deem to have final authority in matters of faith and practice, they themselves stand under the Law's curse as does the crucified Christ! Put otherwise, Paul here cites the Scripture as an authority in order to show that the Law functions as a curse, in opposition to the new preachers in Galatia who have been quoting the Scripture in order to demonstrate to the Galatians that the Law of which Deuteronomy speaks is a source of blessing. The Law is a cursing force, not one that mediates the blessing promised to Abraham. And the Scripture to which the new preachers appeal can be summoned to underline the point. Paul's use of the Scripture is here a matter of expediency and serves his rhetorical agenda, which is to prevent the Galatians from consenting to the Law-based version of the gospel being proclaimed by the new preachers.

Consistent with this argument, in 3:16, Paul cites and interprets the phrase "and to your offspring," spoken to Abraham by God in LXX Gen 17:8, to refer to Christ himself (and, by implication, those who belong to him on the basis of faith), thus not to the people of the Law who stand in genealogical and historical continuity with the biological descendants of Abraham, as the new preachers are claiming. Paul does not cite the relevant phrase as proof for his own understanding of the gospel; he introduces the quotation simply with the words "it says" (*legei*). At issue is the "right"

---

27. See de Boer, *Galatians*, 211.

28. LXX Deut 21:23 reads: "Cursed (*kekatēramenos*) by God is everyone who hangs on a tree." Paul changes the first word to match that of Deut 27:26 as cited in 3:10. Paul also significantly omits the phrase "by God" (*hypo theou*) found in LXX Deut 21:23. On the significance of these changes, see de Boer, *Galatians*, 213.

interpretation of the phrase. Paul arguably interprets it against the grain.[29] For Paul, "the promises" which "were spoken to Abraham and his offspring" (3:16a) all concern Christ, the Christ through whom justification occurs on the basis of faith, not on the basis of Law observance.

That Paul is thinking "historically" about the promises spoken to Abraham in Genesis (cf. esp. Gen 17:1–8) is indicated by his remark that the Law "came four hundred thirty years" (3:17) after God made those promises. In underlining the exclusive christological significance of the promises to Abraham and his offspring in 3:16, Paul also deprives the event whereby the Law came on the human scene of any salvific importance whatsoever (cf. 3:19–21; 4:24–25). Its coming could not invalidate God's previously ratified "covenant" with Abraham "so as to void the promise" (3:17).[30]

Galatians 4:21–5:1

In 4:21, Paul addresses the Galatians explicitly as "you who are wanting to be under the Law," and he challenges them to listen to, and thus to understand, "the Law" in a new way: "do you not hear the Law?" With this question, Paul for the first time in the letter does not use the term "the Law" (*ho nomos*) to encapsulate the Sinaitic legislation with its many commandments and prohibitions. He now uses it in a play on words to mean "the Scripture" (4:30; cf. 1 Cor 14:21; Rom 3:19), in particular the Pentateuch in which the Sinaitic legislation is recorded (cf. Rom 3:21). In this usage Paul follows existing Jewish (and Jewish-Christian) custom and precedent (cf. Prologue to Sirach: "the Law and the prophets and the others that followed them"; Luke 24:44: "the Law of Moses, the prophets, and the psalms"; John 1:45: "Moses in the Law, and the prophets"). The new preachers, who are Christian Jews, are therefore probably also using the term in this way. The use of the term "Law" with this double meaning points to the intimate connection between the written text and the legislation it contains in the thought of the new preachers. In what follows, Paul will use this (positive) meaning of "the Law" as Scripture to undermine the importance and value of "the Law" as legislation to be observed.

What is particularly noteworthy is that when Paul asks the Galatians to listen to "the Law" he refers them not to a portion of Scripture containing legal regulations (*halakah*) but to a *story* (*haggadah*) found in Genesis 16–21 (16:1–16; 17:15–27; 18:9–15; 21:1–21), the story of Abraham and his two sons by two different women: "for it stands written that (γέγραπται γὰρ

---

29. See de Boer, *Galatians*, 221–24.

30. See the treatment of 3:15–22 in de Boer, *Galatians*, 216–36.

ὅτι) Abraham had two sons [Ishmael and Isaac], one from the slave woman [Hagar] and one from the free woman [Sarah]" (4:22). In this case, and unusually, the introductory formula "for it stands written that" (cf. 3:10, 13) does not introduce a direct quotation from the OT but a paraphrase of a *story* found there. Again, the introductory formula probably has a rhetorical motivation: to remind the new preachers who will be listening to the letter with the Galatians that this story is to be found in "the Scripture" to which they appeal for their own interpretation of the gospel. But it is to the story itself rather than to the text mediating the story that Paul here ascribes authority.

The paraphrase in 4:22 constitutes a brief summary and indicates that the Galatians are already familiar with the basic story found in Genesis 16–21. The new preachers have probably been telling the Galatians their own version of this story, one that supports their own version of the gospel.[31] This surmise explains not only why the Galatians seem to be familiar with the story (Paul nowhere mentions Sarah or Ishmael by name) but also why Paul feels compelled to call the attention of the Galatians to a passage whose value, as C. K. Barrett has noted, "from his point of view is anything but obvious."[32] For, as Barrett argues, by following the "plain, surface meaning" of the passage, the new preachers in Galatia can claim that "the Jews, who live by the law of Moses, are the heirs of Abraham" through the line established by his son Isaac, who was begotten by Sarah. "It is to Jews that the promise [made to Abraham] applies. . . . Here are the true people of God; and it will follow that Jerusalem is the authoritative centre of the renewed people of God, now called the church. Those who are not prepared to attach themselves to this community by the approved means (circumcision) must be cast out; they cannot hope to inherit promises made to Abraham and his seed."[33] In this light, it can probably be said that the new preachers regard the Galatians as offspring of Abraham through the line established by Ishmael, begotten by Hagar, Sarah's slave woman.[34] As those who do not practice circumcision and observe the Law, the Galatians, despite being believers in Christ, would not have the status of God's people, but that of Gentile "Ishmaelites" (Gen 37:27).

In his periphrastic summary of the story in 4:22, Paul introduces a word not found in Genesis itself: While Hagar (vs. 25) is called "the slave woman" (*paidiskē*)[35] in Gen 16:1–10; 21:10–13, Sarah (whose name Paul does

31. Cf. Barrett, "Allegory"; cf. de Boer, *Galatians*, 286–88.

32. Barrett, "Allegory," 162.

33. Barrett, "Allegory," 162; cf. Gal 3:15–18.

34. Longenecker, *Galatians*, 201; cf. Gen 16:10.

35. The word is the diminutive of *pais* (girl, or boy) and is commonly used in

not even mention) is never there called "the free woman" (*hē eleuthera*). Indeed, the word and its cognates are completely absent from Genesis. Already in his initial summary, then, Paul establishes the contrast between slavery and freedom that determines the dominant polarity of the passage. He thereby associates Sarah explicitly with freedom, the freedom from slavery that Christ has effected for believers in him (cf. 3:13; 4:1–7; 5:1). Paul clearly assumes that the Galatians will know to whom he is referring with his mention of "the free woman."[36]

In 4:23 Paul expands the summary of the Genesis account by pointing to the different circumstances of the births of the two sons: "But (*alla*) [the decisive point is that] the one from the slave woman has been born according to the flesh, [whereas] the one from the free woman [has been born] through a promise." Paul here uses another term (in addition to "the free woman") not found in LXX Genesis 16–21, the verb "to be born" (*gennaō*).[37] In addition, the phrases "according to the flesh (*kata sarka*)" and "through a promise (*epangelia*)"[38] are also absent from the Genesis account. Paul is clearly not bound by the wording of the original (Greek) text.

The *story*, as Paul understands it, is the key. In that story, Sarah was unable to bear children, leading her to allow Abraham to beget a child by Hagar, her slave woman (Gen 16:1–4). The result was that Hagar bore Abraham a son, Ishmael (16:15). God, however, also promised Abraham that Sarah would bear him a son despite the fact that she was far beyond child-bearing age (Gen 17:17; 18:11). The promise is repeatedly made (17:21; 18:10, 14; cf. 15:4). Despite the initial skepticism of both Abraham and Sarah (17:17–18; 18:12), Sarah does bear Abraham a son (21:1–3). Paul's contrast between the slave woman's son "born according to the flesh" and the free woman's son "[born] through a promise" clearly reflects this account but he casts it in his own words.[39]

On this foundation, Paul goes on to give the passage his own "allegorical" interpretation, i.e., as saying one thing while actually intending

---

contemporary Greek literature to designate a female slave (BAGD, 749–750).

36. For this reason, it is possible that this designation for Sarah has been derived from the teaching of the new preachers in Galatia. For them, too, Sarah, Isaac, and freedom undoubtedly belong together (cf. John 8:33 where "the offspring of Abraham" claim to be "free").

37. This verb can also mean "to beget" as well as "to bear." The verb *tiktō* is used in Genesis 16–21 with the latter meaning (Gen 16:15; 21:1–3), as it is in LXX Isa 54:1 which Paul quotes in Gal 4:27. For discussion, see de Boer, *Galatians*, 292–93.

38. This term and its cognates are absent from the LXX text of Genesis.

39. Paul says nothing here with which the new preachers in Galatia will have disagreed.

something else, in 4:24–26. In doing so, he is, as Barrett observes, "*correct-ing the exegesis*" of the passage by the new preachers.[40] According to Paul's allegorical reading, the two women of the story represent "two covenants" (4:24): Hagar the covenant of the Law given on Mt. Sinai (vss. 24–25) and Sarah the covenant of the promise God made to Abraham (cf. 3:15–18) and, in fact, to Sarah as well. "The slave woman" (Hagar) is thus to be aligned with "the present Jerusalem" (4:25), evidently standing for the church now spon-soring the new preachers and their Law-centered gospel, whereas "the free woman" (Sarah) is to be aligned with "the Jerusalem above" (4:26), standing for the truly liberated people of God (5:1a; cf. 3:13; 4:4–5). In short, for Paul believers in Christ who are now free from the Law (Paul and his converts in Galatia) are the (spiritual) descendants of Abraham, following the pattern of his son Isaac who was begotten through God's promise by Sarah, "the free woman" (4:22–23, 30–31), whereas those believers in Christ who observe the Law beginning with circumcision and now want Gentile believers in Galatia to do the same (the new preachers in Galatia and their sponsors in Jerusa-lem) are actually the (fleshly) descendants of Abraham via his son *Ishmael* who was begotten by Hagar, "the slave woman" (4:22–23, 30–31)! The "chil-dren" of the free woman (the Jerusalem above) are also free, just like their mother, whereas the "children" of the slave woman (the present Jerusalem) are also slaves, just like *their* mother. Paul has thereby managed to "reverse the family relationships of the descendants of Abraham"[41]—he has evidently turned the (seemingly much more plausible) interpretation of the Genesis account by the new preachers in Galatia on its head!

In 4:27, Paul explains where his thinking about the two Jerusalems originates, in LXX Isa 54:1:[42] "For it stands written: Rejoice, barren one who does not bear, break forth and shout, you who are not in labor, for many [will be] the children of the desolate woman, more than of the woman who has a husband." Neither the LXX text nor Paul's citation of it has a verb in the third line (the corresponding text in the MT also has no verb), but the context of the verse within Second Isaiah seems to demand that a future tense of the verb "to be" is presupposed (cf. RSV, NRSV, REB; present tense: NJB, KJV, NIV). Paul applies the word of consolation and the promise he hears in the words of (Second) Isaiah, not to the earthly Jerusalem (as Second Isa-iah does), but to the new or heavenly Jerusalem, represented by Sarah: once barren but now, solely as a result of God's faithfulness to his promise, with

---

40. Barrett, "Allegory," 158, emphasis added; cf. Martyn, *Galatians*, 450.

41. Barrett, "Allegory," 167.

42. For more detail and argument, see de Boer, *Galatians*, 302–5, and chapter 10 below.

many children ("our mother"). The promise Paul hears in Isa 54:1, therefore, has come to fulfillment in the free children of the heavenly Jerusalem, or, perhaps better, is now in the process of being fulfilled.[43] Ever since Christ, the one seed of Abraham (3:16, 19), "came" (3:19, 23, 25) into the world to "redeem" those "under the Law" (4:4–5), the (eschatological) future belongs, according to Paul's reading of Isa 54:1, to the children given birth by the Jerusalem above. Paul's understanding of the gospel of Christ in terms of promise (cf. 4:23, 28) finds its confirmation in Isaiah.[44] But it is Christ who here validates the Scripture and not the other way around.

In 4:28, Paul comes to the penultimate goal of his allegorical reading of the story of Abraham and his two sons by Hagar and Sarah, which is to confirm once again (cf. 3:8–29) the identity of the believers in Galatia as the descendants of the promissory covenant God made with Abraham and Sarah: "[Despite what the new preachers are saying] You (hymeis), brethren (alelphoi), like Isaac (kata Isaak),[45] are children of promise." The new preachers are probably pointing out to the Galatians that those who observe the Law are the direct heirs of Abraham via the line of descent established through Isaac, his son by his wife Sarah. The observers of the Law, i.e., the members of the covenant people of Israel, including those who have embraced Jesus as the Messiah, stand in direct, historical continuity with Abraham and the covenant God made with him. That covenant found its continuity in Isaac and the latter's physical descendants. Paul agrees that the birth of Isaac represents the continuity of the covenant with Abraham, but he presents Isaac, whose conception and birth occurred as a result of God's promise, merely as the "type" for believers in Christ in the present, and then particularly and emphatically of the Galatians ("You"). The "right" interpretation of the event of Isaac's birth is here at issue. According to Paul, believers in Christ are offspring of Abraham (cf. 3:29) not by physical descent ("according to the flesh") but "by a promise" (4:23), a promise that found its fulfillment in Christ and the Spirit (3:14, 18). The birth of these children is as miraculous as that of Isaac was to the aged Sarah, which is to say that it was brought about by God. Paul has already established the identity of the Galatians as "sons of Abraham" (3:8) and as "offspring of Abraham" (3:29) on the basis of the faith rather than works of the Law. The idea that the Galatians were thereby children of promise was

43. See also Paul's use and interpretation of Lev 19:18 in 5:14 as a promise that has been fulfilled in Christ (de Boer, *Galatians*, 341–54).

44. On the particular importance of Isaiah for Paul, see Wilk, *Die Bedeutung des Jesajabuches für Paulus*; Wagner, *Heralds of the Good News*.

45. Literally, "in accordance with Isaac," here probably meaning "in the pattern of Isaac" (Martyn, *Galatians*, 443).

already implicit in that argument; it is here made explicit. It is once again the *story* of Abraham along with his son, Isaac, that is here at issue between Paul and the new preachers rather than "the Scripture" as such.

The same is true in 4:29, where Paul resorts to another typological comparison: "But (*alla*) just as at that time the one who was born according to the flesh (Ishmael) was persecuting the one [born] according to the Spirit (Isaac), so also now." Just as Ishmael "was persecuting" Isaac, Paul claims, "so also now" the new preachers, who are promoting fleshly circumcision (cf. 3:3; 6:12–13), are "persecuting" those of the Spirit, the Gentile churches of Galatia (cf. 3:1–5; 5:13–24). The Genesis account does not actually indicate that Ishmael persecuted Isaac. It is also unclear in what sense persecution is occurring "now." Whatever the case may be,[46] Paul is not here appealing to "the Scripture" but to an element of the story of Abraham and his two sons whereby he implies that the new preachers, who are presumably the ones doing the persecuting in the Galatian situation, are the descendants not of Isaac but of Ishmael.

Paul's perception and characterization of the situation in Galatia makes sense of the following verse and its use of Gen 21:10: "But what does the Scripture say? 'Throw out (*ekbale*) the slave woman [Hagar] and her son, for the son of the slave woman shall certainly not (*ou* μή) inherit [what was promised] with the son of the free woman [Sarah] (Gen 21:10)'" (4:30). In Genesis, the quoted words are those of Sarah to Abraham: "Throw out this slave woman and her son, for the son of this slave woman shall not inherit with my son Isaac." God approves these words in Gen 21:12, telling Abraham to "listen to her voice, because in Isaac shall be your offspring." The point is the exclusion of Ishmael as Abraham's legitimate heir. Paul makes Sarah's words to Abraham into words of "the Scripture" addressed to the Galatians in the present, even though the imperative in Greek is singular in form (*ekbale*). He adapts the text accordingly, changing the last phrase "my son Isaac" into "the son of the free woman" (cf. 4:22–23). The question "What does the Scripture say?" is therefore not to be taken as Paul's acknowledgement of the authority of Scripture and the bringing of that authority to bear in his argument.[47] The point is that the new preachers in Galatia attribute primary authority to Scripture and Paul now uses this attribution against them (see above on 3:10 and 13). According to the Scripture they hold dear, they are in fact to be "thrown out" of the churches of Galatia! Paul is not here pursuing an exegetical argument, but

46. For discussion, see de Boer, *Galatians*, 306–7.

47. This is the third time in the letter that Paul personifies "the Scripture" (3:8, 22). See the discussion of 3:8 above for the possible significance of this.

summoning the Scripture to which the new preachers attach primary authority for his own agenda, which is to undermine their influence on the churches of Galatia and thus to prevent the Galatians from taking up the practice of circumcision and the remainder of the Law.

Because of Paul's peculiar, not to say strained, interpretation of the story of Abraham and his two sons in 4:21—5:1, it is difficult to maintain, as Tolmie does in this connection that Paul here pursues an argument "based on the authority of scripture."[48] Paul's argument is based rather on a christologically informed authoritative *interpretation* of Scripture. Paul's christologically informed allegorical and typological appropriation of the text indicates that Paul's concern is the *story* of Abraham and his two sons and not so much the text itself. His allegorical and typological reading of the text arguably highlights the contemporary relevance of the story of Abraham and his two sons at the expense of the literal meaning of the text being interpreted.

Conclusion

My initial question was: What is the status of the OT text for Paul in Galatians and what is the value, or the authority, of OT history for him in this letter?

With respect to the latter, it has become evident that *selected* features of the story of Abraham in Genesis are important for Paul's understanding of what he calls "the gospel of Christ" (1:7). At the same time, the event of the coming of the Law is deprived of any saving significance.[49] Paul is reacting to new preachers in Galatia, who are preaching a "different gospel" (1:6) there, who emphasize other aspects of the story of Abraham, particularly in connection with the rite of circumcision, and who regard the event of God's giving of the Law by the hand of Moses at Mt. Sinai as central (cf. 3:19–21; 4:24–25).

With respect to the status of the OT text in Galatians, it is very unlikely that "Paul regarded the words of Scripture as having absolute authority for his predominantly Gentile congregations."[50] Such a claim attributes to Paul what is probably true of the new preachers in Galatia. For Paul, the gospel is the standard of all truth, including that of "the Scripture." He selects texts that support his own understanding of the gospel (such as Gen 15:6 in Gal

48. Tolmie, *Persuading the Galatians,* 169.

49. See above chapters 3, 4, and 8.

50. So Stanley, *Paul and the Language of Scripture,* 338; cf. similarly Tolmie, *Persuading the Galatians,* 111.

3:6 or Isa 54:1 in Gal 4:27), ignores those that do not (such as Gen 17:9–14), and cites others that undermine the views of the new preachers in Galatia and their attempt to convince the Galatians to begin practicing circumcision and observe the Law (such as Deut 27:26 in 3:10 or Deut 21:23 in Gal 3:13). Paul also resorts to allegorical and typological interpretation to make the texts witnesses of the gospel as he understands it (in Gal 4:21—5:1). He seeks in other words to make "the Scripture" that functions as an absolute authority for the new preachers in Galatia captive (cf. 2 Cor 10:5) for the gospel that he preached when he founded the churches in Galatia (1:11; 4:13) and that he still proclaims among the Gentiles (2:2).

Chapter 10

Paul's Quotation of Isaiah 54:1
in Galatians 4:27

Introduction

THE IMPORTANCE OF THE quotation of Isa 54:1 in Gal 4:27 for understand-ing Paul's allegorical reading of the story of Sarah and Hagar (Genesis 16–21) in Gal 4:21—5:1 has often been underestimated. In this chapter, I argue that Paul uses this quotation to give his interpretation of this story an eschatological dimension that, unlike the eschatology of Second Isaiah, is both profoundly christological and apocalyptic.

Paul quotes from the Greek Old Testament (LXX) a number of times in his Letter to the Galatians, as we have seen in the previous chapter. The quotations are sometimes more or less clearly marked as such (in 3:8, 10, 13, 16; 4:30; 5:14), sometimes not (in 3:6, 11, 12). The quotation of Isa 54:1 in 4:27 is one that is clearly marked, being introduced with an introductory formula "for it is written" (*gegraptai gar*), as are the quotations in 3:10 (also *gegraptai gar*) and 3:13 (*hoti gegraptai*). Paul's citation follows the text of LXX Isa 54:1 exactly:[1]

> *euphranthēti, steira hē ou tiktousa,*
>
> *rhēxon kai boēson, hē ouk ōdinousa:*
>
> *hoti polla ta tekna tēs erēmou*
>
> *mallon ē tēs exousēs ton andra*

> Rejoice, barren one who does not bear;
>
> break forth and shout, you who are not in labor;
>
> for many [will be] the children of the desolate one,
>
> more than [the children] of her who has a husband.

---

1. Verhoef, "*Er staat geschreven*," 91–95; Smith, "Pauline Literature," 271; Stanley, *Paul and the Language of Scripture*, 248n231.

Neither the LXX text nor Paul's citation of it has a verb in the third line (the corresponding text in the MT also has no verb), but the context of the verse *within Second Isaiah* (= Isaiah 40–55) seems to demand that a future tense (of the verb *eimi*) be mentally supplied.[2] In Isaiah, these words look to the future and thus promise the restoration of Jerusalem which is here likened to a barren woman, now desolate because she is without children and thus without a future. However, there will come a time when she will have many more children than the woman who is married. This second woman is probably meant to represent Babylon where the exiles to whom Second Isaiah is addressed live.[3]

Paul's use of this verse from Second Isaiah thus gives his so-called allegory[4] of Hagar and Sarah in 4:21—5:1[5] an *eschatological* dimension, as

2. Cf. RSV, NRSV, REB (present tense: NJB, KJV, NIV). Second Isaiah was probably written to and for Jerusalemites who had become exiles in Babylon (43:14; 48:20) following the destruction of Jerusalem (44:26–28; 49:14–23) early in the sixth century BCE. Second Isaiah (ca. 550 BCE) consoles and encourages its intended readers with the promise of a new future for Jerusalem and its exiled inhabitants (41:21–23; 42:9; 43:1–7; 44:26–28; 54:1–17).

3. Martyn's observation that there "are not two woman and two cities" in Isa 54:1 but only one woman representing Jerusalem in two phases of her history, "first in desolation, then in fecund affluence" (*Galatians*, 442) applies only to the first three lines of Isa 54:1 (cf. 443, and Martyn, "Covenants of Hagar and Sarah," 195). Isa 54:1 clearly contrasts two women in the third and fourth lines, the one now desolate (abandoned) but soon to be fecund, the other married and already fecund. As Childs writes: "In vss. 1–3 the portrait of the desolate mother is set over against the joyous surprise of suddenly experiencing an abundance of children, greater in number than those conceived by a woman who was not barren" (*Isaiah*, 428; also Bonnard, *Second Isaïe*, 289). The second woman, then, may represent Babylon for Second Isaiah (on Babylon as a woman, see Isa 47:1–4). The Targum to Isaiah (from the rabbinic period) assumes two women in Isa 54:1, with the second representing Rome (the rulers of Judea at that time): "For the children of desolate Jerusalem will be more than the children of inhabited Rome, says the Lord" (translation Chilton, *Isaiah Targum*, 105). The link between Babylon and Rome was commonly made in Jewish (and Christian) apocalyptic works, namely, *4 Ezra* (3:1–2, 28), *2 Baruch* (11:1–2; 67:6), and Revelation (14:8; 16:19; 17:5, 18; 18:2). We will argue below that Paul also assumes that there are two women mentioned in Isa 54:1.

4. Note Paul's use of the verb *allegoreō* in 4:24 (on which see Büchsel, "*allegoreō*," *TWNT*, 1.262–64). It is not clear, however, whether Paul regards the story of Hagar and Sarah in Genesis as in fact an allegory, or makes the story into an allegory through the new elements he adds to it (cf. Witherington, *Grace in Galatia*, 321), or simply gives the story an allegorical interpretation (Verhoef, "*Er staat geschreven*," 263–64). I will use the expression "allegorizing interpretation" to cover the latter two possibilities, with "allegorical interpretation" as a synonym. See further nn. 6 and 18 below.

5. There is disagreement among the commentators about whether 5:1 belongs to the unit (e.g., Martyn, *Galatians*; Vouga, *Galater*) or not (e.g., Burton, *Galatians*; Betz, *Galatians*; Longenecker, *Galatians*). In my view, it belongs to the unit because it picks up and rounds off the opposition between freedom and slavery that is introduced in

commonly recognized.[6] The question we seek to answer in this short study however is: *How and why* does Paul make use of Isa 54:1 to articulate *his own* eschatology which, unlike that of Second Isaiah, is both profoundly *christological[7] and apocalyptic*?[8]

Since Galatians is often regarded as a letter from which apocalyptic eschatology (understood to involve a future expectation, i.e., of the Parousia) is largely absent,[9] a brief word needs to be said about apocalyptic.[10] I here focus on those aspects which are particularly important for Paul's adaptation of Jewish apocalyptic eschatology in the passage chosen for analysis. Fundamental to (Jewish or Christian) apocalyptic is the notion of two world ages ("this age" and "the age to come"), both of which are matters of revelation (cf. Rev 1:1). The two ages are not simply, or even primarily, temporal categories, referring to two successive, discontinuous periods of world history ("ages"); they are also (at least in one prominent strand of Jewish apocalyptic thinking)[11] spatial categories, referring to two spheres or orbs of power both

---

4:22 and is a recurrent theme throughout (4:23, 24, 25, 26, 30, 31).

6. See e.g., Betz, *Galatians*, 248; Longenecker, *Galatians*, 215–16; Dunn, *Galatians*, 255. Cf. Str-B 3.574–75 for the text's role in Jewish eschatological expectations.

7. Christ is explicitly named in 5:1 and in 4:19 and thus provides the larger theological context within which Paul presents and interprets the allegory of Hagar and Sarah, as well as the citation from Isa 54:1. The words of Büchsel (*"allegoreō,"* 264) concerning Paul remain pertinent: "Seine Allegorese wird etwas Besonderes gegenüber der jüdische—sowohl der palästinensischen als der alexandrinischen—dadurch, dass er die Schrift auslegt als einer, der in der Zeit der Erfüllung lebt . . . so dass nun die eigentliche Sinn des AT erkannbar wird. Die Allegorese wird ihm zum Mittel, sein neues christozentrisches, 'staurozentrisches' Schriftverständnis durchzufuhren." See Koch, *Die Schrift als Zeuge des Evangeliums.*

8. Aside from the commentaries, there have been a number of studies of this passage in recent years: Barrett, "Allegory"; Koch, *Schrift*, 204–11; Bouwman, "Die Hagar- und Sara-Perikope"; Malan, "The strategy"; Perriman, "Rhetorical Strategy"; Jobes, "Jerusalem, our Mother"; Borgen, "Some Hebrew and Pagan Features"; Martyn, "Covenants"; Bachmann, "Die andere Frau"; Sellin, "Hagar und Sara"; Elliott, "Choose Your Mother"; Tolmie, "Allegorie"; Brawley, "Contextuality." Only Jobes and Brawley focus specifically on the citation of Isa 54:1, both building on the treatment of Hays, *Echoes*, 105–121. Their concern is the phenomenon of intertextuality, not the apocalyptic import of Paul's use of this text. Both Jobes and Brawley, furthermore, fail to take sufficiently into account how Paul's Gentile-Christian hearers/readers in Galatia would have heard the text, i.e., whether and to what extent they would have recognized the intertextual echoes laid bare in their respective analyses.

9. See Beker, *Paul the Apostle*, 97–105; Martyn, *Theological Issues*, 85–156, 176–82.

10. See in addition to de Boer, *Defeat of Death* and "Paul and Apocalyptic Eschatology," chapters 1 and 2 in this volume.

11. Identified in chapter 1 above as the "cosmological" pattern, which is to be distinguished from the "forensic" pattern. Martyn has made creative use of this distinction in *Galatians*, esp. 97–98; cf. Martyn, *Theological Issues*, 298–99.

of which claim sovereignty over the world. In "this age," alien, destructive powers have taken complete control of God's creation, including the cosmos of human beings, and perverted it. "This age" is, then, the realm of sin, death, and evil (what Paul in Gal 1:4 refers to as "the present evil age"). Human beings are slaves of evil, malevolent powers who have usurped God's rightful claim on the world. In "the age to come," which in Jewish apocalyptic eschatology is to be revealed in the future even as it already exists in heaven above, God will (once more) reign unopposed over the whole creation. For this reason, "the age to come" is the realm of righteousness, life, and peace. The powers of the new age (God and those whom he delegates, e.g., the Messiah) will thus at the end of time reveal themselves, i.e., invade from heaven above the orb of the powers on Earth below (the orb of Satan and his minions), and aggressively defeat them, thereby removing them from the creation and liberating human beings from their malevolent, destructive control. Within the framework of the apocalyptic dualism of the two world ages understood spatially as well as temporally, this end-time event (traditionally known as the "Last Judgment") is necessarily (1) cosmic in scope and implication (all peoples and all times are affected), (2) an act of God (God invades the human cosmos since human beings are in no position to liberate themselves from the evil powers), (3) rectifying (God puts right what has gone wrong in and with the world) and (4) eschatological (i.e., final, definitive, and irrevocable). In ancient Jewish apocalyptic eschatology, the turn of the ages, when "this age" is brought to an end and "the age to come" takes its place, will signify God's eschatological act of cosmic rectification.

In *Paul's* view, God has initiated this eschatological act of cosmic rectification in the person and the work of Jesus Christ. When God sent forth his Son into the world (Gal 4:4) to liberate human beings from enslaving powers (4:3–4), God began a unified apocalyptic drama of cosmic rectification that will reach its conclusion at Christ's Parousia (1 Thess 4:13–18; 1 Cor 15:20–28). Believers live neither in the old age nor in the new; they live at the juncture of the ages where the forces of the new age ("the kingdom of God") are in an ongoing struggle with the forces of the old age (especially Sin, Death and, surprisingly, the Sinaitic Law).[12] Paul's christological adaptation of Jewish apocalyptic eschatology thus contains the well known

12. This point is controversial, but one may note how *in Galatians* Paul can speak of (all) human beings before and apart from Christ as being *hypo nomon*, "under the Law" (3:23; 4:4–5, 21; 5:18), whereby the Law is presented as an oppressive, enslaving power from which Christ redeems human beings (3:13; 4:4–5). To be "under the Law" is to be "under a curse" (3:10), "under a custodian" (3:25), "under guardians and overseers" (4:2), "under the elements of the cosmos" (4:3) and indeed "under Sin" (3:22). See Martyn, *Galatians*, 370–73. Cf. Rom 6:14–15.

tension between an "already" (God has already acted apocalyptically to liberate human beings from enslaving powers)[13] and a "still more" (God has not yet finished the job).[14] In Galatians, the emphasis falls decisively upon the "already" of God's apocalyptic action in sending forth his Son into the human world to liberate human beings from suprahuman, enslaving powers, thereby "rectifying" (*dikaiō*) what has gone wrong in their relationship with God (1:4; 2:16; 3:13; 4:1–6).[15]

Paul's peculiar interpretation of the stories of Hagar and Sarah (and Abraham, Ishmael, and Isaac) in Gal 4:21—5:1 also places the emphasis on the "already," as 5:1a makes absolutely clear, and this means that the promise of Isa 54:1 has for Paul been fulfilled, or at least is in the process of being fulfilled now that Christ and his Spirit have come into the human world (cf. 3:1–5; 4:1–7).

The Function of Isa 54:1 in Paul's Argument[16]

As noted above, Paul cites the verse in his allegorizing interpretation of the stories about Hagar and Sarah in Genesis. Abraham had sons by both women (4:22), Ishmael and Isaac respectively (cf. Gen 16:1–16; 17:15–27; 18:9–15; 21:1–21).[17] Paul is scarcely interested in the two women or the two sons, however, except insofar as they serve as symbols for realities and developments in the past (i.e., in the history of Abraham and his descendants) and as types pointing beyond themselves to realities and developments in

---

13. Cf. Gal 5:1: "For freedom Christ has set us free; stand fast therefore, and do not submit again to a yoke slavery" (NRSV).

14. Cf. Gal 5:5: "For through the Spirit, by faith, we wait for the hope of righteousness" (NRSV).

15. See Martyn *Theological Issues*, 121–22: "It is [in Galatians] the time after the apocalypse of the faith of Christ (3:23–25), the time of things being set right by that faith, the time of the presence of the Spirit, and thus the time of a new war of liberation commenced by the Spirit." For "rectify" and "rectification" as translations of *dikaioō* and its cognate noun *dikaiosynē*, see Martyn, *Galatians*, 249–50.

16. In this section we focus on *how* Paul deploys Isa 54:1 in his *argumentation in a way that will have made sense to his readers or hearers in Galatia*, in the next section on *why* he does so. The separation between the "how" question and the "why" question is merely a matter of convenience and emphasis however. The two can scarcely be neatly separated since both questions seek to discover Paul's *intention* (his message to the churches in Galatia) in making use of Isa 54:1.

17. Paul quotes Gen 21:10 in 4:30, but 4:22–23 seems to be a summary of the Sarah-Hagar material that begins in Genesis 16.

Paul's own time and situation (Paul's allegorical reading of the Genesis narrative thus has typological dimensions).[18]

Allegorically interpreted, the two women represent "two covenants" (4:24) for Paul, even though Genesis in fact mentions only one covenant with Abraham and his offspring (Gen 15:18; 17:1–8), as Paul knows (Gal 3:15–17). According to Gen 17:19–21, this one covenant was valid only for the line of descent established through Isaac, not for the line of descent established through Ishmael. For Paul, Hagar allegorically represents another covenant, namely, the one with Moses on "Mount Sinai" (Gal 4:24–25),[19] despite the fact that this covenant came into effect, by Paul's own reckoning, some "four hundred and thirty years" after the covenant with Abraham (3:17; cf. Ex 12:40 LXX). Paul thus plays the covenant with Abraham off against the covenant at Sinai, using polarizing language (slave/free, flesh/promise).[20] When Paul says "two covenants," he clearly means "two *different* covenants," or even "two mutually exclusive covenants."[21]

18. Neither Sarah nor Ishmael are mentioned by name, which probably means that the Galatians are presumed to be familiar with the basic story (cf. Barrett, "Allegory," 161; for a different explanation, see Elliott, "Choose Your Mother," 671, 682). Philo also allegorizes the two women (e.g., *Congr.* 23), but for him they signify, as Martyn writes (*Galatians*, 436), "timeless human qualities (Sarah as self-taught virtue and Hagar as imperfect training)." Paul's allegorical reading has a historical (typological) aspect that Philo's lacks. Longenecker conveniently presents the texts from Philo (*Galatians*, 204–5).

19. Such is the case no matter how the difficult text-critical problem at the beginning of 4:25 is resolved. The clue to Paul's identification of Hagar with Mount Sinai (and thus with the Mosaic covenant) seems to lie in 4:25a but this half-verse has proved notoriously difficult to understand. For a survey of opinion, see Tolmie, "Allegorie," 170–71. If one accepts the reading of Nestle-Aland[27], one can translate "Now 'Hagar' is Mount Sinai in Arabia" (cf. Borgen, "Some Hebrew and Pagan Features," 157: the initial *to* is equivalent to quotation marks). How Paul comes to this conclusion is not clear and the Galatians would in any case have heard it as a simple assertion: "I would have you know that the Hagar mentioned in the Genesis stories is actually a reference to Mount Sinai in Arabia, and thus to the covenant that enslaves." For a recent attempt to solve this enigma, see Elliott, "Choose Your Mother," who sees a link to "the familiar image of a Mountain Mother" in an Anatolian context (667); see, however, the pertinent critique of Brawley, "Contextuality," 115n62.

20. The metaphorical contrast between slavery and freedom is prominent throughout, occurring six times in the passage (4:22, 23, 24–26, 30, 31; 5:1), followed by the contrast between flesh and promise/spirit (4:23, 28, 29). See Tolmie, "Allegorie," 166–67.

21. Brawley ("Contextuality," 99–100, 114–16) attempts to show that Paul actually wants to "synthesize" the Abrahamic and Mosaic covenants (in his view, the troublemakers in Galatia sought to separate them) with "a salvation history perspective" (116n66) whereby the "present" Jerusalem (symbolizing slavery) is superseded by the one "above" (symbolizing freedom): "The supersession is not temporal (Gentiles after Israel), nor ethnic (Gentiles or Israel), but qualitative (freedom over slavery)" (116). But Brawley misconstrues what Paul says about the two Jerusalems (see n. 31 below).

In 4:25–26, moreover, Paul correlates the two distinct covenants with two distinct Jerusalems and thereby provides a contemporizing interpretation of the Hagar and Sarah stories. Allegorically representing adherence to the Mosaic covenant in Paul's own time and situation,[22] Hagar, the slave woman (4:22, 30; cf. Gen 21:10), whose son Ishmael was "begotten according to the flesh" (4:22), corresponds (*systoichei*)[23] to "the *present* Jerusalem, which is "in slavery [to the Sinaitic legislation] along with her children,"[24] whereas Sarah, the free woman (4:22–23), whose son Isaac was "begotten through [God's] promise" (4:22; cf. Gen 17:16), corresponds[25] to "the Jerusalem above" which is "free [from the Sinaitic legislation]" and "our mother" (4:25–26).[26] Here it becomes evident that Paul posits what Martyn calls "a distinctly apocalyptic contrast"[27] between "the present Jerusalem" and "the Jerusalem above," the

22. Note the repeated use of the present tense from 4:24 onwards.

23. More strongly, "stand[s] in the same line [with]" (BAGD, 979); cf. Borgen, "Some Hebrew and Pagan Features," 160 ("stand[s] in the same rank or line") and Martyn, *Galatians*, 432, 449 ("located in the same oppositional column with"). Brawley ("Contextuality," 111n46) and Koch (*Schrift*, 205n14) disagree; according to Brawley, one would then expect *antistoichei* to be used (cf. LSJ, 163: "stand opposite in rows or pairs"); according to Koch, one would then expect *hē sustoichei hē nun Ierousalēm* ("to which the present Jerusalem corresponds"). LSJ (1735) suggests "corresponds" for Gal 4:25. Either way there are pairs of opposites that can be arranged in two columns.

24. The subject of the verb "corresponds" (*systoichei*) in 4:25 could be either "Hagar," "Mount Sinai," or even "one (covenant)." In the latter case, 4:25a would be parenthetical: "For these women are two covenants: the one from Mount Sinai bearing children for slavery, which is Hagar (4:24)—now "Hagar" is Mount Sinai in Arabia (4:25a)— corresponds to the present Jerusalem" (4:25b). However, the fact that "the Jerusalem above" in the next verse is called "our mother" and thus likened to a woman indicates that Hagar is the intended subject in 4:25b. A choice is not essential since "Hagar" is taken to symbolize "Mount Sinai" and thus also the covenant ratified there.

25. See n. 23.

26. Having introduced the present Jerusalem and her enslaved children in 4:25, Paul rushes on to mention the Jerusalem above and label her "our mother" in 4:26 without explicitly mentioning Sarah either by name or as "the free woman," as in 4:22–23 and 31. But these latter verses provide the literary "frame" of the intervening allegorical interpretation and this frame demonstrates that the Galatians are to understand that Sarah/the free woman is presupposed in 4:26. There is also the characterization of the Jerusalem above as "free," marking the link to "the free woman" of 4:22–23, 31. One can paraphrase 4:26 as follows: "But the Jerusalem above, who is our mother, is free, just as Sarah the mother of Isaac was." The citation in 4:27 makes it certain that Sarah is simply being presupposed in 4:26 (see just below), just as 4:28 makes it certain that the promissory covenant with Abraham (3:14, 15–18; cf. Gen 17:2, 4, 7), though not explicitly mentioned, is also being presupposed in 4:26 (cf. Sellin, "Hagar und Sara," 66, 70).

27. *Galatians*, 440. This contrast could presumably also be characterized as "an apocalyptic antinomy" by Martyn ("Apocalyptic Antinomies"; *Theological Issues*, 111– 24, esp. 115), akin to the antinomy between the Flesh and the Spirit in 5:16–17, which is anticipated by the same contrast in 4:29 (cf. 3:3). See also Bouwman, "Die Hagar– und

former being a reality of the old age and the latter a reality of the new.[28] From the one, children are now being born "according to the Flesh," from the other, "according to the Spirit" (4:29; cf. 5:16–17).[29] These two realities are engaged in an apocalyptic struggle in the present, i.e., in the time of Paul and the Galatians (cf. 4:30). The outcome of the struggle is not in doubt for Paul, *as the quotation from Isa 54:1 with its eschatological promise makes plain.* The quotation of this particular verse, in its original Isaian context a consolatory and prophetic word spoken to the barren and desolate Jerusalem, follows immediately upon the interpretation of Sarah as "the Jerusalem above," who is "our mother" (4:26). The "free woman" (Sarah) had also been barren, having borne no children (Gen 11:30), as the Galatians know,[30] and she too had been in need of consolation, that consolation being God's stunning promise (received by Sarah when she was in fact already far beyond child-bearing age!) that she would indeed bear a child despite the seeming hopelessness of her situation from a human point of view (Gen 18:9–15). And that promise had come to pass (Gen 21:1–2, 6–7), as the Galatians also know (cf. 4:28: "like Isaac"). Paul thus applies the word of consolation and the promise he hears in the words of (Second) Isaiah not to the earthly Jerusalem (as Second Isaiah does) but to the new or heavenly Jerusalem, represented by Sarah, once barren but now, solely as a result of God's faithfulness to his promise,

---

Sara-Perikope," 3149.

28. Cf. Rev 3:12; 21:2, 10; 4 Ezra 7:26; 8:52; 10:27, 44–46, 54; 13:35–36; 2 *Bar.* 4:2–6. One would expect the counterpart to the "present" Jerusalem to be the future Jerusalem ("the Jerusalem to come") or, conversely, the counterpart to the Jerusalem "above" to be the Jerusalem on earth below. Paul mixes temporal and spatial categories, a common feature of apocalyptic thinking since the age to come already exists in heaven above while the present evil age is located on the earth (see Bouwman, "Die Hagar- und Sara-Perikope," 3152). For Paul, moreover, the Jerusalem above is already making its presence felt on earth over against "the present Jerusalem."

29. Martyn, *Galatians*, 435, 444: The phrase "according to the Flesh" is adverbial, not adjectival, as is also the corresponding phrase "according to the Spirit." They can be rendered "by the power of the Flesh" and "by the power of the Spirit" (Martyn, *Galatians*, 435).

30. The Galatians would have seen the connection, knowing enough of the story of Sarah (and that of Hagar) to make that connection. Sarah can remain anonymous and be called "the free woman" instead precisely because of this familiarity. Paul summarizes this story, as familiar to the Galatians as to himself, in Gal 4:22–23 so that he can then give his allegorizing interpretation in the verses that follow (4:24–25). By calling Sarah "the free woman" (*eleuthera*, absent from Genesis 16–21) in 4:22–23, he anticipates that allegorical interpretation, allegorizing the story in the process (see n. 4 above). That the Galatians are assumed also to be familiar with Hagar is indicated by the fact that when Paul mentions her by name in 4:25 he does not pause to identify her as "the slave woman" mentioned in 4:22–23. Similarly, Paul also assumes that the Galatians know that Mount Sinai was the place where the Mosaic covenant was ratified.

with many children ("our mother").[31] The Isaian text is thus brought by Paul into the service of his christologically determined apocalyptic eschatology: The promise contained in Isa 54:1 has come to pass, as his application of the text to the Galatians in the next verse bears out:[32] "You, brethren, are children of promise like Isaac" (4:28).[33]

Jobes appropriately raises the question of the importance of barren-ness in the quotation since that theme provides the crucial link to the figure of Sarah in Genesis.[34] Her own approach is to provide a wide-ranging dis-cussion of this theme in the Old Testament. The theological importance of the barrenness of Sarah and thus of the Jerusalem above, in my view, is that their offspring are born only as a result of God's faithfulness to his promise (cf. Gen 21:1–2 LXX: "And the Lord visited Sarah, just as he had said [he would], and the Lord did to Sarah, just as he had spoken, and Sarah con-ceived and bore Abraham a son . . . "). Isaac was thus "a child of promise," and the Galatian Christians are likewise "children of promise."[35]

31. According to Brawley ("Contextuality," 114), "Jerusalem assumes two identities in Isaiah, a Jerusalem in captivity and a free Jerusalem. . . . So also Jerusalem assumes two identities in Galatians 4, a Jerusalem in captivity and a free Jerusalem. As Isaiah contrasts captivity and restoration, so Galatians contrasts captivity and freedom" (in a similar way, Jobes, "Jerusalem," 311). But in Paul's application of Isaiah 54:1, it is only the Jerusalem above which assumes a double identity, that of barrenness and desola-tion on the one side and that of fecundity on the other (see n. 3 above). The pres-ent Jerusalem has only *one*, constant identity, that of slavery. The two Jerusalems are mutually exclusive and stand opposed to one another. Further, according to Brawley ("Contextuality," 116), "Paul considers the two Jerusalems, of slavery and freedom, to have been a possibility in the course of history" for Ishmael and Isaac, for the Israel of the exile and beyond to his own time. But Brawley fails to see that "the Jerusalem above" is an apocalyptic category and that Paul's notion of freedom concerns what he later calls "new creation" (6:15) whereby those in slavery (including the children of "Hagar," the present Jerusalem) are being liberated through the apocalyptic intrusion of God into the world in Christ. The contrast between the two Jerusalems is thus one that has come into being only with the arrival of Christ onto the world stage (3:23–25).

32. As Jobes ("Jerusalem," 303) observes: "The force of Paul's argument is based on the major premise that the barren one of Isa 54:1 has given birth."

33. Martyn argues convincingly (*Galatians*, 443–44) that *kata Isaak* can probably best be translated "after the pattern of Isaac," since Paul's intention is surely not to es-tablish a historical, genealogical line from the Galatians back to Isaac. "Isaac" functions here as the type of a Christian in Paul's own time, someone who was "begotten" by God, true to his promise, and thus "by the power of the Spirit" rather than by "the power of the Flesh" (4:29).

34. Jobes, "Jerusalem," 307. See further the next section below on this connection.

35. Cf. Martyn, *Galatians*, 444: Paul "sees a divine correspondence between the two *points*, God's action in the birth of Isaac and God's action in the birth of the Galatian congregations" (emphasis original). Between those two points is nothing, certainly no salvation history leading from Isaac to Christ; cf. Gal 3:16 (Christ is Abraham's one

The quotation from Isaiah is introduced with the connective particle *gar*, "for (it stands written)." Burton sees this particle as "justifying or illustrating his [Paul's] conception of a new redeemed Jerusalem whose glory is to surpass that of the old."[36] For Vouga, the citation functions as "Autoritätsargument . . . um sowohl die Gleichzeitung von Sarah und *anō Ierousalēm* als auch ihre Bezeichnung als *mētēr hēmōn* zu begründen."[37] "The *gar* indicates," according to Jobes, "that Paul intends the quotation to somehow advance, explain or ground his previous thought, which includes at least vs. 26."[38] It is more probable, however, that Paul has here placed the cart before the horse, i.e., his interpretation of the text precedes his citation of it, as is the case in 3:10: "For all who rely on works of the Law are under a curse, for it is written (*gegraptai gar*): Cursed be every one who does not abide by all things written in the book of the Law, and do them."[39] The citation from Scripture does not carry the argument forward; it states the source of that argument, in particular the claim that "the Jerusalem above" is "our mother,"[40] but also the apocalyptic contrast posited between "Sarah/the Jerusalem above/her many children" and "Hagar/the present Jerusalem/her children." For it is Isa 54:1 that has enabled Paul to link Sarah, the once barren, then fecund free woman, with the promise of a once barren, newly fecund Jerusalem and to call this Jerusalem "our mother." The latter can be characterized as "the Jerusalem above" (a heavenly Jerusalem) because her children have, "like Isaac," been begotten through the divine promise, not "according to the flesh." The daring part of Paul's interpretation of Isa 54:1 is that this newly fecund, heavenly Jerusalem is distinguished from, indeed, apocalyptically set over against "the present Jerusalem," represented by Hagar. Isa 54:1 itself concerns only one Jerusalem, the woman in the last line probably representing another city, Babylon, as noted previously. Paul, however, discerns two distinct Jerusalems in that text, not only "the Jerusalem above" but also "the present Jerusalem," the latter having about as much to do with the former as Babylon had to do with the Jerusalem of

---

"seed") and 3:19 ("until the seed [Christ] should come"). See Sellin, "Hagar und Sarah," 71: "Das Geburt Isaaks ist als *di' epangelias* geschehene ein *Wunder*" (emphasis original).

36. Burton, *Galatians*, 264.

37. Vouga, *Galater*, 118.

38. Jobes, "Jerusalem," 302.

39. Betz, *Galatians*, 144. The same is true in 3:13 (also 3:8).

40. Jerusalem is not specifically called "mother" in Second Isaiah, but that is clearly implied in 54:1 (as in 51:18; cf. 51:2 where Sarah is explicitly mentioned and then in terms of her role as mother). See Isa 1:26 LXX: "The faithful mother-city Zion," *mētropolis pistē Siōn* (Jobes, "Jerusalem," 310). See also for the notion of Jerusalem as mother, 4 *Ezra* 10:7; 2 *Bar.* 3:1.

Second Isaiah. The last line of Isa 54:1, which introduces a second female figure with a husband and children, is evidently taken by Paul to represent Hagar and thus "the present Jerusalem" who along "with her children is in slavery (*douleuei*)" (4:25).[41]

But now the question is: Where does that second Jerusalem in Paul's reading of Isa 54:1 come from and who does she represent? It is clear from the foregoing analysis that "the Jerusalem *above*" does not refer to a heavenly city in the literal sense, but to the *church* that has been called into being by God (1:6; 5:8) as the eschatological people of God.[42] God is as it were the husband of this heavenly Jerusalem and she his bride.[43] Through Paul's proclamation of the gospel of God's unconditional grace and love as apocalyptically revealed in Christ (1:6, 12, 15–16; 2:20), God begets (4:23, 29) "children of promise, like Isaac" (4:28; cf. 4:23 with Gen 18:14) by the Jerusalem above.[44] The Galatian Christians, addressed directly in 4:28, are such children of promise, as indeed is Paul himself (4:31; cf. 1:12, 15–16; 2:20). The children of promise, begotten in accordance with the Spirit rather than with the Flesh (4:29; cf. 3:1–5), comprise the church(es) made up of former Jews and Gentiles (3:28), free from the enslaving power of the Law (cf. 3:23–25; 4:1–6). These children thereby also become residents of "the Jerusalem above" which, like a mother, gives birth to new children.

Analogously, when Paul refers to "the present Jerusalem" (represented by Hagar) he undoubtedly does not have the earthly city as such in view but a particular community corresponding to the church(es) represented by the heavenly Jerusalem.[45] In the traditional interpretation, "the present Jeru-

---

41. See Bligh, *Galatians*, 403, as cited by Verhoef ("*Er staat* geschreven," 242n257): "He [Paul] understood the second couplet [of Isa 54:1] as a contrast between two distinct women (not between two stages in the life of one woman), and between two Jerusalems." See n. 3 above.

42. According to Martyn (*Galatians*, 440), "Paul may picture this church as the community that is both above and future, being ready to descend to earth, at the parousia," though he also observes (440n142) that the "image is that of churches [cf. Gal 1:2: "churches of Galatia"] on earth that are descended from a church in heaven."

43. Cf. Isa 54:5 where Yahweh is the husband of the earthly Jerusalem and she his bride. See H. Leene on Jerusalem as bride and mother in the Old Testament, especially Second Isaiah ("Sion als moeder").

44. Because of his role in God's work among the Gentiles, Paul could himself be regarded as the spiritual father of the Galatian Christians. He writes in 1 Cor 4:15 that he "begot" (*gennaō*) the Christians in Corinth "in Christ Jesus through the gospel"; he is thus their "father" in Christ, as he was of the runaway slave Onesimus according to Phlm 10. See Martyn, *Galatians*, 451. In Galatians, Paul maintains with particular emphasis that his gospel and his apostleship both originate in God (1:12, 15–16); he thus regards his apostolic work and his gospel as God's own.

45. Bachmann ("Die andere Frau," 127) rightly notes that Paul has two communities

salem" and her children represent contemporary non-Christian Judaism, whose geographical center was Jerusalem.[46] Martyn, however, has recently argued convincingly that, just as earlier in Galatians (1:17, 18; 2:1), the word "Jerusalem" is being used as a metonym not for the Jewish community in Jerusalem, but for the Law-observant, Jewish-Christian church located there.[47] This church, according to Martyn, sponsored its own mission to Gentiles, as Galatians itself attests.[48] Until about 50 CE, the church in Jerusalem was under the apostolic leadership of the three "pillars," James, Cephas/Peter, and John (2:9; cf. Acts 1–15). In the 50s, when Galatians was probably written,[49] it apparently came under the primary leadership of

in view from the outset, as the reference to "children" in 4:25 and 4:28 indicates.

46. E.g., Betz, *Galatians*. See the various critiques of this interpretation by Hays, *Echoes*, 116–17; Martyn, *Galatians*, 447–66; idem, "Covenants"; Bachmann, "Die andere Frau"; and Brawley, "Contextuality."

47. Martyn, *Galatians*, 440, 458–66; *Theological Issues*, 25–36; cf. Mussner, *Galaterbrief*, 325. In Gal 1:17, 18 and 2:1, Paul uses the neuter plural spelling of Jerusalem, *Ierosolyma*, perhaps for the sake of his Gentile readers in Galatia (cf. Murphy-O'Connor, "IEROSOLYMA/IEROUSALEM in Galatians," 280–81). In Gal 4:25–26, he changes to the feminine singular spelling (*Ierousalēm*), which he commonly uses elsewhere (Rom 15:19, 25, 26, 31; 1 Cor 16:3), probably for two reasons: it is the form preferred by the LXX (the neuter plural spelling is found only in later deutero-canonical works) and this form is needed for his allegorical-typological interpretation. Along the same lines, see Bachmann ("IEROSOLYMA und IEROUSALEM im Galaterbrief," 288–89), against Murphy-O'Connor ("IEROSOLYMA/IEROUSALEM in Galatians") who attributes the switch to the influence of "the intruders" who were using the feminine form in connection with "the Mother Church" in Jerusalem.

48. Martyn, "Covenants," 194n9: "Paul's interpretive point of departure [is] the two Gentile missions in his own time." Bachmann ("Die andere Frau," 144n46), however, followed by Brawley ("Contextuality"), rejects Martyn's thesis that the issue underlying this passage is a conflict between two different missions to Gentiles. He argues that the "we" of 4:26 and 4:31 militates against this thesis, as against the thesis that Paul is opposing "am Gesetz festhaltende Judaisten" (citing Mussner, *Galaterbrief*, 327). With this "we," according to Bachmann, Paul includes not only Gentiles but also Jews like himself who have become believers. That is true enough, but the letter is written to the Gentile Christians of Galatia who were brought to faith in Christ by Paul and who are being tempted by "a different gospel" for the Gentiles (1:6), one that involves observing the Law, beginning with circumcision, in addition to believing in Christ (Gal 5:2–4; 6:12–13). Brawley ("Contextuality," 114n59) argues that since "the two Jerusalems are metaphors for slavery and freedom," "the present Jerusalem cannot be identified with the Jerusalem church as Martyn avers." It is not clear, however, why the metaphorical meaning of necessity excludes the metonymical use of the name for a community/ church, especially since the two Jerusalems are expressly said to have "children."

49. Galatians, it is important to remember, was written after Paul's traumatic break with the church of Antioch (Gal 2:11–14; cf. Acts 15:34–41), which also involved a break with his colleague Barnabas (Gal 2:13; cf. Acts 15:39) and Peter (Gal 2:14). Furthermore, the dispute leading to Paul's break with Antioch was initiated by the arrival of "emissaries from James" (*tinas apo Iakōbou*), who are associated with (and perhaps

James (cf. 2:12; Acts 21:18). The "husband" mentioned in the fourth line of Isa 54:1 may thus *in Paul's thinking* refer primarily to James who metaphorically "begets" (*gennaō*) children by "the present [church in] Jerusalem" and does so "according to the flesh" (4:23, 29), i.e., through requiring fleshly circumcision of Gentile converts (cf. 3:3; 6:12).[50] Paul likens the missionary successes of "the present Jerusalem" among Gentiles to "bearing (*gennōsa*) children for slavery" (4:24).[51] Other agents or residents of this "present Jerusalem" in Paul's view are "the false brothers" (2:4) who sought to undermine his work in Antioch and/or Jerusalem (2:1, 11), "the circumcision party" active in Antioch at the behest of James and his emissaries (2:12), and the Christian Jews who have made their way into the Galatian churches (1:7–9) in order to "compel" (6:12; cf. 2:3, 14) the Gentile Christians in Galatia to practice circumcision and adhere to all the commandments of the Sinaitic Law as a precondition for obtaining righteousness or rectification (5:2–4, 7–12; 6:12–13). They may well have referred to the church in Jerusalem as "our mother."[52] In 4:29, Paul intimates that these Christian-Jewish evangelists[53] are "now" persecuting the Galatian Gentile-Christians with their

---

identical to) "the circumcision party" (*tous ek peritomēs*) mentioned in the same verse (Gal 2:12; cf. Acts 10:45; 11:2). Gal 2:11–14 indicates at the very least that Barnabas, Peter *and James* did not have the same understanding of the agreement reached in Jerusalem (Gal 2:7–9) as Paul did, particularly in connection with its implications for the Gentile mission. If Gal 2:11–14 is any indication, James seems also to have fallen under the influence of "the circumcision party" after the conference recounted in Gal 2:1–10 (cf. Acts 21:18–21), as did Barnabas and Peter.

50. The verb *gennaō* which is strikingly absent from the Genesis account, has both a masculine meaning ("beget a child"; 4:23, 29) and a feminine one ("bear a child"; 4:24). For Paul, it is a missionary verb (see Martyn, *Galatians*, 434, 451–54; cf. Phlm 10; 1 Cor 4:14–15). Martyn (*Galatians*, 443) thinks that the church in Jerusalem is for Paul not only the "mother" (cf. 4:24) but also the "husband" referred to in Isa 54:1 (4:27). Martyn recognizes that this combination causes an "inconsistency," but he explains it with the comment that inconsistency "is characteristic of allegorical interpretation." The hypothesis that James is the missionary father of the children of the present Jerusalem makes such an explanation unnecessary, since there is then no inconsistency. Martyn himself (*Galatians*, 463) refers to the Jerusalem church "under the leadership of James" (cf. *Galatians*, 460–461). What Martyn says about the role of the "husband," that he "sponsors—and on a human level—legitimates" the Law-observant mission to the Gentiles, would still apply and perhaps make better sense in view of 2:12 ("emissaries from James").

51. The passage is thus not about the old covenant (Judaism) having been superseded by the new covenant (Christianity). According to Martyn (*Galatians*, 453), the present tense shows that "Paul refers here to the work of the Teachers [Martyn's term for the troublemakers in Galatia] in the Law-observant mission to Gentiles" (see also 4:20: "so also now").

52. See Martyn *Galatians*, 462–63.

53. I call them "Christian-Jewish [rather than Jewish-Christian] evangelists"

insistence on circumcision and full Law-observance.[54] In 4:30, he clearly implies (adapting a citation from Gen 21:10 to the Galatian situation) that the new evangelists are to be expelled from the Galatian churches forthwith ("but what does the Scripture say?").[55]

"So, brethren," Paul sums up, addressing the Galatian Christians directly once more (4:31), "we are not children of the slave woman [of the present Jerusalem, i.e., of the Law-observant church in Jerusalem run by James with its own mission to the Gentiles] but of the free woman [of the Jerusalem above, i.e., the church God has called into being through the gospel of His unconditional grace which I, Paul, proclaimed to you]."[56] Paul then concludes with a ringing announcement and an urgent exhortation: "For freedom Christ has set us free; stand fast therefore, and do not submit again to a yoke of slavery!" (5:1). The beginning of the passage with its reference to those who "wish to be under the Law" (4:21) and the subsequent verses (5:2–4) make clear that the yoke of slavery referred to is the Mosaic Law, beginning with circumcision. The children and the residents of "the present Jerusalem," because (and only because) they sponsor a mission to the Gentiles requiring circumcision and observance of the Mosaic Law in addition to faith in Christ, are part and parcel of the old age of

---

because (a) they seemed to have taken their firm theological point of departure from the Mosaic Law rather than from Christ (cf. Gal 2:15–16; 3:1–5; 6:12–13)—hence they can be more accurately described as Christian Jews than as Jewish Christians—and because (b) they "proclaimed" or "preached" (*euangelizomai*, "evangelize") what they regarded as "gospel" (cf. Gal 1:6–8).

54. I leave aside a consideration of what this "persecution" may have consisted of or whether the Christian-Jewish evangelists would have shared this assessment of their activity among the Galatians. When Paul refers to persecution elsewhere in Galatians (1:13, 23; 5:11; 6:12), he seems to have in view persecution of Christian Jews by non-Christian Jews (see Baasland, "Persecution"). Here, however, the issue is the persecution of Gentile Christians and it seems unlikely that (non-Christian) Jews would bother to persecute tiny groups of Gentiles (living far outside Palestine) who had embraced as the Messiah someone recently crucified as a criminal by the Romans with the cooperation of their leaders in Jerusalem.

55. Gal 4:29–30, addressed to the Gentile Christians in Galatia, further shows that "the present Jerusalem" cannot refer to non-Christian Jews as in the traditional interpretation of the passage. Paul would not need to ask the Gentile Christians in Galatia to expel non-Christian Jews from their churches; such Jews would not be found there (Martyn, *Galatians*, 452n171); contra Nanos, *Irony of Galatians*, who makes an unconvincing case for the contrary; see de Boer, "Review of *Irony of Galatians*."

56. This verse is clearly the goal of Paul's allegorical interpretation (cf. Bachmann, "Die andere Frau," 136–41), namely, to re-establish the identity (also Martyn, *Galatians*, 446, 451) of the Galatian Christians as children of "the free woman," of the Jerusalem above, begotten by the power of the Spirit and now children of God (cf. 4:6–7). Only then can Paul utter the exhortation in 5:1 to stand fast.

slavery,[57] whereas the children and the residents of "the Jerusalem above" are the beachhead of the new age of freedom. Second Isaiah's oracle is understood by Paul to have had in view the new age inaugurated by Christ, the age in which a new community has been created, free from enslaving powers, in this case the Sinaitic Law.

According to Genesis, God promised many descendants to Abraham through *both* Isaac *and* Ishmael (Gen 15:1–6; 17:2–6, 16, 20; 22:17–18) and Paul may have this in mind in his christologically shaped apocalyptic interpretation of Isa 54:1. In Paul's reading of the verse, the children of the free woman (Gentile Christians free from the Law) will be many, surpassing those of the slave woman (Gentile Christians compelled to observe the Law, thereby becoming Christian Jews). It is possible that Paul (if not Second Isaiah) presupposes a present tense in the third line of Isa 54:1, instead of a future: "for many *are* the children of the desolate one."[58] It is difficult to know, however, whether the Gentile Christians converted by Paul in accordance with his Law-free gospel already outnumbered (in his perception at any rate) the Gentile Christians converted by Christian-Jewish evangelists emanating from Jerusalem. He evidently believes that the promise has been fulfilled or, perhaps better, is now in the process of being fulfilled. Ever since Christ, the one seed of Abraham (3:16, 19), "came" (3:19, 23, 25) into the world to "redeem" those "under the Law" (4:4–5), the (eschatological) future belongs, according to Paul's reading of Isa 54:1, to the children begotten by the Spirit.[59]

What prompted Paul to make use of Isa 54:1?

"Why does Paul" Martyn asks, "turn from Genesis 16–21 to this prophetic text with its contrasting picture?"[60] The appeal to material from Genesis 16–

---

57. Paul can refer positively to the Law-observant churches in Jerusalem and Judea (cf. Gal 1:22; Rom 15:27) since for him circumcision, like uncircumcision, is now a matter of indifference (Gal 5:6; 6:15). What matters is "believing in Christ" (Gal 2:16). In Galatians, Paul finds unacceptable the *imposition* of circumcision and the Mosaic Law on Gentile Christians since this imposition presupposes that Christ's faithful death is insufficient for their rectification (2:21). See Martyn, "Covenants," 204–5.

58. So e.g., NRSV; and the commentators Burton, Betz, Longenecker, and Martyn; otherwise Vouga.

59. That "those under the Law" includes, theologically speaking, Gentiles is evident in 3:13–14; 4:1–7. See Martyn, *Galatians*, 334–36. It certainly includes Gentile Christians who were beginning to place themselves under it, as the Christians in Galatians seemingly were doing (cf. 1:6; 3:1; 4:10, 21), in response to the pressure put on them by Christian-Jewish evangelists, such as those who came into the Galatian churches (6:12).

60. Martyn, *Galatians*, 442. Barrett ("Allegory," 164) poses a similar question ("Why does Paul use this passage?"). See Jobes ("Jerusalem," 303) who suspects that "if this

21, which is summarized in 4:22–23, is readily explicable from the situation in the Galatian churches. The Christian-Jewish evangelists who invaded the churches undoubtedly had their own favorite scriptural passages to convince the Gentile Christians in Galatia to take upon themselves the practice of circumcision and thus the other commandments of the Law. A prime candidate is Gen 17:9–14, which mandates circumcision for Abraham and his male offspring, including Ishmael (17:23, 25–26). For Isaac and his descendants circumcision functioned as a sign of the covenant God made with Abraham (17:19–21; cf. 21:4), thereby setting them apart from the other (Ishmaelite) descendants of Abraham.[61] Ishmael and his descendants (the Gentiles), they would maintain, may well be the children of Abraham alongside Isaac and his descendants (the Jews), but without circumcision, i.e., without becoming Jews subsequently obedient to the whole Law (cf. Gal 5:3), they cannot inherit (cf. Gen 15:3–8 LXX) the promises made to him. Concerning the Genesis material, Barrett writes:

> Two points are clear: (1) This is a part of the Old Testament that Paul would have been unlikely to introduce of his own accord; its value from his point of view is anything but obvious, and the method of interpretation is unusual with him. . . . It stands in the epistle because his opponents used it and he could not escape it.[62] (2) Its plain, surface meaning supports not Paul but the

---

passage were excised from the text, most modern interpretations of this passage would not be substantially altered."

61. See *Jub.* 16:16–18 which interprets the Genesis account surrounding the birth of Isaac as follows: "And through Isaac a name and seed would be named for him. And all of the seed of his [Abraham's] sons would become nations. And they would be counted with the nations. But from the sons of Isaac one [Jacob] would become a holy seed and he would not be counted among the nations [Gentiles] because he would become the portion of the Most High and all his seed would fall (by lot) into that which God will rule so that he might become a people (belonging) to the Lord, a (special) possession from all people, and so that he might become a kingdom of priests and a holy people." Translation O. S. Wintermute in Charlesworth, *Old Testament Pseudepigrapha*, 2.88.

62. Tolmie ("Allegorie," 164–65) rejects this claim, even though he admits it is possible. He does not explain how or why the Galatians were familiar with the story, as he concedes, if not through the teaching of "die opponente." According to Borgen ("Hebrew and Pagan Features," 153), "it seems improbable that Paul, by a fresh interpretation of his own making, could identify the gentile Hagar with the Jewish covenant of the law. Paul's way of arguing would then hardly stand up against the view of his opponents." Borgen's solution is to look at the depiction of Hagar in Philo (dismissed by Barrett as not helpful) who emphasizes that Hagar was an Egyptian (Gen 16:1–2) who became a Hebrew by choice. Even if Barrett is right, writes Borgen, Paul is still "drawing on other Jewish expository traditions, traditions which see the slave girl Hagar and her son with Abraham within the context of Jewish thought about gentiles who become proselytes and live under the law of Moses" (163). But why would the use of other

Judaizers: the Jews, who live by the law of Moses, are the heirs of Abraham and it is to Jews that the promise applies. . . . The true descendants of Abraham are the Jews, who inhabit Jerusalem. Here are the true people of God; and it will follow that Jerusalem is the authoritative centre of the renewed people of God, now called the church. Those who are not prepared to attach themselves to this community by the approved means (circumcision) must be cast out; they cannot hope to inherit promises made to Abraham and his seed.[63]

Paul responds with his allegorical (and typological) interpretation of the Genesis account.[64] Through this reading of what "stands written" in Genesis about Abraham, Hagar and Sarah, and Ishmael and Isaac, Paul declares that Christian Jews emanating from Jerusalem with their own mission to the Gentiles are not the offspring of Sarah allegorically interpreted, nor then children of promise as Isaac was. They are the "children" of the slave woman, thus slaves themselves, and can trace their descent back to Abraham only through Ishmael to whom the Abrahamic covenant did not in fact apply even if he was also circumcised![65]

Jewish expository traditions convince the Gentile Galatians more than Paul's own way of arguing? Witherington (*Grace*, 324) also turns to Philo and discovers "that for Philo Hagar symbolizes elementary learning or education," that is, "grammar, geometry, astronomy, rhetoric, music, and all other branches of [elementary] intellectual study" (*Congr.* 11). "In short," concludes Witherington, "she symbolizes something very close to what Paul calls the *ta stoicheia tou kosmou* in Gal 4:3 (cf. 4:9). However that may be, it is clear that the Christian-Jewish evangelists and Paul share a common starting point with respect to Hagar: she represents the slavery under which Gentiles are presumed to live (Martyn, *Galatians*, 449). Paul's radical move, anticipated by earlier parts of the letter, especially 4:1–10, is to equate being "under the Law" (*hypo nomon*) with the slavery "under the elemental spirits of the universe" (*hypo ta stoicheia tou kosmou*) from which the Gentile Christians in Galatians have been freed.

63. Barrett, "Allegory," 162.

64. One may ask how Paul could ignore Genesis 17:9–14 (apart from the possible allusion contained in the term "flesh") and the circumcision commandment (contrast Romans 4). We can only speculate, of course, but a possible answer is that he works from the assumption that God's promise to Sarah and Abraham concerning the birth of a son (Gen 15:1–6; 17:1–8), to which the term "covenant" is applied apart from any mention of circumcision (Gen 17:2, 4, 7), preceded the commandment to circumcise (17:9–14), just as the fulfillment of the promise in the birth of Isaac (21:1–3) preceded his circumcision (21:4). The promise and the fulfillment of that promise thus had nothing whatsoever to do with Abraham obeying the commandment to circumcise his sons.

65. The principle Paul enunciates in Gal 3:18 thus remains operative in his allegorical reading of the Genesis narrative: "If the inheritance were obtainable on the basis of the Law, it would no longer be on the basis of a promise. But God granted it to Abraham through a promise." Paul clearly implies that the Abrahamic covenant and circumcision do not go together, despite what Genesis 17:9–14 plainly says (see previous note and

According to Martyn, Isa 54:1 was "of no service" to "the Teachers" (as he labels the Christian-Jewish evangelists in Galatia),[66] but that judgment may be questioned especially if, as Martyn also claims, "the Teachers" referred to the Jerusalem church as "our mother" in its role of sponsoring a Law-observant mission to Gentiles.[67] They were in any event as capable of seeing a connection between the story of Sarah and the oracle of Isa 54:1 as Paul himself, as the later rabbinic evidence that Isa 54:1 was used as the *haftarah* to Genesis 16 in the liturgy of the synagogue demonstrates.[68] The step from the story of Sarah to Isa 54:1 is not so great in view of two facts and one possibility:

1. Jerusalem in Isa 54:1 is said to be "barren" (LXX: *steira*), as was Sarah, according to Gen 11:30 (LXX: *steira*).[69] In fact, as Barrett rightly observes, "[t]he whole story of Genesis proceeds from the fact that Sarah was barren.[70] . . . This word provides a link with Isa 54:1."[71] Paul exploits that link.[72] As indicated above, however, Paul's use of Isa 54:1 assumes that his Galatian readers can also see the link, if not exactly between Isa 54:1 and Gen 11:30, at least between the barrenness of Jerusalem in the citation and that of Sarah in Genesis 16–21 (even if the word itself does not occur in those chapters).[73]

2. In the whole Old Testament, Sarah is mentioned by name outside Genesis only in Second Isaiah (51:2). Here too her role as a mother is recalled:

Romans 4).

66. Martyn, *Galatians*, 441.

67. Martyn, *Galatians*, 441, 462–63.

68. See Mann, *Bible as Read and Preached in the Old Synagogue*, LII–III, 122 (cf. Barrett, "Allegory," 169n29; Bouwman, "Die Hagar- und Sara-Perikope," 3150). Evidence for such *haftarah* readings do occur in the NT (Acts 13:15; Luke 4:17; John 6:45), though there is no firm evidence that the cycle of readings was fixed or uniform in the New Testament period. The evidence compiled by Mann points to considerable diversity even in the rabbinic period and great uncertainty about earlier times. Sellin ("Hagar und Sara," 66n14) suggests that the earliest attestation of a link between Sarah and Isa 54:1 may be found in Philo, *Praem.* 158f.

69. See Jobes, "Jerusalem," 306–7.

70. Barrett cites here the Hebrew word, but the link is provided for Paul (and the Galatians) by the LXX, not the MT.

71. Barrett, "Allegory," 164.

72. Paul is thus making use of the technique of *gezēra šāwā*, as Barrett points out.

73. Gen 11:30 is the only passage in Genesis in which the word *steira* ("barren") occurs in connection with Sarah, but her childlessness is repeatedly emphasized in Genesis 16–21.

emblepsate eis Abram ton patera hymōn

kai eis Sarran tēn ōdinousan hymas

hoti heis ēn kai ekalesa auton kai eulogēsa auton

kai ēgapēsa auton kai eplēthuna auton

Look to Abraham your father,

and to Sarah who bears you in travail,[74]

for he was one and I called him, and blessed him,

and loved him, and multiplied him.

The verb *ōdinō*, here used transitively to mean "bear children in travail," occurs only once more in Second Isaiah, in Isa 54:1, where it is used intransitively to mean "to be in labor."

3. Given Isa 51:2, it is possible that the writer of Second Isaiah *intended* to make an allusion to Sarah and her barrenness in Isa 54:1.[75] If so, it explains why the link between Genesis 16–21 and Isa 54:1 could be easily made by Paul and by Jews in the rabbinic period.

In view of these two facts and the one possibility, one must judge the Christian-Jewish evangelists in Galatia of having been capable of interpreting Isa 54:1 in accordance with their own views about Hagar and Sarah and their respective offspring. There are good indications, however, that Paul chose the quotation from Isa 54:1 himself.[76] There is, first, no contemporary evidence to suggest that anyone else had associated Isa 54:1 with the Genesis account.[77] Second, Paul uses Isa 54:1 as the scriptural basis for his peculiar, allegorizing interpretation of the Genesis account. He could scarcely have done so without further ado had the troublemakers in Galatia also used this text for *their* understanding of the Genesis account. Isa 54:1 provides Paul with the lens through which to read Genesis 16–21 and he shares it here with his Galatian readers. It is unlikely, then, that Paul took this text from the

---

74. The present tense of the participle is striking. An alternate translation could be: "and to Sarah, the one bearing you in travail." The present tense is then presumably timeless, and the sense demanded by the context might then be "that bore you" (so the English translation given in *Septuagint Version*), which is also how the corresponding Hebrew verb of the MT is commonly translated (KJV, NRSV; cf. BDB, 297).

75. So Beuken, "Isaiah LIV"; see the discussion in Childs (*Isaiah*, 427–28) who, however, rejects this proposal. Jobes ("Jerusalem," 306–7) claims that "Isaiah develops the barren-woman theme by echoing the Genesis account of Sarah."

76. Barrett, "Allegory," 164; Martyn, *Galatians*, 441.

77. Barrett, "Allegory," 164.

exegetical arsenal of the new evangelists in Galatia in order to give it another interpretation for the Galatians, one consistent with the gospel of liberation from the Law. Paul found support for his peculiar interpretation of the Abrahamic covenant in words that also "stand written" in the Scripture, namely in the words of Isa 54:1, through which Paul can, as Barrett writes, "reverse the family relationships of the descendants of Abraham."[78]

There is, third, also strong evidence that Paul was thoroughly familiar with Second Isaiah when he wrote Galatians and that he made grateful use of its language and *Vorstellungen* in order to articulate his own christologically shaped apocalyptic eschatology and his own apostolic vocation at the turn of the ages. Gal 1:15–16 ("God . . . set me apart from the womb of my mother and called me through his grace . . . that I might proclaim him among the Gentiles") appears to be indebted primarily to Isa 49:1–6;[79] Gal 4:19 ("My children, with whom I am again in labor until Christ be formed in you") recalls Isa 45:10 in its Isaian context;[80] and Gal 6:15 ("a new creation") evokes the imagery of Isa 43:18–19 (also 65:17–25).[81] It is distinctly possible, then, that Isa 51:2 was known to Paul and that it led him to Isa 54:1.[82] Paul chose to cite Isa 54:1, instead of 51:2,[83] probably because the passage mentions two women, corresponding to Sarah and Hagar in Paul's interpretation, and also alludes to their respective children, corresponding to the apocalyptic contrast (antinomy) between the two Jerusalems. It is true that Sarah in Genesis was not only barren, she was also married, whereas Hagar was not. Paul's use of

78. Barrett, "Allegory," 167.

79. See Koet, "Roeping of Bekering?," 83.

80. Martyn, *Galatians*, 428–29. It may then be significant that the verb *ōdinō* (bear, be in travail) occurs in this passage, in Isa 51:2 (where Sarah is explicitly mentioned), and in Isa 54:1 (see Brawley, "Contextuality," 113); this word and its cognates occur nowhere else in Second Isaiah. Witherington (*Grace*, 325, 329) tentatively suggests on this basis that Paul plays the role of Sarah in the allegory; he is the Jerusalem above who has given birth to the Galatian children. Witherington finds support in the fact that Paul quotes words Sarah said to Hagar in 4:30 (Gen 21:10): "The voice of Sarah is now also the voice of Paul" (325). A difficulty (recognized by Witherington) is that Paul includes himself when he refers to this Jerusalem as "our mother." Another is that the words cited from Gen 21:10 are attributed to "the Scripture," not Sarah.

81. One may also note that one quarter of the approximately hundred quotations from the OT in the letters of Paul come from Isaiah (see Smith, "Pauline Literature," 273). Most of these come from Second Isaiah.

82. So Verhoef, "*Er staat geschreven*," 207; Hays, *Echoes*, 120; Brawley, "Contextuality," 99. See n. 74 above.

83. One might think that the present tense used in connection with Sarah in Isa 51:2 ("Sarah who bears you in travail") would be attractive to Paul and his allegorical equation of "Sarah" with "the Jerusalem above."

Isa 54:1 may thus seem somewhat "arbitrary"[84] and inappropriate, at least at first sight. However, the "fit" between the Isaian text and Paul's allegorical-typological interpretation of Abraham's two sons and their respective mothers is close enough to leave open the possibility that Paul's reflection on Isa 54:1 from the perspective of the gospel and in light of developments in Galatia prompted his allegorical-typological interpretation of the Genesis account in the first place.[85] Isa 54:1 with its picture of *two* contrasting women provides Paul with a pair of opposites (or, better, an apocalyptic contrast or antinomy) that enables him then also to find other pairs in the Genesis stories: two covenants instead of one, slave/free, flesh/promise, Flesh/Spirit, and even the two Jerusalems. Paul's reversal of the family relationships of the descendants of Abraham is thereby brought into the service of an eschatology that is both christological and apocalyptic.[86]

84. Barrett, "Allegory," 167.
85. Cf. Brawley, "Contextuality," 99.
86. See further de Boer, *Galatians*, 302–5.

Chapter 11

Paul's Use of LXX Psalm 142:2
in Galatians and Romans

Introduction

THERE ARE NUMEROUS REFERENCES to the various books of the Old Testament in Paul's genuine letters, including the Psalms.[1] There are three kinds of references.[2] First, there are *formal quotations* which can be identified by an introductory formula (e.g., "it is written") indicating that Paul is quoting a Psalm text from what he calls "the Scripture."[3] Second, there are *material quotations*, citations without an introductory formula. In such cases the text of the Psalm in question is recognizable even if it has been more or less interwoven with that of Paul. The quotation can be recognized as such if the reader has attained some basic familiarity with the wording of the source text.[4] Third, there are *allusions*, when Paul's formulation is reminiscent of a certain Psalm text but his wording is too unlike that of the source text to qualify as a material citation.[5] In practice, the difference between a material quotation and an allusion cannot be definitively established, in part because Paul also adapts material quotations to the context or his argumentation.

---

1. See the index "Loci citati vel ellegati" in Nestle-Aland[28] (851–55) which lists about seventy "quotations and allusions" (the quotations are differentiated from the allusions by the use of italics) from the Psalms in Paul's undisputed letters. Cf. Harmon, "Aspects of Paul's Use of the Psalms"; Harrisville, "Paul and the Psalms"; Keesmaat, 'The Psalms in Romans and Galatians."

2. See E. Verhoef, "*Er staat geschreven,*" 19.

3. See chapter 10 above. I use the term "quotation" synonymously with the term "citation" in this essay.

4. One may think of an ancient reader with some basic knowledge of the Old Testament Scripture and its contents or of a contemporary reader who may also have access to all sorts of reference books including concordances both printed and electronic.

5. Nestle-Aland[28] lists nineteen "quotations" from the Psalms. The remainder are regarded as "allusions."

Such interventions in the text of a Psalm (e.g., additions, deletions, modifications in the word order) also occur in formal citations.[6]

According to Harmon's tabulation, there are twenty-four citations from the Psalms in the Pauline letters, all but three in the undisputed four main letters,[7] Romans (3:4b, 11–12, 13a, 13b, 14, 18, 20; 4:7–8; 8:36; 10:18; 11:9–10; 15:3, 9, 11), 1 Corinthians (3:20; 10:26; 15:25, 27), 2 Corinthians (4:13; 9:9), and Galatians (2:16).[8] Of these twenty-one citations, seventeen are formal quotations, the four exceptions being the material quotations in Rom 3:20; 10:18; 1 Cor 10:26; and Gal 2:16.[9] It is noteworthy that Galatians contains only one quotation from the Psalms, in Gal 2:16, compared to the fourteen in Romans, a letter with which Galatians otherwise has numerous affinities, including the many quotations from other parts of the Old Testament as well as the prominent role of Abraham and the question of justification on basis of "faith" or "works of the Law" (Galatians 2–3; Romans 3–4). In Rom 3:11–18, there is a cluster of five quotations from the Psalms, mixed with quotations from other books of the OT and all introduced by the introductory formula "just as it stands written that (*kathōs gegraptai hoti*)" in 3:10a. These verses are part of the discrete literary unit that extends from 3:9 to 3:20. The latter contains a material quotation from LXX Ps 142:2 (= MT Ps 143:2), the same verse that is (partially) quoted by Paul in Gal 2:16. Rom 3:20 represents the only instance of Paul deliberately using (the language of) a specific Psalm text a second time.[10] In this chapter I will examine how Paul uses LXX Ps 142:2 in these two passages.[11]

6. See Koch, *Schrift als Zeuge*; Smith, "Pauline Literature"; Hays, *Echoes of Scripture*; Stanley, *Paul and the Language of Scripture*; Stanley, *Arguing with Scripture*; Hays, *Conversion of the Imagination*; Moyise, *Pauland Scripture*; Stanley, *Paul and Scripture*.

7. Harmon, "Aspects of Paul's Use of the Psalms." The three exceptions are all found in Ephesians (1:22; 4:8, 26).

8. A number of scholars have shown that Paul used available Greek translations of the writings of the Hebrew Old Testament (see e.g., Stanley, *Language of Scripture*, 48), commonly and conveniently referred to as the Septuagint (LXX). On the problems with this label, see Stanley, *Language of Scripture*, 41n24. The standard edition remains that of Rahlfs.

9. Not everyone will agree that these are material quotations as opposed to allusions (see further below).

10. In this article I adopt without supporting argument the consensus view that the letter to the Galatians was written before the letter to the Romans.

11. On the basis of data he has collected, Harrisville ("Paul and the Psalms") maintains that there can be no question of a single hypothesis about Paul's use of the Psalms.

First Observations

Paul writes in Galatians 2:15–16:[12]

> (15) We Jews by birth and not sinners of the Gentiles, (16) because we know that someone is not justified on the basis of works of the Law, but through the faith of Jesus Christ,[13] we too came to believe in Jesus Christ, that we might be justified on the basis of the faith of Christ and not on the basis of works of the Law, because on the basis of works of the Law shall all flesh not be justified.

The quotation from LXX Ps 142:2 takes place in the very last clause of this passage, vs. 16d: "because on the basis of works of the Law all flesh will not be justified," *hoti ex ergōn nomou ou dikaiōthēsetai pasa sarx.*

The second line of LXX Ps 142:2 (henceforth 142:2b) reads as follows: "because every living being will not be justified before you," *hoti ou dikaiōthēsetai enōpion sou pas zōn.*[14] Paul's version of LXX Ps 142:2b deviates at three points from the LXX:

4. The phrase *enōpion sou* ("before you ") does not occur in Galatians 2:16d, not even in an adapted form (e.g., "before him").

5. Paul writes *pasa sarx* ("all flesh") instead of *pas zōn* ("every living being").

6. The words *ex ergōn nomou* ("on the basis of works of the Law") do not occur in the source text.

For some, such as the editors of Nestle-Aland, these differences weigh heavily enough to classify this instance not as a material quotation but as an allusion and perhaps not even that.[15] For others, however, the remaining agreements justify the conclusion that we are dealing here with a material quotation.[16] In both Gal 2:16d and LXX Ps 142:2b, the following words occur in the same order:

> *hoti . . . ou dikaiōthēsetai . . . pas/pasa . . .*

---

12. I here use the translation made and defended in de Boer, *Galatians.*

13. On the translation of *pistis Christou* as "the faith of Christ," see chapter 6 above.

14. The Greek text is a literal translation of the underlying Hebrew of the MT.

15. Nestle-Aland[27] (788) lists Gal 2:16 as an "allusion," rather than as "quotation," but Nestle-Aland[28] (855) omits it altogether from its list of OT quotations and allusions. Similarly, Nestle-Aland[27] contains references to the Psalm verse and to Rom 3:20 in the margin at Gal 2:16 whereas Nestle-Aland[28] omits both marginal references.

16. See e.g., Verhoef, *"Er staat geschreven,"* 39–44; Betz, *Galatians,* 118.

The conclusion that we are dealing here with a material quotation finds support in Paul's use of the text of LXX Ps 142:2b in Rom 3:20, more precisely Rom 3:20a. Paul here writes: "Therefore by works of the Law shall all flesh not be justified in His sight," *dioti ex ergōn nomou ou dikaiōthēsetai pasa sarx enōpion autou*. The phrase *enōpion autou* ("before him [God]") is apparently a slightly adapted version of the phrase *enōpion sou* ("before you") of LXX Ps 142:2b.[17] This agreement with the text of the LXX confirms the suspicion that in Gal 2:16d as in Rom 3:20a Paul is making conscious, intentional use of language derived from LXX Ps 142:2b. If so, then Gal 2:16d and Rom 3:20a both involve not an (incidental or subconscious) allusion but a (conscious, intentional) material quotation.[18]

Romans 3:20a provides additional information that is relevant to the interpretation of Gal 2:16d. The quotation deviates from the LXX in four ways. In addition to the conversion of *enōpion sou* into *enōpion autou*, Paul replaces *hoti* ("because") with *dioti* ("therefore"). Furthermore, as in Galatians 2:16d, he writes *pasa sarx* ("all flesh") instead of *pas zōn* ("every living being") and also adds here the words *er ergōn nomou* ("on basis of works of the Law"). The first two deviations in Romans 3:20a can be explained as stylistic adaptations to a new literary and argumentative context. The other two deviations are more substantive in nature. It is striking how the same two deviations also occur earlier in Gal 2:16d. So the key question must be: How can these two extraordinary deviations be explained? This question leads naturally to a second: What is the purpose (or function) of Paul's use of this Psalm text in, respectively, Galatians and Romans?

Galatians 2:16d

The two substantive deviations identified above are different in kind. I discuss them each in turn.

1. The term *pasa sarx* ("all flesh") is a Hebraism (*kol-basar*), and occurs regularly in the LXX (cf. e.g., LXX Ps 64:3; 135:25; 144:21). Since the text of the LXX was not yet fixed in Paul's time, a possible explanation

---

17. Why Paul omitted this phrase in Gal 2:16d is difficult to assess. In any case, we may assume that Paul did not find the omission detrimental to his argument.

18. Verhoef, *"Er staat geschreven,"* 19. Whether the intended readers, the non-Jewish Galatians (cf. Gal 4:8–10) will have recognized the words of Gal 2:16d as a quotation from "the Scripture" (Gal 3: 8, 22) remains an open question. It is more likely that Paul's opponents in Galatia (cf. 1:6–9, 3:1: 4:17; 5:2–4, 7, 10–12; 6:12–13) will have been able to do so, for they were of Jewish origin and knew the Old Testament inside out. See de Boer, *Galatians*, 50–61.

of this deviation from the LXX is that Paul had access to the Greek text of this Psalm with the reading *pasa sarx* instead of *pas zōn* ("every living being"). The fact that the words *pasa sarx* also occur in Rom 3:20a could support this possible explanation. There is, however, no text-critical evidence for the existence of such a reading. Another possibility is of course that Paul himself has changed the words of the LXX. In terms of meaning, there is little or no difference between *ou dikaiōthēsetai pasa sarx* and *ou dikaiōthēsetai pas zōn*. Consistent with the underlying Hebrew, the phrase in both cases emphatically means that "*no one* will be justified."[19] Paul chooses the words *pasa sarx* because they fit well with his argumentative agenda. With these words he emphasizes the difference between God and human beings (cf. Gal 2:20), indicates that human beings are by nature susceptible to the power of Sin (cf. Gal 2:17; 3:22), which he can also refer to as "the Flesh" (cf. Gal 5:13–21), and establishes a link to fleshly circumcision (cf. Gal 3:3; 6:12–13), a rite he wants to keep the Galatians from adopting at all costs (cf. Gal 5:2–4).

2. The words *ex ergōn nomou* ("from works of the Law") do not occur in LXX Ps 142:2b. In fact, the expression *erga nomou* ("works of the Law") does not occur anywhere in the LXX and also has no equivalent in the Masoretic text.[20] Paul has used the expression *ex ergōn nomou* twice before in Gal 2:16, each time to emphasize that justification does *not* occur on the basis of works of the Law. The conclusion that Paul himself added the words *ex ergōn nomou* to the text of LXX Ps 142:2b therefore lies to hand. In other words, he quotes this text as if the words *ex ergōn nomou* are also part of it.

How can he get away with this addition? Paul's argument in Gal 2:16 is about justification (God's approval and vindication of the just).[21] Does justification occur on the basis of faith or on the basis of works of the Law? Paul seeks unequivocally to exclude justification on the basis of works of the Law (= doing what the Law prescribes) and he makes use of the language of LXX Ps 142:2b to strengthen his argument. In the first line of LXX Ps 142:2, the writer calls on God not go into judgment with him (*kai mē eiselthēs eis krisin meta tou doulou sou*), "because," as he continues, "before you no living being

19. Cf. BDR16 #302.1; BDF #302.1.

20. The expression "works of the Law" (*maʿăśê ha-torah*) does appear in manuscripts of the Dead Sea Scrolls, in particular 4QMMT. There are also indications in the letter to the Galatians that Paul himself did not invent the expression; in 2:16 he assumes that the expression is familiar. See chapter 6 above.

21. See chapter 7 above.

will be justified." Ps 142:2b therefore explains why the writer does not want to end up in judgment: because (*hoti*) *no one* will be justified before God. Paul reads these words through a christological lens. In Gal 2:16a–c he has already emphasized that justification can only take place "on the basis of *pistis Christou*." Works of the Law are excluded. For Paul, the words of Ps 142:2b really signify that *no one* will be justified *apart from pistis Christou*. That also then means that works of the Law, which Paul has mentioned twice already earlier in the verse, cannot provide the basis for justification (cf. Gal 2:21). For this reason, Paul can add the words *ex ergōn nomou* ("on the basis of works of the Law") to Ps 142:2b. That represents for him the contextually relevant implication of that text.[22] Paul adds the words in order to clarify the significance of the text and to make it relevant to the situation at hand.[23] It is to be noted, however, that Paul does not indicate in any way that he is relying upon or quoting from LXX Ps 142:2b. The words from the Psalm are simply incorporated into what amounts to a declaration.[24] He has made the words from the Psalm his own.

Romans 3:20a

As noted above, Paul quotes LXX Ps 142:2b in Rom 3:20a in almost the same way as he has done in Gal 2:16d. The same two substantive changes that he made to the text of the Psalm in Gal 2:16d also occur in Rom 3:20a and thereby remain relevant now for his argument in Romans.

Rom 3:20 concludes a discrete literary unit that begins in 3:9 and must be interpreted in that light. In 3:9 Paul writes that the preceding argument has shown that "all people, " both "Jews" and "Greeks" (cf. 1:16; 2:9; 14:17) are "under the [power of] Sin," *pantas uph' hamartian einai*.[25] Like 3:20a, this verse has a point of contact with Galatians, because in Gal 3:22 Paul writes that "the Scripture (*hē graphē*) shut all things (*ta panta*) up under the [power of] Sin (*hypo hamartian*)." Paul does not indicate here which texts from "the Scripture" he has in view. He does do that in Romans, however. He supports the claim that all people are under the power of Sin with a series of quotations from the Old Testament (the LXX) in verses 10–18. There

---

22. Paul's opponents in Galatia, the new preachers who have come there with their own version of the gospel, will undoubtedly object strenuously to this exegesis of the text.

23. See Verhoef, *"Er staat geschreven,"* 150.

24. De Boer, *Galatians,* 152.

25. On Sin as a cosmological and cosmic power, see chapter 4 above.

are five quotations from the Psalms,[26] one from Isaiah (in Rom 3:15–17). The whole series of quotations is introduced with the quotation formula "just as it stands written," *kathōs gegraptai* (Rom 3:10a).

> In 3:10–12, Paul cites from LXX Ps 13:1–3 (MT 14:1–3)[27] and does so selectively. The words in vs. 10b, *ouk estin dikaios oude eis* ("there is not one person who is just") cannot be found as such in LXX Psalm 13. Nevertheless, the import of vs. 10b is consistent with the last line from LXX Ps 13:1, which is repeated in vs. 3 of the Psalm and cited by Paul in vs. 12: *ouk estin ho poiōn chrēstotēta, ouk estin heōs enos,* "there is no one who does good, there is not one." Verse 10b can then be regarded as Paul's brief summary of the import of this line.[28] Paul begins that summary with the same words, *ouk estin* ("there is not"), but follows with the adjective *dikaios* ("just, righteous") because the existence of humanity "under Sin" (vs. 9) indicates a lack of *dikaiosynē,* justness or righteousness (cf. Rom 6:18).[29] It is also the case that justness and justification are prominent themes in Romans (cf. e.g., 1:17; 2:5; 3:21–26; 5:1–21).

Verse 10 functions as the heading of the whole series of quotations that now follow. In vs. 11, Paul cites words taken from LXX Ps 13:2, modifying them with the twofold use of the phrase *ouk estin* already used in vs. 10: "there is not (*ouk estin*) one person who understands, there is not (*ouk estin*) one person who seeks God." As a result, three times in a row a line begins with the words *ouk estin,* "there is not":

> "there is not one person who is just"

> "there is not one person who understands"

> "there is not one person who seeks God"

In this light, vs. 12, containing a quotation from vs. 3 of Psalm 13, constitutes a first climax: "all have deviated, together they have become useless, there is not (*ouk estin*) anyone who does good, there is not (*ouk estin*)[30]

---

26. The quotations from the Psalms agree with the text of the LXX (3:13a, 3:13b) or vary slightly from that text (3:10–12, 14, 18).

27. See also LXX Ps 52:2–4 (MT 53:2–4).

28. It is probably coincidental that the first three words of vs. 10b (*ouk estin dikaios*) are also to be found in in Eccl 7:20 (cf. 1 Sam 2:2).

29. *Hamartia* ("sin") and *dikaiosynē* ("justness, righteousness") are antithetical correlates for Paul, especially in Romans 6.

30. Nestle-Aland puts the phrase in brackets because the reading is uncertain.

even one." The repetition of *ouk estin* is rhetorically very effective. The point is that there is no exception, not a single one.

The remaining quotations, with small adaptations from the source texts, drive the point home:[31] "Their throat is an open grave" (vs. 13a; Ps 5:10), "the venom of asps is under their lips" (vs. 13b; Ps 139:4), "their mouth is full of curses and bitterness" (vs. 14; Ps 9:28), "their feet are swift to shed blood, in their paths are ruin and misery, and the way of peace they do not know" (vss. 15–17; Isa 59:7–8), "there is no (*ouk estin*) fear of God before their eyes" (vs. 18; Ps 35:2). With its use of *ouk estin*, here taken directly from the source text, vs. 18 functions as an *inclusio*, recalling the opening citation in vs. 10.

Verses 19–20 are a summing up and provide a transition to the following passage (3:21–26).[32] Verse 19 repeats in different words the point of vs. 9 ("the whole world" in vs. 19 has the same referent as "all people" in vs. 9), taking the import of the intervening citations into account: "Now we know that whatever the Law says, it speaks to those in the Law, that every mouth may be stopped and the whole world be held accountable to God." Paul here describes the preceding citations as coming from "the Law" (*ho nomos*), even though they actually come from the Psalms and Isaiah. He could have written "the Scripture" here, as he does in Gal 3:22.

It is evidently for rhetorical reasons that Paul now refers to the (whole) Scripture as "the Law" (cf. 1 Cor 14:21).[33] He directs his words to those who stand "in the Law (*en tō nomō*)," here evidently using the term "Law" to refer to the Mosaic legislation in particular (cf. 2:12; 3:21a). Those who stand "in the Law" are those who acknowledge its authority by observing its commandments (cf. 7:7–12; 13:9). The words from the (scriptural) Law that Paul has just cited mean that everyone, even those who live according to the (legislative) Law, are equal in the eyes of God, "that *every* mouth may be stopped and the *whole* world be held accountable to God." There are no exceptions, not even those who are Law-observant. As Ridderbos writes: "Paul turns the weapon with which they thought to defend themselves against them."[34] The Jews have their advantages (to them "have been entrusted the

---

31. The following quotations are also present in manuscripts of the LXX at the end of Ps 13:3 and given within brackets in the standard edition of Rahlfs. As Stanley (*Paul and the Language of Scripture,* 88) writes: "The presence of this entire section . . . in countless manuscripts of the Septuagint is perhaps the clearest evidence . . . for the influence of the New Testament citations on the textual tradition of the Septuagint."

32. Cf. Hays, "Psalm 143 and the Logic of Romans 3."

33. In 3:21b he uses the term to refer to the Pentateuch in particular ("the Law and the prophets").

34. Ridderbos, *Romeinen,* 79.

oracles of God"; Rom 3:2), but not when it comes to the universal condition of humanity "under the power of Sin" (3:9).[35] "For there is no distinction; since all have sinned and fall short of the glory of God" (3:22b–23).

In vs. 20, Paul draws a conclusion with respect to the issue of justification, which will be the main topic in the paragraphs that follow: "Therefore, all flesh will not be justified before Him on the basis of works of the Law, for through the Law comes knowledge of Sin." Paul adapts the language of LXX 142:2b to the argumentative context. For the subordinatin conjunction *hoti* ("because") found in Ps 142:2b and retained by Paul in Gal 2:16b, he now substitutes, as noted above, the coordinating conjunction *dioti* ("Therefore"), which begins a new sentence and introduces a conclusion. As in Gal 2:16d Paul makes use of the language of LXX Ps 142:2b but does not indicate in any way that he is quoting. By using the words *enōpion autou* ("before him") instead of *enōpion sou* ("before you"), Paul changes the Psalm text from a statement addressed to God into a general statement. With the omission of these words Paul had achieved the same effect in Galatians 2:16d. As we have seen above, the words *ou dikaiōthēsetai pasa sarx* ("all flesh shall not be justified") mean that *no one* will be justified and that message corresponds to, and here sums up, that of vss. 10–18.

Furthermore, as mentioned earlier, the two substantive changes that occur in Galatians 2:16d with respect to the LXX text of the Psalm are retained in Rom 3:20a (the use of *pasa sarx* instead of *pas zōn* and the inclusion of the phrase e*x ergōn nomou* as if it were part of the source text). That first modification plays no further role in the immediate context of Romans 3:20, although Paul mentions "flesh" in connection with (literal) circumcision in 2:28 (cf. LXX Gen 17:11–14; see also the references to "the flesh" in Rom 7:5, 18, 25; 8:1–3). Works of the Law do play an important role in the following paragraphs in connection with Paul's teaching on justification (3:27–28; 4:2, 6). The material quotation from LXX Ps 142:2b thus constitutes a transition to the subject of "justification on the basis of the faith of (or: in) Christ" in the following paragraphs, whereby "works of the Law" are irrelevant and excluded (3:21–5:11). The final clause, "since through the Law comes knowledge of Sin (*epignosis hamartias*)" (3: 20b), anticipates this exclusion of the Law for justification. The verse functions literarily as an *inclusio* with 3:9 ("all people are under the power of Sin") and it indicates that the (legislative) Law is not a solution for Sin, but to the contrary functions merely to make human beings aware of the Sin under which they are enslaved (cf. 5:13, 21; 6:12–18; 7:7–25).[36]

---

35. Cf. Keck, "The Function of Romans 3:10–18," 153.

36. See chapter 4 above.

Conclusion

We posed two questions at the beginning: (1) How are the two noteworthy deviations of LXX Ps 142:2b in Galatians 2:16d and Romans 3:20a (the use of *pasa sarx* instead of *pas zōn* and the inclusion of the phrase ex *ergōn nomou*) to be explained?

And (2) what is the function of Paul's use of this Psalm text in the Letters to the Galatians and to the Romans?

1. For an answer to the first question we first briefly return to the catena of citations in Rom 3:10–18 which precedes the citation from LXX Ps 142:2b in Rom 3:20a. Given the tight composition and rhetorical aspects of the series, the view that Paul cites "from memory"[37] can be put aside. According to Keck, Paul did not compile the catena of quotations himself; rather, he is dependent on pre-Pauline tradition.[38] This hypothesis is rejected by Koch and Stanley,[39] who hypothesize that Paul himself compiled this catena some time before writing the Letter to the Romans. In short: Paul probably made use of an anthology that he compiled himself.[40] The comparison between Galatians 2:16d and Romans 3:20a leads to the same conclusion.[41] The retention in Rom 3:20a of the two substantive changes in the citation of LXX Ps 142:2b made in Galatians 2:16d can then be readily explained.

2. In order to be able to answer the second question, it must first be noted that Paul's insights into the human condition are based on (his understanding of) the gospel of the crucified Christ (cf. 1 Cor 1:18–2:5; Gal 3:1; Rom 3:21–26; 5:6–11, 12–21),[42] not on the authority of "the Scripture" (Gal 3:22) or "the Holy Scriptures" (Rom 1:2). In certain circumstances, however, Paul makes an appeal to texts from the OT, in particular from the Psalms, to underscore the seriousness of the human condition. In connection with the latter, he provides a

37. Ridderbos, *Romeinen*, 77. See the criticism of this view by Stanley, *Paul and the anguage of Scripture*, 16–17, 69–70.

38. Keck, "Function," 141–57.

39. Koch, *Schrift als Zeuge*, 180–83; Stanley, *Paul and the Language of Scripture*, 88.

40. For a parallel, compare CD 5:13–17. According to Keck these and other parallels suggest "that in apocalyptic circles the OT may have been sifted to locate passages which could be connected to catenae or indictments against sinners" (Keck, "Function," 149); Paul "appropriates a piece of apocalyptically-shaped tradition" (153).

41. Verhoef, *"Er staat geschreven,"* 249. On the basis of more general considerations, Stanley (*Language of Scripture*, 71–79) also concludes that Paul has compiled his own anthology of texts.

42. See de Boer, *Defeat of Death*.

catena of texts, almost all from the Psalms, in Rom 3:10–18 to further *illustrate* the dire human condition before and apart from Christ and to undermine all self-deception about this reality.[43] In both Galatians and Romans Paul seeks to show that "works of the Law" are a dead end and provide no solace for the human condition. Before and apart from Christ all people are held captive "under the power of Sin," which is a core insight of the gospel for Paul. The works of the Law do not offer a way out of this prison. The Law (as Scripture) itself confirms this view according to Paul: "on the basis of works of the Law *no one* will be justified."

For those who know and value the OT, Paul's use of texts from this body of literature comes across as selective and misleading. And that is in fact the case.[44] Paul quotes texts from the OT, the Psalms in particular, in Gal 2:16d and Rom 3:9–20 to highlight the human inability to receive justification from God on the basis of keeping the Law. Paul uses these texts to illustrate his understanding of the human condition as informed by the gospel of the crucified Christ. By quoting words from "the (scriptural) Law" (Rom 3:19), Paul seeks to convince readers who rely on the Scripture as the authoritative word of God that their position on "the (legislative) Law" is untenable.

---

43. Paul's appeal to Scripture (the OT) thus does not serve as proof, but as an illustration of knowledge that he has attained from the gospel. If the quotations were meant to serve as proof, readers who possess a good knowledge of the OT could rightly protest and provide alternate readings, as Ridderbos does in his comment on Rom 3:10–12, where Paul cites from LXX Ps 13 (MT Ps 14). Ridderbos notes that while it is true that vss. 10–12 repeatedly says that "there is no one . . ." and that this charge also has a very general scope, the Psalm obviously does not intend to say that there are no other people to whom the charge does not apply (cf. vs. 5). And that is even more true of the other Psalms cited, where very clearly only the behavior of the ungodly is being described and contrasted with that of the pious. This, he concludes, is "of course" not denied by Paul (*Romeinen*, 78). In this way, the specific words which Paul does in fact quote (and apply in his further argument) are completely disarmed and domesticated.

44. See Koch, *Schrift als Zeuge*; Stanley, *Paul and the Language of Scripture*.

Chapter 12

Apocalyptic as God's Eschatological Activity in Paul's Theology

Introduction

IN PUBLICATIONS DEVOTED TO "apocalyptic Paul," I have consistently used the term "apocalyptic" as an adjective modifying the noun "eschatology." The focus of my research has been Paul's "apocalyptic eschatology."[1] But I am not averse to using the term "apocalyptic" also as a noun.[2] When I do, I employ it as convenient shorthand for this particular form of eschatology.[3]

In using the expression "apocalyptic eschatology," I have profited from a three-fold distinction propounded by Paul D. Hanson in an article published in 1976.[4] He distinguishes "apocalyptic eschatology" from an "apocalypse," on the one hand, and "apocalypticism," on the other. John J. Collins has propounded a similar distinction.[5]

1. See de Boer, *Defeat of Death*; de Boer, "Paul and Jewish Apocalyptic Eschatology" (chapter 1 above); de Boer, "Paul and Apocalyptic Eschatology"; de Boer, *Galatians*, 31–35. This paper takes these publications as a point of departure, as also the following articles: "Paul, Theologian of God's Apocalypse" (chapter 2 above) and "Paul's Mythologizing Program in Romans 5–8" (chapter 3 above). I am also deeply indebted to the work of J. Louis Martyn, in particular his article, "Apocalyptic Antinomies," and his magisterial commentary, *Galatians*, esp. 97–105.

2. This usage has probably occurred under the influence of the German noun *Apokalyptik*. Since the 1980s, some scholars have found the nominal use of the English word "apocalyptic" deeply problematic, but the nominal use has become ingrained in biblical scholarship in English through the publication of such influential works as Russell, *Method and Message*, and Rowland, *Open Heaven*. This usage can no longer be undone, nor does it need to be as long as authors are clear about how they are using the term.

3. I here use the term "eschatology" to mean simply human expectations concerning "the (very) last things," i.e., the final destiny of human beings and the world in which they live. *Apocalyptic* eschatology is a particular form of such expectation, to be further specified below.

4. Hanson, "Apocalypticism." See Introduction above.

5. Collins, *Apocalyptic Imagination,* 2–11. See also Collins, *Apocalypticism in the Dead Sea Scrolls,* 1–11. It is, I think, unfortunate that this threefold distinction is not

The term *apocalypse* for Hanson designates a literary genre. This has become the accepted and ubiquitous academic use of the term, mainly through the efforts of Collins.[6] The paradigm of the genre is the NT book of Revelation, also known as the Apocalypse. In fact, the genre designation is derived from this book whose first word is *apokalypsis*, "apocalypse/revelation."[7] It is not clear, however, whether the term here already functions as a genre designation[8] or simply as a description of the book's content(s): "An *apokalypsis* of Jesus Christ, which God gave him to show his servants what must soon take place; and he made it known by sending his angel to his servant John" (Rev. 1:1, RSV, 2nd ed.). The *apokalypsis* of Jesus Christ, it may be noted, concerns *events* that must soon occur. As the rest of the book makes plain, these coming *events* are *eschatological*.[9]

---

maintained by Murphy, *Apocalypticism*, 5.

6. See his influential and much quoted definition in Collins, *Morphology*, 6: "a genre of revelatory literature with a narrative framework, in which a revelation is mediated to a human recipient, disclosing a transcendent reality which is both temporal, insofar as it envisages eschatological salvation, and spatial insofar as it involves another, supernatural world." Collins subsequently expanded this definition with words taken from Yarbro Collins (*Early Christian Apocalypticism*, 7) concerning the social and rhetorical function of such writings: they were "intended to interpret present, earthly circumstances in light of the supernatural world and of the future, and to influence both the understanding and behavior of the audience by means of divine authority" ("Introduction," xiii).

7. Both the Greek noun *apokalypsis* and the English noun "revelation" (from the Latin *revelatio*) literally mean "unveiling" ("veil" in Greek is *kalumma*, in Latin *velum*), just as the corresponding Greek verb *apokalyptō* and the English verb "reveal" (from the Latin *revelare*) both literally mean "to unveil" and thus "to uncover (what was hidden)."

8. The book actually has the formal features of a (circular) letter to seven churches (cf. 1:4; 22:21).

9. Moreover, the value of the genre designation for books written before the second century CE is dubious, since according to Collins the "use of the Greek title *apokalypsis* (revelation) is not attested in the period before Christianity." Works written before Revelation, he notes, "had not yet attained the generic self-consciousness" evident in later works and thus "have affinities to more than one genre" (*Apocalyptic Imagination*, 3). An "apocalypse" is thus to be regarded as "a generic framework" incorporating other literary genres (letter, testament, parable, hymn, prayer, etc.) and "is not constituted by one or more literary themes but by a distinctive combination of elements, all of which are found elsewhere" (*Apocalyptic Imagination*, 8–9). (Similar remarks are made by Hanson, "Apocalypticism"). Such observations make any clear definition of the genre whereby an apocalypse (as a self-contained book) can be usefully distinguished from other literary genres (other books) well-nigh impossible (see the confusion about the matter in Murphy, *Apocalypticism*, 4–8). Collins notes that the formal definition offered in *Morphology* actually applies only "to various sections" of such works as *1 Enoch*, *4 Ezra*, and *2 Baruch* (*Apocalyptic Imagination*, 4), but this has not prevented many scholars, including Collins himself, from referring to *1 Enoch*, *4 Ezra*, *2 Baruch*, etc. in their entirety as "apocalypses" (cf. Collins, *Apocalyptic Imagination*, 5–7). In *Defeat of Death*

Hanson uses the term *apocalypticism* to describe "the symbolic universe in which an apocalyptic movement codifies its identity and interpretation of reality." "This symbolic universe," he continues, "crystallizes around the perspective of apocalyptic eschatology which the movement adopts."[10] Since apocalyptic eschatology is evidently the defining characteristic of an apocalyptic movement's symbolic universe and is also given separate treatment by Hanson, a more appropriate definition of "apocalypticism" would be: "a social movement adopting an apocalyptic perspective on reality,"[11] or "a group having recourse to apocalyptic eschatology as its symbolic universe."[12] It is important for our purposes to note that, for Hanson, apocalyptic eschatology is not confined to historical apocalyptic movements to the extent such can be traced; it can be embraced by different social groups in diverse circumstances.[13]

That brings us then to Hanson's understanding of *apocalyptic eschatology*. He defines it as "a religious perspective, a way of viewing divine plans in relation to mundane realities."[14] For understandable reasons, apocalyptic eschatology as a perspective or worldview has been closely associated with the book of Revelation—the Apocalypse—and other ancient literature sharing (at least some of) its generic features,[15] especially the so-called "historical apocalypses" found in such works as Daniel and *4 Ezra*.[16] The eschatol-

---

(1971n4), I suggested that Collins's definition in *Morphology* amounts to a definition of a "vision" (more accurately, "a written report of a vision"), a genre designation not normally applied to whole books. The various parts of works such as Daniel, *1 Enoch*, or *4 Ezra* are often labeled "visions." It may thus be better to think of an apocalypse as a smaller literary genre (*Form*) akin to prayer, parable or hymn, and not as a larger literary genre (*Gattung*) for a whole book such as letter, gospel, or history. By this definition Mark 13 and 1 Thess 4:13–18 are apocalypses (as generally recognized), but Mark and 1 Thessalonians of course are not. The same would apply, e.g., to Isa 24–27 ("the Isaiah Apocalypse") or *1 Enoch* 83–91 ("the Animal Apocalypse"). See n. 3 above for a brief, working definition of "eschatology."

10. Hanson, "Apocalypticism," 30.

11. Cf. Collins, *Apocalyptic Imagination*, 10 ("a historical movement"), though in *The Encyclopedia of Apocalypticism*, Collins uses the term to designate "a worldview" ("Introduction," xiv), as does Murphy (*Apocalypticism*, 8).

12. Cf. Cuvillier, "Das apokalyptische Denken." *Apokalyptik*, according to Cuvillier, concerns three things: a literary genre (*Gattung*), a social movement, and a worldview or ideology characterized by apocalyptic eschatology (2). See the summary of Hanson by Sturm, "Defining the Word 'Apocalyptic'," 35.

13. See further Hanson, "Apocalypses." See also de Boer, *Defeat of Death*, 41.

14. Hanson, "Apocalypticism," 29. This perspective, says Hanson, is not to be confused with "a system of thought."

15. But see the discussion in n. 9 above.

16. See Collins, *Apocalyptic Imagination*, 5.

ogy found in Revelation is itself strongly indebted to Jewish antecedents and traditions, even if it goes far beyond them in its use of imagery and symbolism and has a specifically Christian focus.[17] Apocalyptic eschatology, whether Christian or Jewish, is assumed to bear at least a "family resemblance" to the eschatology found in the book of Revelation.[18] For this reason, among others, it has been called *apocalyptic* eschatology instead of something else.[19] Hanson notes that this perspective, or worldview, is not confined to Revelation nor to apocalypses generally, but that it can also find expression in or through other genres of literature (parables, hymns, letters, testaments). As a perspective, it is not genre specific, it is not genre bound.[20]

Hanson's definition of apocalyptic eschatology as "a religious perspective, a way of viewing divine plans in relation to mundane realities" is rather vague and needs elaboration. This Hanson in fact provides. He points out that as a religious perspective *early* Jewish apocalyptic eschatology, which was Hanson's particular area of expertise,[21] concerns *God's* "final saving acts" and these final divine saving acts involve "deliverance out of the present order into a new transformed order" of reality. Hanson appeals in this connection to Isa 65:17: "For behold, I [God] create new heavens and a new earth; and the former things shall not be remembered or come into mind" (RSV).[22] We may compare Rev 21:1–2: "Then I [John] saw a new heaven and a new earth; for the first heaven and the first earth had passed away . . .

17. See Bauckham, *Revelation*, 9–12.

18. The actual "touchstone" for any definition of apocalyptic eschatology, therefore, is not "the kind of eschatology found in the apocalypses" generally (Collins, *Apocalyptic Imagination*, 9) but the kind of eschatology found in the book of Revelation specifically.

19. It may go without saying that the expression "apocalyptic eschatology" is "a construct of scholars that purports to epitomize certain phenomena discernible in the primary sources" (de Boer, *Defeat of Death*, 181; see chapter 1 above). As I have pointed out repeatedly, any definition of the term is partly a matter of scholarly tradition and convenience even though it is based, as it should be, upon the data of the available sources, primarily Revelation but also such conceptually related works as (parts of) Daniel, 1 Enoch, and 4 Ezra. There may be ancient apocalypses that contain no eschatology or an entirely different one, or that use the language of revelation outside the framework of apocalyptic eschatology, but that is of no consequence for the soundness of the definition since there is enough data to support it.

20. See Collins, *Apocalypticism in the Dead Sea Scrolls*, 8: "A worldview is not necessarily tied to one literary form, and the apocalyptic worldview could find expression in other genres besides apocalypses." On the problem of genre definition, see above. The nature of the relationship of apocalyptic to the literary genre apocalypse has bedeviled biblical scholarship since the pioneering work of F. Lücke in 1832. See R. Sturm, "Defining the Word 'Apocalyptic.'"

21. Cf. Hanson, *Dawn of Apocalyptic*.

22. Hanson, "Apocalypticism," 30.

And I saw the holy city, new Jerusalem, coming down out of heaven from God" (RSV). The expected new order of reality will not be a rehabilitation or a reconfiguration of the present (social and political) order of reality ("this age"), as is generally the case in OT prophetic eschatology,[23] but its termination and *replacement* by something completely new ("the age to come").[24] The new Jerusalem will replace the old Jerusalem.[25] The new order of reality will replace the old order of reality, and it will do so definitively, finally, and irrevocably, i.e., eschatologically. This act of replacement will be initiated and brought about by God and God alone, which is to say that it cannot be initiated by human beings or effected by them.

The word "apocalyptic" in scholarly discussion especially since the work of Johannes Weiss, and after him Albert Schweitzer,[26] Ernst Käsemann,[27] and more recently J. Louis Martyn,[28] evokes this expectation of God's own eschatological activity of putting an end to the present order of reality ("this age") and replacing it with a new, transformed order of reality ("the age to come"). As Weiss wrote, in connection with Jesus' proclamation of the kingdom of God: "By force and insurrection men might establish a Davidide monarch . . . but God will establish the Kingdom of God without

23. On this issue, see Hanson, *Dawn,* and Collins, "From Prophecy to Apocalypticism."

24. Cf. Vielhauer ("Einleitung," 413) for whom the eschatological dualism of the two ages is *the* defining characteristic apocalyptic eschatology (against Wright, *Paul and His Recent Interpeters*, 158; Frey, "Demythologizing Apocalyptic?," 509). The classic text is *4 Ezra* 7:50: "the Most High has not made one age, but two." There are scattered references to "this age" and/or "the age to come" in the relevant literature (cf. *1 Enoch* 71:15; *4 Ezra* 7:112, 119; *2 Bar.* 44:8 15; 83:4, 9; see *m.'Abot* 4:1; *m.Sanh.* 10:1; *m.Ber.* 9:5), including the NT (e.g., Eph 1:21; Matt 12:32; Luke 20:34–35). For Paul, see below. This dualism should probably not be called a doctrine (as Russell does in *Method and Message,* 269), as if it were some carefully worked out principle or teaching. It is better to think of it as the basic presupposition of an apocalyptic-eschatological worldview, whether that be Jewish or Christian and whether or not the specific terms are used. The dualism of the two ages can be given expression in a rich diversity of imagery, symbolism, and concepts, derived from a wide variety of sources. It is thus somewhat misleading and even futile to provide a list of "characteristics" of the apocalyptic worldview or of apocalyptic literature, as is often done. The "family resemblance" between apocalyptic texts in all their diversity lies in the eschatological dualism of the two ages.

25. The new age does not merely succeed the old age as on a time line; it *replaces* this age with another age. For the two ages are not merely temporal epochs; they are also, perhaps even primarily, orbs or spheres (spaces) in which certain activities take place. The two ages are fundamentally distinct, mutually exclusive "orders of reality" (to use Hanson's terminology), i.e., "worlds."

26. Schweitzer, *Mysticism of Paul.*

27. Käsemann, "Beginnings" and "Primitive Christian Apocalyptic."

28. Martyn, "Apocalyptic Antinomies"; idem, *Galatians.*

human hands, horse or rider, with only his angels and celestial powers"; "God himself must come and make everything new"; "The actualization of the Kingdom of God is *not* a matter for human initiative, but entirely a matter of God's initiative."[29] Weiss described such views as "eschatological-apocalyptic." They are not just apocalyptic (matters of divine revelation) and not just eschatological (expectations of events concerning "the last things"), but both—what I would call (reversing Weiss's word order) "apocalyptic-eschatological"! Apocalyptic (as I use the term) is a form of eschatology that expects God to come and establish a new order of reality for human beings.[30] That new order of reality will have a "heavenly" character because it will come from heaven, which is to say from the realm of God (cf. Rev 21:1-2, cited above). For that reason, this new world will be nothing like what has been seen before (cf. 1 Cor 2:9: "what no eye has seen, nor ear heard, nor the heart of a human being conceived . . . ").

To adopt an apocalyptic perspective, then, is not "to concentrate on the theme of the direct communication of heavenly mysteries in all their diversity,"[31] but on the expectation of God's own visible eschatological activity, what I have called the Apocalypse of God[32]—where the term "apocalypse" obviously does not denote a literary genre, nor does the term signify only divine revelation or disclosure of previously hidden information, but also visible divine movement and activity on a cosmic scale.

In the view of Paul (but also in that of John, the seer of Revelation), this Apocalypse of God occurs in the event of Jesus Christ. So Paul writes: "When the fullness of time of time came, God . . . ." God did something. He "sent forth his Son . . . so that he might redeem those under the Law, so that we might receive adoption as sons" (Gal 4:4-5; cf. Rom 5:8; 8:3-4). At part of this same Apocalypse of God, "God sent forth the Spirit of his Son into our hearts" (Gal 4:6). As Martyn has written, "The advent of the Son and of his Spirit is thus *the* cosmic, apocalyptic event."[33] The difference here from ancient Jewish apocalyptic eschatology is the conviction that in

29. Weiss, *Jesus' Proclamation*, 102, 108, and 132 (original emphasis), respectively.

30. Let that serve as a concise definition of apocalyptic eschatology. See n. 20 above.

31. Rowland, *Open Heaven*, 14. See my critique of Rowland's approach in chapter 2 above.

32. See chapter 2 above. It is true that neither Paul nor Revelation uses this expression but both do use the expression "an apocalypse of Jesus Christ" (Gal 1:12; Rev 1:1) and for both God is effectively present in the person and the work of Christ. The apocalypse of Jesus Christ, then, is for both tantamount to the Apocalypse of God (I capitalize the term here to indicate the finality of the event). See further below on Paul's use of the terms *apokalypsis* and *apokalyptō*.

33. Martyn, *Theological Issues*, 121.

the coming of Jesus Christ God has inaugurated "the final saving acts" (to use Hanson's phrase) that mark the definitive end of the old order of reality ("this age") and its irrevocable replacement by the new order of reality ("the age to come," which for Paul and John of Revelation is no longer solely a future expectation).[34] It is therefore a mistake to limit apocalyptic eschatology in Paul (or in Revelation) to the future acts of God (or Christ), i.e., to the Parousia (1 Thess 4:15; 1 Cor 15:23) or the End (1 Cor 1:8; 15:24).[35] For Paul (as for John of Revelation), apocalyptic eschatology involves an "already" and a "still more."[36] The death and resurrection of Christ has inaugurated a unified apocalyptic drama that reaches its conclusion at the Parousia/the End (1 Cor 15:20–26).[37] The Apocalypse of God in Jesus Christ covers events from

34. As noted earlier, Paul refers specifically to "this age" (*ho aiōnios houtos*) in several passages (Rom 12:2; 1 Cor 1:20; 2:6, 8; 3:18; 2 Cor 4:4. He can also call it "this world" (*ho kosmos houtos*) in 1 Cor 3:19; 5:10; 7:31; cf. Eph 2:2; *4 Ezra* 4:2; 8:1). He does not use the expression "the age to come" (*ho aiōnios ho mellōn/erchomenos*) in his undisputed letters though it does occur in Eph 1:21 as well as other NT texts (Matt 12:32; Mark 10:30; Luke 18:30; cf. 1 Cor 10:11; Eph 2:7; Heb 6:5). As previously indicated in the Introduction, it would seem probable that such expressions as "the kingdom of God" (Rom 14:17; 1 Cor 4:20; 6:9–10; 15:50; Gal 5:17; cf. Eph 5:5; Col 1:13), "eternal life" (Rom 2:7; 5:21; 6:22–23; Gal 6:8), and "new creation" (2 Cor 5:17; Gal 6:15) in Paul (and elsewhere in the NT as well as in Jewish apocalyptic texts from the period) are often best understood as other ways of speaking about the age to come (looked at from different angles). The absence of the expression "the age to come" can also be explained by the fact that for Paul the new age had already begun to dawn in God's sending the Son and his Spirit.

35. In "Primitive Christian Apocalyptic," Käsemann observes that he speaks of "primitive Christian apocalyptic to denote the expectation of an imminent Parousia" (109n1). It is in this sense that "Apocalyptic was the mother of all Christian theology" ("Beginnings," 102). But Käsemann nuances this strict definition later in the former essay: "Christ is God's representative over a world which is not yet fully subject to God, although its eschatological subordination is in train since Easter and its end is in sight. No perspective could be more apocalyptic. . . . Paul is absolutely unable and unwilling to speak of any end to history which has already come to pass, but, he does, however, discern that the day of the End-time has *already* broken" (133; emphasis added). It is Martyn who has insisted that Paul's present eschatology must also be given the label "apocalyptic," not just his future eschatology, which remains equally important for Martyn's understanding of Paul as an apocalyptic theologian. Cf. Martyn, "Apocalyptic Antinomies in Galatians," 421: "Paul's perception of Jesus' death is, then, fully as apocalyptic as is his hope for Jesus' parousia (cf. 1 Cor 2.8)."

36. For this formulation of the tension, see de Boer, *Galatians*, 34. This tension has often been formulated as an "already" and a "not yet," the latter reflecting "an eschatological reservation" formulated by Paul over against pneumatic enthusiasts in Corinth (Käsemann, "Primitive Christian Apocalyptic," 132). But for Paul himself and other believers, such as those in Thessalonica or Jerusalem, the (eager) expectation of an imminent Parousia was a matter of "still more."

37. Jewish apocalyptic eschatology, it is sometimes asserted, has its own version of "already" and "still more" (or "not yet"). This was already noted by Käsemann,

the initial sending of the Son and his Spirit into the world to the transfer of Christ's messianic sovereignty to God at the End (1 Cor 15:23–28).[38]

God's Apocalypse and the Human Plight

But now the question arises: What makes God's eschatological intervention necessary in ancient Jewish apocalyptic eschatology and in Paul's christologically informed adaptation? [39] Why, in other words, is it that human beings are not capable of putting an end to the old order of reality ("this age") and replacing it with a new one ("the age to come")?

The answer is that "this age" is characterized above all else by death.[40] The term "death" is applied not only to the physical demise of human beings (bodily death) but also (in a metaphorical extension) to sinful behavior (moral or spiritual death) and to damnation or perdition (eternal or eschatological death).[41] In all these usages, death signifies separation from God and from life which is understood to involve being in the presence of God and there acting according to God's will. A presupposition of this picture is that human beings are incapable of doing anything about

---

"Righteousness of God," 178. The point has received new emphasis in the work of Stuckenbruck, "Overlapping Ages" and "Evil in Johannine and Apocalyptic Perspective," 229–32. However, the term "eschatology" in the expression "apocalyptic eschatology" involves finality and irrevocability, things that cannot be said of earlier divine interventions, also in the history of Israel. Furthermore, for Paul, previous divine interventions did not (in retrospect) deal with the problem (the human plight). Only Christ has done that. See Martyn, "Apocalyptic Antinomies," 121: "For the true war of liberation has been initiated not at Sinai, but rather in the apocalypse of the crucified one and in the coming of his Spirit." Until the coming of Christ, the promise to Abraham remained just that, a promise (cf. Gal 3:6–29). See further n. 47.

38. See de Boer, *Defeat of Death,* ch. 4. Cf. Martyn, *Galatians,* 105: Paul's "view has, in fact, three foci: Christ's future coming [his Parousia], Christ's past advent (his death and resurrection), and the present war against the powers of evil, inaugurated by his Spirit and taking place between these two events."

39. The revelation of the age to come simultaneously unmasks the present time and everything leading up to the new age as the old age that is doomed to pass away, usually very soon, when it will be replaced by the new age. Apocalyptic eschatology thus involves not only the expectation of the new age but also the assessment of the past (up to the present moment) as the order or realm of evil, as what Paul calls "the present evil age" in Gal 1:4. Both ages, then, are matters of revelation.

40. This was a fundamental point of my book, *Defeat of Death,* where the relevant texts are scrutinized. The key texts in the letters of Paul are 1 Corinthians 15 (esp. vss. 20–28) and Romans 5 (esp. vss. 12–21).

41. See de Boer, *Defeat of Death,* 83–84, 143–44.

death. Death signifies the end of all human possibilities and hopes.[42] The understanding of "this age" as marked by death (irremediable separation or alienation from God) explains why there is no continuity between "this age" and "the age to come." It is only God who can bring life out of death, something out of nothing (cf. Rom 4:17b), and for that reason there is no remedy for the human plight apart from God's own intervention. It is also for this reason that the resurrection of the dead, however it may be conceived anthropologically and whatever its scope may be, is an apocalyptic event. It is in fact, soteriologically speaking, *the* apocalyptic event, for through it God rectifies what has gone wrong with the human world and does so once and for all. Without this divine intervention, physical and moral death are tantamount to eternal death.

As indicated in chapter 1 above, there are two basic and competing explanations in the relevant sources for the human plight (death in its threefold form) and thus also for the solution to this situation. In the first explanation, represented especially by *1 Enoch* 1–36 (cf. also chs. 37–71), the human plight is attributable to evil angelic powers (Satan and his minions). These angelic powers are (ultimately) responsible for human sinfulness (idolatry in particular) and its primary consequence, the violent death of those who seek to acknowledge God's rightful sovereign claim on the world. In the second explanation, represented especially by *2 Baruch* (cf. also *4 Ezra*), human beings are themselves responsible for their plight (cosmological powers play no role). All human beings beginning with the first, Adam, have sinned and thus deserve the death that overcomes each and every human being.

The expected solution must address or correspond to the plight. For the first explanation of the human condition, therefore, the Last Judgment is expected to entail a victorious cosmic war against the evil cosmological powers,[43] at which time God also vindicates their primary victims, the righteous few who have not allowed themselves to become complicit in the hegemony of the evil powers, often at the cost of persecution and death. God raises the righteous martyrs from the dead (a limited resurrection)

---

42. Cf. 2 Sam 14:14: "We must all die; we are like water spilled on the ground, which cannot be gathered up"; Job 7:9: "As the cloud fades and vanishes, so those who go down to Sheol do not come up." It is a characteristic of apocalyptic that (bodily) death is no longer regarded as a naturally necessary event or reality as it is in the OT. Death has become *the* indication that something has gone terribly wrong with the world.

43. Cf. *1 En.* 1:3–9: "The God of the universe, the Holy Great One, will come forth from his dwelling. And from there he will march upon Mount Sinai and appear in his camp emerging from heaven with a mighty power. And everyone shall be afraid, and Watchers [fallen angels] shall quiver. . . . Behold, he will arrive with ten million of the holy ones in order to execute judgment upon all" (trans. E. Isaac, in Charlesworth, *Old Testament Pseudepigrapha*).

and rewards them with eternal life (cf. Dan 12:1–2). For the second explanation, the Last Judgment is expected to involve a cosmic courtroom before which all human beings appear before God for sentencing on the basis of their deeds.[44] To make this possible all those who have already died are raised (a general resurrection) so that God can reward the righteous (a small number) with eternal life in the new age and condemn the wicked (a much larger group) to eternal death (perdition), what Revelation calls "the second death" (Rev 2:11; 20:6, 14; 21:8). For the former group, the sentence of death passed on Adam and his descendants is overturned; for the latter, it is confirmed and made eternal.[45]

In both of these distinguishable patterns of ancient Jewish apocalyptic eschatology, the Last Judgment is a cosmic event (involving all people from all times) in and through which the Creator God of Israel eschatologically (i.e., finally, definitively, and irrevocably) rectifies (puts right) the world God has created: "this evil age" ceases to exist and "the age to come" in which God reigns unopposed takes its place. From a soteriological angle, the realm of life replaces the realm of death. In both patterns of ancient Jewish apocalyptic eschatology, furthermore, the righteous (or saints) are those who have acknowledged the sovereign claim of Israel's God (the First Commandment) and have done so by committing themselves to God's Law, which is God's standard for determining who is to be rewarded and punished at the Last Judgment.[46] The Law, then, is God's proffered remedy for death and its underlying cause, sin (the repudiation of God, which is the fundamental sin of Adam and each of his descendants).[47] With the gift of the Law, God gives human beings a weapon to withstand evil powers (in the first explanation of the human plight) or a second chance to get it right (in the second explanation). In other words, when chosen and observed, the Law functions as a bridge for crossing the otherwise unbridgeable chasm—death—that separates human beings from God and thus from life in the world to come.

There is nevertheless a fundamental difference between the two patterns, as indicated above: in the first or "cosmological" pattern, human beings

44. Cf. 4 Ezra 7:33–38; 2 Bar. 49–52. According to 4 Ezra 7:113, "the day of judgment will be the end of this age and the beginning of the immortal age to come."

45. The preceding paragraph is a brief summary of a complex set of data. For more detail and nuance, see de Boer, Defeat of Death, ch. 3. The same can be said for the paragraph that now follows.

46. For this reason, the righteous in a sense already proleptically experience and possess the eternal life that will be their reward at the Last Judgment.

47. See chapter 4 above.

are *victims of forces beyond their control*,[48] whereas in the second or "forensic" pattern, human beings are held to be *fully accountable moral agents*.[49] As a result, the Apocalypse of God is also differently conceived, either primarily as a cosmic war against evil cosmological powers which have usurped his sovereignty or primarily as a cosmic courtroom in which all human beings are held accountable for what they have done or not done.[50]

Paul adapts elements from both patterns of ancient Jewish apocalyptic eschatology.[51] As Albert Schweitzer pointed out nearly a century ago, however, Paul's own perspective stands "closer"[52] to the apocalyptic eschatology of *1 Enoch* than to that of *2 Baruch* (or *4 Ezra*) which is to say, closer to the cosmological pattern of Jewish apocalyptic eschatology than to the forensic pattern. For Paul, according to Schweitzer, the present world-age is "characterized not only by its transience, but also by the fact that demons and angels exercise power in it," whereas the coming world-age "will put an end to this condition."[53] Salvation is "thus cosmologically conceived,"[54] i.e., as the expurgation of evil demonic or angelic powers from the cosmos. This has also been the view of Käsemann and Martyn. I in turn have sought to show that in Romans Paul appears to be in conversation with Jews holding to a contemporary version of the forensic pattern, whereas in Galatians he is seeking to rebut Christian Jews (preachers who have invaded the Galatian

---

48. This counts, though in different ways, both for those human beings (usually rulers) who are morally complicit in the hegemony of the evil powers and for those (the righteous) who resist the powers and are persecuted and even put to death as a result.

49. For the nomenclature "cosmological" and "forensic" to describe the two patterns or "tracks" of ancient Jewish apocalyptic eschatology, see chapter 1 above. The "forensic" pattern is a weakened form of the "cosmological" pattern, that is to say, the former is a form of apocalyptic eschatology from which cosmological evil powers have disappeared, to be replaced by the notion of human guilt and responsibility. The cosmological pattern can have, and normally does, forensic elements (the evil powers or angels are judged as are the human beings who have been complicit in their hegemony; cf. *1 Enoch* 1) but the forensic pattern seeks to suppress or remove "cosmological" explanations for evil, as demonstrated in chapter 1 above.

50. At the Last Judgment, God can be expected to provide an effective remedy, usually the Spirit, in the new age for the strong human inclination to sin either by submitting to the powers that be (in the cosmological pattern) or by making the wrong choice between life and death (in the forensic pattern). Cf. Ezek 11:19–20; *Jub.* 1:23–24; 1QS 4:20. For Paul, see especially Gal 3:1–5; 4:6, 16–25; Rom 8:1–26, where the Spirit is God's powerful weapon against the works of the Flesh.

51. The same is true of Revelation. Furthermore, the relevant Jewish texts also often exhibit elements from both patterns, especially the Dead Sea Scrolls. See chapter 1 above.

52. Schweitzer, *Mysticism of Paul*, 57.

53. Schweitzer, *Mysticism of Paul*, 55.

54. Schweitzer, *Mysticism of Paul*, 54.

churches) holding to a modified ("Christianized") version of the very same pattern. In both letters, Paul does not reject or abandon the forensic categories, terms, and perspectives dear to his conversation partners,[55] but he does circumscribe or recontextualize them with notions that are fundamentally indebted to the cosmological pattern of Jewish apocalyptic eschatology. Sin and death, for example, are no longer simply matters of human behavior or experience but are also conceptualized as evil cosmological powers that oppress and thus *victimize* human beings—hence Sin and Death (see esp. 1 Cor 15:20–28, 54–56; Rom 5:12–21). Paul sees all human history as a monolithic whole in which Sin and Death reign in tandem over the world and have done so from Adam's transgression onward. In such an understanding of the human plight, the Law is not only too weak and ineffectual for expurgating Sin and thus also Death from the cosmos, it has also (ironically and lamentably) become a major tool in the hands of Sin for solidifying its Death-dealing hegemony over human beings.[56]

When God's Apocalypse is conceived of as the defeat and destruction of evil cosmological powers, God's intervention at the Last Judgment has the character of an invasion, a military metaphor Martyn has consistently used with respect to Paul.[57] With the coming of Christ and his Spirit, God has begun a war of liberation against and from evil powers that have ruined, distorted, despoiled, and perverted human life.[58] God's eschatological saving activity in Jesus Christ is from beginning to end apocalyptic in the sense that it entails a war of cosmic proportions against evil cosmological forces that have oppressed and victimized human beings.[59]

As indicated, the Law for Paul functions as a tool in the hands of Sin, solidifying its Death-dealing grip on the human world. Especially in Galatians,

---

55. See de Boer, *Defeat of Death*, and chapter 7 above.

56. See chapter 3 above. The way in which the Law functions in the dual reign of Sin and Death shows that Israel does not constitute an exception any more than Abraham does. Abraham is placed among the ungodly (Rom 4:5) and thus among the dead (4:17), as is Israel (11:15). There is for Paul "no distinction" with respect to either the plight or the solution (3:22; 10:12).

57. Martyn, *Galatians*, 105: "Specifically, both God's sending of Christ to suffer death in behalf of humanity (the cross) and Christ's future coming (the parousia) are *invasive* acts of God. And their being invasive acts—into a space that has temporarily fallen out of God's hands—points to the liberating war that is crucial to Paul's apocalyptic theology. It is this apocalyptic vision, then, that has given Paul his perception of the nature of the human plight. . . . The root trouble lies deeper than human guilt, and it is more sinister" (emphasis original). Cf. Käsemann, *Romans*, 134.

58. Cf. Martyn, "Antinomies," 122. See further, Gaventa, "Rhetoric of Violence."

59. As noted above, Paul does not abandon or reject forensic elements, such as a final judgment for deeds (cf. Rom 14:10; 1 Cor 5:10). It is this combination of elements that makes Paul a great and challenging thinker.

but also in Romans, Paul regards being "under the Law" as being tantamount to being "under Sin" (Gal 3:22–23; cf. Rom 3:9; 6:14–15). Christ's crucifixion is understood by Paul to be *the* event that announces and effects the end of the "world" (*kosmos*) determined and given structure by the Law (Gal 6:14–15).[60] For Paul, a world has been judged and destroyed in Christ's crucifixion, and that is what Paul wishes to emphasize in Galatians with his repeated references to Christ's cross and his crucifixion, instead of merely to his (atoning) death (cf. 2:19–20; 3:1, 13; 5:11, 24; 6:12, 14).[61] To be crucified is to be killed, to be violently put to death, and that is what happened to Paul—he was crucified with Christ (Gal 2:19; 6:14)—of course not in a literal but in an extended sense: The "world" (Gal 6:14) that he had known had been utterly destroyed, that world given structure and meaning and coherence and hope on the basis of the Law (cf. Rom 6:6, 14). In short, the cross is understood to be an apocalyptic event which destroyed Paul's earlier conviction that by being Law-observant and so creating his own righteousness based on the Law (Phil 3:9) he could bridge the gap of death that separates the present evil age from the kingdom of God. He came to understand that the bridge from the one to the other can only be the righteousness that comes as a divine gift through the faith(fullness) of Christ (*pistis Christou*: Gal 2:16, 20–21; Rom 3:21–26; Phil 3:9)[62] and the Spirit that came into the world as a result (Gal 3:1–5, 14; 4:6; 5:16–18, 22–23; Rom 5:5; 8:1–26).

Paul's Apocalyptic Language and Faith

In contrast to the book of Revelation itself, Paul often uses the Greek noun *apokalypsis* "apocalyptically," i.e., to signify God's eschatological activity in and through Christ, as he does the cognate verb *apokalyptō*.[63] In 1 Cor 1:7, in particular, he refers to the Parousia as "the *apokalypsis* of our Lord Jesus Christ." In the next verse, he asserts that God "will strengthen" the

60. In 1 Corinthians 1–2, Paul uses the rhetoric of crucifixion to establish the end, i.e., the destruction, of human "wisdom" for the believers in Corinth.

61. Cf. de Boer, *Defeat of Death*, 176–77.

62. *Pistis Christou* can be translated either as "(human) faith *in* Christ" (the traditional rendering) or as "the faith(fulness) *of* Christ," which has received increasing support in recent years. See de Boer, *Galatians*, 148–50; and further below. My point would still stand if one were to adopt the traditional interpretation and translation.

63. Cf. Martyn, *Galatians*, 362: "On the whole . . . his [Paul's] apocalyptic language refers not to an *unveiling* of some *thing*, but to an *invasion* carried out by some *one* who has moved into the world from outside it" (emphasis original). I sought to provide a firmer basis for this claim in chapter 2 above. This material was incorporated into an excursus on "Paul's Language of Apocalyptic Revelation" in *Galatians*, 79–82. What follows is a brief summary of some relevant points.

Corinthian believers "to the End (*telos*)" (1:8; cf. 15:24) so that they "may be blameless on the day of our Lord Jesus Christ" (1:8). These two verses clearly point forward to chapter 15 where Paul refers explicitly to Christ's Parousia.

> . . . all will be made alive in Christ. But each in his own order: Christ the first fruits, then at his *Parousia* those who belong to Christ. Then is the End (*telos*), when he hands over the kingdom to God the Father, after he has destroyed every ruler and every authority and power. . . . The last enemy to be destroyed is Death. (1 Cor 15:23b–24, 26)

The *apokalypsis* of Jesus Christ concerns, then, his visible eschatological appearance at his Parousia and this is clearly an apocalyptic *event*, whereby the cosmological principalities and powers of this evil age, especially Death, are finally and irrevocably brought to submission "so that God may be all in all" (cf. 1 Cor 15:24–28). The *apokalypsis* referred to is no mere disclosure of previously hidden heavenly secrets, nor is it simply information about future events, but rather concerns eschatological activity and movement, an invasion of the world below from heaven above, which is also in a sense an invasion of the present by the future.[64] According to 1 Thess 4:15–16, where Paul uses the imagery of war, "the *Parousia* of the Lord" means that Jesus "himself will descend from heaven with a cry of command, with the archangel's call, and with the sound of the trumpet of God" (cf. 2 Thess 1:7).

As noted in chapter 2, Paul also uses this language in connection with the gospel he preaches. In Romans 1:16–17, he claims that in the gospel "the righteousness of God *is being revealed* (*apokalyptetai*) from faith for faith." This gospel is "the power of God (*dynamis theou*) for salvation." Paul here relates the verb *apokalyptō* directly to the notion of "the power of God." The righteousness of God becomes visible and powerful, or powerfully visible, in the gospel itself and for that reason within the sphere of faith (*pistis*). Faith is elicited or created by the gospel of God's powerful righteousness and it is evidently for Paul a form of sharing in God's eschatological revelation, that is, in God's eschatological activity and movement.[65] Among other things, faith signifies for Paul that a believer can truly see and perceive this action, this movement, of God *into* (and then *in*) the world. The movement and presence of God are to be seen in the crucified and risen Christ and his Spirit. Furthermore, that this activity and movement of God involves

---

64. Paul uses these terms in other passages (Rom 2:5; 8:18; 1 Cor 3:13) in a similar way, that is, in connection with a *future* apocalyptic-eschatological event.

65. This eschatological activity and movement are a sign and a confirmation of God's liberating love: cf. e.g., Rom 5:8. Further, faith itself "works through love" (Gal 5:6: cf. 1 Cor 13).

judgment upon "this world" is evident in Rom 1:18–32: The revelation of God's righteousness "through faith for faith" also means that "the wrath of God," normally associated with the Parousia (cf. Rom 2:5; 5:9; 1 Thess 1:10), "is [now also being powerfully] revealed (*apokalyptetai*) from heaven upon all ungodliness and wickedness of those who by their wickedness suppress the truth" (Rom 1:16–18). The creation of something eschatologically new in the world, faith, also entails God's judgment of a world marked by its absence before and apart from Christ.

That the terms *apokalypsis* and *apokalyptō* are also being used "apocalyptically" in Galatians was suggested by Martyn: "it is precisely the Paul of Galatians who says with emphasis that the cosmos in which he previously lived met its end in God's apocalypse of Jesus Christ," with references to Gal 1:12, 16; and 6:14. "It is this same Paul who identifies that apocalypse as the birth of his gospel-mission (1.16), and who speaks of the battles he has to wage for the truth of the gospel as events to be understood under the banner of apocalypse (2.2, 5, 14)."[66] The basis for these claims actually lies in Gal 3:23: "Now before faith came (*elthein*) [into the world], we were confined under the Law, being shut up until faith should be revealed (*apokalyphthēnai*)." The noun "faith" (*pistis*) is the subject of the verb "came" as well as of the verb "revealed" (both infinitives in the Greek text). As Martyn points out, this parallelism indicates that the latter verb must mean something more than simply "unveiling (of previous hidden information)" for Paul.[67] Paul is redefining the word in terms of God's eschatological *movement into* the world.

Furthermore, the context indicates that Paul here understands faith to be a metonym for Christ himself (cf. 1:23). According to 3:24, the "Law was our custodian until Christ [came on the scene], so that we might be justified on the basis of faith [i.e., on the basis of Christ]. But now that faith has come [i.e., now that Christ has come on the scene], we are no longer subject to a custodian [that is to say, the Law]." The *pistis* in view is in the first place that of Christ himself.[68] By identifying *pistis* with Christ in this way, Paul makes clear that faith as a human activity (or "response") does not involve an innate or natural human possibility but an apocalyptic-eschatological possibility, which becomes an anthropological reality when elicited (in effect, created) by the proclamation of Christ's faithful death "for our sins" or "for us" (cf.

66. Martyn, "Apocalyptic Antinomies," 417 (emphasis removed).

67. Martyn, "Apocalyptic Antinomies," 417, 424n29.

68. The evidence of 3:23 is one of the reasons that the phrase *pistis Christou* (see n. 62 above) is probably to be construed as "the faith(fullness) *of* Christ," referring specifically to his death as the defining mark of that faithfulness (cf. Gal 2:20–21; Rom 3:21–26).

1 Cor 15:3; Gal 1:4; 2:20–21; 3:13; Rom 3:21–26; 2 Cor 5:21). Faith is the visible mark of the "new creation" (Gal 6:15),[69] an apocalyptic-eschatological *novum* inseparable from Christ as God's Apocalypse. Faith itself is a mark of the divine activity, of God's invasion of the cosmos with God's Son and the Spirit of that Son. Or as Martyn puts it: "Paul envisions, then, a world that has been changed from without by God's incursion into it, and he perceives that incursion to be the event that has brought faith into existence."[70]

Paul's distinctively "apocalyptic" use of the noun *apokalypsis* and its cognate verb *apokalyptō* may be indebted to two passages from Second Isaiah, a portion of Scripture Paul often cites from or alludes to in his letters, Galatians and Romans in particular.[71] According to Isa 52:10, "the Lord shall reveal (*apokalypsei*) his holy arm (*brachion*) in the sight of all the nations (*panta ta ethnē*); and all the ends of the earth shall see the salvation that comes from our God" (cf. Rom 1:5, 16–17; Gal 3:8; LXX Ps 97:1–2). And in Isa 53:1, whose initial question Paul cites in Rom 10:16, we read: "O Lord, who has believed our report? and to whom has the arm of the Lord been revealed (*apokalyphthē*)?" The "revelation" of God's "arm" (a symbol of power and military might) is no mere disclosure of previously hidden information or of a heavenly mystery, but the visible coming of God to effect salvation in the world. Paul frequently uses the term in a very similar, though more "apocalyptic" way, to describe God's eschatological invasion (in and through Christ) of the human cosmos under the hegemony of cosmological powers destructive of human life and opposed to God's will and intention for the world (especially Sin, Death, and the Flesh).

Conclusion

In one long-standing tradition of scholarship of ancient Judaism and Christianity, apocalyptic concerns the (ancient Jewish) expectation of God's own

69. See the parallel between "faith working through love" in Gal 5:6 and "new creation" in 6:15.

70. Martyn, *Galatians*, 363. For Martyn, the epistemological implications of Christ's apocalypse are crucially important. About this Stuckenbruck has perceptively written: "Martyn's approach to apocalyptic does not obligate the interpreter to find any essential continuity with comparable or contrasting Jewish paradigms. Once God has disclosed God's self in the Christ event as a new way of knowing, all that came before becomes functionally irrelevant, not only for Paul but even for Paul's interpreters" ("Overlapping Ages," 317).

71. The two terms are rather rare in secular sources; cf. Oepke, "*apokalyptō, apokalypsis*," 570–71. The noun occurs in the LXX only three times, with the meaning "disclosure" or "revelation" (1 Sam 20:30; Sir 11:27; 22:22), though the verb occurs much more frequently.

eschatological activity whereby God will put an end to the present evil order of reality ("this age") and replace it with a new, transformed order of reality ("the age to come"). Paul is an apocalyptic theologian in this sense, though it must also be noted that his apocalyptic theology (a) is closer to the cosmological pattern exemplified by *1 Enoch* 1–36 than to the forensic pattern exemplified by *2 Baruch*, and (b) assumes (as does the book of Revelation) a christological modification to this expectation: The coming of Christ (or, if you will, of Jesus as the Messiah) represents God's apocalyptic-eschatological invasion of the human world whereby God has begun to wage a war of cosmic proportions against evil cosmological forces that have oppressed and victimized all human beings and brought about their separation from God and from life; this war will end in God's sure triumph at Christ's Parousia.

Bibliography

Adams, Edward. *Constructing the World: A Study in Paul's Cosmological Language.* Studies in the New Testament and its World. Edinburgh: T. & T. Clark, 1999.

The Apocrypha: Revised Standard Version of the Old Testament. New York: Thomas Nelson & Sons, 1957.

Augustine. "Nature and Grace." In *Three Anti-Pelagian Treatises of St. Augustine,* translated and edited by F. H. Woods and J. O. Johnston, 87–166. London: David Nutt, 1887.

Baasland, Ernst. "Persecution, A Neglected Factor in the Letter to the Galatians." *ST* 38 (1984) 135–50.

Bachmann, Michael. "4QMMT und Galaterbrief, הרותה םעשי und ΕΡΓΑ ΝΟΜΟΥ." In Bachmann, *Anti-Judaism in Galatians? Exegetical Studies on a Polemical Letter and Paul's Theology.* 19–31. Grand Rapids: Eerdmans, 1999.

———. "Die andere Frau. Synchrone und diachronische Beobachtungen zu Gal 4:21–5:1." In *Antijudaismus im Galaterbrief? Exegetische Studien zu einem polemischen Schreiben und zur Theologie des Apostel Paulus,* 127–58. Freiburg: Universitätsverlag; Göttingen: Vanderhoeck & Ruprecht, 1999.

———. "IEROSOLYMA und IEROUSALHM im Galaterbrief." In *ZNW* 91 (2000) 288–89.

Barclay, John M. G. *Paul and the Gift.* Grand Rapids: Eerdmans, 2015.

———. "Paul's Story: Theology as Testimony." In *Narrative Dynamics in Paul. A Critical Assessment,* edited by Bruce W. Longenecker, 133–56. Louisville: Westminster John Knox, 2002.

Barrett, C. K. "The Allegory of Abraham, Sarah, and Hagar in the Argument of Galatians." In *Essays on Paul,* 154–69. Philadelphia: Westminster, 1982.

Bartchy, S. Scott. "Slavery (New Testament)." In *ABD* 6 (1992) 65–73.

Barth, Karl. *The Christian Life, Church Dogmatics IV, 4: Lecture Fragments.* Grand Rapids: Eerdmans, 1981.

Bauckham, Richard J. *The Theology of the Book of Revelation.* Cambridge: Cambridge University Press, 1994.

Baumgarten, Jürgen. *Paulus und die Apokalyptik: Die Auslegung apokalyptischer Überlieferungin den echten Paulusbriefen.* Neukirchen-Vluyn: Neukirchener Verlang, 1975.

Beilby, James K. and Paul Rhodes, eds. *Justification: Five Views.* Downers Grove, IL: IVP Academic, 2011.

Beker, J. Christiaan. *Paul the Apostle: The Triumph of God in Life and Thought.* Philadelphia: Fortress, 1980.

Betz, Hans Dieter. *Galatians. A Commentary on Paul's Letter to the Churches in Galatia.* Hermeneia. Philadelphia: Fortress, 1979.

Beuken, W. A. M. "Isaiah LIV. The Multiple Identity of the Person Addressed." In *OTS* 19 (1974) 2970.

Black, Matthew. *Book of Enoch or 1 Enoch.* SVTP 7. Leiden: Brill, 1985.

Blackwell, Ben C., et al., eds. *Paul and the Apocalyptic Imagination.* Minneapolis: Fortress, 2016.

Bligh, John. *Galatians: A Discussion of St. Paul's Epistle.* London: St. Paul, 1969.

Blinzler, Joseph. "Lexikalisches zu dem Terminus *Ta stoicheia tou kosmou* bei Paulus." In *Studiorum Paulinorum Congressus Internationalis Catholicus 1961, Vol. 2,* 429–43. Rome: Pontifical Biblical Institute, 1963.

Bonnard, P. -E., *Le Second Isaïe.* Études Bibliques. Paris: J. Gabalda, 1972.

Bonner, Campbell, ed. *The Last Chapters of Enoch in Greek.* SD 8. London: Christophers, 1937.

Borgen, Peder. "Some Hebrew and Pagan Features in Philo's and Paul's Interpretation of Hagar and Ishmael." In *The New Testament and Hellenistic Judaism,* edited by Peder Borgen and Søren Giversen, 151–64. Aarhus: Aarhus University, 1995.

Bouwman, Gijs. "Die Hagar und SaraPerikope (Gal 4,2131). Exemplarische Interpretation zum Schrifbeweis bei Paulus." In *ANRW* 2.25.4 (1987) 3135–55.

Bornkamm, Gunther. *Paul.* New York: Harper & Row, 1969.

Brandenburger, E. *Adam und Christus: Exegetisch-religionsgeschichtliche Untersuchung zu Röm 5.12–21 (1 Kor. 15).* Neukirchen: Neukirchener Verlag, 1962.

Brauch, Manfred T. "Perspectives on 'God's Righteousness' in recent German discussion." In E. P. Sanders, *Paul and Palestinian Judaism,* 523–43. Philadelphia: Fortress, 1977.

Branick, Victor P. "Apocalyptic Paul?" *CBQ* 47 (1985) 664–75.

Brawley, Robert L. "Contextuality, Intertextuality, and the Hendiadic Relationship of Promise and Law in Galatians." In *ZNW* 93 (2002) 99–119.

Büchsel, F. "ἀλλεγορέω." *TWNT* (1933) 1.262–64.

Bullinger, E. W. *Figures of Speech Used in the Bible.* London: Eyre & Spottiswoode, 1898 (repr. Grand Rapids: Baker, 1968).

Bultmann, Rudolf. "Adam and Christ According to Romans 5." *Current Issues in New Testament Interpretation: Essays in Honor of Otto A. Piper,* edited by William Klassen and Graydon F. Snyder, 143–65. New York: Harper & Brothers, 1962.

———. "ΔΙΚΑΙΟΣΥΝΕ ΘΕΟΥ." *JBL* 83 (1964) 12–16.

———. "Ist Apokalyptik die Mutter der christlichen Theologie?" In *Apophoreta: Festschrift für Ernst Haenchen,* 64–69. BZNW 30. Berlin: Töpelmann, 1964.

———. "New Testament and Mythology: The Problem of Demythologizing the New Testament Proclamation." In *New Testament and Mythology and Other Basic Writings,* edited by Schubert M. Ogden, 1–43. Philadelphia: Fortress, 1984.

———. "On the Problem of Demythologizing." In *New Testament and Mythology and Other Basic Writings,* edited by Schubert M. Ogden, 95–130. Philadelphia: Fortress, 1984.

———. *The Presence of Eternity: History and Eschatology.* Westport, CT: Greenwood, 1975.

———. *Primitive Christianity in its Contemporary Setting.* New York: Meridian, 1965.

———. *Theology of the New Testament,* 2 Volumes. New York: Scribner's Sons, 1951, 1953.

Burton, Ernest DeWitt. *A Critical and Exegetical Commentary on the Epistle to the Galatians*. ICC. Edinburgh: T. & T. Clark, 1921 (reprint, 1971).

Campbell, Douglas A. "The Story of Jesus in Romans and Galatians." In *Narrative Dynamics in Paul*, edited by Bruce W. Longenecker, 97–124. Louisville: Westminster John Knox, 2002.

Charlesworth, James H. *The Old Testament Pseudepigrapha*. 2 vols. Garden City, NY: Doubleday, 1983, 1985.

Childs, Brevard S. *Isaiah*. Old Testament Library. Louisville: Westminster John Knox, 2001.

Chilton, Bruce D. *The Isaiah Targum. Introduction, Translation, Apparatus and Notes*. The Aramaic Bible, Vol. 11. Wilmington, DE: Michael Glazier, 1987.

Cohen Stuart, G. H. *The Struggle in Man Between Good and Evil: An Inquiry into the Origin of the Rabbinic Concept of the Yeser 'Hara*. Kampen: Kok, 1984.

Collins, John J. "Apocalypses and Apocalypticism (Early Jewish Apocalypticism)." In *ABD* 1:282–88.

———. *The Apocalyptic Imagination. An Introduction to the Jewish Matrix of Christianity*. New York: Crossroad, 1984.

———, et al. *Apocalypticism and Mysticism in Ancient Judaism and Early Christianity*. Ekstasis: Religious Experience from Antiquity to the Middle Ages 7. Berlin: De Gruyter, 2018.

———. "From Prophecy to Apocalypticism: The Expectation of the End." In *The Encyclopedia of Apocalypticism*, Vol. I, edited by John J. Collins, 129–61. New York: Continuum, 1998.

———. "Introduction to Volume 1." In *The Encyclopedia of Apocalypticism*, Vol. I, edited by John J. Collins, xiii–xvii. New York: Continuum, 1998.

———, ed., *The Morphology of a Genre = Semeia* 14 (1979).

Conzelmann, Hans. "Die Rechtfertigungslehre des Paulus: Theology oder Anthropologie?" *EvT* 28 (1968) 389–404.

Croasmun, Matthew. *The Emergence of Sin: The Cosmic Tyrant in Romans*. Oxford: Oxford University Press, 2017.

Cuvillier, E. "Das apokalyptische Denken im Neuen Testament: Paulus und Johannes von Patmos als Beispiele. *ZNT* 22 (2008) 2–12.

Das, Andrew A. "Another look at ἐὰν μή in Galatians 2:16." *JBL* 119 (2000) 529–39.

Davies, J. P. *Paul Among the Apocalypses? An Evaluation of the 'Apocalyptic Paul' in the Context of Jewish and Christian Apocalyptic Literature*. LNTS 562. London: T. & T. Clark, 2016.

de Boer, Martinus C. "Apocalyptic as God's Eschatological Activity in Paul's Theology." In Blackwell et al., *Paul and the Apocalyptic Imagination*, 45–63. Minneapolis: Fortress, 2016.

———. "Cross and Cosmos in Galatians." In Downs and Skinner, *The Unrelenting God*, 208–25. Grand Rapids: Eerdmans, 2013.

———. *The Defeat of Death: Apocalyptic Eschatology in 1 Corinthians 15 and Romans 5*. JSNTSS 22; Sheffield: JSOT, 1988 / LNTS 22; London: Bloomsbury Academic, 2015.

———. "De Psalmen bij Paulus: LXX Psalm 142:2 in Galaten 2:16 en Romeinen 3:20," *Amsterdamse Cahiers voor Exegese van de Bijbel en zijn Tradities* 25 (2010) 83–94.

———. *Galatians: A Commentary*. New Testament Library. Louisville, KY: Westminster John Knox, 2011.

———. "The Meaning of the Phrase τὰ στοιχεῖα τοῦ κόσμου in Galatians." *NTS* 53 (2007) 204–24.

———. "The New Preachers in Galatia: Their Identity, Message, Aims, and Impact." In *Jesus, Paul, and Early Christianity. Studies in Honour of Henk Jan de Jonge*, edited by Rieuwerd Buitenwerf, Harm W. Hollander, and Johannes Tromp, 39–60. NovTSup 130. Leiden: Brill, 2008.

———. "N. T. Wright's Great Story and its Relationship to Paul's Gospel." *JSPL* 4.1 (2014) 49–57.

———. "Observations on the Significance of the Old Testament in Galatians." In *The Scriptures of Israel in Jewish and Christian Tradition: Essays in Honour of Maarten J. J. Menken*, edited by Bart J. Koet, Steve Moyise, and Joseph Verheyden, 211–26. NovTSup 148. Leiden: Brill, 2013.

———. "Paul and Apocalyptic Eschatology." In *The Encyclopedia of Apocalypticism*, Vol. I., edited by John J. Collins, 345–83. New York: Continuum, 1998. Reprinted in *The Continuum History of Apocalypticism*, edited by B. McGinn, J. J. Collins, and S. J. Stein, 166–94. New York: Continuum, 2003.

———. "Paul and Jewish Apocalyptic Eschatology." In *Apocalyptic and the New Testament. Essays in Honor of J. Louis Martyn*, edited by Joel Marcus and Marion L. Soards, 169–90. JSNTSS 24. Sheffield: JSOT, 1989.

———. "Paul's Mythologizing Program in Romans 5–8." In *Apocalyptic Paul: Cosmos and Anthropos in Romans 5–8*, edited by Beverly Roberts Gaventa, 1–20. Waco, TX: Baylor University Press, 2013.

———. "Paul's Use and Interpretation of a Justification Tradition in Galatians 2.15–21." *JSNT* 28.2 (2005) 189–216.

———. "Paul, Theologian of God's Apocalypse." *Interpretation* 56 (2002) 21–33.

———. "Paul's Quotation of Isaiah 54.1 in Galatians 4.27." *NTS* 50 (2004) 370–89.

———. Review of *Irony of Galatians*, by Mark D. Nanos. *BibInt* 12 (2004) 421–24.

———. "Salvation History in Galatians? A Response to Bruce W. Longenecker and Jason Maston," *JSPL* 2.2 (2012) 105–114.

Desjardins, M. "Law in 2 Baruch and 4 Ezra," *Stud Rel/SciRel* 14 (1985) 25–37.

Downs, David J., and Matthew L. Skinner, eds., *The Unrelenting God: God's Action in Scripture*. Grand Rapids: Eerdmans, 2013.

Dunn, James D. G. *The Epistle to the Galatians*. Black's New Testament Commentaries. Peabody, MS: Hendrickson, 1993.

———. "The New Perspective on Paul." *BJRL* 65 (1983) 95–122. Reprinted in Dunn, *Jesus, Paul and the Law*, 183–206, with an "Additional Note," 206–14. London: SPCK, 1990.

———. "Once More ΠΙΣΤΙΣ ΧΡΙΣΤΟΥ." In Richard B. Hays, *The Faith of Jesus Christ. The Narrative Substructure of Galatians 3:1–4:11*, 249–71. 2nd edition. Grand Rapids: Eerdmans; Dearborn: Dove Booksellers, 2000.

———. *Theology of Paul the Apostle*. Edinburgh: T&T Clark, 1998.

———. "Works of the Law and the Curse of the Law (Gal. 3.10–14)." *NTS* 31 (1985) 523–42. Reprinted in Dunn, *Jesus, Paul and the Law*, 215–36, with an "Additional Note," 237–41. London: SPCK, 1990.

Eastman, Susan Grove. *Paul and the Person: Reframing Paul's Anthropology*. Grand Rapids: Eerdmans, 2017.

Elliott, Susan M. "Choose Your Mother, Choose Your Master. Galatians 4:21—5:1 in the Shadow of the Anatolian Mother of the Gods." In *JBL* 118 (1999) 661–83.

Fee, Gordon D. *God's Empowering Presence: The Holy Spirit in the Letters of Paul.* Peabody, MA: Hendrickson, 1994.

Fitzmyer, Joseph A. *Romans. A New Translation with Introduction and Commentary.* Anchor Bible 33. New York: Doubleday, 1993.

Foster, Paul. "The First Contribution to the πίστις χριστοῦ Debate: A Study of Ephesians 3.12." *JSNT* 85 (2002) 75–96.

Frey, Jörg. "Demythologizing Apocalyptic? On N. T. Wright's Paul, Apocalyptic Interpretation, and the Constraints of Construction." In *God and the Faithfulness of Paul: A Critical Examination of the Pauline Theology of N. T. Wright,* edited by Christoph Heilig et al., 489–531. Tübingen: Mohr Siebeck, 2016.

Fung, Ronald Y. K. *Galatians.* NICNT. Grand Rapids: Eerdmans, 1988.

Furnish, Victor Paul. *Theology and Ethics in Paul.* Nashville: Abingdon, 1968.

García Martínez, Florentinio, and Eibert J. C. Tigchelaar, eds. and trans. *The Dead Sea Scrolls: Study Edition.* 2 Vols. Leiden: Brill, 1997.

Gathercole, Simon. *Defending Substitution: An Essay on Atonement in Paul.* Grand Rapids: Baker Academic, 2015.

———. "'Sins' in Paul." *NTS* 64 (2018) 143–61.

Gaventa, Beverly Roberts, ed. *Apocalyptic Paul: Cosmos and Anthropos in Romans 5–8.* Waco, TX: Baylor University Press, 2013.

———. "The Cosmic Power of Sin in Paul's Letter to the Romans." In *Our Mother Saint Paul,* 125–36. Louisville: Westminster John Knox, 2007.

———. "Galatians 1 and 2: Autobiography as Paradigm." *NTS* 28 (1986) 309–26.

———. *Our Mother Saint Paul.* Louisville: Westminster John Knox, 2007.

———. "The Rhetoric of Violence and the God of Peace in Paul's Letter to the Romans." In *Paul, John, and Apocaplyptic Eschatology: Studies in Honour of Martinus C. de Boer,* edited by Jan Krans et al. Novum Testamentum, Supplements, vol. 149. Brill, 2013.

Hanson, Paul D. "Apocalypse, Genre." In *IDBSup,* 27–28.

———. "Apocalypses and Apocalypticism (Genre, Introductory Overview)." In *ABD* 1: 279–82.

———. "Apocalypticism." In *IDBSup,* 28–34.

———. *Dawn of Apocalyptic. The Historical and Sociological Roots of Jewish Apocalyptic Eschatology.* 2nd ed. Philadelphia: Fortress, 1979.

Harmon, A. M. "Aspects of Paul's Use of the Psalms." *WTJ* 32 (1969) 1–23.

Harnack, Adolf von. "The Old Testament in the Pauline Letters and in the Pauline Churches." In *Understanding Paul's Ethics: Twentieth Century Approaches,* edited by B. S. Rosner, 27–49. Grand Rapids: Eerdmans, 1995 (German original 1928).

Harnisch, Wolfgang. *Verhängnis und Verheissung der Geschichte. Untersuchung zum Zeit- und Geschichtsverständnis im 4. Buch Esra und syr. Baruchapokalypse.* FRLANT 97. Göttingen: Vandenhoeck & Ruprecht, 1969.

Harrisville, R. A. "Paul and the Psalms: A Formal Study." *Word & World* 5/2 (1985) 168–79 .

Hayman, A. P. "The Fall, Freewill and Human Responsibility in Rabbinic Judaism," *SJT* 37 (1984) 13–22.

Hays, Richard B. *The Conversion of the Imagination: Paul as Interpreter of Scripture.* Grand Rapids: Eerdmans, 2005.

———. *Echoes of Scripture in the Letters of Paul.* New Haven: Yale University, 1989.

———. "Galatians." In *The New Interpreter's Bible*, Vol. XI, edited by Leander E. Keck et al., 181–348. Nashville: Abingdon, 2000.

———. "Πίστις and Pauline Christology: What Is at Stake?" In Hays, *The Faith of Jesus Christ. The Narrative Substructure of Galatians 3:1–4:11*, 272–97. 2nd ed. Grand Rapids: Eerdmans; Dearborn: Dove Booksellers, 2000.

Hengel, Martin. *Judaism and Hellenism*. 2 Volumes in 1. Philadelphia: Fortress, 1974.

Henze, Matthias. "*4 Ezra* and *2 Baruch*: Literary Composition and Oral Performance in First-Century Apocalyptic Literature." *JBL* 131 (2012) 181–200.

Jobes, Karen H. "Jerusalem, our Mother. Metalepsis and Intertextuality in Galatians 4:2131." In *WTJ* 55 (1993) 299–320.

Kabisch, Richard. *Die Eschatologie des Paulus in ihren Zusammenhängen met dem Gesamtbegriff des Paulinismus*. Göttingen: Vandenhoeck & Ruprecht, 1893.

Käsemann, Ernst. "The Beginnings of Christian Theology." In Käsemann, *New Testament Questions of Today*, 82–107. Philadelphia: Fortress, 1969.

———. *Commentary on Romans*. Grand Rapids: Eerdmans, 1980.

———. "God's Image and Sinners." In Käsemann, *On Being A Disciple of the Crucified Nazarene*, 108–19. Grand Rapids: Eerdmans, 2010.

———. "Justification and Salvation History." In Käsemann, *Perspectives on Paul*, 60–78. Philadelphia: Fortress, 1971.

———. "On Paul's Anthropology." In Käsemann, *Perspectives on Paul*, 1–31. Philadelphia: Fortress, 1971.

———. "On the Subject of Primitive Christian Apocalyptic." In Käsemann, *New Testament Questions of Today*, 108–37. Philadelphia: Fortress, 1969.

———. "Paul and Early Catholicism." In Käsemann, *New Testament Questions of Today*, 236–51. Philadelphia: Fortress, 1969.

———. "The 'Righteousness of God' in Paul." In Käsemann, *New Questions of Today*, 168–82. Philadelphia: Fortress, 1969.

Keck, Leander E. "Paul and Apocalyptic Theology." *Interpretation* 38 (1984) 229–41.

———. *Paul and His Letters*. Philadelphia: Fortress, 1979.

Keesmaat, Sylvia C. "The Psalms in Romans and Galatians." In *The Psalms in the New Testament*, edited Steven Moyise and Maarten J. J. Menken, 139–61. London: Bloomsbury, 2004.

Kertelge, Karl. '*Rechtfertigung*' *bei Paulus*. NTAbh. 2nd ed.. Münster: Aschendorff, 1967.

Klijn, A. F. J. "2 (Syriac Apocalypse of) Baruch." In *The Old Testament Pseudepigrapha. Volume I: Apocalyptic Literature and Testaments*, edited by J. H. Charlesworth, 615–52. Garden City, NY: Doubleday, 1983.

Koch, Dietrich-Alex. *Die Schrift als Zeuge des Evangeliums. Untersuchungen zu Verwendung und zum Verständnis der Schrift bei Paulus*. BHT 69. Tübingen: Mohr [Siebeck], 1986.

Koet, Bart J. "Roeping of Bekering? Paulus volgens Handelingen vergeleken met de Paulus van Galaten." In *Eén auteur, twee boeken. Lucas en de Handelingen van de Apostelen*, edited by Peter Schmidt, 77–95. Leuven/'s-Hertogenbosch: Acco, 1991.

Leene, Henk. "Sion als moeder en als bruid. Bijbelstheologische betekenissen van Jeruzalem." In *Jeruzalem. Beeld en Realiteit*, edited by W. Haan et al., 24–38. Kampen: Kok, 1996.

Lightfoot, J. B. *Saint Paul's Epistle to the Galatians: A Revised Text with Introduction, Notes and Dissertations*. London and New York: Macmillan, 1887.

Longenecker, Bruce W., ed. *The Road to Damascus: The Impact of Paul's Conversion on His Life, Thought, and Ministry*. McMaster New Testament Studies. Grand Rapids: Eerdmans, 1997.

———. "Salvation History in Galatians and the Making of a Pauline Discourse." *JSPL* 2.2 (2012) 65–88.

———. *The Triumph of Abraham's God. The Transformation of Identity in Galatians*. Edinburgh: T. & T. Clark, 1998.

Longenecker, Richard N. *Galatians*. WBC 41. Dallas: Word, 1990.

Lührmann, Dieter, *Galatians: A Continental Commentary*. Minneapolis: Fortress, 1992.

Luther, Martin. *Lectures on Galatians 1535. Chapters 1–4*. Luther's Works, Vol. 26. St. Louis: Concordia, 1963.

Malan, F. S. "The strategy of two opposing covenants." In *Neotestamentica* 26 (1992) 425–40.

Mann, J. *The Bible as Read and Preached in the Old Synagogue. Vol. I. The Palestinian Triennial Cycle. Genesis and Exodus*. New York. KTAV, 1971.

Marcus, Joel, and Marion L. Soards, eds., *Apocalyptic and the New Testament. Essays in Honor of J. Louis Martyn*. JSNTSS 24. Sheffield: JSOT, 1989.

Martyn, J. Louis. "Afterword: The Human Moral Dilemma." In *Apocalyptic Paul: Cosmos and Anthropos in Romans 5–8*, edited by Beverly Roberts Gaventa, 157–66. Waco, TX: Baylor University Press, 2013.

———. "Apocalyptic Antinomies in the Letter to the Galatians." *NTS* 31 (1985) 410–24.

———. "The Covenants of Hagar and Sarah: Two Covenants and Two Gentile Missions." In Martyn, *Theological Issues in the Letters of Paul*, 191–208. Studies of the New Testament and its World. Edinburgh: T. & T. Clark, 1997.

———. "Epilogue: An Essay in Pauline Meta-Ethics." In *Divine and Human Agency in Paul and his Cultural Environment*, edited by John M. G. Barclay and Simon J. Gathercole, 173–83. London: T. & T. Clark, 2007.

———. "Epistemology at the Turn of the Ages: 2 Corinthians 5.16." In *Christian History and Interpretation: Studies Presented to John Knox*, edited by W. R. Farmer et al., 269–87. Cambridge: Cambridge University, 1967.

———. "From Paul to Flannery O'Connor with the Power of Grace." *Katallagete* 6 (1981) 10–17.

———. *Galatians: A New Translation with Introduction and Commentary*. AB 33A. New York: Doubleday, 1997.

———. "The Gospel Invades Philosophy." In *Paul, Philosophy, and the Theopolitical Vision*, edited by Douglas Harink, 13–33. Eugene, OR: Cascade, 2010.

———. "A Law-Observant Mission to Gentiles: The Background of Galatians." *SJT* 38 (1985) 307–24.

———. "On Hearing the Gospel both in the Silence of the Tradition and in its Eloquence." In *From Jesus to John. Essays on New Testament Christology in Honour of Marinus de Jonge*, edited by Martinus C. de Boer, 129–47. JSNTSS 84. Sheffield: Sheffield Academic, 1993.

———. *Theological Issues in the Letters of Paul*. Studies of the New Testament and its World. Edinburgh: T. & T. Clark, 1997.

Maston, Jason. "The Nature of Salvation History in Galatians." *JSPL* 2.2 (2012) 89–104

Matera, Frank J. *Galatians*. SP 9. Collegeville, MN: Glazier, 1992.

Matlock, R. Barry. "'Even the Demons Believe': Paul and πίστις Χριστοῦ," *CBQ* 64 (2002) 300–318.

————. *Unveiling Apocalyptic Paul. Paul's Interpreters and the Rhetoric of Criticism.* Sheffield: Sheffield Academic, 1996.

Menken, Maarten J. J. "Observations on the Significance of the Old Testament in the Fourth Gospel." In *Theology and Christology in the Fourth Gospel,* edited by G. Van Belle, J. D. G. Van der Watt, and P. Mauritz, 155–75. Leuven: Peeters, 2005). Originally in *Neot* 33 (1999) 125–43.

Metzger, Bruce M. "The Fourth Book of Ezra." In *The Old Testament Pseudepigrapha. Volume I: Apocalyptic Literature and Testaments,* edited by J. H. Charlesworth, 516–59. Garden City, NY: Doubleday, 1983.

Meyer, Paul W. "Pauline Theology: A Proposal for a Pause in its Pursuit." In *The Word in This World: Essays in New Testament Exegesis and Theology,* edited by John T. Carroll, 95–116. New Testament Library. Westminster John Knox, 2004.

————. "The Worm at the Core of the Apple: Exegetical Reflections on Romans 7." In *The Word in This World: Essays in New Testament Exegesis and Theology,* edited by John T. Carroll, 57–77. New Testament Library. Louisville: Westminster John Knox, 2004.

Milik, J. T. *The Books of Enoch: Aramaic Fragments of Qumran Cave 4.* Oxford: Clarendon, 1976.

Mininger, Marcus A. *Uncovering the Theme of Revelation in Romans 1:16–3:26.* WUNT 445. Tübingen: Mohr Siebeck, 2017.

Moyise, S. *Paul and Scripture.* London: SPCK; Grand Rapids: Baker Academic, 2010.

Müller, Christoph. *Gottes Gerechtigkeit und Gottes Volk.* FRLANT 86. Göttingen: Vandenhoeck & Ruprecht, 1964.

Murphy, Frederick J., *Apocalypticism in the Bible and its World: A Comprehensive Introduction.* Grand Rapids: Baker Academic, 2012.

Murphy-O'Connor, Jerome. "IEROSOLYMA/IEROUSALHM in Galatians." In *ZNW* 90 (1999) 280–81.

Mussner, Franz. *Der Galaterbrief.* 5th ed. HTKNT 9. Freiburg: Herder, 1988.

Nanos, Mark D. *The Irony of Galatians. Paul's Letter in First-Century Context.* Minneapolis: Fortress, 2002.

Novum Testament Graece [Nestle-Aland], 28th ed. Münster: Deutsche Bibelgesellschaft, 2012.

Oepke, A. "ἀποκαλύπτω, ἀποκάλυψις." In *TDNT* 3 (1965) 563–592.

Perriman, A. C. "The Rhetorical Strategy of Galatians 4:21–5:1." In *EvQ* 65 (1993) 27–42.

Prothro, James B. "The Strange Case of Δικαιόω in the Septuagint and Paul: The Oddity and Origins of Paul's Talk of 'Justification.'" *ZNW* 107 (2016) 48–69.

Rahlfs, Adolf, ed., *Septuagint. Id est Vetus Testamentum graece iuxta LXX interpres .Id est Vetus Testamentum graece iuxta LXX interpres.* Stuttgart: Deutsche Bibelstiftung, 1935.

Räisänen, H. "Galatians 2:16 and Paul's Break with Judaism." *NTS* 31 (1985).

Reynolds, Benjamin, and Loren Stuckenbruck, eds. *The Jewish Apocalyptic Tradition and the Shaping of New Testament Thought.* Minneapolis: Fortress, 2017.

Ridderbos, Herman. *Aan de Romeinen: Commentaar op het Nieuwe Testament.* Kok, 1959.

Rowley, H. H. *The Relevance of Apocalyptic.* London: Athlone, 1963.

Rowland, Christopher, "Apocalyptic." In *A Dictionary of Biblical Interpretation,* edited by Richard J. Coggins and J. Leslie Houlden, 34–36. London: SCM, 1990.

————. *The Open Heaven. A Study of Apocalyptic in Judaism and Early Christianity.* New York: Crossroad, 1982.

————. "Paul as an Apocalyptist." In Reynolds and Stuckenbruck, *The Jewish Apocalyptic Tradition*, 131–54. Minneapolis: Fortress, 2017.

Rusam, Dietrich. "Neue Belege zu dem stoicheia tou kosmou (Gal 4,3.9; Kol 2,8.20)." *ZNW* 83 (1992) 119–25.

————. "Was versteht Paulus under der Πίστις (Ἰησοῦ) Χριστου *pistis (Iêsou)* (Röm 3,22.26; Gal 2,16.20; 3,22; Phil 3,9)?," *Protokolle zur Bibel* 11 (2002) 47–70.

Russell, D. S. *The Method and Message of Jewish Apocalyptic, 200 BC–AD 100.* Old Testament Library. Philadelphia: Westminster, 1964.

Saldarini, Anthony J. "The Uses of Apocalyptic in the Mishna and Tosephta," *CBQ* 39 (1977) 396–409.

Sanders, E. P. *Paul.* Past Masters. Oxford: Oxford University Press, 1991.

————. *Paul and Palestinian Judaism.* Philadelphia: Fortress, 1977.

————. *Paul, the Law, and the Jewish People.* Philadelphia: Fortress, 1983.

Schäfer, P. "Die Lehre von den zwei Welten," In *Studien zur Geschichte und Theologie des rabbinischen Judentums*, 244–91. Leiden: Brill, 1978.

Schnelle, Udo. "Die kosmische Auseinandersetzung zwischen Christus und die Sünde nach dem Römerbrief." In *Paulus und Petrus: Geschichte-Theologie-Rezeption*, edited by Heike Omerzu and Eckart David Schmidt, 79–100. Arbeiten zur Bibel und ihrer Geschichte. Leipzig: Evangelische Verlagsanstalt, 2016.

Schütz, John H. *Paul and the Anatomy of Apostolic Authority.* Cambridge: Cambridge University Press, 1975.

Schweitzer, Albert. *The Mysticism of Paul the Apostle.* New York: Seabury, 1968.

————. *Paul and His Interpreters: A Critical History.* New York: Schocken, 1964.

Schweizer, Eduard. "Slaves of the Elements and Worshipers of Angels: Gal 4:3, 9; Col 2:8, 18, 20." *JBL* 107 (1963) 455–68.

Segal, Alan F. "Paul's Thinking about Resurrection in its Jewish Context." *NTS* 44 (1998) 400–419.

————. *Paul the Convert: The Apostolate and Apostasy of Saul the Pharisee.* New Haven: Yale University Press, 1990.

Seifrid, Mark A. "Paul's Use of Righteousness Language Against its Hellenistic Background." In *Justification and Variegated Nomism*, Vol. 2, edited by Donald A. Carson, Peter T. O'Brien, and Mark A. Seifrid, 39–74. Tübingen: Mohr Siebeck, 2004.

Sellin, Gerhard. "Hagar und Sara. Religionsgeschichtliche Hintergründe der Schriftallegorese Gal 4,21–31." In *Das Urchristentum in seiner literarischen Geschichte. Festschrift für Jürgen Becker zum 65. Geburtstag*, edited by Ulrich Mell and Ulrich B. Müller, 59–84. BZNW 100. Berlin and New York: Walter de Gruyter, 1999.

The Septuagint Version of the Old Testament and Apocrypha with an English Translation. Grand Rapids: Zondervan, 1976.

Smith, D. Moody. "The Pauline Literature." In *It is Written. Scripture Citing Scripture. Essays in Honour of Barnabas Lindars SSF*, edited by Donald A. Carson and H. G. M. Williamson, 265–91. Cambridge: Cambridge University Press, 1988.

Stanley, Christopher D. *Arguing with Scripture: The Rhetoric of /Quotations in the Letters of Paul.* New York: T. & T. Clark, 2004.

———. *Paul and the Language of Scripture.* SNTSMS 74. Cambridge: Cambridge University Press, 1992.

———., ed. *Paul and Scripture: Extending the Conversation.* Atlanta: Society of Biblical Literature, 2012.

Stuckenbruck, Loren T. "Overlapping Ages at Qumran and 'Apocalyptic' in Pauline Theology." In *The Dead Sea Scrolls and Pauline Literature,* edited by Jean-Sébastien Rey, 309–26. Studies on the Text of the Desert of Judah, vol. 102. Brill, 2014.

Stuhlmacher, Peter. *Gerechtigkeit Gottes bei Paulus.* Göttingen: Vandenhoeck & Ruprecht, 1965.

Sturm, Richard E. "Defining the Word 'Apocalyptic': A Problem of Biblical Criticism." In Marcus and Soards, *Apocalyptic and the New Testament,* 17–48. JSNTS 24. Sheffield: JSOT, 1989.

Timmins, Will N. *Romans 7 and Christian Identity.* SNTSMS 170. Cambridge: Cambridge University Press, 2017.

Tolmie, Francois D. "Allegorie as argument. Galasiërs 4:21—5:1 in retoriese perspektief." In *Acta Theologica* 2 (2002) 163178.

———. *Persuading the Galatians: A Text-Centred Rhetorical Analysis of a Pauline Letter.* WUNT. Tübingen: Mohr Siebeck, 2005.

VanderKam, James C. "Messianism and Apocalypticism." In *The Encyclopedia of Apocalypticism,* Vol. I, edited by John J. Collins, 193–228. New York: Continuum, 1998.

Verhoef, Eduard. *"Er staat geschreven . . . ." De oud-testamentische citaten in de brief aan de Galaten.* Meppel, Netherlands: Krips Repro, 1979.

Vielhauer, Philipp. "Apocalypses and Related Subjects: Introduction." In *New Testament Apocrypha, Vol. II: Writings relating to the Apostles; Apocalypses and Related Subjects,* edited by Edgar Hennecker and Wilhelm Schneemelcher, 581–607. Philadelphia: Westminster, 1965.

———. "Apokalypsen und Verwandtes: Einleitung." In *Neutestamentlichen Apokryphen in deutscher Ubersetzung, Band II: Apostolisches. Apokalyptik und Verwandtes,* edited by Edgar Hennecker and Wilhelm Schneemelcher, 407–42. Tubingen: J. C. B. Mohr [Paul Siebeck], 1964.

Vielhauer, Philipp, and Georg Strecker, "Apocalypses and Related Subjects: Introduction." In *New Testament Apocrypha. Vol. II: Writings relating to the Apostles; Apocalypses and Related Subjects,* edited by Wilhelm Schneemelcher, 542–68. Rev. ed. Cambridge: James Clarke & Co; Louisville: Westminster John Knox, 1992.

Vouga, Francois. *An die Galater.* HNT 10. Tübingen: Mohr Siebeck, 1998.

Wagner, J. Ross. *Heralds of the Good News: Isaiah and Paul "in Concert" in the Letter to the Romans.* NovTSup 101. Leiden: Brill, 2002.

Walker, William. "Does the 'We' in Gal 2.5–17 Include Paul's Opponents?," *NTS* 49 (2003) 560–65.

———. "Translation and Interpretation of ἐὰν μή in Galatians 2:16." *JBL* 116 (1997) 515–20.

Wedderburn, A. J. M. "The Theological Structure of Romans V.12." *NTS* 19 (1972–73) 339–54.

Weima, Jeffrey A. D. "Gal 6:11–18: A Hermeneutical Key to the Galatian Letter." *CTJ* 28 (1993) 90–107.

Weiss, Johannes. *Jesus' Proclamation of the Kingdom of God*. Edited by Richard H. Hiers and David L. Holland. London: SCM-Canterbury, 1971.

Westerholm, Stephen. *Israel's Law and the Church's Faith. Paul and his Recent Interpreters*. Grand Rapids: Eerdmans, 1988.

———. *Perspectives Old and New. The 'Lutheran' Paul and his Critics*. Grand Rapids: Eerdmans, 2004.

Wilk, F. *Die Bedeutung des Jesajabuches für Paulus*. FRLANT 179. Göttingen: Vandenhoeck & Ruprecht, 1998.

Williams, Sam K. *Galatians*. Abingdon New Testament Commentaries. Nashville: Abingdon, 1997.

———. "*Pistis Christou* Again." *CBQ* (1987) 431–47.

Winger, Michael. "From Grace to Sin: Names and Abstractions in Paul's Letter." *Novum Testamentum* 41 (1999) 145–75.

Witherington, Ben III. *Grace in Galatia. A Commentary on St Paul's Letter to the Galatians*. Edinburgh: T. & T. Clark. 1998.

Wrede, William. *Paul*. London: Philip Green, 1907.

Wright, N. T. *Paul and His Recent Interpreters*. London: SPCK, 2015.

———. *Paul and the Faithfulness of God*, 2 Vols. London: SPCK, 2013.

———. "Paul in Current Anglophone Scholarship." *Expository Times* 123 (2012) 367–81.

———. *What Saint Paul Really Said. Was Saul of Tarsus the Real Founder of Christianity?* Oxford: Lion, 1997.

Yarbro Collins, Adela, ed. *Early Christian Apocalypticism: Genre and Social Setting*. Semeia 36, 1986.

Ziegler, Philip. *Militant Grace: The Apocalyptic Turn and the Future of Christian Theology*. Grand Rapids: Baker Academic, 2018.

Ziesler, John. *The Epistle to the Galatians*. Epworth Commentaries. London: Epworth, 1992.

Name Index

Scripture Index

4 Ezra

2 Corinthians